THE BOOK OF WIT AND HUMOUR

THE BOOK OF
WIT AND HUMOUR
A Public Speaker's Treasury

by
PETER CAGNEY

THORSONS PUBLISHERS LIMITED
Wellingborough, Northamptonshire

Originally published as *Treasury of Wit and Humour*
First paperback Edition 1976
This Edition first published 1984

ISBN 0 7225 1122 1

Printed and bound in Great Britain.

PRE-ESTABLISHED COPYRIGHT

to
Deirdre, Stephen, Pennie
and Alayne

CONTENTS

FOREWORD

PETER CAGNEY has devoted the whole of his writing career to the lighter side of life in the belief that comedy is a commodity sadly lacking in many areas of human endeavour, and that laughter is a vital antidote to the pressures and stresses of modern existence.

He began work as a contributor to humorous magazines, and to a variety of international newspapers in which his articles and pieces were syndicated. He is also the author of several scores of novels and other books, many of them in the "thriller" vein. In the early fifties he began writing comedy material for a number of impressarios in show business, and for several comedians working in Variety and radio. The pressure of preparing comedy routines for artistes whose individual styles and requirements had different technical aspects, and often to urgent deadlines, compelled him to abandon his publishing contracts for thrillers and to devote all his time to the stage, radio and subsequently to television.

It was a difficult decision because the fictional books were being reprinted throughout the world, and he had been producing four titles a year. But the demand for scripts was growing, partly due to the expansion of the leisure industry which was branching out into the Club area, and to the advent of more markets in the realm of video.

The Peter Cagney Script Service was fully established by the middle sixties, and he was writing for several hundred artistes and acts, including such greats as Ken Dodd, Harry Worth, Jimmy Logan, Jack Hylton, Alan Clive, George Moon, Clarkson Rose, the late Max Miller, Jack Trip, Nat Mills, Ben Lyon, Tommy Cooper, Les Dawson and many more. To cope with the demand the publishing side of the P.C.S.S. was developed, and comedy material was licensed to entertainment companies ranging from holiday camp managements to cruise lines and revue theatres, as well as many of the new and lavish cabaret clubs that were opening up in every town in the country.

Today the P.C. Script Service has an international flavour, supplying light-entertainment scripts and acts to every type of show-business medium. He has also produced a number of comedy plays and television programmes, and has developed a unique training course for aspiring newcomers to the showtime world. Peter Cagney has made several television appearances in recent years, including an appearance in "Whickers World" in which his work was discussed.

The Press has always been interested in comedy entertainment and Cagney has been a frequent target for the reporters. It provides the newspapers with an opportunity to quote a few current jokes and gags, and at the same time invent striking headlines such as Donald Zec's claim that Peter Cagney is the "Nation's Jester", and Donald Walker's gushing tribute, doubtless tongue-in-cheek, which included the banner headline "Peter the Great – King of a Million Laughs" *(Daily Mirror)*. *The Observer,* perversely, showed a picture of Cagney holding a pile of his books stacked in his cupped palms beside the headline "The Deadly Serious Business of Being a Funny Man".

The total output of this author over the years exceeds 84 novels and other books, more than 2,000 scripts, plays and entertainment routines, and a wide range of articles and stories published in the world's press media. A formidable harvest of words running into several millions. This prodigious output may not as yet merit recognition in the *Guinness Book of Records,* but Cagney is quite content to know that, as far as his humorous works are concerned, he has enjoyed liaison with several hundred of the world's most talented entertainers and the friendship of innumerable personages in the fields of show business and publishing.

From the prolific cache of original stories, jokes, gag-lines and showtime material that has accumulated during his career Peter Cagney has selected the most amusing individual items for inclusion in a series of anthologies. Books which are useful for many people outside the immediate sphere of professional show business who are sometimes elected to speak in public; or who like to be the life and soul of the party whenever folk congregate for relaxation, be it a dinner function or a celebration or a company meeting. These volumes are unique inasmuch as they are composed of original extracts from entertainment scripts, and not merely collections of humour edited from various books, or quotations from sundry other sources. In other words, somewhere and at some time the material has been successfully performed before audiences and has proved that it works.

In a world so constantly torn apart by stress, anxiety and tension, laughter is the principal factor in relieving some of the misery. Very few people today are entirely free from insecurity, uncertainty and everyday problems. Peter Cagney's anthologies contain the ammunition that combats tension: a good burst of laughter is as good as a tonic. Whether his books are used as bedside reading, a source of usable humour for speakers, company directors, comperes, amateur entertainers, party wags, travelling salesmen, stars of stage, radio and television, or simply for dipping into when you feel overwrought, there is little doubt that they accomplish their aim.

So here's to laughter, you'll feel better after!

GERALD HELLIWELL

GAGS, WISECRACKS AND WITTICISMS

GAGS, WISECRACKS AND WITTICISMS

1 Henry was buying an expensive long-playing opera on hire purchase. He got two months behind with the payments, and the firm took back two violinists and an oboe-soloist.

2 He bought her a camel coat. When she's got it on you'd think the camel was still in it.

3 A local beatnik was off work for three days. He had woodworm in his sideboards.

4 Have you noticed that they always have Spring Sales when the shops are crowded? Why don't they wait until things are quieter?

5 Never let the grass grow under your feet. Especially if you're ticklish.

6 His mother told him that eating plenty of spinach, like Popeye, would put colour in his cheeks. And it did. He's the only kid in the street with green cheeks.

7 Overcautious—like the man who has a combination lock on his garbage pail.

8 You owe it to yourself to become a great success. After that you owe it to Inland Revenue.

9 Flying Saucers are manned by little cosmic explorers coming over the sky to see.

10 Some husbands come in handy around the house. Others come in unexpectedly.

11 Mr. and Mrs. Offentiff have been married now for twelve years and they are still in love. She with her doctor and he with the maid.

12 He's a chap with lofty ideas. All he needs is the farmer's daughter and a hay loft.

13   When John was an adolescent the family were so poor they had to share clothes with each other, which wasn't very practical because he had five sisters.

14   Hollywood movies would improve greatly if they shot less film and more producers.

15   Mammy's little boy loves shortenin' bread . . . he also likes shortenin' his little sister's hair, the legs of the table, and anything else he can get a. with his scout's knife.

16   Christopher Robin is saying his prayers:
        Dad tripped over the skates Chrissy left on the stairs.

17   This Workers' demarcation-line business is making things tough. All offices now have to employ a full-time carpenter to sharpen the pencils.

18   Don't cry over spilt milk—save it for when you spill the whisky.

19   Agatha bought herself some body-building equipment, and a pair of shorts to wear around the gymnasium. And with her gymnasium she needs a pretty large size of shorts.

20   Any girl who can spend three or four hours spooning obviously isn't the type that's easily stirred.

21   She stood underneath the mistletoe at Christmas waiting for someone to kiss her, and she was still there at Whitsun.

22   You can always tell when there's been a national calamity in the U.S. The American president puts black armbands round his golf clubs.

23   The radio station lists it as Chamber Music, but it must come from their torture chamber.

24   She's such a large girl that an engineering company uses her to test tubular armchairs for metal fatigue.

25   Next Christmas he isn't going to buy his family presents. He's come to the conclusion that money is thicker than water.

26   Income Tax is an awful drain on one's resources. It's like buying oats for a dead donkey.

27 Mr. Fred Tomkins wrote to the National Health Service for an address of a specialist where he could go to get inoculated against poverty.

28 He couldn't even afford to buy his little boy a yo-yo last Christmas. He just managed to get him a yo.

29 Lizzie couldn't get a man however hard she tried. But one day a gypsy sold her a special Chinese love potion for 50 pence —and it worked. A week later she married the Chinese Ambassador.

30 Those Sunday newspapers will go to any extremes to make a scoop sensation. They've just threatened to name the girl who was with Drake in his hammock just before the Armada arrived.

31 Of all the songs of Solomon the most pathetic is the dirge his wives wrote the night they went on strike. "No, no, a thousand times no."

32 An East End docker won £50,000 on the pools, so they couldn't very well refuse his lavish subscription when he wanted to join the golf club. All they can do is look the other way as he spits on his hands before wielding his mashie.

33 Things were so bad at a night club that when a customer offered the manager a five-pound note and wanted change they had to make the guy a partner . . . .

34 There's an old couple living next door who are enjoying a Soccer-Romance—each is waiting for the other one to kick off.

35 A great big hairy stevedore went home one night, unshaven, unkempt; struck his wife, kicked the dog, pulled the cat's tail, drank another pint of whisky, smoked a cigar, kicked his boots off through a window, then went into the bathroom, ran the water and shouted to his six-year-old daughter: "Maggie, where the hell have you put me perishing lilac bath salts?"

36 He found a lost blonde in the street and took her to the police station. The sergeant said: "If nobody claims her in three days, she's yours."

37 He heard someone fiercely pounding the door . . . once, twice, five times. Then he murmured: "Well, I guess that can't be opportunity."

38 Then there's the tailor who goes awfully giddy making eight hundred consecutive circumnavigations on the merry-go-round because the circus proprietor owed him for a suit. . . .

39   Dumb Dora said that she was thin, and her friend Mavis was thin, but that Miss Brugg in the typing pool was as thin as the two of them put together.

40   The vicar was asked to retract the statement in his parish magazine to the effect that a proportion of the Rebuilding Fund was being used to get the choir well plastered.

41   If you see a journalist staring vacantly at the blank paper in his typewriter, that'll be the man who writes the Society page for the *Daily Worker*.

42   Some years ago he was in the Tory Cabinet. He was a pickle fork.

43   Here's a most useful household hint. How to carry two gallons of milk in a leather bag without spilling any. Leave it in the cow.

44   Fascinated by the intricate job of folding road maps in a baby car, Lionel practised until he became a famous accordion player.

45   They move house so often that his wife can't keep pace. She sold the vacuum cleaner because they were never in any one place long enough for the dust to settle.

46   They awarded a medal to a man who saved a girl from drowning at the local baths. He was annoyed about it—they pinned it on him before he could get dressed.

47   A fellow put 20 pence   into the air mail stamp machine at Northolt airport . . . and an air hostess fell out . . .

48   With mass unemployment on the way in the States, due to automation, the Government is busy inventing jobs for thousands of people. The latest stunt is to provide doormen for telephone kiosks.

49   It was a Frenchman who invented the best cure for dandruff. He called his machine the guillotine.

50   At a fashion show yesterday eight lovely models were showing a new range. I've seen wounds dressed better.

51   When a famous concert pianist was booked for a recital at Wakefield Prison last week they had to cancel it. Someone stole the piano.

52   She was a lieutenant in the American Woman's Army Corps. She looked real cute in her new strapless off-shoulder evening gown. Her only problem was where to pin the epaulettes.

53   He got a letter from his wife: "Bert, I missed you yesterday. Come home and let me have another shot—Ethel."

54   He joined the Foreign Legion to try and forget his wife but six of the Legionnaires looked just like her.

55   They went to Brighton last November; why November? It's only at that time you can get a deckchair.

56   His wife is very safe driving on the roads, but a menace on the pavements. Once she knocked down an old man. He didn't look both ways before crossing. Why should he, in his own front parlour?

57   They had a huge St. Bernard dog in the boarding house who carried a barrel of brandy round his neck. The poor animal was an alcoholic. He took a liking to me the first day. Jumped straight into my lap and crushed four ribs.

58   They went into a restaurant and ordered chicken fricassee. . . . The fowl was so old a chunk of wood was found on one plate and the waiter explained that it was the remains of the bird's crutches.

59   The man at the hotel stared at the red-skinned guest and asked: "Do you have a reservation?" The guest answered: "Sure have, heap big place near Rio Grande. How!"

60   When he went to the police and reported that his wife was missing they asked her husband to give them a detailed description. It was four hours before they stopped laughing.

61   When his young son said he wanted to be a farmer, Mr. Twitson sent him to an agricultural college. He should have sent him to a pharmacy.

62   He went to see her last picture. What a terrible actress she must be. Frankenstein, Dracula and The Thing were waiting in the same queue.

63   You can tell how long their marriage lasted—they didn't even have time to hear the flip-side of the 12-inch L.P. Auntie gave them as a present.

64   Edna was given one of those electric automatic toasters for her birthday. You put in a piece of plain bread, switch on, and three minutes later up pops a sheet of flame.

65   Donald's wife had been serving him so many burnt offerings for supper that he's bought her an altar cloth for the dining table.

66   You can tell how poor they are: this Christmas they're going to eat up last Christmas's leftovers.

67   There's a theatre in Liverpool where they're giving shows on hire purchase. The audience goes in and laughs, and a week later the comic comes and tells them a joke.

68   It was the best wedding he had ever attended. They even got forty-nine   pence   back on the empties.

69   An old lady visited her G.P. and told him: " It's awful, doctor. My leg. The pains come on every twenty minutes and last a week."

70   Slimming is a fallacy. One girl we know went on a strict water and fruit diet for two weeks and all she had lost at the end of that time was a fortnight.

71   Norman would never have married Harriet, but she got so fat that he couldn't get his engagement ring off her finger.

72   Angus McTavish spent the first week of his holidays in Torquay. And that's all he did spend.

73   His wife keeps asking him for new clothes, but he can't afford to buy them. He just can't keep her in clothes. He bought her a new house last year and he can't keep her in that, either.

74   Common sense would save a significant number of marriages. If men used it, there wouldn't be any.

75   A midget walked into a coffee bar and ordered a glass of condensed milk and a slice of shortbread.

76   You just can't count on anyone these days. You have to use your own hands.

77   Poor old dear—she waited years and years for her ship to come in and then her jetty collapsed.

78   Sticks and stones may break no bones, but the bathroom soap is different.

79   George is so bald, he has to wear dark glasses when he dusts his head, to avoid the dazzle.

80   Chinese couples always have coloured children because two Wongs don't make a white.

81   When she asked him why he had suddenly stopped loving her, he said he had a train to catch.

82   The show was a tremendous success. It took the audience two hours to file out after the final curtain. He was lame.

83   The tailor made him a suit which was padded with horse-hair. One day he tore the lapels, and they had to shoot the whole jacket.

84   There ought to be a law against those side-street clubs where the music is soft and the lights are low. Twice this week a regular customer has bashed his head on the lamps.

85   It's one marriage that seems doomed to failure. They even started a row about who should cut the wedding-cake.

86   There's an hotel in Swansea that's so dirty, everyone has to change for dinner—into overalls.

87   That new perfume "Irresistible" is a knockout. Gladys used some last night, and her boy-friend caught her kissing herself in the full-length mirror.

88   The only Government measure that has increased productivity in Britain is Family Allowances.

89   The family is very poor. Their mother has to take in brain-washing. The children have no shoes—they paint their feet brown and lace up their toes. Dad gives the children sixpence to go to bed without supper, to save food. And in the morning he charges them ninepence for breakfast.

90   She's so rich she even has her monogram printed in gold on the bags under her eyes.

91   The shop steward struck his small son for using a dirty word. "Work."

92   He was trying to explain to her about nuclear plants but he wasn't getting across to her. Eventually she said: "Yes, but what colour are the petals?"

93   There was a fan-dancer in the show who had a far better fifth movement than anything Beethoven ever dreamed of.

94   The American serviceman kidded her that he was a big cattle dealer in Texas, but when she got out there, she found out he was a butcher's delivery man.

95   She's not exactly beautiful but she has good bone structure. Anyway, all the dogs love her.

96   Farmer Brown had a good day yesterday, reaping in the long meadow. He got forty-eight bushels of wheat and six courting couples.

97   Mr. Forster had his wife crawling on her hands and knees yesterday. She kept shouting: "Come out from under that bed, you coward!"

98   Sam painted his bath, and unknowingly his mother-in-law got into it. She stuck fast.   So Sam wrote to the manufacturers for advice.

99   Dumb? He didn't even know that two and two make four until his uncle bought him a ready-reckoner.

100   He never knew what it was to feel wanted. Then he saw his name in the Police Gazette.

101   Paris is a Sink of Iniquity: henpecked husbands enjoy going there to wipe up a few dishes.

102   When the ham actor visited the Grand Theatre again after an absence of five years he found the place changed. They'd filled in all the bullet holes with plaster.

103   The dress fitted her like an old sack. When she wanted to get undressed she just pulled a ripcord and baled out.

104   His wife was crying her eyes out because he threatened to leave her. "You're all I've got left!" she sobbed. And he said: "I'm all you started out with."

105   Mr. Frampton muttered a few words in church and found himself married. A couple of years later he muttered a few words in his sleep and found himself divorced.

106   He knows that you really can't take it with you, but he's wrapping his up in asbestos just in case.

107   When he promised that he would take her to the races at Doncaster she rushed down to the lingerie shop and bought herself a betting slip.

108   Little Tommy fell against the piano. Fortunately he didn't hurt his head badly—it struck the soft pedal.

109   Matches are made in heaven, and then sold to the other place.

110   At school, Roger never made the first cricket eleven, but in later years he did marry an old bat.

111   For her birthday he gave his wife a complete mink outfit—two traps, some bait and a twelve-bore rifle.

112   He began his prison sentence in Dartmoor and was then moved to Wormwood Scrubbs . . . a sort of two-way stretch.

113   He was the only heel in a town of some 50,000 souls.

114   They are not going to bury General Sir Mortimer Wretchington with full military honours. He isn't dead yet.

115   Her husband loved her and left her. He left her £50,000.

116   My uncle fought with General Sir Hugh Toshenten in the Second World War. It was over a French actress in Paris.

117   The beatnik took his girl-friend to Brighton on the pillion of his ton-upping 750-c.c. motor-bike, and ever since she hasn't spoken to him. He thinks she's sore about something.

118   He breeds some pretty hopeless horses. They never win, and most of them even have a bit of a struggle to come in last.

119   Never make a date with a schoolmistress. If you show up five minutes late you have to go home and get an excuse from your mother.

120   There's a hard-headed businessman in Leeds who is meticulous about all his deals. Last month he gave his daughter away in marriage and when he handed her over to the groom, he demanded a receipt.

121   COMMERCIAL: Use Snowsoft Cream Soap. It's made to make lovely women lovelier still. It refreshes and stimulates. You just jump out of the bath ready to meet all comers.

122   They gypped poor old Stan in Paris. They sold him a ticket to see "The Best Leg Show in France"—and it turned out to be the Six Day Bicycle Race.

123   There was a nasty thing on the television last night when I called round to see Jim. His mother-in-law's photograph.

124   The sort of woman who can make a fool of a man, could also make a man out of a fool.

125   You can get a full-scale eight-course dinner at the Pacardi Restaurant in Barcelona for about forty pesetas. They don't put finger-bowls on the table, of course. But they supply free stomach-pumps.

126   Tom Parkes had a nasty experience in Bournemouth. He walked into the wrong room at his hotel, and surprised a young girl who was just going to bed. He was so embarrassed he stood in the doorway for an hour, apologising.

127   Scotch is a wonderful drink. It not only makes you see double it makes you feel single.

128   The victim was discovered lying on the floor with two bullet holes in his back, a knife sticking out of his stomach and a tight rope pulled round his throat. The local police suspected foul play.

129   All the new cars are being fitted with fabric upholstery now, instead of leather. It makes it so much easier for the mechanics to wipe their hands after checking the gear-box oil.

130   Father Christmas left a full case of pale ale on the roof of the house and left a note in the letterbox stating: "The drinks are on the house."

131   His brother lives from hand to mouth—he's a dental surgeon. On the shingle outside it says: "Filling Station."

132   Never envy a rich man. A rich man is nothing but a poor man with money.

133   Have you ever wondered what pink elephants see when *they* get drunk?

134   If you feel below par, go to a nudist club and get some colour back into your cheeks.

135   Remember, girls, if you're putting on weight don't put on slacks as well.

136   A titled lady from Dorset went to a London beauty-parlour to have her face lifted. Twice the crane broke. And finally, when they saw what was under her lifted face, they dropped it again.

137   Moths are usually friendly little things. Never disturb them when you open your wardrobe or they might spit buttons at you.

138 She's so ugly, even plastic flowers wilt on her.

139 He cultivates the most gorgeous bloodshot orchids. His secret? Gin-and-tonic fertiliser.

140 Stereophonic equipment makes the music go round and around and then it comes out here, and there, and there, and here . . .

141 While out with the car one day last week, his wife ran across some old friends. May they rest in peace.

142 Bert was marooned on an island for four years. In prison on the Isle of Wight.

143 He was so mean that when the police put a price on his head he gave himself up.

144 They were a very argumentative married couple. The husband eventually changed the name of his house from "Chez Nous" to "Wigwam" because it was the home of a brave.

145 Class hatred—that's when a lad hates everyone else in his class.

146 Never lend money to an optimist. He'll expect to get it back.

147 If all the motor cars in this country today were laid end to end you'd have a fair representation of the Exeter by-pass, every summer Sunday.

148 He received a belated gift from Santa Claus. He wanted a soldier suit when he was eight, and ten years later he joined the army.

149 He's the one who runs things around his own home. Such as the floor polisher and the vacuum cleaner . . .

150 She was given a divorce by the judge merely because her husband had flat feet. They were always in the wrong flat.

151 Television enables people with nothing else to do to watch people who can do nothing.

152 He might have been captain of his soul, but his wife was the skipper. She skipped with the lodger.

153 He thought his shirt had shrunk in the wash until he realised he was trying to get his head through a buttonhole.

154 The wife visited her husband in the condemned cell and she took a piece of rope with her. She explained: "They don't tell you anything. I wasn't sure whether or not you were supposed to provide your own."

155 Top of the Pops is a modern song that stays popular for about seven days.

156 What we want to know is this—if matches are made in heaven why do they cost 5p a box?

157 When she played golf she couldn't hit a darned thing. Now she's learned to drive a car, and she hits everything.

158 Did you hear about the absent-minded scientist who took his wife out to dinner instead of his assistant?

159 When you sometimes think you're sitting on top of the world it turns out to be the little bit that sticks out above the axis.

160 A lazy German is a man who lives by the sweat of his frau.

161 It's ridiculous to call money "dough". Money doesn't stick to your hands.

162 He left his job and went to work in a jazz band but the noise was so terrible he applied for his job back again. In a panel-beating workshop.

163 Columbus discovered America. He peered behind a long row of garrish billboards and there it was.

164 We ate at a seafood restaurant last week. The fish was so fresh it was still chewing the bait.

165 She entered for the Beauty Contest but didn't get anywhere. However, the judges did give her a small recommendation. They recommended that she went home and stayed there.

166 The novel he wrote was so utterly naïve and incomprehensible that the editor had to rewrite half of it to make it good enough to throw away.

167 Carl Poster's first book was called: "How To Avoid Taxation". He is now writing his second book, entitled: "My Life In Pentonville".

168 Things were pretty rough when he was a child—and they couldn't afford talcum.

169   They say it is unhealthy to be too fat. It is also unhealthy to be too thin. There's a girl in Galway who is so thin, when she gets lumbago and stomach ache they are both in the same place.

170   Their house is so damp, they've had to fit the piano with stabilizers.

171   Then there's the secretary of a very influential shipping magnate who hung her coat behind the office door and took her boss to the cleaners.

172   Under the bright shining moon as they meandered down Lover's Lane she whispered in his ear those three wonderful words—"Go hang yourself".

173   There's a very exclusive private school in Berkshire; they have bars up at all the windows to prevent inquisitive people breaking in.

174   According to the advertisement Atilla Airways can put a girdle round the earth in thirty-two hours. We know a lot of big women who could do with this service.

175   Aren't the shops crowded in these days of easy money? A school-teacher who went into a large city store to buy some Christmas cards waited so long for attention that by the time she was served they were selling Easter eggs.

176   It seems suspicious; a butcher in Halifax was given a pound note by a woman who bought half a pound of beef sausages, and she got her change in horse-shoes.

177   Two Hebrew gentlemen boarded a train going north. About eight miles from London one said to the other: "I feel so hungry. I think I'll it it mine lunch. I've got it en haddock." The other looked up from his newspaper and said: "Moishe, if you've got it en haddock, why don't you take an aspirin?"

178   When he came out of the army he was like a fish out of water. His wife soon cured that. She made him take a bath with carbolic soap.

179   They've solved the problem of getting rid of all those unwanted worn-out cars. There's a new machine which crushes the entire vehicle into a slab of battered metal. You've probably seen some of them on the roads after they've been crushed.

180   Some girls are basically dishonest but Evelyn is as straight as a die: 28–28–28.

181 Pop singer Colin Cyclone has just made a new record. You can tell how bad it is—the little dog on the colour-sleeve is sitting with his paws in his ears.

182 When his mother-in-law spent a week with them shortly after the wedding, he realised why his wife was so fond of calves' feet.

183 A hospital is a place where they wake you up at five in the morning to give you a sleeping pill.

184 Milk keeps a lot of people awake. The delivery man comes at half-past four in the morning.

185 A drunk went up to the box-office window of the Grand Theatre and backed numbers 3 and 5, reversed.

186 The banks are making fantastic profits. Money no longer seems to have any meaning for them. If you go into the main branch of any of the big five banks to cash a cheque for two, three or four pounds, they get it out of the waste-paper basket.

187 British recording companies are awarding trophies for the best new pop songs being composed. Six times last month they had to exhume Tchaikovsky and Strauss.

188 He stayed in Folkestone at a wonderful hotel, but he had to share the bathroom . . . with another fellow forty yards up the street.

189 He told the doctor he was suffering with stomach trouble. The doctor asked: "What sort of trouble?" and he replied: "I can't get my trousers over it."

190 Arthur bought his suit from Robinson and Cleaver. And what can you expect from a third-hand suit?

191 He invented Nickelised steel. It's made from a mixture of pig-iron, magnesium, carbon, and Nick who stood too close to the side of the vat.

192 She uses such greasy lipstick that he has to sprinkle her face with sand to get a better grip.

193 Have you noticed that while all the pretty girls go out with any Tom, Dick or Harry, plain girls stay home with the willies?

194 The girl was half Swedish and half French, and she had a pretty useful half-nelson.

195 Things are now getting so bad so quickly that the Good Old Days seem only a week old.

196 An angler in Scotland poured whisky into the river and the salmon came up ready canned.

197 He's so ugly, the only thing he ever took out on a moonlight night is an insurance policy.

198 What some restaurants call chicken soup is usually hot water in which some old hen has been wrung out.

199 She's just like Venus de Milo, that girl. As cold as marble, and harmless.

200 Nature created woman. And anyone can make a mistake.

201 It is better to have loved and lost than never to have lost at all.

202 The best buy in Britain today is a 10 pence call to the right girl.

203 He complained to the police that someone was sending him threatening letters. They came from the Rates Office.

204 There's a man at the local fairground who has been fasting for forty-two days and nights. There are restaurants like that in our street, too.

205 A worried little man walked into a psychiatrist's office carrying a packet of biscuits and said to him: "Doc, do something for these will you? They're crackers."

206 Scientists inform us that all human life begins in a single cell. For many of today's delinquents it ends there, too.

207 The American West is a place where men are men, but in Soho you can never be sure.

208 He was explaining how he met his girl-friend. "I just bent down to pick up a pound I dropped in the gutter, and there she was."

209 Mr. Henry Fortescue of Harley Street is making a fortune, according to his press agent. He sells advertising space on psychiatrists' ceilings.

210 They got a local handyman to make the sedan chair for the Pageant. He bought himself a do-it-thyself book.

211 A man from Newcastle got his throat cut. He went to the Wimbledon tennis finals wearing a starched collar.

212 West Side Story—in which the schoolchildren don't rub out the blackboard, they rub out the teacher.

213 An artist painted her picture and it was hung at the Academy with its title beneath it: "September Moron".

214 Sybil has left the Nudist Club. She says she is getting ready for the wedding in June and she wants to be married in white.

215 Sign in a baker's shop: "Tarts like Mother used to make— 10p ." . . . "Tarts like she thinks she used to make— 25p ."

216 There's an artist in Chelsea who has been bitten by the new Action-Painting trend. He does three-dimensional abstracts by nailing his models straight on to the canvas.

217 There was far too much interference while he was watching television so he fitted a suppressor—to his wife.

218 Albert is a scratch golfer. His wife knitted him a hair shirt.

219 People who live in glass houses must present a delightful spectacle to the casual passer-by.

220 He spent a fortune on deodorants before he found out that people didn't like him anyway.

221 An artist and his model were necking on the sofa in the studio when there was a loud knocking at the door. The artist jumped up and cried out: "For goodness' sake, Sylvia—that might be my wife. Get your clothes off, quick, and let's pretend to be working."

222 The office manager heard a terrific commotion in the general office. As he stepped out to investigate he saw that one of the clerks had gone berserk and had shot two other employees dead. Angrily the manager roared: "Wilkins! How dare you! You're sacked."

223 A deep-sea fisherman was looking over the side of the trawler when he saw a pretty young girl in trouble in the water. She said that her swim-suit had been washed off. Thinking fast the fisherman threw her a fishing net to cover herself with.

224 The chap's a sadist. He works at the Labour Exchange finding jobs for other people.

225 Prisoners now prefer to be sentenced in the winter because they're scared of having to do double-summer-time.

226 Miss Dumbelle thinks that a surgeon is an operating theatre organist.

227 Notice on a greengrocer's display: "God help those who help themselves."

228 Miss Dumbelle thinks that an octopus is a cat that's had eight kittens.

229 It gets awfully cold on the French Riviera, especially around the Overcote d'Azure.

230 Remember that a motorist who breaks down on a lonely road doesn't want you to lend a hand—he wants a tow.

231 We know a civil servant who makes over two thousand a year—cups of tea.

232 A pretty girl is like a melody; that's why guys whistle her.

233 Until things start humming in the building trade you have to B sharp to get A flat.

234 What a lot of dreadful people you meet at the Underground club in Soho. All corduroy trousers, thin moustaches and crew-cut hair. And the men are just as bad.

235 An American officer's wife is suing him for divorce on the grounds that every night in bed she gets scratched to death by the pins of his medals on his pyjama jacket.

236 There was once a parson who started as a missionary in Africa and got captured by cannibals. The tribal chief got annoyed when the cook served him the victim's nose.

237 Then there's the woman driver who drove into a garage and told the mechanic that she had a short circuit in the ignition and asked him to lengthen it.

238 The last time he had to go in hospital he took my bicycle with him. It was easier to chase the nurses when he was convalescent.

239 Wouldn't it be nice for once if cinemas had as good a picture on one week as the one the trailers say they're going to have the week following?

240   When he claimed his money back under their "satisfaction-or-money-refunded" guarantee, they assured him that they were *perfectly* satisfied with his money.

241   When he was in the Army they had a sergeant who was a proper cissy. Every time there was boiled barbed-wire for dinner, he used to put sugar on his.

242   Did you hear the story of the fly who walked up a window pane and then had to go back? He'd left his specs behind.

243   The cuckoo got rather confused when the clocks were changed. The end of summer-time was a problem for him. So on the hour he just came out, shrugged his shoulders, raised his eyes to the ceiling and slammed his little door.

244   A new sexy novel written in France is so hot that the British edition is an expurgated version . . . all the saucy parts of the original have been taken out and used for the British book. The rest is being serialised in a Sunday paper.

245   Have you ever seen a Jewish chess set?—Two rooks, two castles, a king and a queen, two rabbis and eight pawnbrokers.

246   He's a visiting psychiatrist. When he has to make an urgent call he never calls a taxi, he calls a van . . . has to take his couch along.

247   When he was in the Army he went through thick and thin. Through thick underwear and thin soup.

248   A marriage certificate. That's just another name for a work permit.

249   Always remember that true beauty always comes from within . . . from within bottles, jars, phials, compacts, tubes. . . .

250   If music be the food of love, what's for afters?

251   Had an awful time last night—I fell over sixty feet. . . . Trying to get along the back row at the cinema to find the girl I'd promised to meet there.

252   You've seen all those shiny new cars on the road with signs in the rear window—Running In? You should see the sign in the rear window of MY car. It says "Running Out".

253   A Sioux Indian walked into a bookstore in New York and asked "Have you any good Easterns?"

254 Russian hotels are better than ours in some ways. Do you know every Russian hotel has television in every bedroom? But you don't watch it—it watches you.

255 Modern advertisements on TV for breakfast cereals always insist that cereals give you good straight limbs and good square shoulders. . . . What do you have to do? Eat the packets?

256 The King of Saudi Arabia has had all his teeth out. At the next official meeting of Middle East Monarchs all speeches have to be in Gum Arabic.

257 He lost all his fingers in an accident at work, and when he sued them for damages they offered to re-engage him as a shorthand writer.

258 The only thing that will rid a fat wife of her three chins is a guillotine.

259 When he saw his wife's sleeping suit on the bedroom floor he said: "Well, if that isn't the cat's pyjamas!"

260 The best cure for a really bad cold is to slowly squeeze the juice out of two pints of best Scotch.

261 When he was playing on the beach at Brighton he found nine lovely little stones . . . she was blonde too.

262 His wife says she is looking forward to her twenty-fourth birthday, but she's facing in the wrong direction.

263 He pointed to the fly swimming in his soup and the waiter said: "I'm afraid you'll have to go in for it yourself, I can't swim."

264 Girl we know has the longest nails in the country; she recently entered them for an amateur talon contest and won first prize.

265 A well-known photographer claims that nearly everybody has a double. Well, that's his problem—he shouldn't give so many parties.

266 When she said she was going to change the baby, her dumb husband told her to get a quieter one.

267 The reason why Jayne Mansfield gave up her job playing a clarinet in a dance band. Every time she took a deep breath she knocked over the music-stand.

268 Once upon a time an antique dealer discovered a very old, cracked and splintered gramophone record among his stock. . . . He tape-recorded it and sold it to a new recording company and it became a hit "pop".

269   He doesn't believe in all this current emphasis on giving kids a good sound walloping instead of using psychology. He's never hit one of his kids, except in self defence.

270   "What's the big idea of you fooling around with my daughter?" "Believe me, Pop, I wasn't fooling."

271   Miss Dumbelle thinks that Blue Serge is an unhappy Russian.

272   Before going on to the links, the new member was warned to watch out for lady drivers.

273   A violinist keeps moving his fingers up and down the strings because he's looking for the place.

274   Her boy-friend seldom buys her anything. He's a man of rare gifts.

275   When he heard that Parisian women wouldn't be wearing dresses much longer this season, he decided to take his summer holidays there.

276   The darkest hour is just before the pawn.

277   We know a country where they have the deuce of a job establishing a president.

278   The cannibal chief told his wife to put on all her ceremonial regalia as they were having a baronet for dinner.

279   Alimony is the best policy—that's a man's cash surrender value.

280   His hair is neatly departed in the middle.

281   She hit him with a paddle as he rowed her up the river. He was completely oar-struck.

282   Miss Dumbelle thinks that a thimble is a thort of thign.

283   The jury declared that they wished to add a rider, so the judge got on his high horse.

284   She objected that he referred to her as his awful wedded wife.

285   He was summoned by the railway company for not paying his fare on almost a score of occasions. The fellow should have known better than to twist on nineteen.

286 The bounder left her standing in the church. In fact she was cast away on an aisle.

287 She married a sailor because she wanted to have children and rear admirals.

288 There was the rehearsal of a new play by the local amateurs yesterday. At the end of Scene 1 the curtain comes down to denote the passing of time. It stays down for sixty minutes and then opens to show the same scene sixty minutes later.

289 Mr. Phelps waited in the restaurant for his lunch for twenty minutes. Then he got annoyed and asked the waiter what the hold-up was. The waiter explained that the chef had popped over the road to get his dinner.

290 A team of salvage experts were trying to raise the wreck of an old steamer off the Cocos Islands. They say that all the mermaids thereabouts moved to another part of the ocean—for divers reasons.

291 There'd been a robbery at the farm about ten miles away, so the police got out their bloodhound and set him off on the scent. For an hour the bloodhound sniffed his way over the bog and through the forest and then suddenly stopped. And started making eyes at a lady bloodhound who'd been dodging him for weeks.

292 Jones met a very supercilious St. Bernard dog when he was climbing the Alps in Switzerland. After being lost in the snow for three days, up comes this St. Bernard with the brandy-barrel swinging from his collar . . . and makes him sit up and beg for a drink.

293 The latest thing in men's clothing is women.

294 I saw the biggest crowd at church last Sunday—it was on fire.

295 Marriage is NOT a lottery . . . in a lottery you have a chance.

296 We had no trouble in winding up my grandfather's estate . . . he only left an old cuckoo clock.

297 An apple a day only keeps the doctor away, but you should see the result when you take onions.

298 My wife and I moved the piano this morning. Well, she moved the piano and I carried the stool.

299 Never known anyone so absent-minded as Alf. The other day he went out of the french windows to look around the garden—forgetting that two days earlier they'd moved out of the bungalow into a tenth-floor flat.

300 Mike used to work in the Inland Revenue office, making up tax forms. But now he's had all the experience he needs and he's starting up in business for himself. Going to be a pickpocket.

301 McCarthy was a traffic warden before he became an M.P. His pals in the police used to pull his leg by asking him every night: "Have you booked any good Reds lately?"

302 Maisie went to see her psychiatrist. He asked her what she'd dreamt of the night before and she told him that she hadn't had any dreams that night. So he got angry and said that if she didn't do her homework he couldn't help her.

303 The village is so behind the times! Last month they were celebrating their four hundredth anniversary and decided to have illuminations. So they bought a second-hand set of traffic lights and a zebra-crossing beacon.

304 He used to cut quite a dash when he had a full head of curly hair. Now he cuts a much balderdash.

305 Little girl presenting term-end report to her parents: "Of course it's a rotten report. What do you want me to be when I grow up—one of those precocious know-alls?"

306 Definition of a miner: A man who labours in a vein.

307 In accordance with their policy of discovering everything before anyone else, the Russians now claim to have invented the parigonameter; their spies are busy in America trying to find out what the durned thing is for.

308 He's invented a turntable for playing records at 92 revolutions a minute, so that you can run through records you don't like as quickly as possible.

309 Men are supposed to be the gay deceivers, but it's the women who wear them.

310 Girl to boy: You never sent me any nice incriminating letters. . . .

311 Modern proverb: Nothing recedes like success.

312   Betty says she doesn't believe in chasing after a man, unless he's getting away.

313   He's just lost his entire fortune. The family's living in the lapse of luxury.

314   He reckons that his wife is an outspoken woman. Having met her we'd be mighty interested to know who outspoke her!

315   When she told her husband that everything she had was worn out he said he was beginning to feel the effect himself.

316   He complained to the waiter that his egg hadn't been cooked long enough, or soon enough.

317   We know a woman whose hard exterior covers a heart of stone.

318   She egged him on to become an actor and his very first audience egged him off.

319   He's become very keen on gardening since the chorus-girl came to lodge next door. He keeps looking over the hedge to admire their curvaceous boarder.

320   All she wanted was three rooms in some ritzy hotel. She was just a suite young thing.

321   She was off to Europe on a husband-seeking trip; all her friends wished her bon boyage.

322   Owing to a misprint in the local paper Miss Evergreen, an enthusiastic member of the women's cricket eleven, was picked to keep wicked this season.

323   The difference between the cautious blonde and the plain blonde— one must make her mind up and the other must mind her make-up.

324   And remember, girls—if you keep men dangling on the end of a string you'll never tie the knot.

325   He's the only man who can play a tune on a tuba—but this is a tuba toothpaste.

326   The difference between a king and a dictator—a dictator sits on the overthrown.

327 She's the kind of wife who spends her evenings dining and whining.

328 Labour trouble: strikers should know by now that it'll never get better if you picket.

329 An auctioneer has no friends. Only nodding acquaintances.

330 A public executioner was put on the retired list in his prime. Pity, because he was just getting the hang of the thing.

331 Britons have an infinite capacity for churning themselves up into a terrific calmness.

332 A cynic is a man who never reads a book before he reviews it in case it prejudices him.

333 She was wearing a vagabond dress—one with no visible means of support.

334 The Ministry of Agriculture is advertising for a poet to produce some advertisements to popularise reindeer meat. Expect the job to go to Alfred Lord Venison.

335 You've probably heard about the angler who never had any luck. When there was an epidemic he only caught one measle.

336 Our medical expert says that fat men and tall men are more prone to rheumatic troubles. Big stiffs.

337 Since Grandma did a backwards-somersault while knitting, she's gone off her rocker.

338 Report in a society gossip column: "Lady V—— is expecting a happy event in August and has been compelled to cancel her engagement for that month."

339 He wanted a divorce from his wife, a professional clairvoyant. He alleged that she sat up in bed all night reading palms.

340 She's got the sort of figure that pulls their eyes over her wool.

341 They were kicking their heels on the carpet of the night-club, waiting to see the floor show.

342 The vicar asked the beautiful young widow to give another little talk to the village Temperance Society because he and the men liked her short addresses.

343 She fell out with her officer boy-friend. She had a rift with the lieut?

344 Marriage is a bed of roses from which the blooms have been plucked.

345 With so many re-issues of ancient pre-war films on TV, one Hollywood studio is convinced it has solved the problem of perpetual-motion pictures.

346 One word of censure makes Dad hold his tongue, and Mum's the word.

347 Did you hear the story of the sanitary inspector who missed the last drain?

348 When a woman gets explosive a guy forks out.

349 When the pet-store salesman said that the dog was a bloodhound, Mr. Hayseed wanted to know what group.

350 The chemical firm wanted to call their new hair-cream product "Britannia" because it rules the waves.

351 A woman accidentally fell out of a Fulham window into a dustbin just as a Chinaman was passing. He sagely reflected: "What waste! In China she would have been good for ten years yet!"

352 Did you hear about the moths who buy at hole sale prices?

353 Never slam the door of a restaurant after you've had a quick lunch. It's no good closing the door after you've bolted the horse.

354 Extract from *Farmers' Union Weekly*: "Westminster has just been declared a foot-in-mouth area."

355 We know a salesman who claims that his ancestors were the most successful salesmen in the world, and one of them introduced the first loose-leaf system to Adam.

356 When Barbara's tennis coach asked her to name two ancient sports she suggested Anthony and Cleopatra.

357 Every married man knows that the most perfect husband in the world belongs to the woman next door.

358   When she came home she was exhausted. She'd been playing squash —at a bargain sale.

359   Her father calls the sitting-room where his youngest daughter entertains her boy-friends, the mush-room.

360   We know a beautiful nurse who's so conceited when she takes a male patient's pulse she subtracts five.

361   Angus was a cat burglar. When the police raided his apartment they found a hundred stolen tabbies.

362   He was living in the lap of luxury and then one day it sagged.

363   An angler's wife asked her husband for some money. He gave her three fivers, two pound notes and a   50p piece   . She threw the small one back.

364   He was looking for a girl who didn't smoke, didn't drink and didn't keep asking for money for clothes. At last he came across one—she was nine.

365   He was living in a flat near Whitehall because he wanted to be near his money.

366   A Cherokee in the American Army was fined four dollars for beating his Indian wife. They're trying to do away with all this squaw-bashing.

367   It was so hot on the beach, fellers were lying around baked in their jackets.

368   The waitress in the café opposite the Stock Exchange has got into the habit of asking her customers: "One slump or two, sir?"

369   After twenty years of married life, Harvey's wife is still as pretty as ever; but it takes her fifteen minutes longer.

370   Every week he goes through the list of phone numbers and takes away the little number he thinks of.

371   On the day of his wedding he took out a maritime insurance policy.

372   Saw an unusual sight while out deep-sea fishing the other afternoon. A dwarf-mermaid: half woman and half sardine.

373   The critic wrote of a new play: "I can't remember the author's name but his farce is familiar.

374 A comedian was telling some friends that he looked like having to give up the entertainment lark owing to ill health. He kept making his fans sick.

375 A woman's place is in the home but few men have the courage to put her there.

376 They say that things are so bad in the circus business that even the elephants forget when they last had a booking.

377 A couple had dinner at a very expensive restaurant and when the waiter gave the man the bill, the House Charge was so steep he had to go out and sell his car.

378 Atkinson is the sort of chap who could move mountains if there weren't any hills in the way.

379 A cinema critic says he went to a sneak preview of a new Sophia Loren film last week, and every other sneak in town was there.

380 The guide had escorted thousands of people around the show without trouble, but last week he handled a small party of eighteen and was injured. She kicked his shin.

381 A lumberjack was picking up some logs the other day when one of them turned to him and said: "Boy, I slept like a man last night."

382 She went out with a musician and has never been composed since.

383 Frank is awfully good-mannered. If a lady drops anything he kicks it over to her so that she can pick it up without trouble.

384 We've got another advantage over the Victorians—to find out if a girl was knock-kneed *they* had to listen.

385 Agnes always thought that a pantry was where the butler kept his underwear.

386 The producer of a big West End revue which has thirty gorgeous girls in the chorus had rehearsals every day for a month. He was stocktaking.

387 I'll say this for Freda—spending money is her only extravagance.

388 Hawkins took his mongrel dog to a flea circus and the clever animal stole the show.

389   A plain girl is one who always comes home wearing the same amount of lipstick she started out with.

390   One germ said to another: "Steer clear of me, Cedric—I've got a touch of the penicillins."

391   He's so mean if he found a bottle of indigestion mixture, he would eat a jar of pickled onions.

392   Cynthia wanted a Ming coat to go with her Ming vase.

393   His wife's putting on a lot of weight but he's stuck with her because he vowed to cherish her in thickness and in health.

394   A painter who dropped a can of red enamel over a dowager apologised for not being able to hold his lacquer.

395   She was a woodworker's daughter, the brazen bit.

396   Katie just bought one of those Paris Biblical gowns. The low-and-behold type.

397   He told her he was a meat-packer when all the time he was just a corset-maker.

398   A sleuth is a guy who finds out who sleu wheu.

399   The trouble with strong liquor is that one and a half pints make one cavort.

400   Taking his idea from the kangaroo, a fellow we know has just patented a process for sewing pockets on nudists.

401   A detective-sergeant who found the dead body in the *living*-room wanted to know what it was doing there.

402   The price of silver is coming down. Go and get your clouds re-lined.

403   The smart girl always hitches a caravan to the car when a guy takes her for a ride, so that she won't have far to walk home.

404   The purring sound from the lecture-room was just the professor talking in his student's sleep.

405   Redundancy is when a fellow has nothing to do and is given an assistant to help him.

406 He's in a very unique profession. He goes around night-clubs dishypnotising patrons.

407 She's got her husband eating right out of her hand. It saves the dishwashing.

408 He got a job as an extra in a big studio, and he stole the picture. You can't leave anything lying about these days.

409 George joined a girl to forget the Foreign Legion.

410 He winters at Juan les Pins and springs at any girl in sight.

411 He's in the Navy now. Actually he wanted to join the N.A.A.F.I. but he couldn't spell properly.

412 A visitor from Monte Carlo went into a fried-fish shop, asked for a shilling's worth of chips, and then put them on the red.

413 They say that things are so tough in Glasgow, if you see a man with a whole set of teeth and a straight nose, he's a sissy.

414 From the very first day at school I was teacher's pet. It saved her having to buy a dog.

415 In Eire the restaurants serve steaks that are so big you can milk them.

416 The spotlight of publicity has been on her for so long, everything she had has faded.

417 For exercise he goes to see a horror film and lets his flesh creep.

418 We heard a very haunting melody from the ballroom. It was haunting because the band was murdering it.

419 When he criticised the scantiness of her swim-suit she just laughed it off.

420 When she volunteered as a blood donor they asked her what type she was and she said she was the sleek, sultry type.

421 On these cold nights one good turn gets most of the blanket.

422 He's been chased by so many girls he's had his head turned, and now he's the only guy I know who can read a newspaper over his own shoulder.

423 He's so thin he can make one stud do for both back and front of his collar.

424 He claims that one of his ancestors was such a villain he was beheaded three times.

425 He did very well with his bees last year; didn't get much honey, but they stung his mother-in-law four times.

426 They say beauty is only skin deep but did you ever try skinning a lady?

427 He finishes off all his letters: "Always at your service." Except those he writes to the vicar.

428 He refused to buy her the pair of budgerigars she wanted because he said that one could cheep as lively as two.

429 He bought a vase from the curio shop, thinking he was getting Ming. He only got Stung.

430 Great are the uses of advertisement, which is why millions rush from poster to pill.

431 We know a typist who has changed her boss six times in the last six months, but she's on the last lap now.

432 A radio comic we know never goes anywhere without a retinue of five scriptwriters because he likes to keep his wits about him.

433 She's hungry for love and she doesn't know where her next male is coming from.

434 Stupidity is hereditary—you often hear of a chip off the old blockhead.

435 Joe has just received an invitation to the Bachelors' Annual Thanksgiving Service.

436 An aunt of ours heard a BBC announcer say that they were closing down, and wrote to ask what day the sale would be.

437 The doctor said he'd given Mrs. Neverwell something to fortify her. What she really needed was something to twentify her.

438 Statesmen are people who have to watch their appease and accuse.

439 Television always catches his worst side: the outside.

440 There are three types of women: the beautiful, the intelligent, and the majority.

441 Able-Seaman Watkins found a passenger in Number Three Hold. So he took her on deck to show her Number Four Hold.

442 His parents took him away from Manchester when he was three and a half—there wasn't enough work there for him.

443 I wouldn't say she's old but there were so many candles on her birthday cake at the party, the ceiling caught alight.

444 She's going out with a French count now . . . you know what a French count is? Un, deux, trois. . . .

445 She went out with an officer—he was just a lemon with three pips.

446 Sailors—the fellers who don't really start their manoeuvres until they get shore leave.

447 Bureaucracy is all right if you keep your eye on it—they say that Whitehall once mislaid a sheaf of papers and a detachment of Royal Engineers waited fifty years in the Fiji Islands for further instructions.

448 She was a very lovable sort of girl; you'd often find her at the zoo feeding the little monkeys . . . to the lions.

449 She was a pretty girl of some twenty summers and twenty-nine winters.

450 I remember Jack—he died with his boots on. One of them was on the accelerator.

451 He described the one that got away, using finger and thumb. He was a shrimp-boat skipper.

452 Three men wanted to think out a cheap way of committing suicide with one bullet, so they put their heads together.

453 He went into town to get a bottle of brandy for his wife. One of the best swops he ever made.

454 When she left him, all the shine went out of his life. She took all the silver with her.

455   He says he always knows when he's had enough to drink—he falls flat on his face.

456   They really ought to move the head offices of Inland Revenue to Andover.

457   The idiot painted his sundial with luminous paint so that he could tell the time at night.

458   Five minutes after he was born the gangster's baby spoke. He said: "You can't pin this wrap on me."

459   While he was house-hunting he saw a model home . . . but she didn't invite him in for a drink.

460   Life is divided into two parts. Some of us are in the swim and the rest in the soup.

461   Most women get their good looks from their mothers. But she gets hers from a chemist.

462   Some people who pat you on the back are only looking for a soft spot to knife you on some future occasion.

463   Recent bank robberies have resulted in special watches being employed as floor-walkers by city banks. The guarding of the change.

464   When he saw her swimming about in the sea he thought she was a girl worth wading for. . . .

465   There are probably several better cures for a cold than three double whiskies, but who cares?

466   He told the gold-digger that she'd be a lot of use in medical research because she was obviously a human gimme-pig.

467   He was going to have a few words with his wife but then found that she'd cornered the market.

468   Quite a number of sheep have been killed by vixen since a cinema was opened in a small village. While shepherds watch the flicks by night.

469   Lady Bilberry is dreadfully worried about her heir. She can't do a thing with him.

470 There's something to the notion that a bachelor is a guy who failed to embrace his opportunities.

471 Beware of women who slip their brains into neutral and let their tongues free-wheel.

472 He paid too much for the car because he didn't feel like driving a bargain on an empty stomach.

473 Epitaph to El Pico! The bull tossed him and he came down heads.

474 A tight dress never yet stopped a girl's circulation.

475 She was a real blushing bride. The groom had failed to show up.

476 Before he left her he settled the furniture on his wife. In fact he settled so much furniture on her it took the neighbours three hours to help her out from under.

477 He said that his wife reminded him of her mother. At every conceivable opportunity.

478 It took a certain author twenty years to realise that his writings were extremely mediocre, but he was then far too famous to do anything about it.

479 He took a good long look at the menu prices and ordered sal volatile.

480 She was accused of assaulting the cheerful spiritualist. She struck a happy medium.

481 The prisoner took the stand. And the judge made him put it back.

482 He's got a brain fit for a kink to live in. . . .

483 Then there was the young barber who spent his holiday helping on the land. He lathered the fields before scything them.

484 If you're superstitious, and use a rabbit's foot, remember it didn't do the rabbit much good.

485 The commercial traveller had it all down on his expense sheet—in black and blonde.

486 The man who boasts he got up at dawn to see the sun rise could hardly have picked a better time!

487　Sign outside a plastic surgeon's office: Alterations as usual during business.

488　Careful make-up can reduce a woman's apparent age by twenty years but you can't pull the wool over a steep hill.

489　We saw a terrible show last night. It started at 8 p.m. sharp and finished at 10.30 blunt.

490　An old man always looks at the past but a young man looks at what's passing.

491　Short Hollywood marriage: "I do"—"Adieu".

492　The difference between magnesia and amnesia is that amnesia can be kept a secret.

493　When he asked her if she liked Kipling she said she might do, but she didn't know how to kipple.

494　The way things are going, marriage licences will soon be issued complete with a detachable coupon for a speedy divorce.

495　She was very badly sunburned, but she only got what she'd been basking for.

496　Never let life get you down; always remember that when one door shuts, another closes.

497　It's sad to know that those old narrow lanes in which two vehicles could so easily collide are now being turned into broad highways where several vehicles can collide.

498　A nursery is where you keep your little mistakes until they grow bigger.

499　He's in debt, up to his eyes. The hat is paid for.

500　They've sacked the advertising specialist who wanted to start Government advertisements for army recruitment with the words: The British Army Needs New Blood. . . .

501　They say that film actress's husband insisted on hiring a cook because he couldn't bear the idea of his wife leaning over a hot stove all day in case it ruined her career.

502 Ornithologists are getting excited about some of the new species of birds recently seen for the first time in Britain, namely: the double-breasted seersucker, the morning pee-wee, the electric crane and the extramarital lark. . . .

503 My wife complained that they had made a shapeless mess of her costume at the cleaners. When she put it on it fitted her perfectly.

504 Because a guy makes overtures it doesn't mean he's a musician.

505 For a girl who was studying law she didn't put up much of a defence.

506 Evening newspapers up north have a wonderful economy idea. They leave the two centre pages blank, for fish and chips.

507 Both Johann and Richard Strauss wrote beautiful music—what a wonderful pair of Strausses they were. . . .

508 And how about old Alcoholic Joe? Every time he hears there's a storm brewing he rushes out into the night with a tankard.

509 Science is wonderful. Someone has just invented a machine that does the work of fifty-seven men. It's got a built-in strike-leader.

510 Did you hear about the lazy bank robbers who didn't bother to count their haul—they just waited for the morning papers to tell them.

511 They've moved into a new place. The house is so small they have a ceiling that is on eye-level. They've only been there a week, and now they've got the only round-shouldered armchairs in town.

512 The garden fell forty yards into the river yesterday, and that's a long way for a window-box to fall.

513 They live so far away from civilisation; when neighbours drop in to borrow a cupful of sugar they have to put them up for the night.

514 His wife is always losing her temper over *small* things. Like that 5 ft. 1 in. blonde he was out with last night.

515 She wears tight-fitting slacks to prove that she's made of stern stuff.

516 A new television show for rabbits, called Double Your Bunny.

517 Did you hear about the lady chiropodist who married a dentist? They fought tooth and nail.

518   There's been a vast improvement in Government forms lately. Whitehall is hiring ex-Folliesgirls as part-time typists.

519   Our M.P. was born stupid and then he had a relapse.

520   Progress.—The modern world has got rid of the idle rich. Now we've got the idle poor.

521   They say that when you go to France you should spend some time at the *Folies Bergère*, but this isn't easy when you've only two weeks holiday.

522   He's an exhibitionist. Like a beat singer who actually lets you hear the words.

523   When she window shops she takes the car in with her. I wish she was as interested in lakes.

524   Once in the heart of the African jungle she was pawed by a ferocious beast . . . named Colonel Arthur Dingle-foot-Alstruther.

525   The news from Italy was bad this morning. The announcer read it in garlic.

526   The perfume she wears is like the breath of spring . . . onions.

527   My brother is making pictures. Not in Hollywood. In Rowley Regis with a Brownie No. 2.

528   Modern times. When dirty pictures on walls are known as contemporary murals.

529   It was so wet all the week in Wigan the buses didn't have brakes— they were fitted with anchors.

530   Last night I saw two shooting stars.—Matt Dillon and Wyatt Earp.

531   She's got the sort of figure that makes a sack dress look like a form-fitting sheath gown.

532   A Russian scientist has invented a forty-foot-long telescope which curves over and down at the end. He uses it to study the earth.

533   The young couple should be very happy. Both of them are very much in love with the bridegroom.

534 She uses eight pigeons in a strip-tease act. For an encore the pigeons take their feathers off.

535 Party politics—that's an argument that takes place when the wife wants to go to the Joneses' anniversary party and you want to go to Higgins's stag party, on the same night.

536 His girl has just bought something for her bottom drawer. It's a cure for dry-rot.

537 He thinks that a parquet floor is an ice-rink.

538 The latest craze in Scotland. Sporrans for men and women, each labelled clearly HERS and HIS.

539 She's so fat she doesn't use a girdle, she uses a converted hammock.

540 The Martian had a nervous breakdown. His doctor wrote on the medical certificate: Metal Fatigue.

541 The latest candid-camera for news-photographers—it's fitted with a key-hole-shaped lens.

542 Life Insurance is so cheap in Eastern Europe. You only have to pay the premiums for a couple of years.

543 Then there's the comedian who goes to all the big variety shows at the leading theatres. Just to hear what he's going to say in his new act next week.

544 She was so angry she could hardly contain herself. And that goes for the dress she was wearing too.

545 A man is getting old when he chases after women, and having caught them, forgets why.

546 There's more things in life than money. There's hire purchase, provident checks, overdrafts, car finance, extended credit. . . .

547 Another M.P. is following in his father's footsteps and it isn't easy getting them on that desk in Whitehall every morning.

548 The reason why George Washington's little lad never became a politician . . . he told the truth.

549 There's only one thing that isn't taxed in this country and that's a politician's brain-power.

550 The park was a terrible disgrace yesterday, all the lawns smothered with bits of paper . . . half of them were leaflets reading "Keep Britain Tidy".

551 It was a shady lady who brought the sunshine into his life.

552 This pay-as-you-view television is a splendid idea. It's about time we got paid for watching the rubbish.

553 We ate so many rice puddings as kids that even to this day I keep getting an urge to do my own hand laundry.

554 Never marry for money. Even in days of inflation it's cheaper to borrow it.

555 He's so cautious he even looks both ways before crossing his legs.

556 A greedy taxidermist is just a guy who stuffs himself.

557 It's very easy to get spare parts for pre-war cars. On many main roads you just find them lying around after another pre-war car has passed by.

558 It's embarrassing to have a wife who's so ugly the neighbours think you must have married for her money.

559 Last week our M.P. put forward two ideas. . . . They'd been in his family for generations.

560 He dreamt he was eating a carton of shredded wheat and awoke chewing the mattress.

561 She's got a baby's complexion and frankly I think the baby was glad to get rid of it.

562 He's mean enough to take his wife's teeth to work with him every morning to stop her eating between meals.

563 Petrol stations serve you well. The mechanics not only top up your petrol tank and wipe dead insects off the windscreen and check your oil, they even scrape pedestrians off your bumpers.

564 In Brighton the police are trying to stop gambling . . . it's taken such a hold over them.

565 His son will be home for a day's holiday from reform school. They always give the lads a day off to celebrate Crippen's birthday.

566 She's so thin, when she puts on a fur coat she looks like a pipe-cleaner.

567 We fully realise that you can't take it with you, but what's the position when you haven't even got it here?

568 He bought some shares in that soap firm that advertised on TV and now he's stinking rich.

569 Politicians are worried because there are so many old folks in this country. They just can't understand how people can live so long under such terrible conditions.

570 What he likes best is doing the washing-up in a sink of iniquity.

571 Of course politics was always a gamble. Every new government breaks the seal on a new pack of lies.

572 Eat, drink and be merry and tomorrow you diet.

573 Always meet your difficulties like a man. Blame them on your wife.

574 He's only got three friends in all the world. And when that three quid's gone he doesn't know what he'll do. . . .

575 If you don't think that things are as bad as they look, sell your radio set and buy a TV.

576 He's so stupid he thinks a bar-bell is a blonde who hangs around cocktail saloons.

577 His girl's brother is as strong as a lion—and you know how strong lions smell.

578 I wouldn't say that he goes to the Burlesque Theatre too often; but he's worn out six pairs of opera glasses.

579 Did you hear that they had to turn down Gina Lollobrigida for a part in a new film? Seems she had flat feet.

580 She used to be a bubble-dancer but there came a time when four woodpeckers got loose on the stage, and her career blew up in her face.

581   He's a smart cinema manager; he always books X-certificate French films. That way, they sell more ice-cream.

582   Men DO make passes at girls who wear glasses—if they've got the right frames.

583   In Glasgow there's a man who took all his money out of the bank for a holiday, gave it a week's rest in his pocket and then took it back.

584   The difference between an Italian model and an English model is that the Italian model owes everything she's got to spaghetti and the English model owes it to foam rubber.

585   What a baby-sitter she was; she woke the infant up three times during the evening, so that he could adjust the TV picture for her.

586   What a typist she turned out to be. Every time the bell rang on her machine, she broke for tea.

587   This is the time of the year when lots of women are haunting the holiday hotels, looking for husbands. And most of them aren't particular about who's husband he is.

588   Men like going to the local library. The shelves are so well stacked with good things to browse over and so is the blonde librarian.

589   Mr. Gould's wife has had her picture done in oil. He accidentally dropped her photograph in the chip pan.

590   He thinks of everything; his latest scheme is to launch a fund to save the natural wild-life of Soho. . . .

591   The other day in the country, two glow-worms were slowly working their way across a branch. The rear one was pushing the other one because his battery was flat.

592   Then there's the boss who found a way to save his firm thousands of pounds a year. He fired his secretary.

593   I was reading one of those historic novels. You know the sort. You just can't put them down. You have to throw them away.

594   When George's wife parks at a parking meter it costs her 50p just to get the car into position.

595 The Post Office lost a lot of money on its telephone service last year. That accounts for the new system they've got. This morning a caller put a coin in the box and a voice from the slot said: "God bless you, sir!"

596 The quickest way to make your own anti-freeze is to hide her nightie.

597 Down in the forest something stirred. It was a teaspoon. The Websters were having a picnic.

598 Shape: that's what happens to a swim suit when you put a girl in it.

599 Below-par golfer: a man who always takes two or three lumps with his tee.

600 Never offer to buy dinner for a fat girl. It's like rolling stones into a cavern.

601 Courting is like a boxing tournament. The preliminaries last so long you never know when the main event will start.

602 Growing pains are what you get if your wife makes you do the garden.

603 A tactician is a fellow who never hits a man when he's up.

604 Modern music: anything that isn't worth saying, made into a song.

605 What a shame it is when a girl has a loving disposition and wastes it on herself.

606 For your holiday this year why not go to Italy and see some old Roman ruins. Why stay in London and see the old English ones?

607 One night Fred got fed up and said: "Aw, come on Clara, let's take all the money we've been saving up for a car, and blew it all in on a fish supper."

608 French dress designers never leave much to the imagination because they know few Englishmen have any.

609 It's no good dieting to preserve a youthful figure if you haven't got enough strength left to shift it around.

610 A bore is a fellow who, when you ask him the time, starts telling you how watches are made.

611   Whoever said you can't get wounded by a blank has obviously never received an Income Tax form.

612   He has definite tastes about women's clothes. He can't stand his wife in anything over four-pounds.

613   If your wife keeps dyeing her hair different shades refuse to go out with her. You might get arrested for bigamy.

614   After dinner, the hostess said they would take coffee in the library. But when they drove over there the library was shut.

615   His mother would be most upset if she knew he was an actor. She thinks he's still in Tangier peddling dope.

616   Money won't help you to make friends, but you'll have a much better class of enemies.

617   A man of forty knows about half as much as he knew when he was twenty.

618   An alderman on the city council has dreamed up a great idea for keeping youngsters off the streets at night. He suggested the pavements should be taken up at dusk and stored overnight.

619   If you think you can cut down smoking by just having one cigarette after each meal, you'll find yourself struggling to eat twelve meals a day.

620   Running into debt is no problem. Just watch you don't run into any creditors.

621   A frustrated woman is one whose husband has his trousers made without pockets.

622   It's no wonder people never go to the local Palais de Dance—the place is so crowded.

623   Wives have a perfect right to do as they wish. Some of them also have a perfect left.

624   They dismissed a detective from the Stockport force. When a woman witness refused to give evidence he held her for further questioning. Round the waist.

625   If your old car needs a repaint job and you can't afford it, why not wallpaper it?

626 Here's to happy days. Any fool can have a good time at night.

627 When a young husband saw his baby for the first time, he was so astonished at its ugliness that he didn't know whether to dash off and buy a crib or a cage.

628 There's a modern composer who got fed up with writing pops and started to drink. This gave him the idea of writing drinking-songs. But when he started he found he couldn't get past the first two bars.

629 The fat man met a fat woman at a protest meeting. He said to her: "I'm a one-woman man and you're a one-man girl, so how about you and me making up a foursome and going out tonight?"

630 The age of adolescence is when growing children start questioning the answers.

631 If you cannot give up alcohol the next best thing is to have your knees soled and heeled.

632 Green stuff is excellent for eyesight. Did you ever see a rabbit wearing a monocle?

633 He thought he was having a really wonderful time. Living the life of O'Reilley. Then O'Reilley came home unexpectedly.

634 On a trip to France to see the old battlegrounds a touring party visited Vignonne, but all they saw were courting couples.

635 He's a cave-man type. One kiss and the girls cave in.

636 Ellis is a lucky chap. He's got a wife and a transistor radio and they both work.

637 His wife isn't one of those flighty women who run around with other men. She's too fine, too upstanding, too decent—and too old.

638 If your hair is getting a little thin on top, don't worry. Fat hair isn't healthy.

639 Never buy gloves which are marked: "Genuine Cowhide". They'll probably only have four fingers.

640 The slowest horse in the race was so sluggish that the jockey took a library book with him for the journey.

641 They do a double musical act on the stage; he's a pianist and she's an off-coloratura. He plays on the white notes and the black notes and she sings in the cracks.

642 French windows in the lounge bring the great outdoors flooding into the house. They also bring in a lot of large muddy feet.

643 His wife used to have a nice firm chin, but now the firm has taken on a couple of partners.

644 He used to think out all his worries and troubles over a cigarette. Now the cigarettes are causing him more worry and trouble than his other problems.

645 A boxing gymnasium: that's a sort of guided-muscle research station.

646 A week-end driver is one who enjoys sitting in a long lane of immobile traffic breathing in deep gulps of diesel-laden smog and trying to fold up road maps.

647 Bills and final notices come shooting through the letter-box. How true it is that there is nothing more deadly than the mail.

648 Landed gentry: Men who have been tricked into marriage.

649 A cross-section of the British Public: Taxpayers.

650 If your wife keeps leaving jobs undone it only shows that she lacks finishitive.

651 A Gossipping Woman: One who, when you tell her a secret, lets it go in one ear and out on the ether.

652 My father had success written all over him. The kids did it with ballpens.

653 When he was twenty-nine he was a seven-stone weakling; now he's forty—and a twelve-stone weakling.

654 The army made a man of him—so he's suing them. When he joined up he was a girl.

655 The widow was asked if her husband was in a comfortable position when he died. She said: "No—he was half-way under a bus."

656 Jack was so poor when he was demobbed from the Army, he had to join the Air Force to get a suit.

657 Sign at a cheap café: "All you can eat for £5."

658 At the hotel I stayed in on the Margate front, they changed the bed-sheets every day. From one room to another.

659 His father was an old newspaperman. He didn't sell many—nobody wanted old newspapers.

660 His lordship added a new east wing to the country mansion. Then he added a new west wing. A month later there was a bit of a cyclone and the house took off.

661 Did you hear about the rich old jewel-thief who couldn't get a house? He threw a bag of diamonds through the window of a building firm and stole a pile of bricks.

662 The doctors may be right when they tell us that garlic ensures a long and healthy life, but who wants to live that long and be so lonely?

663 A fellow who spends his youth sowing wild oats can always sell his life story to the Sunday papers for cerealisation.

664 His fans are enthusiastic. They throw flowers at his feet; the girls throw themselves at his feet; men throw money at his feet. He isn't much of an artist, but his feet are popular.

665 You can consider yourself poor when you have to have ox-tongue for lunch and the other end for supper.

666 Throughout the war Britons fought for dear life. And success crowned all their efforts—the cost of living was never dearer.

667 The stores are now open only from 9 a.m. to around 5 p.m. Britain is becoming a nation of closed-shop keepers.

668 She was such a lovely-looking colleen, the porter put her with the goods.

669 In America there's a Californian psychiatrist who guarantees patients a sure cure or their mania back.

670 Could a half-wit work part-time for Intelligence?

671   The human body is an interesting phenomenon. Often a pat on the back will result in a swollen head.

672   His doctor put him on a stable diet. Three times a day—oats and hay.

673   There was a driver on the M1 last week-end who must have been travelling at well over 150 m.p.h. Only two things passed him between Birmingham and Watford—an Air Force jet-bomber and a Boeing.

674   Then there's the crook who is so fond of policemen that he has two mounted cops in his house—over his mantelpiece.

675   Those new army quarters are not so lavish as people think. In some of them things are so bad that sergeants have to share one television set between two of them.

676   Some television programmes are so bad that viewers actually welcome a bit of interference.

677   Until he was sixteen he had had bad eyesight, then his father gave him 50p to get a haircut.

678   There's a woman in Coronation Street who has lovely Titian hair . . . it's imitition.

679   He can trace all his family back to the theatrical profession. Even his great-grandmother was an old trouper—and she swore like one, too.

680   A woman in a suburban street complained to the police that there was a neighbour constantly spying on her. She said that every time she peered through her curtains she saw this neighbour peering through hers.

681   She's decided to get a job as a theatre usherette. . . . It looks as though that's the only chance she'll ever get of walking down the aisle.

682   Harassed husband to wife: "Money, money, money! Those are the only three things you're interested in."

683   Thieves escaped with over £600,000 in a robbery in Birmingham. Police are trying to fathom a motive for the crime.

684   There was a fire at the Rates Office in Weston. Firemen were able to get the blaze under control before any serious good was done.

685   The most conceited crook in the world is the one who forges his own tickets for the Police Ball.

686   Politicians think that if they keep people always with their backs to the wall, the public will never see the writing on it.

687   In the West End of London it's growing more and more difficult to find a restaurant that gives same-day service.

688   A tattooed lady in Blackpool realised that the best pictures were those on her back, so she had the letters P.T.O. tattooed on her stomach.

689   Buyers in the motor-car market are complaining about the high price of bargains.

690   An optician is a man who is always up to the eyes in other people's work.

691   The Government has a plan to impregnate treasury notes with synthetic fibre to make them last longer, but a pound still won't go further than the width of a counter.

692   Whoever said that figures can't lie has never spent a day on the beach at Brighton.

693   When he bought a cheap third-hand pre-war car and took it home, his wife told him he was too old to play with a rattle.

694   On his day off an employee of the Gas Board stays in bed reading meters.

695   What a cornet player! He felled the entire audience with one blow.

696   Pessimist. That's a girl who wears water-wings in the bathtub.

697   There's a club comedian in Liverpool who keeps his wife in stitches all day. But she keeps asking for clothes.

698   She has sandy hair, eyes like bright little pebbles—and a complexion like a beach.

699   It's come to a fine thing when a packet of cigarettes costs almost the same as a smoking-jacket.

700   In his spare time he races pigeons. But he never comes in first.

701   Definition of a Shakespearian actor. Tall, dark and some ham.

702   Since Legal Aid became available in Britain, men have discovered a drop in the cost of leaving. You can get a divorce for £10.

703   Property Speculators. Men who are building and cooing.

704   Did you know you can even buy your meat on hire purchase? Dash down to the butcher's and open a joint account.

705   She married a contortionist who said he was rich, but he turned out to be just another rotten twister.

706   He's got the world's worst typist. If it takes her an hour to write a letter, how long will it take her to write the alphabet?

707   Proverb: A thing of beauty has joy for ever, especially if she's fair.

708   James Bond proverb: Variety is the life of spies.

709   There's money in fertiliser these days. It's one of the phew things with real export possibilities.

710   Gravity doesn't always work. It's harder to drop a girl than to pick one up.

711   Definition of a crowbar: A place where women gather for a glass of port.

712   If you want to understand the rudiments of English, get yourself one of those best-selling banned books.

713   Two beatniks saw a sign in a mens-wear store: "Clothes to Rent"— so they went in and slashed a few.

714   A modern song composer doesn't need to know how to carry a tune. Just how to lift one.

715   Marriage is a mutual partnership. The mute is the husband.

716   A gunman swept into a local post office and shocked the staff. Four women counterhands dropped stitches.

717   Irony is when a woman runs off with the milkman and leaves a note for her husband telling him about it, but signs it "Yours Faithfully".

718   A dealer is a man who goes around the houses buying old junk, and returns to his lair with an armload of valuable old antiques.

719   Hollywood actresses do not lightly dismiss their husbands. They wait until they need the publicity.

720   When you see two married people sitting in a restaurant holding hands you can bet they're not married to each other.

721   It's no good making your mind up to stay in if your wife has made up her face up to go out.

722   Never marry an ugly woman. People will think you married her for her money. Which you probably did.

723   A restaurant in Manchester has stopped putting Swiss cheese sections on the cheese board of adjacent tables. They kept yodelling across to each other.

724   If you want to keep your wife, tell her to go to the devil. Then she daren't go home to mother.

725   Hollywood is the place where an actress takes a man for better or for worse but not for keeps.

726   It gets colder in Scotland than anywhere else in the United Kingdom. Last winter in the Highlands, a snowman was seen making a little boy.

727   A woman gave birth to a baby on the London underground last week. The things some girls will do to get a seat.

728   When buying bacon make sure that it has been properly cured. You don't want it to have a relapse.

729   It's no good trying to judge a woman by her clothes these days. Insufficient evidence.

730   In Russia fewer people are living under canvas these days. There are more dresses in the stores.

731   Bachelor. A man who doesn't have a better half, so he has better quarters.

732   A nagging wife is a woman with an interferiority complex.

733   How to tell if a man is married. Watch him when he is driving a car, with a woman beside him. If he drives with both hands on the wheel, he's married.

734 A monologue is a conversation between you and a motor-car salesman.

735 Generally speaking a woman is generally speaking.

736 A wife is a person who cannot see the garage door at ten yards but can see a blonde hair on her husband's lapel a mile away.

737 A man who held the chair of applied electricity at a well-known American Institution has just died. He was electrocuted in Sing Sing.

738 A tailor in Macclesfield has an entirely new system for bespoke suits. He doesn't measure you. You just walk through a sheet of thin brown paper and he makes you a suit to fit the hole.

739 A shaggy dog is one where you don't know if it's wagging its tail or panting for breath.

740 There's a toreador in Madrid who always goes into the arena with a white cloak instead of a red one. He wants to be sure he can signal surrender if the bull gets too playful.

741 On a crowded beach one sunny day last summer a girl was sunbathing in a string of beads. And those were perspiration.

742 Marriage is a three-ring circus: first the engagement ring, then the wedding ring, then the suffering.

743 The three ages of woman are as follows: at twenty-three they are attentive, at thirty-five they are attractive, and at forty-five they are adhesive.

744 People who live in Scotland make their money go further than people who live in, say, Birmingham. It is further from Aberdeen to Westminster than it is from Birmingham.

745 A modern mother is a girl who knows how to hold a cigarette and a safety-pin in her mouth at the same time.

746 British politicians are considering the inauguration of England's first triangular postage stamp, to commemorate the tricentenary of the invention of the napkin.

747 A political party is a banquet at which M.P.s eat caviar and talk boloney.

748 Some city police forces have had instances of corruption in their ranks. This could never happen in the village of Moulting-in-the-Ditch near Aylesbury. The police force there is not only feverishly honest, but he's also a very nice chap.

749 Supercineramascope Vistavision is a new process for projecting 3-dimensional films on to a circular screen. The screen is in fact so broad that in the new Lassie picture, the dog is played by a disguised crocodile.

750 In the world of club cabaret it is no longer essential for a girl to have the right background to become a star. It is the right foreground that matters.

751 In a feverish effort to combat inflation the Chancellor of the Exchequer is going round all the car-parks stabbing car tyres.

752 Did you know that bookmakers have special wrist-watches for timing races? They don't go tick-tock, they go tic-tac, tic-tac.

753 Most women are just average—egotistical, avaricious, spiteful, mean and argumentative.

754 Every time we get another financial crisis a barber in Soho puts up the price of a shave according to how much longer his customers faces have grown.

755 At a village fête they were selling tea at 5 pence a mug. The queue of mugs was eighty yards long.

756 The optician's daughter went to a cocktail party. Two glasses and she made a spectacle of herself.

757 As a hostess Lady Farling was hopeless. She couldn't even entertain a doubt.

758 Women with time on their hands usually show it on their faces.

759 The manager said he was putting Mavis in the typing pool, so she went home and put on her swimsuit.

760 There's a new one-day cleaning business open in town. You leave your suit there to be cleaned and one day you might get it back.

761 If you are going to learn music, start on the violin. Later, switch to the piano—then you'll have somewhere to rest your beer.

762   Frankie was Number One on the Hit Parade for three weeks. Everyone was hitting him.

763   If you feel as though you need more exercise, why not lie down until the feeling wears off?

764   Jack is a great poker player. Give him a poker, and he'll play anything from the national anthem to "Smoke Gets In Your Eyes".

765   A man was arrested for stealing bicycles. In mitigation he confessed that he was a chain-smoker and couldn't get enough chains.

766   The government is putting jokes and cartoons on the back of Income Tax forms now, so that taxpayers can see the funny side.

767   Documentation has been simplified in Whitehall offices by the switch-over to red-tape recorders.

768   A misanthrope is a man who listens to his conscience with his hearing-aid switched off.

769   New York's mayor is determined to clean up the city. Every cop has been issued with a mop and pail.

770   There's a mercenary family in the north of England who save money every winter by sitting around a painting of a log-fire, eating peppermints.

771   Who says British workmen are bone idle? A foreman came across a road-mender last week with *two* spades in his hands. And clubs were trumps.

772   A man in Dover advertised for a daily woman, and hired 365 of them.

773   A man who goes in for breeding goats will sooner or later have to come out for fresh air.

774   Lightning Artist. A man who does his best paintings during a storm.

775   Newspapers are full of calamities. Just read the Births and Marriages columns.

776   Irene is always singing happily in the bath-tub. Not because she has a good voice—there's no lock on the door.

777   Ingrate: A man who turns the milk of human kindness sour.

778 Tattooist: A man who has designs on women.

779 Men and women go to nudist camps to air their differences.

780 A firm of dry cleaners hired two girls as invisible menders and they haven't seen them since.

781 It is terribly hard to keep young these days. Especially if you have four or five of them.

782 Do you find when smoking one of those new special filter-tip cigarettes that you get a sharp tingling, burning sensation in your mouth? If so, you've got the wrong end in it.

783 Big Chief Yellow Feather is no longer a full-blooded Indian. They threw him out of the tribe just because he became a blood donor for the Red Cross in Wyoming.

784 When he left the R.A.F. he had a D.F.C. and two bars. The D.F.C. was given to him by a grateful government. The two pubs, he bought with his gratuity.

785 There's a short-sighted tailor in Saville Row who works with a needle that has to wear a monocle in its eye.

786 Diana has a dress in her wardrobe that is so skimpy the moths have to stand on one leg.

787 A topless dress is just an ordinary dress with shoulder straps twenty-four inches long.

788 Edna said she wanted to become a policewoman. Now she's on the local beat. It's not much of a job but it's better than walking the streets.

789 A dope-ring is four or five guitarists standing round a microphone putting people to sleep.

790 Do you wake up in the morning feeling tired, fed-up, disgruntled, tetchy and irritable? With a rotten personality like that you ought to stay asleep.

791 He was the feather-weight champion of Shepton Mallet. He used to tickle his opponents to death.

792 He thinks he's a strong-man type, but the only bar he can bend between his teeth is a chocolate bar.

793 George's old grandmother is a noted artist. She spends most of the day drawing corks.

794 She makes the kind of records that send your head spinning at 45 r.p.m.

795 The BBC announcer said that as it was summer-time and people kept their windows open, listeners ought to keep their radio sets low down. So Bert put his on the floor.

796 When they sent Jim to Borstal, the Governor escaped by tunnelling his way out.

797 He was so poor he couldn't afford new shoes so he had his spats soled and heeled.

798 If, at sea, you want to tell port from starboard, look at the label.

799 While they were touring through Cornwall, their old car ran like a top. It kept spinning all over the road.

800 There was a big Indian uprising in the Sioux country. Big Chief Two Rivers accidentally sat down to a pow-wow on a cactus.

801 Venice, the city where omnibuses are fitted with anchors instead of brakes.

802 There's a new directory just been published in Hollywood listing all the actors and actresses. It's called "Who's Whose?"

803 The first thing a pilot does is learn how to control the air hostess.

804 Horace is a shift worker in an engineering works. Every time someone mentions work, he shifts.

805 Phyllis likes a drink. She went to a party where the hostess was noted for her culinary experiments. The gravy-boat was full of a new sauce laced with brandy. Phyllis ate four dinners.

806 She was wearing a faint perfume. One sniff and you fainted.

807 She entered two beauty contests at the same time. One was for the Most Beautiful Back and the other was the Most Beautiful Figure. Honestly, she didn't know which way to turn.

808 Crime may not pay but at least you're your own boss.

809   She's the sort of girl who doesn't mind what sort of a line you use on her as long as it's a supply line.

810   A staggering line is the shortest distance between two joints.

811   The reason why etiquette demands that a man should walk on the edge of the pavement nearest the traffic when out with a woman is so that she can be closer to the shop windows.

812   I saw a fat woman fall down yesterday and rock herself to sleep trying to get up again.

813   My wife made me a beach-suit out of awning canvas and now every time the sun goes down my trouser legs roll up.

814   Always put your girl on a pedestal, and then take the ladder away.

815   They lived in a small room in a very small house and he invited friends home to meet 'the little woman'. Turned out to be a midget.

816   Remember that when you have to decide whether to give up women or wine, consider the vintage.

817   When you feel old and the night's still young, frankly it's time to quit.

818   One of the benefits of being a failure in show business is that you never have to worry about making a come-back.

819   They're doing a new serial on BBC television next month that is a must for all viewers. Come to think of it, they mussed up the last one, too.

820   My neighbour has the loveliest kids. But the little boy will keep biting his nails. He cured him quite easily . . . pulled all his teeth out.

821   The joke about Beryl is that she weighs fourteen stone and when she got engaged started a *little* bottom drawer.

822   The first time Beryl took Tom home, her father was so pleased he told him to feel like one of the family . . . to treat the house as if it were his own . . . so Tom went and sold it.

823   My mother-in-law is coming to stay for a few days so I've been redecorating the spare room—with travel posters.

824   We know a desperate spinster who bought a broken-down old ice-box just to have an excuse for the ice-man to call.

825   He's invented a most marvellous gadget for speeding up production in all kinds of factories. He's calling it a whip.

826   He's not in a very good state of health, today. His wooden leg keeps bothering him. His wife hits him over the head with it.

827   Question of the day. . . . Instead of making ballet dancers prance around on tip-toe, why don't they just get taller showgirls?

828   She knew she'd made a mistake marrying Sandy Mackintosh Ferguson. On their wedding night she caught him trying on all the old shoes tied to the car.

829   Grandfather still chases after women. The only way Grandma can slow him down is by removing the tyres from his wheelchair.

830   Confucius said that a man who covers chairs instead of territory is a salesman who's always on the bottom.

831   Television was invented by an impatient man who wanted pictures to look at while he was waiting for something good on the radio.

832   When elections are in full swing I often think it's a pity the candidates don't follow suit.

833   Just look at this country. Millions of people are still so stupid that they continue to live in the past. . . . Come to think of it, why not? It's so much cheaper.

834   I bought a second-hand piano and started to learn to play it. My neighbours loved my music—they broke all the windows in my room so that they could hear me better.

835   Beryl's hands are so big that once when they were playing whist she went to scoop up a trick and picked up the whole table.

836   There's a brand-new singing star in Hollywood who is breaking all Bing Crosby's records. He's breaking them over his knee.

837   The cost of living is so high that the next step is for the Government to collect everyone's wages, and give them a voucher each week for a bottle of water and a bread roll.

838   FRED: Fred is a Communist now—one of those fellows who's got nothing and wants to share it with everyone. He does an honest day's work

and expects a week's pay. He's never kept any one job for longer than four hours but now he's decided to train as a labourer so as to know what sort of work he's out of if anyone asks. The only people who like him are the chaps at the Employment Exchange because with the way things are today, he's their only client. If they lose Fred they'll have to close the office up. Last week Fred refused to vote with the other men because he thought they were voting for a four-day week; as it happened they were voting for a four-day week-end.

839   He bought her a bikini swim-suit on the instalment plan. Unfortunately she wore it before he bought the second instalment.

840   She went on a summer cruise and gave the captain the glad aye aye.

841   He was arrested for using unsuitable language in the street and pleaded that he was only sowing his wild oaths.

842   There was a wealthy financier who took a tumble for a blonde and lost his balance at the bank.

843   Then there's the film actress who fell upon hard times; her ten-year-old daughter now has to wear her cut-down wedding gowns. . . .

844   He couldn't help getting drunk. He had two bottles of whisky and the fellows he asked to share them were teetotallers.

845   Now the building industry's in more trouble. Labourers want padded handles on their spades to prevent chafing when they're leaning on them.

846   Everyone talks about the weather but nobody does anything about it. Except me. I stay indoors.

847   There are only two specimens of a Neanderthal moron's head in existence. The British Museum has one and Bill's got the other.

848   A beatnik-type thug jumped at him in the darkness and dug a revolver into his stomach and said: "One peep out of you and I'll blow your brains out."

849   If you want your car remodelled double fast just leave it on a packed unattended car-park at rush hour for speedy action.

850   They were so poor, every Thursday their father used to make them bite their tongues so that they wouldn't grow up not knowing what meat tasted like.

851 She's a queer sort of woman. When you meet her you don't raise your hat, you raise your eyebrows.

852 Modern employers have to give their staffs five weeks' holiday every year so that they can go to the seaside and build up enough energy to come back and strike. . . . At one factory car engines are coming off the assembly line at a rate of three thousand a day; it's about time somebody did something to stop the things falling off before they're finished. . . .

853 The lady ordered a whisky at the bar, and as she looked worried the barman asked: "Would you like a chaser?" and she said: "I might—how old is he and what's he look like?"

854 In days of old when knights were cold, men didn't go to a tailor for a new suit; they went to an engineering works.

855 They've been married for ten years and they are still in love. He with the maid and she with the chauffeur.

856 The killer was so meticulous about his appearance that when they hanged him he insisted on the rope being tied with a Windsor knot.

857 He had so much fun at the bachelor party that he postponed the wedding.

858 The glove compartment of his new car is so small he has to wear finger-stalls.

859 When you go bald you may save a little time brushing your hair but it's taken up by the extra face you have to wash.

860 All she ever learned at High School was how many minks make a stole.

861 She joined a troupe of strip-tease dancers going to Morocco. Not that she liked dancing, but she was crazy about the uniform.

862 When Bill took her home after the dance she said: "Would you like to come in for a little while and I'll make you a nightcap." They went inside, and she got out her needles and knitted him a super little nightcap in blue and pink.

863 Little Miss Muffet sat on a tuffet eating her curds and whey. Down came a spider and she squashed it flat with her big feet.

864 This girl was beautiful and it was obvious that she was used to being picked up. She had handles on her hips.

865 The idiot was eating his lunch out of a toolbag—wallpaper sandwiches filled with paste, jelly, paint and bits of brocade curtain. "Fancy loading all that stuff into your stomach," said his friend. "Why not—I'm an interior decorator," the idiot replied.

866 The hotel had forty-two bedrooms, an eighteen-hole golf-course and nine-hole sheets. At the end of the week, the weather was still unsettled and so was their bill.

867 The local cafés were so dirty even the flies wouldn't eat there.

868 He's fed up. He wasted a whole week in a field making a clever hide-out where he could do some bird-watching—and then she moved to Worcester.

869 In Britain we have a wonderful climate. If only the weather didn't spoil it.

870 He's one of the new-style comedians. Wherever he's performing his act, queues start to form long before dawn. At the Emigration Office.

871 "And now the orchestra is going to play four choruses of 'Colonel Bogey'. If any of you in the audience know the words . . . keep quiet!"

872 He's got the most interesting girl-friend now. They like the same films, the same books, the same kinds of people. They laugh at the same jokes. There's only one problem. They don't like each other.

873 Britain is having some say in Anglo-American Nuclear Co-operation. The man who will push the button to set off the rockets might be an American, firing off an American missile from an American-based launching-pad, but the button he pushes will be British made.

874 Annie was a Western girl who always wore buttons and bows. She was the boys' favourite because all the other girls wore dresses.

875 In 1964 a man was cast away on a lonely Pacific Island with only a young redhead for company. . . . A petty-officer named Shaun O'Reilly.

876 Up in the Wyoming hills four Indian Chiefs were having a pow-wow. Bashing each other about with their pipes of peace.

877 In Oxford Street a street-salesman with a tray of nylon stockings hanging from his neck was surrounded by four men—his accountant, his bank manager, his chief buyer and the Income Tax inspector.

878 She's so gentle, so sweet, so obliging. She wouldn't hurt an elephant.

879 The filly turned to her young colt who was running round the paddock splay-legged: "If your father could see you now, he'd turn over in his gravy."

880 Hammer-Toes the Third was the smartest horse in the race. He only used three of his legs to run with. He used the fourth leg to trip up the other runners.

881 The jockey got down from his mount, tenderly rubbing his seat. He said: "I don't know how anything stuffed with hay can be so damned hard!"

882 If you want a horse to stand still you don't have to hitch him to a post, you just have to back him in a race.

883 A dreadful accident happened at the race-course last Thursday. One of the judges fell and broke his leg, and the vet shot him.

884 Give your dog WAGGO dogfood; it's the only dog food that tastes like a postman's leg.

885 Last week we found that the woman who'd been sitting watching TV with us for the past eight years was a complete stranger. My wife thought she was my mother, and I thought she was hers.

886 There he was, standing in the dock, a fine figure of a man—tall—dark—and handcuffed.

887 How about a Freeze-Eye dinner tonight? Frozen Chicken Broth and Frozen Peas, followed by Frozen Strawberries and Frozen Mousse. Then off to bed with a hot-water bottle to thaw out.

888 A romantic Westerner was in trouble way back in the old days. He came back to town with two black eyes. Fancy thinking Jesse James was a girl!

889 Every Wednesday he used to take his pigs to market but he never sold a single pig. No wonder—Market Day was Friday.

890 Then there's the farmer who couldn't keep his hands off his wife; so he sacked them and hit her himself.

891 Things are so hard financially, his only hope of salvation is to find a bad poker player with good money.

892 The television cameras always catch her worst side. The outside.

893 The latest thing in skiffle L.P. discs are American pop numbers with English subtitles.

894 When teacher asked Charlie to name a beast of burden, he said "Dad".

895 Just look at what's happened in the past twenty years! Your wife has got five years older.

896 In Texas there used to be a one-horse town called Oldsberg. It isn't even a one-horse town any more. The horse got sick of the place too, and moved to Houston.

897 There he was, strumming a folk-song on his guitar. It was a lousy song, but then, so were his folks.

898 The only reason she keeps getting divorced and remarried is because she's crazy about wedding cake.

899 Then there's the artist who's model is a bit touched.

900 Do you ever feel stiff in the joints? Then keep away from damp joints and go to a warmer pub.

901 I wouldn't say she's got a big mouth, all I know is that a lipstick only lasts her a week.

902 There's a new toothpaste on the market which has stripes. One girl's been using it for weeks now. Every other tooth is red.

903 His wife went to the fishmongers to buy a pair of kippers, but they hadn't got a pair so she bought two odd ones.

904 Have you noticed that everything's full of sex these days? Books are full of sex, movies are full of sex, newspapers are full of sex. . . . Everything except girls.

905 Veronica is in a quandary. She's got a lovely figure, and a very expensive new coat and she can't decide how to show them both off at the same time.

906   Zeke thought he had a club foot for thirty years until he died and they discovered he had his boots on the wrong feet.

907   The idiot invented a special low stool for milking coconuts.

908   She hit her fiance over the head with a bottle of Bitter Lemon. Lucky for him it was a soft drink.

909   Those Italian suits might *look* all right but they're not practical. The pockets are so small you can't get a tin of spaghetti into them.

910   He formed a strong attachment for a girl; and fitted it over her mouth.

911   Many hands might make light work, but also give you a peculiar appearance.

912   Do you know what he does with his fan mail? He uses the back of the envelope to make notes on.

913   Girl you shouldn't marry. The one who puts a bucket under a gas leak.

914   Milk keeps her awake at night. She's in love with the milkman.

915   They say you can't take it with you so Bert's not bothering to get any.

916   Every time he plays "Gypsy" on his violin it makes you think of home. That's how he plays—awful.

917   He doesn't need to look at comic strips in the newspapers. He's seen his wife getting ready for bed.

918   To start the car there's a little button on the dashboard with the word "Push" written on it. All you have to do is get out and push.

919   A woman is a person who will stand in the rain on a street corner waving a flag for two hours while waiting for a Royal Procession, yet wouldn't cross the road to buy a piece of cod for her husband's dinner.

920   A Liberal is a man who makes enemies left and right.

921   When you see how brilliantly white and clean modern detergents make our laundry, what an awful lot of dirty folk we must have been in the good old days.

922   Kennedy's great-grand-grandfather is the only Irishman who went to America in the *Mayflower* and had enough money for the fare.

923 She hasn't voted for eight years. Not because she isn't on the voting register, but because she's too fat for the polling booth.

924 It is the way of the world that a full sweater is ample compensation for an empty head.

925 Always remember, when you feel that you are ordinary and nondescript, that a fast clock is never right, and a slow clock is never right, but a clock that is broken is right at least twice a day.

926 The Corps Diplomatique racket has become a farce in London. During the typhoid epidemic, a Spanish attaché refused to catch it—he claimed diplomatic immunity.

927 Roger has been taking a body-building course which consists of three long-playing records. He's only been through the discs four times and already his pick-up arm has developed 2-inch biceps.

928 He's invented a short two-runged ladder. It's specially adapted for young women who want to elope from bungalows.

929 It's no good telling Mabel not to go out with strange men—what other types of men could such a strange girl get?

930 Show business isn't good for some pop singers. One week their latest disc is sweeping the country, and the next week, *they* are.

931 We know a fellow who is crazy about fish. He'd walk a mile for a packet of frozen fish fingers. And that's not all. Yesterday at Caxton Hall he married a mermaid.

932 One show in Leeds last week was so bad the manager was giving people their money back as they walked in.

933 Percy was stopped by a footpad on his way to the theatre, in a dark alley. The thief said: "Come on, put your hands up." and Percy said: "Up what?"

934 There was a Russian spy ship off the Dogger Bank last week. Secretly trawling for fish.

935 The new £20 banknotes are smaller; about the size of an American dollar, and worth just as much.

936 Mike is never going to the local barber again. Right alongside the chair there was a drip-transfuser.

937 When he visited his girl, her father answered the bell, and shouted into the house: "Evelyn—there's something to see you."

938 William has a new girl-friend. She reads a lot, likes classical music and modern art, loves visiting museums and memorials. But then, nobody's perfect.

939 He's an associate producer. Associates with all the girls in the cast.

940 What a girl! Just like Venus de Milo. Old, cold as marble, and chipped in places.

941 The singer confessed: "All the time I'm singing in front of a mike or a TV camera, I just don't know what to do with my hands." The producer said: "Have you tried clamping them over your mouth."

942 The BBC is always careful not to annoy viewers. Because of complaints about cruelty they cancelled a programme about bullfighting in Spain and put on a war film instead.

943 A fool and his money are soon parted, but boy, what memories.

944 Girls; never marry an alcoholic! The first night he carries you over the threshold—and after that you carry *him*.

945 He's just invented a revolutionary deaf-aid. It's a card which the deaf person hangs across his chest, with the word "SHOUT" printed on it, and it sells for only ten guineas.

946 When he wanted to forget, instead of joining the Foreign Legion, he joined the W.R.E.N.S. He wanted to do it the hard way.

947 Utopia is a place where all men will be equal and someone else will have to empty the dustbins.

948 Remember, folks, that if your baby-sitter rings you at the party to tell you that one of your twins has blown up, she's fed one of them twice by mistake.

949 A diamond can cut through the hardest metal, and it's not bad for softening blondes, either.

950 Remember—a girl takes hours and hours to get ready to go out to dinner, and the longer she takes the more hungry she gets.

951 When he needs someone to pour out his troubles to, he doesn't have to waste money on a psychiatrist—he picks a barmaid.

952 She's a business woman. She's always sticking her nose into other people's business.

953 He didn't know what to do for a career, then one day he found himself bitten by the Entertainment bug—it was his own fault for going to such a cheap theatre.

954 They're starting up the Great Western Railway again . . . they need it to bring all the TV westerns down from Liverpool docks to Lime Grove.

955 There's not much Dan doesn't know about horses. He worked in a Soho restaurant for four years.

956 The only thing that doesn't strike in a Midlands motor works is the clock.

957 The two birds are perched on an oak tree branch. Says one to the other: "Have you bred any good *rooks* lately."

958 News item: 240 young girl students at Grossmere Girls High School have complained to the Grossmere Council about the new observatory which has been built opposite their dormitory.

959 In the corner of the bar there were two chimney-sweeps telling smutty stories.

960 Letter from Convict 445 in Wormwood to his solicitor: "Long time no she."

961 The garage mechanic looked over Ernie's car and said: "If I were you I'd keep the oil and change the car."

962 In Montreal there's a boarding house owned by a Catholic and a Jew. It's called the Saint Isadore Hotel.

963 She wore a restless evening gown. It kept coming out and going in.

964 If a girl is too beautiful for words, who wants to waste time talking?

965 He shaves oranges. The barber of Sevilles.

966 Annie hadn't had a meal for a week and her doctor is worried about it. She's thirty-six doses of medicine behind.

967 You've heard of that song, "Carry Me Back to Green Green Pastures"? If you've ever been there you'll know why you *have* to be carried.

968 He is one of the country's popular recording artists. Some of his records are now collector's items. Garbage collector's. He's so fond of himself that he's had his telephone specially rigged so that it doesn't ring —it claps.

969 Her father was in the Navy; he was a sub-human lieutenant.

970 She's the best touch-typist in the firm. In fact, there's no one else to touch her, except the general manager.

971 Once when Julian Scrogg played his violin at Stratford, the audience cried and cried. But the management refused to give them their money back.

972 He's a very happy man tonight. His wife has presented him with a little bundle. It won't be the first time he's done his own laundry, either.

973 He was so good last time that the management have doubled his salary. He used to get ten pounds a week, now he's getting ten pounds every two weeks.

974 He's got the sort of a voice that, when other people have got it, they say, "Excuse me" afterwards.

975 He got his wallpaper from a mail-order catalogue . . . and still had eighteen pages left over after he'd papered four rooms.

976 Eat? She's the only woman who goes into a restaurant with her own fork-lift.

977 The hotel had a winding staircase. Last man in wound it up.

978 I asked the bartender for a dry Martini. He pushed the bottle at me and said: "Dry your own, you can see I'm busy."

979 My wife didn't have the slightest sympathy for me when I injured my foot. All she said was: "Well—you shouldn't have kicked Mom so hard."

980 Magnum cigarettes do not leave nasty, filthy dark-brown stains all over your fingers . . . only round your mouth.

981 The butler went down to the cellar and fetched up something so old it was covered with cobwebs . . . her ladyship.

982 He kisses all the girls goodbye even when he isn't going anywhere.

983 We decided to have something novel for lunch. Food.

984 It's the sort of cheap hotel where if you pull down the blinds the building collapses.

985 They served chicken that really tickled your palate. They left the feathers on.

986 The best way to keep a stiff upper lip is to starch your moustache.

987 The manager said: "If you play ball with me I'll play ball with you", so they spent the afternoon kicking each other round the office.

988 How about that famous politician who's been advocating peaceful co-existence for years? . . . He's been incompatibly married eight times.

989 She's the sort of girl who helps you kill time if you prefer your time dead.

990 She uses toothpaste twice a day. If she didn't stick them with paste they'd drop out.

991 One girl kept her brief swim-suit in an aspirin bottle. A full one.

992 Putting up a deckchair is as easy as bandaging your torn fingers.

993 The latest style of ballpen really does write under water—but what soggy letters my girl gets.

994 He's so musical I've seen him standing in the hall conducting the musical doorbell chimes.

995 Liquor improves with age—the older you get the more you like it.

996 His wife is a kleptomaniac but her sister is worse. *She* walks backwards into stores and leaves things on the counters.

997 One psychiatrist is treating a lot of schizophrenics these days. He had a double couch. For split personalities.

998 Today two can still live as cheaply as one if one is getting National Assistance and the other is on a diet.

999   He's the one sailor in Chatham who *has* to wear bell-bottomed trousers because that's the only kind that fits his shape.

1000   The trouble with Alice is that she's so melancholy. She has a shape like a melon and a face like a collie.

1001   Fred Bloggs has been practising music for years and years. He's got quite a lot to give the world of music—two broken fiddles, an untuned piano and a saxophone with no mouthpiece.

1002   There once was a Frenchman who was so afraid of losing his girl-friend he took fencing lessons and built a fence around her.

1003   He was a Parachute Corps Sergeant until he signed the pledge. Now he says he's never going to take another drop.

1004   You didn't know that Fanny was in pictures, did you? Most of them are by Salvador Dali.

1005   Horace has just written a new book. It's the kind of book you can dip into, if you don't mind getting sludgy fingers.

1006   You can tell how famous he's become on the stage. They put his name under the name of the printer on the playbills.

1007   Sam's got a job now. At last his pockets are full. He hangs around all day with his hands in them.

1008   Lionel says that he didn't know what happiness was until he got married—and then it was too late.

1009   The Indian Chief, Big Chief Running Water, has two daughters. One's very cold, and one's very hot. They do a tap-dance routine on the halls.

1010   When his Aunt got stung by a bee the doctor told her over the 'phone to put some blue-bags on. So she went and put a pair on.

1011   His wife's very strict about some things. He even had to sell his big St. Bernard dog because she wouldn't allow any strong liquor in the house.

1012   In Texas there was a cowhand who weighed nearly thirty stones. He was the only guy in Texas with a bow-legged horse.

1013   Jack was so disgusted with everything he read about the habit of smoking that he's given it up. Not given up smoking—given up reading.

1014   She believes that a ring on the hand is worth two on the 'phone.

1015   After you've tried everything under the sun, why not try a little something under the moon?

1016   On his way to work tomorrow he's going to slip into the barber's and get a quotation for a haircut.

1017   He's a bit of an art critic in a way. He doesn't understand women but he knows what he likes.

1018   Here's a guaranteed method for making an approach to a girl. First tell her her face is familiar, and then act the same way.

1019   Poor Sid. His boss told him he had no brains, so Sid went and blew them out just to prove his boss wrong.

1020   Trouble is she has an impediment in her speech. She can't say No.

1021   The landlady told the vicar that her husband had gone up aloft. The vicar was going to console her when she pointed out that he'd gone up a loft with the maid.

1022   He had a cut-glass accent and he gave her an engagement ring to match.

1023   Stella thinks her eyes are so beautiful. She has them looking into each other all day long.

1024   Girl's don't seem to like Dave. He's been turned down so often he's starting to look like a page in an outspoken novel.

1025   His wife broke her jaw chewing on a steak. He rang up the doctor and asked him to drop in some time next week, if he happened to be passing.

1026   Their house is furnished throughout with period furniture. So much down and the rest over a period of three years.

1027   Ben fell over a prayer-rug the other day. You should have heard his language.

1028   Ever since he had his operation he's been eating like a horse. That's because his wife gives him his meals in a nosebag.

1029   He's just written a new piece of music for summer holiday-resort shows. It's called the "Foreshore Concerto".

1030 When the secret agent took on this mission in the Middle East, he asked if he had to take tropical kit. But Kit was working in another part of the world so he took Brenda instead.

1031 In the room he found a dead spy lying on the floor with two blades sticking out of his back. His shoulder blades.

1032 They told the spy that when dawn came he would die. When Dawn arrived she turned out to be a cheery blonde and for the first time in his life he really lived.

1033 There was a secret message written on the paper with a quill. Maybe the pigeon wrote it himself with one of his feathers.

1034 The beautiful spy was carrying arms. She also had two fully loaded legs.

1035 She was the daughter of Mata Hari on her mother's side. On her father's side was a touch of sciatica.

1036 The intelligence colonel picked up the 'phone and called his secretary six times. Then he remembered he didn't have a secretary.

1037 He was told that he would have to undertake an extremely dangerous mission in Frankfurt. So he started to look up the plane schedules. To New York.

1038 There's nothing in this world as good as a good woman. And nothing so hard to find, either.

1039 The secret message was written in code. Even a baby could have understood it. The colonel studied it for six minutes and then sent for a baby.

1040 John wishes he'd never got married now. His mother-in-law is fed up with her husband and is coming home to her daughter.

1041 He was a dairy farmer and when he was at the conference he shook hands with everyone one finger at a time.

1042 She went out window shopping and came home with nothing except flat flabby feet and a flat nose.

1043 The football pools results weren't so good this week. They say that the winners are all going to get a bag of crisps.

1044   Years ago he used to be very poor indeed, but he's cleaning up now. Sometimes it's the street, sometimes it's the back yard.

1045   Maud has got to have more exercise to get her weight down. The doctors told her to push herself away from the table four times a day before meals.

1046   She's never bothered about make-up. Sometimes when she's got no eye-shadow left she just sticks her head up the chimney and blinks a couple of times.

1047   New Songs on the Hit Parade:
"She used to go with the landlord but now she goes with the lease."
"You can take a horse to water but rhubarb must be forced."

1048   The managing director was off colour the other morning. He rang for his secretary three times and was starting to get annoyed when he noticed she was still on his lap.

1049   Dick says his father has got ten years for highway robbery. He pinched a stretch of the Great North Road.

1050   He went out with a telephone operator who knew her job from A to B.

1051   She was wearing a lovely big string of beads. He knew he could count on her.

1052   A fellow who took his invalid wife to the doctor was told that he would have to keep her very quiet. He worked himself into a nervous breakdown trying to do it.

1053   They're not a political family but his father used to be a bit of a platform speaker. He was at Crewe Station announcing the trains.

1054   Ernie's people are farmers. All the family work on the farm. They're real sons of the soil. In fact, they're just about the dirtiest family in Hampshire.

1055   He's so selfish he wears frosted glasses so that no-one else can see what he's looking at.

1056   He was so upset he was beside himself. And you never saw a more repulsive couple.

1057   What a girl she was. Eighteen stones of her. She wasn't just *in* the front row of the chorus. She *was* the front row of the chorus.

1058 In London there's a travel agent who's so keen on travel that he goes to work in a Charing Cross Road office from Golders Green via Siam.

1059 Washing her hair in cold water every day has given her a warped mind.

1060 At an Olde Tyme Dance a girl wanted to try the St. Bernard's waltz. It was all right for a time, but the St. Bernard she was dancing with kept slapping her with his brandy barrel.

1061 He put his wife on a pedestal. She looks pretty cute on the wash-basin in the bathroom.

1062 She just loves to bury her face in the new-mown hay. Who cares where she buries it as long as it's out of view?

1063 He said she was one of the loveliest roses of the East. But he didn't say whether it was East Acton or East Ham.

1064 Frank is so ugly his shadow insists on walking on the other side of the road.

1065 She's got such a big figure that everything she wears is a pull-over.

1066 His wife is so lovely he's left breathless. Like the time last week when he got the account from her beauty salon.

1067 Tom's wife had a fight with the chimney-sweep and gave him a white eye.

1068 If an actress is good-looking nothing else matters. She can always rely upon the males in the audience to remember her lines.

1069 They had a humming bird for dinner the other day. You know what a humming bird is, don't you? It's a long dead duck.

1070 He used to go around a lot with a beautiful red-head named Patsy, but she threw him over. He's sorry they teach ju-jitsu by correspondence.

1071 They went to a night-club where the only wine they served was so old it had to be brought to the table in a wheel-chair.

1072 There's a brand-new musical play on Broadway. You know the kind of thing—a sort of opera without music and no plot.

1073   Years ago there was a very poor family and the mother used to run a Chinese laundry. You've no idea how dirty some of those Chinese got.

1074   Dick ran away from home when he was fifteen. His mother used to keep a light burning in the window until she got tired of standing there striking matches.

1075   They tried a new local restaurant for dinner. The steaks were so fresh there were two rustlers still on the plate changing the brand.

1076   His wife's got system if nothing else. Especially in the kitchen. She keeps the tea in the cleaning cupboard in a tin of cocoa labelled "sugar".

1077   She's a cleaner at the Folies Bergère. It's her job to go around after the show and pick up all the eyeballs from the stalls.

1078   After a trip to Australia her boy-friend brought Maud back a little present. A boomerang. She was so mad. She nearly went crazy trying to throw it away.

1079   The photographer asked Freda if she wanted a large picture or a small one, and when she said a small one would do, he asked her to keep her mouth shut when she posed.

1080   Fred always called a spade a spade until one night when he fell over one.

1081   Women *do* believe in long engagements. Just you try to get through to a certain number when some woman is on the 'phone.

1082   She lists all her boy-friends in her him book.

1083   Some Members of Parliament are so poor that they will walk miles to save a penny. Quite a lot of them think nothing of going to the Prime Minister half-way through the week for a sub.

1084   The photographer eyed her shrewdly and then walked to his camera, picked up the big black cloth—and covered her face with it.

1085   You know what perfume is don't you? It's smell which is used to smother a worse one.

1086   Hobson's choice? It's not Mrs. Hobson—it's the blonde next door.

1087   The Civil Service—where, when someone dies, or leaves, no vacancy is noticed.

1088   Good for Mike! Since he came out of prison he's been a reformed character. For the last two years he's worked at the City Baths—and he's never taken a bath.

1089   Definition of a conceited actor: Ham and ego.

1090   In my philosophy of life there are three things which never come together; the time, the girl and the place.

1091   They shot Billy the other day, the bullet went right across the room, hit his head, careered into space—and came out behind his ear.

1092   This new show is doing record business, I hear. Folks would rather stay home and play their records.

1093   He's so crafty he wears open-toed sandals and walks in the gutter to pick up cigarette-ends with his hammer toes.

1094   The father was a pigmy. He kept his son in a sty.

1095   At a dance the other night, she had to leave in embarrassment. She was wearing a strapless evening gown, and she got hiccups.

1096   He never looks at girls lying on the beach sun-bathing—unless he's wearing dark glasses.

1097   At school they taught him all about the birds and the bees. Now he's got five birds and every one's a honey.

1098   Mrs. Brough bought a new dress at a bargain sale. Her husband said: "Darling, it suits you absolutely perfectly. It's horrible."

1099   There was quite a heat wave in the South last week. All the banks were doing a brisk trade in iced lolly.

1100   Talking of folks being lazy, the doctor told one woman she ought to exercise more. Now she stands at the window every morning blinking her eyelids.

1101   Fred was quite a crook in the old days. He had all the rackets sewn up. It proved to be valuable experience—now he's working on mail bags.

1102   I went to a smashing party last night. It wasn't very crowded. There was no one else under my table.

1103 Zena bought some new perfume the other day. It's so powerful, she says the makers give away a free course on self-defence with every bottle.

1104 The doctors have warned us again that eating too much luxury food shortens the breath. So—who wants long breath?

1105 Now Fred's on a balanced diet. He has four ounces of white-meal bread and a glass of water each day. He's not at a health clinic—he's in prison.

1106 If an apple a day keeps the doctor away, think how many other people you can keep at bay if you try garlic.

1107 When she stands on the bathroom scales and checks her weight, she only stands on them with one leg.

1108 To gain a little weight Bill has been sticking to starchy foods only. For dinner last night he had nothing but two stiff shirt-collars, a dickey and three cuffs.

1109 The Rainbow Room Nightclub, where the lights are pink, the walls are grey, the table-linen white—and when you get the bill you turn green.

1110 He's the kind of bore who's here today and here tomorrow.

1111 In America a four-poster bed is one with two posters advertising corsets, one advertising toothpaste and the fourth advertising advertising.

1112 She has hammer toes and feet shaped like sickles. They've hired her for the Moscow Ballet.

1113 He was shocked when he learned that he was born out of wedlock. Must have been born on the wrong side of an electric blanket.

1114 What you need is some iron in your blood. But first you must get some blood.

1115 If you were born under Capricorn and are not married, this could be a happy day for you. In fact if you are not married it could be a happy day, no matter what sign you were born under.

1116 Warner Brothers are still churning out those sixty-minute television Westerns. Last year their allotment for bullets alone was a million dollars and statistics prove that Wyatt Earp, Matt Dillon and Cheyenne have between them rubbed out half the Texas and Arizona population. We can only hope the policy spreads right across the States.

1117 We know an Indian called Big Chief Fellow Traveller—a pink Indian.

1118 That advertising mania for marking everything "This week—Three-pence Off" is spreading like mad. Yesterday in Bond Street a Blue Canadian Mink coat was marked "10p off".

1119 Isn't it a shame about the poor Scot who needed money so badly he took some out of his Post Office savings?

1120 Patient speaking to surgeon just about to operate: "I say, a funny thing happened to me as I was coming to the theatre this morning. . . ."

1121 Ben's just written a new mystery novel. The mystery is: who's going to publish it?

1122 Lydia is a fur trapper. She only threatens to open her trap and she gets a mink coat.

1123 Have you seen the face-towels they give you in some hotels when you're taking a bath? Little things that are sent to dry us.

1124 A student reading Law at a university was asked to state the maximum penalty for bigamy and wrote: "Two mothers-in-law."

1125 He's a musical contortionist—plays the harmonica by ear.

1126 She was elected Miss Demeanour of 1976.

1127 American businessmen meeting in Chicago agree that the largest commodity turnover in the States is in chewing-gum.

1128 She's had lots of dates but so far not one of the men has given her a stone.

1129 If a woman does the household chores for £5 a week, that's domestic science. If she does them for nothing—that's matrimony.

1130 Sign in window displaying corsets: We take your breadth away.

1131 We have just learned that it's so cold in Northern Alaska the inhabitants live elsewhere.

1132 In the first-class dining-room of the steamer a fat man was piling so much fodder into his vitals that someone else reported him to the captain as a stowaway.

1133   In a New York store window full of bizarre neckties we saw one simple notice reading: "Listen!"

1134   There is a rumour that the Soviet premier is offering to erect a memorial to sailors who wanted Columbus to turn back.

1135   Mr. Smith bought a house-boat on the Thames. It's great fun living on a boat. You never get nasty rude letters through your letter-box when you owe money. Just a torpedo through the hull.

1136   Fellows used to flock around Jack's girl like flies round a glue-pot. But Jack's the one who got stuck with her.

1137   Lydia always wears a bright red rose in her hair. She never suffers from dandruff. Her trouble is greenfly.

1138   When he took the girl home, her husband welcomed him with out-stretched arms—a Colt revolver and a Winchester repeater.

1139   He's a regular Darby and Joan man. All he thinks about are horses and women.

1140   He's an honest type of actor who doesn't yearn to play Hamlet. He knows that Hamlet would beat him. He also believes that a small role is better than a long loaf.

1141   Her head is empty, but that's more than you can say for her sweater.

1142   He keeps bragging about his ancestors. He claims that they were with Noah in the Ark. So I told him about my ancestors. They weren't with Noah—they had a boat of their own.

1143   About those hotels where they don't provide mirrors in the bathroom. After you've had a wash, you have to look at the towel to see if your face is clean.

1144   The last thing a man wants is a talking doll.

1145   He's a tape recorder in the Army. Keeps a check on how many corporals there are.

1146   There was once a Hollywood actress who was so busy making movies her stand-in had to have her baby.

1147   The game of love has never yet been called off because of bad light.

1148 He polished his boots until he could see his face in them, and frightened himself to death.

1149 The craze for topless dresses is worrying club managers. The other night in a crowded Soho dive the only girls wearing clothes were the strippers.

1150 Then there's Flash Tornado, the latest pop-idol: his manager groomed him for stardom and now he has his own stable.

1151 He's doing very well as a young pop-singer now—just bought his mother a £5,000 bungalow, bought his father a 3-litre car and given his sister his bucket and spade.

1152 They went to a Cypriot restaurant for dinner; a dingy, badly-lit joint, with dirty cracks all down the walls. They couldn't read them because they were written in Greek.

1153 His father came home from the racetrack with a profit of over £50. He didn't pick any horses—just pockets.

1154 The Martians must have discovered a more powerful fuel for their unidentified objects. Last night I saw a flying soup-plate.

1155 He once worked as a cleaner in a computer factory. He did all the electronic brain-washing.

1156 There was once a very shy blonde who was so attractive to men she had to go and live in a bird sanctuary.

1157 After a heavy night out with the boys he went back to the bar next morning and ordered an aspirin on the rocks.

1158 Father lived to be eighty-four. He had a long outdoor life. This was because whenever Mother started nagging him he went out for a walk.

1159 Report in the local about an accidental shooting—"Last night forty-nine-year-old Sir Egbert Doolittle went rabbiting on Dewscombe Common. He is survived by a wife, two sons and a rabbit."

1160 The best time to visit Paris is between your eighteenth and twenty-fifth birthdays.

1161 Layabout beatniks all tell the same story. They're trying to form a new world. Most of them don't even know what the *old* world looks like. They've never had a haircut.

1162   A fellow in the Royal Navy lost a stone in weight in one night. He took off his diving boots.

1163   The pet-shop proprietor was so small that he could clean out the rabbit hutches without stooping. He's the only feller in East Cheam who has turnups on his underpants.

1164   Willie backed a horse at Hurst Park which nearly won the last race. It would have been a photo-finish but by the time he got to the post it was too dark to take pictures.

1165   A Viennese doctor has a new method for getting fat women to lose weight. He sews up three-quarters of the stomach.

1166   Albert stayed at a little pub called the "Saggy Stocking". It used to be the "Star and Garter" but the elastic broke.

1167   A physicist wonders what happens when you immerse a cold body in tepid water. The 'phone usually rings.

1168   In some ways Jack's a bit like Peter Pan. He has to be revived every Christmas.

1169   Bert has just got a new job. He's the official R.S.P.C.A. representative at wrestling matches.

1170   Mr. Phelps bought a very nice little puppy at the pet shop in Soho the other day. He bought it because it was going cheap. Most puppies go bow-bow, so one that goes cheap must be worth a fortune.

1171   Did you hear about the frustrated bank robber? He broke into Barclays Bank, got into the vaults, began to fiddle with the combination on the safe, and got the Light Programme.

1172   A girl in despair is the one who always comes home wearing the same amount of lipstick she left home with.

1173   They had dinner at a very ritzy restaurant. When Jack saw how much the House Charge was, he had to 'phone his solicitor and raise a mortgage.

1174   She was a woodworker's daughter. The brazen bit.

1175   She thinks a lawyer's briefs are his underpants.

1176   He was a painter, and one day he dropped a can of yellow enamel from a fifth floor window. Painted the crowds with sunshine?

1177 A tailor in Stockholm has a wonderful job. Sewing pockets on squirrels so that they can keep young.

1178 He went into a West End restaurant and ordered two boiled eggs. The waiter said they were off because their egg-boiling machine had broken down.

1179 He was a fine upstanding man. Then he fell over a banana skin.

1180 He always gives his girl a lipstick for her birthday. That way he gets most of it back.

1181 Did you hear about the short-sighted snake? He wasted a month trying to make love to a coil of rope.

1182 Two men who didn't trust each other started a private bus service. On the first day of operations they both turned up for work as conductors.

1183 She's the kind of woman who always enters a room voice first.

1184 He's not the kind of man who puts a difficult job off till tomorrow. He puts it off altogether.

1185 While all the other chorus girls were slowly climbing the ladder of success, Marylin took the elevator. She married a producer.

1186 He calls their home "The Elms". That's where they live—in an elm tree.

1187 He's the kind of character girls are scared they might not meet in the dark.

1188 The girl was a nurse, but she gave it up. She didn't like the way things were at the house where she worked. The kids were too backward and their father was too forward.

1189 His wife stayed in the powder-room so long, he sent a message in to her asking her why she didn't write.

1190 It was so hot on the beach, a lot of middle-aged dogs were lying around with their coats unbuttoned.

1191 She went to a spring sale and bought some springs.

1192 She was pretty but her legs were like matchsticks; in fact, the last time I saw legs like that there was a message tied to one of them.

1193 Do you know what I'd do if I had all the money in the world? I'd pay a few of my debts.

1194 At the wedding the bridesmaids wept, the mother wept, the bride wept, and even the cake was in tiers.

1195 When a lifeguard pulled his wife out of the sea at Brighton the husband told him it was very good of him but he really shouldn't have bothered.

1196 Every time there's a new moon why don't you 'phone the Income Tax Office and ask them to turn your money over?

1197 His fiancée was most considerate about her singing. She went abroad to train.

1198 John has opened a restaurant in a poor district. He's flogging a dead horse.

1199 He's a sailor who doesn't start any naval manoeuvres until he gets shore leave.

1200 He was a short-sighted musician. One day he fell over a clef.

1201 He had to go back to the opticians because he'd left his eyes fastened on the blonde receptionist.

1202 She's an iceberg. Her gown is four-fifths below the surface.

1203 His ancestors date back to the time of the Garden of Eden. That's the kind of snake he is.

1204 He's a lightning artist. Frustrated when there's no storm.

1205 It's only the man who carefully puts away a little for a rainy day who ends up with enough money to go and live where it never rains.

1206 If baby is cutting her teeth, take the scissors off her.

1207 They gave him the part of the swashbuckling hero in the play. At rehearsal, he fell and buckled his swash.

1208 She was so nervous even her pearls were highly strung.

1209 There's something odd about Charlie; he can enter a three-legged race without a partner.

1210 Three Scotsmen wanted to find the best way to commit suicide with one bullet, so they put their heads together.

1211 He worries so much even his scratch wig is going bald.

1212 They've invented a new type of life jacket for women: it fits around the chest and acts like a buoy.

1213 She offered herself as a blood donor: when they asked what type she was, she said she was the sleek, sultry type.

1214 Women have conquered this business of fat. Nowadays they can take it off, put it on, and even re-organise it.

1215 On their twenty-fifth wedding anniversary he suggested to his wife that they ought to stand in silence for one minute.

1216 He had his initials embroidered on his pyjamas so that no matter how tight he got he would know who he was.

1217 Just as you are managing to make ends meet some busybody always comes along and moves the ends.

1218 Joe and his fiancée are always together. They're what you call insufferable.

1219 He's so shy for an artist. He can't even paint a bowl of fruit if the wrappers are off the oranges.

1220 The undertaker got fed up with little boys who kept running into his shop asking if he had any empty boxes.

1221 A genial Yid admitted that the reason why he always won money at cards yet lost at the races was because he couldn't shuffle the horses.

1222 She went to the hospital to prevent them operating on her boy-friend. She didn't want anyone else opening her male.

1223 One secretary has changed her job a dozen times in the past couple of years—but she's on the last lap now.

1224 She only had seventeen candles on her birthday cake. Evidently she intended lighting them at both ends.

1225 He's so mean, if he found a bottle of aspirin he'd bang his head against a wall until he got migraine.

1226 He was without money the other day and got a nasty shock from the electricity bill.

1227 He's got a very good head for figures. And two great staring eyes in it.

1228 Daniel, the town's wealthiest painter, died. A couple of night's later his wife switched on the radio and heard him singing "I'm Painting the Clouds With Sunshine".

1229 The married couple had to leave their young son Stanley at home. Apparently he wasn't any good travelling by air. . . . Even collecting airmail stamps made him giddy.

1230 He's so lazy he'd rather not see his wife off at Southampton in case he has to throw a couple of kisses from the dockside.

1231 He only went to church twice in his life. The first time they threw water at him, and the second time they tied him to a nagging woman. The third time he goes they'll throw dirt on him. That's life.

1232 A woman was in church with her crying baby. The parson shouted: "Please keep that baby quiet. He's disturbing me." The woman retorted: "If you ask me, you're disturbing *him*."

1233 Parson's first speech is a little confused as he is nervous. "My brethren," he said. "One thing is certain—there is indeed a hell . . . however, I will not go into that just now."

1234 As he sat down to the first meal she had ever set before him, the young groom realised what lay ahead in the years to come. Supper consisted of wedding-cake and chips.

1235 A man's best friend is his dog. Some men have so few friends the dog just has to be best.

1236 It must be awfully embarrassing for a scout-master who is leading his troop of young lads down the street and one of them whistles after a passing blonde.

1237 How often do you hear a parishioner mutter to the vicar: "By the way, I didn't see you on the links last Sunday?"

1238 All a man can do when his wife complains he isn't paying attention to her is to admit that he heard every stupid word she said.

1239   When a fat woman tries to wear a skimpy Italian sheath-dress, somehow a lot is lost in the translation.

1240   Then there's Ug-Ug, the cave-dweller, who got into trouble with his wife—she complained he hadn't dragged her anywhere for months.

1241   All over the camping ground at Hayling Island she's known as the "Caravan Sight".

1242   He showed her a photograph of himself when he was a kid of eight, sitting on his father's knee. She stared at it, and then said: "Alf—you never told me your father was a ventriloquist."

1243   They cured David of drinking by an operation. They removed a long brass rail that had been pressing against his foot for years.

1244   Owing to many complaints from disgruntled visitors, an old-fashioned hotel has finally done something about its old iron bedsteads. They've oiled 'em.

1245   They've been married for five years, and at long last they are expecting the blessed event—divorce.

1246   Remember that no matter which Chancellor plays Santa Claus, it's you who holds the bag.

1247   What's the good of a topless dress if you've nothing to put in it?

1248   She thinks saddle-bags are the trousers you wear when you're horse-riding.

1249   There's always safety in numbers until you read them off a speedometer.

1250   Women are like newspapers. Back numbers are not in great demand; they are worth looking over; they have a great deal of influence over men's minds; you can't believe anything they say; there's little demand for the bold-faced type. And every man should have his own and not borrow his neighbour's.

1251   He said to this girl: "Come, come, the night is young," and she said: "Aren't you a little envious of it?"

1252   They had an eight-course dinner including some caviare supplied from the Royal College of Sturgeons.

1253 Why crime doesn't pay. It's been nationalised.

1254 Invention is the mother of necessity, and when Man wanted to escape from his wife's nagging tongue he learned to fly faster than sound.

1255 Did you know I used to work for Intelligence? I was posted to the Royal Mint during the war. I was a mint spy.

1256 A mermaid has been working for eighteen months on a new scientific project. She wants to make a pen that writes above water.

1257 They fell in love at first sight. Then he wanted a retake.

1258 This is a free country. The very air in Britain is free. So long as you can afford to stay and breathe it.

1259 The Russian premier visited Vladivostok last week, and what a day it was. All the happy free Russians were clapping and cheering and rattling their chains in delight.

1260 There's a new American musical coming to London. It's a pinch on two other musicals, so they've called it "Chatanuga Choo Choo Choo Chin Chow."

1261 A motorist says that on a cold morning he thinks longingly of those tropical countries where a few determined cranks can start a revolution.

1262 About the time you're important enough to take two hours for lunch the doctor limits you to a glass of milk.

1263 An estate agent committed suicide the day after the news that property prices were tumbling. He'd dreamt that he dealt in marble halls.

1264 Sign over dentist's chair: "Satisfaction guaranteed or your teeth refunded."

1265 Last night she spent three hours setting her hair. And at midnight it went off.

1266 It's no use telling our politicians to go to hell until they've finished building it for us.

1267 It's no wonder Fred Trent-Willson is a wonderful golfer. He cursed the day he was born.

1268 When he saw her off at Southampton it was like listening to a speech from the Dock.

1269 Life is divided into two parts. Some of us are in the swim and the rest in the soup.

1270 There was a terrible tragedy in a supermarket yesterday. A woman shopping for peas leaned over the frozen-food counter and five frozen fish-fingers grabbed her by the throat.

1271 She didn't like sophisticated intellectual city boys, so she started going with a young country lad. This one lacked any polish. He was really rough around the hedges.

1272 Modern scientists have gone stark raving mad. The latest stunt is to send four mice into orbit by rocket. You'd think that with all the advances science has made, they could invent cheaper methods of getting rid of mice.

1273 Dick was fined yesterday under the Clean-Atmosphere Act. What's more the judge confiscated his cigar.

1274 British manufacturers can't win. They produce a new machine and within three months the Russians have invented it, and a month later the Japanese are making it for half the price.

1275 There was a time when you couldn't take it with you, but they've thought of an answer to that. Now you can get *portable* television sets made from mini-transistors.

1276 When he sees a pretty girl in a bikini lying on the sand, he doesn't entertain wicked thoughts. The thoughts entertain him.

1277 They've just released a sequel to that top-ten disc "Mac The Knife" —it's on a jam label and is called Taffy The Tablespoon.

1278 A woman surgeon made a terrible mess of an operation she performed on a chap with heart trouble. She believed that the best way to a man's heart was through his stomach.

1279 According to a football survey undertaken by the Soccer Supporters Association, not one single referee in the game was born in wedlock.

1280 Good news this morning. Ghana is sending a missionary to Brooklyn, U.S.A.

1281 You can't get a divorce without evidence in this country. In other words, although the Ten Commandments say you mustn't commit adultery, the law insists that you do.

1282 A hotel in Scotland boasted that Queen Elizabeth I had spent a night there. To prove it they indicated the ring under the bed where the crown used to be kept overnight.

1283 There's a new book on the market, about primitive life in a South American town noted for its disorderliness. It's the only book ever published whose pages turn *you.*

1284 To avoid being obvious, a wealthy tycoon left his money thus: "To my dear cat Felix I leave my entire estate of £50,000, and to my loyal secretary Miss Phoebe Tanner I leave my dear cat Felix."

1285 Our neighbour spares no expense with his kids. He's just ordered ten tons of quicksand for them to play in.

1286 Frank can't stop his dog from running after bubble cars in the street. And when he catches them he buries them in the garden. . . .

1287 We've just found the only certain way to reduce the cost of living. Drop dead.

1288 At a dinner party last week, for once there were no controversial arguments about politics, religion and money. Everyone discussed sex.

1289 A missionary has just gone out to Africa to help raise the fallen. He's giving away free brassieres to Umbango tribeswomen.

1290 It's terrible trying to travel these days. One man had to stand all the way from Marble Arch to Hendon—and he was in a taxi.

1291 There's a terrible shortage of doctors in the States. They're all making television films. All over Hollywood actors are meeting in the streets and sticking stethoscopes into each other's chests instead of shaking hands.

1292 One pop singer's current hit has a lyric that takes about ten minutes to sing. It needs cutting a lot. Not the song—his throat.

1293 Too bad about the man who was playing the back-end of a horse in pantomime. He sprained his ankle and the vet shot him. His big gag was to say to the man at the front: "Don't look now, but I think you're being followed."

1294　Forty computers went on strike at a motor car plant. They wanted a longer oil break.

1295　He used to play rugger for the Rovers. They called him Neckline Harry. . . . He was always plunging down the middle but never really showing any talent.

1296　Roger got drowned while he was water-skiing in the Bahamas. Oddly enough his father also died on the end of a rope.

1297　The gorgeous concert pianist Vera de Cruz was playing "In A Monastery Garden". We don't know why she was playing there, but four monks were chasing her round the orchard.

1298　After long and exhausting inquiries into modern habits, the Research Council have discovered that nine out of ten viewers have a television set. The tenth has a keyhole.

1299　One thing about Britain's uncertain weather. We're a nation that's famous for inventing more indoor games than anyone else on earth.

1300　Pop artists are young people who have made fortunes by singing words to radio static.

1301　It was so hot on the beach. You can tell how hot it was, a man was chasing a blonde over the sand and they were both walking.

1302　A juvenile delinquent is a youth who sees a sign saying: "Keep Off The Grass" and walks on the flower-beds.

1303　There's another new musical group trying to make the big money in show business. But they're so bad; two play guitars, one plays the drums and the fourth one drives the getaway car.

1304　The other day a Hollywood actress walked into a department store in Hollywood and ordered *another* drip-dry wedding dress.

1305　Have you seen some of the characters in these Horror movies? One big red eye in the middle of the forehead; teeth like fangs; green complexion; long sticky hair matting on the shoulders; ears pointing downwards. And that's only the ice-cream girl.

1306　Fat runs in her family. She had a French great-grandmother who was caught up in the revolution. She was so fat, Robespierre had her guillotined. Three times.

1307 His wife is so ugly! Before he married her all the fellows used to chase after her—giving her forty miles start.

1308 A hotel in Blackpool is so worried about food-poisoning they take special precautions. They don't give you any food.

1309 The housing shortage was so acute they had to take what they could get. It's a tiny tumbledown house, two up and two down. Two families upstairs and two in the basement.

1310 Minnie can't take her dog anywhere. He's a Doberman Pinscher and everywhere we go he pinches dobermans.

1311 His car has three speeds . . . slow, faster and well-your-honour-it-was-like-this . . .

1312 A nudist is a girl who is wearing a dress that hasn't yet been delivered.

1313 Horror Flicks Incorporated have just finished a moronic version of *The Boy Friend*. It's called *The Ghoul Friend*. In the film the heroine drinks a lot so they've given it an XXX certificate.

1314 Ever since he joined the Army he's had to carry an 80-lb. pack on his back. Around the camp he's known as the Hunchback of Hut 56.

1315 Horror Flicks Inc. are planning a new feature to be called *The Thing, On Blood*, as a sequel to *Cinderella On Ice*.

1316 She was having a drink with one of the producers of *The Bride of Frankenstein Rides Again*. As she downed her fifth gin he ordered himself another blood-and-bitter-lemon.

1317 In the orchestra he plays the piano. But at home he plays second fiddle.

1318 I asked Tom to introduce me to his sister, and he said: "I'll let you see her if you're over sixteen, otherwise you'll have to be accompanied by an adult."

1319 Oscar had a happy event at home last week. His wife's mother went back to her blasted heath to meet her two friends.

1320 A television company is trying out a brand-new quiz show. They ask you questions and you have to guess which idiot sent them in.

1321   After seeing all those films starring Lollobrigida, Brigette Bardot, Anita Ekberg, Jane Mansfield and Sophia Loren, it's no wonder he keeps calling his wife "Sir".

1322   There must be something the matter with Fred. All his non-iron shirts have gone rusty.

1323   He used to be so strong he could tear a telephone directory in half; if it was from any village with less than twenty subscribers.

1324   She's got a voice like a 78 being played at 33⅓.

1325   Statistics prove that 50 per cent. of all the people who get married at Easter are girls.

1326   Stereophonic radiograms are all the rage now. Yesterday I saw a tape-recorder in an antique shop.

1327   The doctor told him to keep away from white meat so now he goes out with African women.

1328   He's only five feet ten and he says he was born under Taurus the Bull. I think he was born under Itchus the Flea.

1329   George said to his boss: "I wish I could afford a lovely Rolls Royce like yours." And he said: "So do I."

1330   When she baked her first cake her husband had to shore up the oven before he risked putting it in.

1331   Did you hear the story of the flea who quitted his job in the Flea Circus and got a new job in the House of Lords? He's on knights.

1332   He's got a very good war record. . . . Vera Lynn singing "There'll be Bluebirds . . ."

1333   The theatre used to hold a mirror up to life, but television uses a keyhole.

1334   Every night he used to lie awake sleepless, counting sheep. It went on for weeks until the sheep started picketing him for shorter hours.

1335   It says in the paper that sixty million people go to the cinema every year. And all but two of them have to file past your seat.

1336   Things are so bad I've had to stop lighting matches by scratching them on my seat—they're tearing my underpants.

1337   Under a new Act for Mental Health, all feeble-minded people may be sent to luxury homes. So who is going to write the new pop songs?

1338   Aunt Fanny searched under her bed yesterday looking for a collar stud with a man on it.

1339   The Red Indians are worried sick. There's a rumour that the President of the United States wants to give America back to them.

1340   He doesn't care one bit about his appearance. He's even wearing the tie his wife gave him for Christmas.

1341   They're doing *Eskimo Nell On Ice* next. A story written around the frozen waists.

1342   Their son spends every summer on the Continent, working his fingers to the bone. Thumbing lifts to the South of France.

1343   Last week he made 2,000 people happy at the Empire Theatre in Leeds. He got there too late to do his act.

1344   A barber cut his throat yesterday. He spent half an hour telling his troubles to a customer who turned out to be stone deaf.

1345   He was tricked into marriage. The day his wife landed him she and her mother held a Victory Parade.

1346   When buying a canoe, make sure it is made on the Clyde, because a Glaswegian canoe never tips.

1347   He takes such a dim view of everything he'd make a wonderful photographer.

1348   He used to have a wonderfully easy job at the Moulin Rouge in Paris. He was the guy who carried the can-can back.

1349   Theatrical managers are concentrating on nude shows these days. Show business is a risqué business.

1350   Agatha is so stupid. She thinks that when two flags get married they have baby baby buntings.

1351   Alf was in hospital. There was a chart over the bed with a series of complaints written on it. Nearly all the nurses had written something.

1352   There's only one good thing to be said for all the motor cars on the roads today. It's practically eliminated horse-stealing.

1353   Four hundred years ago a band of ravaging Vikings invaded the shores of Britain. They seized a hundred young English women . . . who all shrieked . . . with delight.

1354   Then there's the weary old businessman who complained to his wife that his secretary didn't understand him.

1355   He met her at a Fancy Dress Ball. She was dressed as an old witch. When the time came to unmask he found out she wasn't wearing one.

1356   The maids at the hotel were a very boisterous and noisy young lot. He had to get out of a warm bed at four in the morning to let them out.

1357   What a luxurious hotel it was. They had a forty-nine-piece orchestra. And that was only in the wash-room.

1358   I've been operated on so many times I look like a slot machine.

1359   A foundation garment? That's the vital difference between facts and the figure.

1360   She always burned the candle at both ends, and what's she got to show for it? Nothing but a lot of old flames.

1361   Do you know how to find out if the lions are hungry when you go hunting? If they eat you—they're hungry.

1362   It was an awful dinner suit. He bought it off a penguin who needed the money.

1363   I rang Phyllis and told her I was speaking from St. Albans, so she wanted to know what I was doing at *his* place.

1364   As she dropped and broke her diamond necklace the actress said: "Damn, another seven years' bad luck."

1365   He's the perfect gentleman. Whenever he meets a lady, he raises his head.

1366 He got fed up with life, so he went home and put his head in the gas oven. His wife basted it every twenty minutes.

1367 She's just turned 32. The way she's turned it makes her 23.

1368 He was the best politician in Ireland. He solved the unemployment problem by sneaking up behind anyone who was unemployed and braining them with a mallet.

1369 They fired twenty-one guns on his grandfather's eighty-fifth birthday. That's what killed him—a firing squad.

1370 They bought a French poodle but the silly animal never did as he was told. Neither of them could speak French.

1371 A Scot who was awaiting execution wanted to send a telegram asking for a reprieve, but he couldn't get it down to twelve words before they came for him.

1372 His parents had their differences of course. One was a man and the other a woman.

1373 They are a musical family. Mother plays the drums, Irene's the pianist, and their Dad's usually on the fiddle.

1374 You know what a hussy is, don't you? It's a girl who, sooner than marry the man she wants, would rather marry the man someone else wants.

1375 I'm so tired through keeping up with the Joneses. I live next door to Tom.

1376 They went to a classy night-club the other day. There was a stiff cover charge for the table, and an un-cover charge for the cabaret.

1377 A composer friend of mine asked me to his home. He wanted to show me his new operetta. She was a telephone operetta.

1378 He used to play in a three-piece orchestra. That's all they had in the repertoire—three pieces.

1379 The reason Alf's hair is a little thin on top is psychological. When he was a young boy his father used to hit him over the head with a large book on child psychology.

1380 They call their butcher the Actor's Physician. He's just opened a new surgery to cure hams.

1381   The price they charge these days for a haircut! A man who was nearly bald went into a West End barber's for a haircut. They charged him 21s. for a trim. That works out at three shillings a hair!

1382   The egg I had for breakfast this morning was as hard as stone. I think it came from a Rhode Island bricklayer.

1383   There are plenty of fish in the sea, Alice says, but she prefers goldfish.

1384   You know what a real musician is, don't you? He's a chap, who, when he hears a girl singing in her bath, puts his ear to the keyhole.

1385   In an optician's window the other day a peculiar thing happened. Two monocles got together and made a spectacle of themselves.

1386   The rich grind the faces of the poor. And that's how their wives get face powder.

1387   I wanted to buy a horse, so the dealer showed me one in the paddock. A great big stallion—eighteen hands. Eighteen hands and no feet.

1388   He's so dim, he can't even read. He married a tattooed lady just so's he could look at the pictures.

1389   He's a deserter from the Army. The corporal who serves the rice pudding in the mess.

1390   There was a time when he could hold his girl-friend very tight, but now he can't do it even though he's teetotal.

1391   Because she's fed up paying high prices for footwear, she's bought herself a shoe tree.

1392   She doesn't like the sound of boys' voices unless it's a voice with a ring to it.

1393   She told her boy-friend she was a leading light in the film world. But she was an usherette in a cinema.

1394   A deaf and dumb man who was lecturing about the government broke four fingers.

1395   The magistrate told the girl that she had no business being in a parked car in the dark. She told him that she wasn't there on business.

1396 He went off for a week-end's fishing, and didn't catch anything until he got home.

1397 A Dorset farmer put such a horrible scarecrow in his field that the birds not only left the crop alone, they even brought back the corn they stole last year

1398 It's funny, but when a girl gets old enough to wear a bikini swim-suit, her parents see less of her than ever.

1399 Children—what a comfort they are in your old age! And how sooner they bring it on.

1400 These new cars have three speeds—fast, furious and well, if-it-isn't-St. Peter.

1401 The views from the hotel window were terrific; you could see for miles through one of the windows—the fanlight, in the roof.

1402 He got married but now he says his wife doesn't understand him. It's his own fault for marrying a Lithuanian girl.

1403 He's training to be a lion tamer, but they won't let him do anything yet except comb their hair and brush their teeth.

1404 When he was in Paris he saw some really beautiful things in the shops. He even followed one or two of them home.

1405 They were very fond of George at the club; they even gave him an Illuminated Address. They set his house on fire.

1406 A clock-and-watchmaker died the other day. They reckon it'll take them twenty years to wind up his estate.

1407 He went all the way to America by sea, and then all the way back again, without having a bath. The dirty double-crosser.

1408 Three ghosts were invited to a party, so they went to the cemetery to dig up a few girls.

1409 In his last job he didn't have much to do. He was a costume designer for the Folies Bergère.

1410 When she asked the captain to show her to the cabin he told her that the purser was the man responsible for all the berths on board.

1411   We went to the dogs the other night and every race started late. An attendant told us that the reason was they'd washed the hare and couldn't do a thing with it.

1412   The last number she sang was called: "I forgot to switch off the electric blanket and now I'm the toast of the town."

1413   He's at that dangerous age when all women look the same . . . desirable.

1414   Aunt Sadie took up bodybuilding four years ago. Now she's an Uncle.

1415   He's had quite a brush with his girl. She was wearing her new white angora sweater and he was in his black barathea suit.

1416   Women? Who's interested in women? Take all that lovely glossy hair away from the twenty-four Miss World Beauty contestants and what have you got left. Two dozen bald-headed girls.

1417   Bill saved at least four lives yesterday. He wouldn't let his wife have the car.

1418   After he committed his last crime he had to lie low in Soho. He had to lie low because the old bed sagged in the middle.

1419   Albert made love to a girl in the reference library. She would have kicked up a commotion but for the fact that there was a big sign saying "SILENCE".

1420   Before Joe got married he often used to have girls sinking into his arms. Now his arms are nearly always in the sink.

1421   She's allergic to mink. . . . Whenever she sees another woman wearing one she feels ill.

1422   He invented foam rubber but couldn't make much money with it. Until one day they invented girls.

1423   During the last war she was mentioned in despatches. . . . *The Sunday Despatch*, the *Evening Despatch* and *The Law Court Despatch*. . . .

1424   She invited him to her home one evening because she couldn't go out as she had to wash her smalls. So they went to her home and she spent the whole evening bathing the twins.

1425 Have you noticed how all the great movies are now being made in Rome instead of Hollywood? Where they used to make films over in Hollywood on a shoe-string, they can now make them on a length of spaghetti.

1426 A Scotsman always says that his good singing voice is a natural gift. It would have to be.

1427 Tom was kicked in the stomach by a beatnik wearing winklepickers and when he went to the doctor he scratched his head and said: "That's the first time I ever saw a stomach with two navels."

1428 I wouldn't say he was shortsighted, but he did once enjoy a television picture so much that he sent the girl a fan letter—then discovered it was the test card.

1429 She's an ex-wife. The X marks the spot where she murdered her husband.

1430 America is well ahead of Russia in the atomb-bomb race. They've got H-bombs in the States that now come in three sizes—King size, Monster size and Hey-Where'z-Everyone-Gone?

1431 When I was in Africa I got caught by cannibals and indignantly demanded to see their chief. They brought a big black chap to me, wearing bangles, straw hat and feathers, with a ring in his nose. He chatted to me in excellent English for some time and I said: "It was good of you to see me, Chief, and to ask so many questions to clear this matter up." He said: "Oh, I'm not their chief—I'm their food inspector."

1432 If you go to Spain for your holidays remember to see a bullfight. These bullfighters really do know their stuff and it's just as well they're proficient. There was one toreador at a bullfight and he took his eyes off the bull for only a fraction of a split second. Now he's a soprano singer with the Madrid Opera.

1433 It gets windier and windier on the beach these summers. On holiday this year at Largs, the wind was blowing so strongly, the rain couldn't land.

1434 Workers at a British motor factory have decided to save up their tea-breaks. This means that every fortnight they can have a week's holiday.

1435 I'm not saying this girl was ugly, or oversized, all I know is that she was voted Mr. Universe at Palm Beach last year.

1436 You've heard about people in despair who slash their wrists? Terrible thing happened in a West End theatre last night—a beatnik slashed his seat.

1437   I don't sleep well at all. There must be something wrong with me. I keep waking up every two or three days.

1438   A credit squeeze is a woman buying a girdle on hire purchase.

1439   A French champagne expert from Bordeaux was taken to the London Clinic for an emergency operation. They stuck him in a large ice-bucket before opening him up.

1440   There's a sex maniac in Worcester who has a wall safe with the combination 38-24-36.

1441   A press photographer drove himself mad trying to take pictures of bathing beauties at different angles, and couldn't find any angles.

1442   Franklin discovered electricity, Marconi invented radio but it was Adam who supplied the parts for the first loudspeaker.

1443   Did you hear about the girl who went to Africa and bought herself a dozen flesh-coloured stockings in a native bazaar? When she got home she found they were black.

1444   He's been saving up for a rainy day. So far, he's saved one dirty raincoat, an old pair of wellington boots and a torn sou'wester.

1445   He'll never forget his first Royal Command Performance. . . . The Queen of Tonga told him to belt up.

1446   She's the most brilliant girl at her college. She uses phosphorescent make-up.

1447   These new detergent powders are being advertised with tremendous vigour. Their message is driven home with a thickening sud.

1448   They say of a certain Hollywood actress who has been much married that she isn't so much a wife as a reissue.

1449   An artist is a man who is very temperamental about colours. In fact, he can look at a hue and cry.

1450   Every time there's a new moon he rings the tax collector and asks him to turn over his money.

1451   When a horse gets to the bottom of his nosebag, I guess it's the last straw.

1452   Definition: Triplets are short excursions.

1453   Mr. and Mrs. Stubbs went on holiday at Torquay this year. They had some smashing digs—they'd only been dug a month.

1454   Old Robert Smith recently took Holy Orders. The local vicar wanted three dozen bibles, a new hassock, twenty-two prayer books and a box of candles.

1455   There's something about Sam that attracts women—to other men.

1456   To find out how popular he was as an entertainer, he held a poll. Her name was Lydia Cracowcz.

1457   They overlooked Ted again on this New Year's Honours List. He can't even get on the Walsall housing list.

1458   The other day a large car whizzed past Charlie and he noticed a pair of old boots dangling from it. He turned to a bystander and said: "Has there been a wedding?" The bystander said: "No, an accident."

1459   I'll never forget the day I met my wife; and heaven knows I've tried hard enough.

1460   I once knew an Irishman named Mick Murphy who would pat you on your back in front of your face and then cut your throat behind your back.

1461   Thank heavens we don't have to keep up with the Joneses any more. Last night they surrendered.

1462   I met a gorgeous girl in Rome on holiday. A real Italian beauty, with the perfect shape—XXXVII-XXIV-XXXVI. . . . The weather there was good, but terribly hot; it was always about 125 in the shade. But I was smart, I kept out of the shade. . . . Later in Venice I tried to kiss a girl in a gondola and she whispered in my ear: "Wait till we get into shallower water, the gondolier is my husband. . . ."

1463   A deputation came all the way from Switzerland to see Agatha Christie's play, *The Mousetrap*. They want to know why their cheese has caught nothing over all these years.

1464   Try smoking those new cigarettes with the miracle filter. . . . If you finish the packet, it's a miracle.

1465   It won't be long now before the Russians have a spaceship that will take them to the moon. America has offered to help build it, provided they can get all 170,000,000 Russians into it.

1466   He got home, made pleasant remarks to his wife, and kissed her ardently on the lips and all she said was: "Why can't you come home exhausted like other men?"

1467   He married her twice. Once in a register office and again in church. So she's got a double wedlock on him.

1468   Last year there were thirty candles on her birthday cake; this year there are twenty-nine.

1469   Sydney was booking into an hotel in Rhyl and the proprietor's pretty daughter showed him to his room. He asked what the rates were. "Three pounds," said the girl.
   "That's wonderful, I'll pay three pounds with pleasure."
   "With pleasure it'll be five pounds," remarked the girl.

1470   A dish with a copper bottom is one who has been sunbathing on her stomach in the South of France.

1471   Oscar went into a record shop and bought a new release which had the words: "Billy Berger Swings" on it. When he got home he found it was a coloured magazine about a chap named Billy Berger who was executed at Winson Green.

1472   There's something wrong with this country when Fords keep building more station-wagons and the Transport Minister keeps closing down more stations.

1473   Then there's the three brass monkeys who went to a party—and had a terribly dull time.

1474   Give a husband enough rope and he'll skip.

1475   Tom reckons a bird in the hand is worth two in a photograph.

1476   The married man I like is the one who went into the local pub for bitter or worse.

1477   Age is something that might not show on a woman's face these days; but it shows when she walks up a steep hill.

1478   A fool and his money are soon married.

1479   Miss Dumbelle thinks that a blunderbuss is one that takes the wrong route.

1480   He told the bank manager he had skin trouble—his wife wanted a mink coat.

1481   He's the kind of chap who has plenty to be modest about.

1482   The front of his shop was too low so he had his facia lifted.

1483   She bought a pair of gloves that fitted her like a swim-suit.

1484   Definition: Heirlooms are what wigs are made on.

1485   The champion gave him a left then a right then a left cross, and another right, and another left . . . so the loser called the ref over and demanded to have the champion's hands counted.

1486   She's quite a clever mathematician. Spends her time circling the square.

1487   History books tell us how Venus fought for her lover; that was doubtless the first application of unarmed combat.

1488   Definition of a wolf: a man who strikes while the eyeing is hot.

1489   They knew my girl was a good cook, so for a wedding present they gave us a carving set—two mallets, eight chisels. My wife is so economical . . . on her thirty-fifth birthday she made do with twenty-four candles. . . . When we got married I promised to endow her with all my worldly goods —that's how she got my golf clubs. . . . It's like Solomon said when he was in a good mood: "My wife is one in a thousand."

1490   The chief maintenance engineer was sitting forlornly on the bench looking bored stiff as he gruntled: "Did you ever have one of those days when nothing seems to go wrong?"

1491   He's been making films since 1956—and coincidentally in those few years 1,295 cinemas have converted to bowling alleys.

1492   Over seventy international records were broken in Manchester last night . . . a maniac got loose in a Deansgate music shop.

1493   If you don't like sleeping in a flock bed, use DDT—that will soon get rid of the flock.

1494   A London landlord is so mean even the worms in his back garden have to pay him ground rent.

1495   She's so fat she has to wear a girdle to keep her corset in.

1496   As the girdle said to the new spring hat: "You go on a head and I'll bring up the rear."

1497   You can tell the sort of man she's going around with; she went to the chemist and asked them if they had any perfume that smelled like boiled-beef and carrots.

1498   To economise on her dress allowance, Martha sends away for patterns of fabrics, and makes sun-suits from them. She's very popular on the beach in the summer.

1499   During the war he was torpedoed in the Pacific and lived eighteen days on one tin of sardines. It was hellishly cramped.

1500   Donald wouldn't have bought the second-hand car but for the fact that the salesman assured him that it had only had one previous owner, a quiet, elderly, reserved, gentlewoman, with county associations. Tomorrow he's taking back the stuff he found when he cleaned the car out—four cigar butts, a meerschaum pipe, two empty gin bottles, a pair of garters with roses on them and the top of a bikini.

1501   Their grandfather died a rich man. He had instructed his executors not to inform the newspapers that he had left a fortune, but that he had been taken away from one.

1502   Moira isn't one of those beatnik girls. She's too honest, too upright, too straight. You don't get them any straighter than 30–30–30.

1503   There are some people who make things happen—some people who like to see things happen—then there's Bill's wife—she doesn't even know anything *has* happened.

1504   When a couple were touring Ireland last year, they took a short cut from Blaggyblog to Ballyfallon and had to go through a deep ford. Finished up with a radiator full of Guinness.

1505   She's so fat she bought one of the first mini-cars made, in 1959— and she's still stuck in it.

1506 Have you seen the new play at the Alhambra theatre? Only one thing spoils it. The ending. It's too far away from the beginning.

1507 There was a nasty accident on a zebra crossing. An Irish navvy knocked over one of those new miniature taxi-cabs. And all sixteen Scotsmen in it were injured.

1508 The vicar of Stuttgart claims that there is a new thirst for righteousness in Germany today. They're opening beer gardens outside all the churches.

1509 Any fool can be a pop-group star. You don't have to have a good voice, and you don't even need any talent for playing the guitar. All you need is a good agent and plenty of pluck.

1510 He's got one aim in life. He's going to devote all his time to making people happy and contented, no matter how much you object to it.

1511 His girl-friend said she wanted a fish-and-chip supper after they came out of the pictures, so he took her to the aquarium and bought her a bag of crisps.

1512 His wife has joined a Secret Society. They meet every Tuesday to discuss their neighbours' secrets.

1513 She embarrassed the chemist by asking him what she could do about all the chaps she had on her hands.

1514 Then there's the idiot who walked into a freshly painted pillar box and got his palm red.

1515 She does her washing at home because of the high cost of laundering and her husband complains that she spends most of her time in the garden. That's where she hangs out.

1516 He asked her if she'd like to see a moving picture and then took her to the art gallery to see the "Last Days of Pompeii"!

1517 It was leap year and she landed right on his back.

1518 He felled the audience with one blow. Some saxophone player!

1519 A boxer we know is well travelled. He gets around and a bout.

1520 He's the cock of the north. Got that way by fowling.

1521   Radio comedians are beginning to sneak material from foreign broadcasts. Especially humour from news flashes. That's probably where they get their alien corn.

1522   The early worm—has to get his own breakfast.

1523   They honeymooned at two hotels because he didn't like the manager at the first place and in the second place the first place was too expensive.

1524   Miss Dumbelle thinks that a Provisional Licence is a permit to sell groceries.

1525   She thought the world was her oyster but all she got was imitation pearls.

1526   I know a girl who's got more brains in her head than I've got in my little finger.

1527   The biggest problem about getting rich is that it costs money.

1528   The United States will in future be referred to by Britain as the I.O.U.S.A.

1529   Milking cows is so simple in these days of mechanisation, that any little jerk can do it.

1530   He's the kind of fellow who makes so many enemies he could do with an enemy agent.

1531   Then there's the beautiful secretary who quit her job because she walked into the boss's office and found his wife on his lap.

1532   They call her Pontoon Peggy. She's thirty-six but she stuck at twenty-one.

1533   He invested in a girl but she didn't yield much. That's the worst of investing in gilt-edged blondes.

1534   Fred tells me his wife is so clever she can talk for hours on any subject under the sun. Some wives don't even need a subject.

1535   The best formula for a holiday is to take twice the money you've got and half the clothes you packed.

1536   Clinging gowns aren't new. Tom's wife had to cling to hers for years.

1537   He found a cure for the hiccups in playing the bagpipes. All he needs now is a cure for playing the bagpipes.

1538   Miss Dumbelle thinks that a marriage settlement is a block of two-bedroom flats.

1539   He chooses his own suits, but his wife picks the pockets.

1540   He's a man who knows a thing or two. And no more.

1541   An awkward child is a living example of the triumph of mind over matter.

1542   He's so weak he sprained his wrist peeling a banana.

1543   His wife talks and nags all day. He bought her some lipstick but it didn't work. He's suing the makers.

1544   There was a girl at the party wearing a convertible French gown. One with the top down.

1545   She said she was entering her declining years so Bill told her that a woman of her age couldn't afford to decline *anything*.

1546   When he first got married he felt he wanted to set the world on fire. He should have started with her mother.

1547   Her folks were in the iron and steel business. Ma ironed and father stole.

1548   She was all right until she took out a toothcomb and started to comb her teeth.

1549   He used to have a penchant for hard work. Now he's only got his old-age penchant.

1550   He asked his girl if she knew a good way to stop falling hair, so she bought him a net.

1551   Miss Dumbelle thinks that a stage-coach is a Drama School teacher.

1552   They arrested a pickpocket at a lecture. His defence was that he was there to take notes.

1553   He was living in the lap of luxury but luxury got up and walked away.

1554   Did you hear the story of the snail, the tortoise and the motor-car having a race along Oxford Street? The snail won.

1555   He was looking for a girl who didn't smoke, drink or swear. The only one he could find was a six-year-old schoolgirl.

1556   Then there's the owner of a fish-and-chip shop who changed his order at the newsagent from one morning paper each day to two, because business was improving.

1557   Billiards is a game demanding long hours of consistent practice. For instance we know a player who spent eighteen days at it without a break.

1558   Miss Dumbelle thinks an off-licence is what a girl gets when she finally hooks her man.

1559   A judge recently awarded £87,000 damages to a man who lost the use of three fingers on his right hand. The claimant explained that his profession was that of a pickpocket and that his career was ruined.

1560   She's training to be an opera singer, but for the moment her "Madame Butterfly's" more of a caterpillar.

1561   A gossip-spreader is a woman with large ears that will swallow anything.

1562   He's an eccentric. His ancestors grace all the walls, he has a portrait of his grandfather over the cocktail cabinet, and his wife hangs over the bannisters.

1563   She's had so many husbands they've formed their own football team.

1564   Did you hear about the two Russian diplomats who rushed forward to meet each other and shake heads?

1565   She complained to the matron that the patient in Ward 4 was always moaning and that she was tired of nursing a grievance.

1566   That story about Adam and Eve takes a lot of believing. It's probably just a rib.

1567   Did you hear the story of the politician who took a girl for a ride in his car and ran out of gas for once?

1568   She believes in making the best of her wonderful figure. And where there's a wool there's a way.

1569 He never gives other women a second look. He makes the first one last.

1570 When asked how he knew that people are now getting less fish-and-chips for their money, he said he saw it in the paper.

1571 Wife to husband sporting the latest technicolour effect in American neckties: "I wish you'd take that tie off Alfred, it's giving me a headache."

1572 He's a plastic surgeon. So brittle he keeps cracking.

1573 He was telling the old fellow that his wife had just spent four pounds on a skirt, and the old fellow said that in his youth he'd spent three thousand on one.

1574 He has one of the highest possible positions with the BBC. He's an aerial maintenance man at Sutton Coldfield.

1575 The Borough insisted that municipal householders must not give their homes fancy titles unless they were approved by the Housing Committee. So he put his council house down for a name.

1576 The airman who baled out without a parachute was simply jumping to a conclusion.

1577 They have a watchdog that reacts violently at the approach of strangers or burglars—he crawls under the bed.

1578 Always remember that a holiday-maker who paddles in the sea showing his braces would look even funnier if he didn't wear them.

1579 Water has killed more people than strong liquor—remember the Flood?

1580 Johnson was born with a silver spoon in his mouth—but it had someone else's family crest on it.

1581 As a child he had a nanny who was paid to wheel him out in the park; and he's been pushed for money for forty years altogether.

1582 She was wearing a flared skirt. A beatnik set fire to it.

1583 A girl who is youth-less is inclined to be ruthless.

1584 Kidnappers took a show-girl from a Strip Club and the police say that she has not yet been recovered.

1585 When he saw the bikini his eighteen-year-old daughter bought for sunbathing, her father tanned her hide himself.

1586 She's a girl who doesn't mind if a man hasn't good looks as long as he has good lucre.

1587 She won the no-belle prize in the Beauty Contest.

1588 If a football pool punter had a bad season last year with his perms, will he change his combinations next winter?

1589 Then there's the munitions salesman who was fired because he had a disarming smile.

1590 A crook who didn't like the price offered by the "fence" for the stolen gems, hit him and knocked him to the floor. He shouldn't have slammed down the receiver.

1591 Marriage—that's the thing which puts a ring on a woman's hand and two rings under a guy's eyes.

1592 I've been married for two years and believe me, when it comes to making a lot of money, I've got to hand it to my wife. Every penny of it.

1593 Percy's got a chip on his shoulder. Probably a little piece that worked loose from his head.

1594 Modern medicine is taking a new turn. They use such wonderful new instruments nowadays. A man went to see a specialist. The specialist put a divining rod over his head and told the guy he had water on the brain.

1595 I took her outside during the dance and I stole a few kisses. She turned to me and asked me not to start a crime wave.

1596 Bert is sick in hospital. He took an overdose . . . of food. Now they've got him on a strict diet to bring down his weight from twenty stones. All he has is one of those new-fangled diet-biscuits, something like a dog-biscuit with a cream centre. The fever that started his trouble was very bad—they put him to bed with 104 . . . and 104 in one bed is too many —especially when one of them is Bert.

1597 Did I tell you about my operation? It was performed, and I use the word loosely, by Dr. McKinsey, known throughout Emergency Ward Thirteen as "Mack the Knife".

1598 We had a sergeant in the army who had been through four years and finished up with a wooden leg. Gee, it was painful. It hurt like the devil. I know because he used to bash me over the head with it.

1599 I had a great time at Goodwood races. I sat down on the wrong end of my shooting-stick and won the two-thirty by four furlongs.

1600 I had to go into town to buy a new mink coat . . . for my mink—he's moulting.

1601 My girl went to book seats at the cinema for a double horror film. The manager took one look at her and screamed.

1602 I wouldn't say my friends are poor but whenever I go there for a meal I notice they give me a dish with the name Rover on it.

1603 I'm exhausted. I've had nothing to eat for three days except meals.

1604 It was a long walk from my dressing-room to the boxing ring. . . . I was glad I didn't have to walk back.

1605 I note that BBC Television is going to start screening a series of Educational Shorts next winter. They're a bit late. I saw some of them on the beach last summer.

1606 I can't sing so I'm advertising for a beautiful girl accompanist who can't play the piano.

1607 The customs officer thought I was a pirate, just because my passport photo looked like a skull and cross-bones.

1608 You can tell what kind of hotel it was. I left a call for seven in the morning . . . and woke up to find seven blondes in my room.

1609 My wife suffers very badly with arthritis. It takes her five times as long now to go through my trouser pockets when I'm asleep.

1610 I was extremely seasick on the trip to New York. The steward asked me if he could get me anything and I told him to get me an island.

1611 Modern fashions are often crazy. I think people in those high-heeled peep-hole shoes look ridiculous. That's why my father's stopped wearing them.

1612 I was so tired I went to the pictures to see a re-issue of *The Return of Doctor Kildare*. I saw it through three times and he never examined me once.

1613 I didn't mind being operated on by a short-sighted surgeon, but when he woke me up and asked me to thread the needle before he could stitch me up, that was the end.

1614 There's a chap I know who is so interested in modern music that he goes from one record shop to another. Setting fire to them.

1615 In such cold regions as Alaska, everyone wears a lot of thick furry clothes. Once, when I was out there exploring, a woman in a thick white fur coat hugged and squeezed me for an hour. Until I found out she was a polar bear.

1616 I took three large bottles of vitamin pills and the third one stuck in my throat.

1617 If they want me on BBC-TV at any time, they only have to say the word. The word is "Money".

1618 Last night I painted the town red and tonight I'm giving it a second coat.

1619 We were so poor as children, and we lived in a poor quarter. A quarter of one room. At Christmas time, Santa Claus didn't come down the chimney —he came up the drain. My parents couldn't really afford to have me. The neighbour's wife had me. My mother hated my father because he was such a drunkard. He hardly left any for her at all. But to look at me today you wouldn't dream I came from a broken home. I did—I can show you the bits I broke.

1620 I came home late one night and my wife complained that the cat upset her. It was her own fault for eating it.

1621 She's the kind of girl I'd go to the ends of the earth for, but I gave her up. She moved to Wigan.

1622 I loved her so much I practically lived on her doorstep. Until her father tripped over my tent and broke his leg.

1623 I went to see Fred the other night. He had a beautiful piece of China on his mantelpiece and I asked him about it. He said her name was Chi Wong Lu.

1624 I'll say this for Lydia. She always wears the last thing in clothes. A nightdress.

1625 To tell you the truth, I'm very homesick. Whenever I go home, I feel sick.

1626 I've got fighting in my veins. I admit it would be better if I had blood. I've done quite a lot of boxing in my time. I used to work in a kipper-packing store. I remember my last fight very well. I was fighting a man named Basher Beauchamp. The punishment that guy's hand took from my nose! When I stepped into the ring and took off my dressing-gown the crowd went wild with excitement. I'd forgotten to put my shorts on. The second nudged me and whispered, "The bell's gone." I said: "Well don't look at me . . . I never touched it." In round two, I had the Basher worried. He thought he'd killed me. The Basher was smothered with blood. Mine. In round four we spent most of the time playing Puss-In-The-Corner. He'd hit me in the puss and I'd lie in the corner . . .

1627 Her husband is very hospitable. I'd hardly been there five minutes before he'd put the kettle on. When it boiled he put boiling water down my neck.

1628 I went home by underground. Mind you, I had to dig my own tunnel.

1629 We went to Clacton one year and my wife was sunbathing. She's so thin I keep telling her she shouldn't wear a swim-suit. Everywhere else there are seagulls hovering overhead, but over my wife—vultures!

1630 My wife's hair is coming out in handfuls. The other night she made a cottage pie for supper. It's the first cottage pie I ever saw with a thatched roof.

1631 I can remember when we were young kids my sister used to play with dolls and I used to play with soldiers. Now we're grown up the positions are reversed.

1632 I went home early one night and found my wife on the sofa with our lodger. But I got my own back. I sold the sofa.

1633 I had dinner in a terribly slow restaurant the other night. I ordered stewed rabbit and pickled herrings. By the time they arrived they were cold sober.

1634 She kept pursing her lips, so every time I wanted to kiss her I had to stick my head in her handbag.

1635   Aren't the shops crowded? I stood in a long queue to buy some hair cream and by the time I got to the counter I was bald.

1636   We share a machine at the launderette. My socks and her nightie have been going around together for weeks. . . .

1637   Last night I got run down by a bubble car and the owner is suing me for damages.

1638   I don't know why they allow Members to get so drunk. I read in my morning paper that one M.P. delivered a speech yesterday from the floor of the House.

1639   I spent two hours fiddling with the knobs on the TV set to try and get rid of all the herringbone lines and spots. In the end I sent for the maintenance engineer and he solved the trouble in two ticks—my spectacle lenses were cracked.

1640   My uncle died of a sore throat—Auntie cut it.

1641   I must dash down to the theatre. I've got to do a repaint job on "Rhapsody in Blue".

1642   I was so scared I couldn't even bite my fingers. I'd swallowed my teeth.

1643   I've got the most wonderful wife in the world. I only hope her husband never comes for her.

1644   For six years I thought I was a dog, and I went to every psychiatrist in the country. I'm much better now. My nose is cold.

1645   I shan't be able to deal with my fan-mail this week. I can't afford a stamp to answer it.

1646   I once had my nose broken in three places. The Colonade Club, Mandy's Restaurant and the Hi-Fi Coffee Bar.

1647   I've just bought my girl something she badly needed. A little thing for round her neck. A cake of soap.

1648   My wife used to open all my letters. Then one day I got one from a former girl friend I'd met in Paris. That one steamed itself open.

1649   When I was in the army, the bugler used to wake me every morning. What a terrible noise he made. Slept in the same bed as me.

1650   When we had burglars the other night, I showed my real spirit. I went down those stairs six at a time. The burglar was on the roof.

1651   The landlady liked me, I think. She gave me three sausages for breakfast. The others were lucky. They only got two.

1652   I spent all last night trying to pull out our neighbour's dog's teeth. But they were too far embedded in my thigh.

1653   My car has perfect lights, a perfect engine, good brakes. It's absolutely flawless. And whoever heard of a car with no floor?

1654   I think I'd do well as a magician. At a restaurant last night I had to saw a sausage in half.

1655   He had a bit of trouble last night. He was with a girl at the pictures and she complained she couldn't see the screen. So he leaned forward and tapped the woman in front on the shoulder and asked her to take her hat off. It turned out to be his wife.

1656   Two convicts were eating their Christmas dinner in the huge dining-hall at Pentonville, and one of them was crying bitterly into his pudding. His comrade said: "Aw, go on, quit being so sentimental!" The other guy sobbed: "It ain't that . . . it's my little boy, Arnold. I ain't home for the festivities and he did so want a stolen scooter for Christmas."

1657   I once went out with a big-game hunting party to the Congo. We hunted deer at night because it was far too cold to hunt bear.

1658   Well, at last, after four years of struggle, we've finally got a car in our garage. There's nowhere to drive it, so that's where it stays—in our garage.

1659   It was one of those warm nights and little old grandma was sitting out on the veranda in her rocker, knitting away like mad. She was knitting a little old man.

1660   I got home from work feeling tired out, and all ready for a nice cosy evening by the fire. You can imagine how I felt when I looked at the hall-stand and realised that my mother-in-law had turned up. Her broomstick was in the umbrella rack.

1661   George is such a slick worker that before a girl can tell him she's not a girl like that, it's too late.

1662 There was one girl at the party who wore the sort of thing that knocks your eye out. Brass knuckles.

1663 The big advantage about being a nudist is that when you go bathing in the summer you don't have to sit around in a wet swim-suit.

1664 There was once a Scotsman who took a ravishing redhead home from a party in a cab. He was so engrossed in her that he could hardly keep his eyes on the meter.

1665 A tramp walked up to Mike Cohen and said: "Say, guv, can you give me a few coppers so I can get a bed tonight?" Mike gave him threepence and said: "Sure, but let's have a look at the bed."

1666 I bought a coat of arms yesterday. It's in blue serge. No front, no back, just plenty of sleeves.

1667 Have you ever wondered how ghosts manage to get through locked doors? They use skeleton keys.

1668 Ada won't drink anything stronger than pop. And her Pop will drink anything.

1669 His wife has a contract to give lectures. Well, actually, it's a marriage certificate.

1670 Tomorrow night he's going on a bender. He can't help it—he's bow-legged.

1671 Miss Simpkins had got a new job as typist in Mr. McReady's office. One morning she said to her boss: "You know, it's rather cool in here. Don't you think it's time we had a fire?" "Don't be silly," said the boss, "I only signed the policy a month ago—it would look too suspicious."

1672 The other day a gorgeous redhead knocked on Joe's apartment door. She said: "Can you tell me where Mr. Perkins lives?" He looked her over and said: "Yes, of course. He lives next door. Come in for a couple of hours and I'll give you the details of how to get there."

1673 When a wife is getting ready to go to a dance all she has to do is put on her face and take off a few clothes.

1674 If it's human to err, what is it to him?

1675 Harold's full of brilliant new money-making ideas. His latest dodge is to cross rabbits with hens to get home-made poached eggs.

1676 Two tired old charwomen were working on the landing of the main office of a government department. They were on their hands and knees, surrounded by a bucket and a floorcloth. One said to the other: "I know, Agnes—you wash and I'll wipe."

1677 Horace won a first prize in a newspaper competition. Telling this to the reporter of the small local newspaper he explained that the prize was a caravan, and that he hadn't had details but was expecting a double-berth. The local reporter provided the headlines for the story: "Horace Piggot Expecting Twins."

1678 Yesterday afternoon I went to see my bank manager. He invited me home for tea. We had cheese sandwiches. The cheese was kept in a strong-box.

1679 Agnes looked so lovely. She must have gone to an awful lot of trouble.

1680 He had a very useful skeleton key. Used to go around winding up skeletons.

1681 He was trapped on the ninth floor with the police barring his way out down the staircase, or by the elevator. There was only one thing he could do. He set the building alight so that he could use the fire-escape.

1682 He was such an efficient burglar, he even wore drainpipe trousers. And you should have seen the trouble he went to to hammer a crease in them.

1683 They sent him out of the drawing-room because he couldn't draw.

1684 The other night Sam tied a piece of string to his finger so that he wouldn't forget something he wanted to remember. And his pyjamas fell down.

1685 When I was on tour in my first revue I stayed in a small hotel in a small town high up in the Irish Highlands. One morning I plugged my electric razor in and started to shave . . . and all the trams stopped.

1686 Elsie is happily married to a Second Lieutenant. The first one got away.

1687 He's the best dentist in town. When he makes dentures the teeth are so real they even ache.

1688 Mavis asked where she could find a mare's nest because she wanted to add the eggs to her collection.

1689   The other day was her twenty-first birthday. Someone bought her a reading lamp. So she bought herself a book and she's learning to read.

1690   Lavinia thinks that good housekeeping is just the name of a magazine.

1691   One of the best remedies for indiscriminate petting is to get married. That puts an end to it altogether.

1692   Did you hear the story of the clever feller who decided to manufacture cheap mink coats by crossing minks with gorillas? He worked hard at it for three years and then committed suicide. The sleeves were too long.

1693   As you get older it always takes longer to get over a good time.

1694   You know what mental trouble is, don't you? It's when you've got a girl on your mind and a wife on your hands.

1695   There was once a man who lived in a semi-detached house which had quite a nice front garden. One Sunday morning he put on his grubbiest, dirtiest clothes and went out to dig up the front flower-bed. A woman who had just moved into the adjoining house passed by on her way to church. Her garden was in a bad state of neglect. So she beckoned the man over and whispered to him: "Look, if you'd like a new job, come and work for me. I'll give you more money and more time off, and once you've got my garden straight, the work won't be very hard. . . ." So the man said: "It's a good offer, but I'm on too good a thing here; you see, I even get to sleep with the lady of the house."

1696   You know the vicar's quite a card. Last Sunday he was at it again. Preaching about sin. Not against it—for it.

1697   Her father comes from a very old Irish family—that's what he likes —plenty of old Irish.

1698   She has an appetite like a bird. A buzzard.

1699   She never stops talking from morning till night. In fact, commercial advertisers are trying to book space on her tongue.

1700   She does all her shopping at the supermarket. Her back-room is full of stuff from the supermarket—baskets, tills, shelves, empty cartons and trolleys.

1701   She got sacked from her job as a herdswoman on the farm because she couldn't keep her calves together.

1702   My bank is just a small local branch. I went in there this morning to cash a cheque for thirty shillings and they gave me an IOU for it.

1703   What a driver! Going down the motorway yesterday only two things passed him—a Concord and a Vulcan bomber.

1704   I admired the red currants he had growing in his hot-house and it was very embarrassing; because they were tomatoes.

1705   The new ten-pound bank notes are smaller, about the size of an American dollar, and worth just as much.

1706   I sent my wife into town to get some anti-freeze and she came home with a new fur coat.

1707   No wonder the British are better than any other race at indoor sports. With a climate like ours, we spend more time there.

1708   Psychiatrist to a new patient who is a Rabbi: "I can't do anything for you—you're just a crazy mixed-up Yid."

1709   Missionary in darkest Africa meets cannibal chief in darkest night. The cannibal immediately goes down on his knees and utters a prayer. Missionary says: "How wonderful it is to find that our teachings spread so far." The cannibal chief grunts: "Stop interrupting me while I'm saying grace before meat."

1710   Then there's that perennial spinster, Maud Garnett. Yesterday she returned to the scene of her former triumphs only to find they'd all got married.

1711   I've been wondering about putting a Private Bill through Parliament. It's my gas bill. Maybe they'll pay it.

1712   If ever they needed an architect to build blocks of slums he'd be just the chap.

1713   To start my car there's a little button on the dash-board with the word "Push" written on it. All you have to do is get out and push.

1714   At his army medical they told him he didn't even have enough life to be a civilian.

1715   Jeffrey has another new job now. He travels for a doctor. Goes around making people sick.

1716   The engineer came from the Post Office to fix my phone and the first thing he said was: "I don't like the look of your dial." I told him that he'd come to mend the telephone and not give me a screen test.

1717   I was once playing in a concert at Carnegie Hall when a string broke. Was I mad! I had to finish the oratorio holding up my trousers with one hand.

1718   In the spring a young man's fancy seldom finishes in the first three.

1719   My girl comes from a very large family, and they're all very careful about money. In fact I've seen them set fire to a cigarette in an ash-tray, and nine of them stand over it and inhale.

1720   They advised me to go to Littlesea for my holidays, so I rented a small cottage. It was advertised as having creepers around the door. There was a bed to match.

1721   I'll never forget how Marilyn looked in the moonlight when I kissed her. She looked utterly disgusted.

1722   Donald's mother was a famous actress. She had twelve children, and all of them were born in the theatre. What a woman she was! Could never resist an encore.

1723   He was such a rich and powerful crook that he always used gold bricks when he did a smash-and-grab raid.

1724   We started to improve our old country house. At Easter we added a new wing to the east side. At Whitsun, we added a new wing to the west side. There was a high wind the week after, and the house just took off.

1725   Fred is so bone idle that if you shot him he'd want someone to help him to the floor.

1726   I've sewn so many wild oats in my time that a Sunday newspaper wants to turn my life story into a cereal.

1727   There was a boarding house I stayed in up north where the dust was so thick on the floor, the cockroaches walked around on stilts.

1728   The man at the bar gave me a nasty look. I didn't need it. I already have one.

1729   The fans followed Arthur around the golf course in droves. For years they'd been waiting to see him swing.

1730   Maisie was telling me about her visit to see her psychiatrist. He asked her what she'd dreamt the night before and she told him that she hadn't had any dreams that night. So he got angry and said that if she didn't do her homework he couldn't help her.

1731   The firm never actually told me I was overpaid. But when I picked up my salary every month it was all done up in a gift wrapper.

1732   Lots of people are buying antiques on the H.P. plan. New stuff, of course, but antique by the time it's paid for.

1733   He had a nasty habit of biting his nails. That was why he always used to wear open-toe sandals.

1734   As a kid I always wanted an air rifle but my father wouldn't buy me one. He said: "As long as I'm head of this family, you're not having any guns." I said: "If I ever do get a gun, you're not going to be head of the family any more."

1735   I'm a real sporting type. For instance, I never hit a man when he's up.

1736   Fred's boss is a slave to habits. He recently bought a tape-recorder to dictate letters on to . . . and he can't work without sitting it on his lap.

1737   The singer on TV wasn't so good last night. She was a bit off-colouratura.

1738   I've got very definite tastes about women's clothes. I can't stand my wife in anything over five pounds.

1739   I've bought a new gadget which keeps the inside of a car quiet. You fit it over your wife's mouth.

1740   Here's to happy days. Any fool can have a good time at night.

1741   The adolescent stage. That's when kids start questioning the answers.

1742   My wife is an expert at making illicit whisky. For all her faults I love her still.

1743   Bill and Edna were married by candlelight. It only lasted a wick.

1744   One evening there was a knock at the door and a woman came in. I stood up and raised my hat like a gentleman, but all she did was slap my face. Maybe that was because I was in the bath at the time.

1745   She's so ugly, when she sucks a lemon, the lemon pulls a face.

1746   Sybil is the kind of girl her mother wouldn't like her to associate with.

1747   I went to Mollie's house for a drink. She gave me a stiff one. A ginger-pop and starch.

1748   She was telling me about a fellow who took her out the night before. She'd had to walk home. I said: "Why?" "Well," she said, "the car had four controls and the driver had none."

1749   My girl went for an audition for a part in a new movie. She telephoned the producer to ask if he wanted her to bring along any references. The producer said: "Not references, honey. Just samples."

1750   A medley of current POP songs: Daddy Wouldn't Buy Me a Bow-Wow; Father Thames; Don't Go Down The Mine, Daddy; and Pop Goes The Weasel.

1751   Her husband is so bow-legged she has to iron his underpants on a boomerang.

1752   He caught Persian 'flu—from a cat.

1753   Things are so bad these days that the next time the wolf's at the door I'm going to have to eat him.

1754   Our M.P. says that when he gets elected he's going to put an end to all this Red Tape. He thinks green is a nicer colour.

1755   My brother tried hard to get a Government post, but now he's doing nothing. He got the job.

1756   The country is full of willing people. Some willing to work and the rest willing to let them.

1757   He's a smart cinema manager; always books X-certificate French films. That way they sell more ice-cream.

1758   Modern advertisements on TV for breakfast foods always insist that cereals give you good straight limbs and good square shoulders. What do you have to do? Eat the packets?

1759   She wears high Italian heels. That way she meets more low American heels.

1760   A man is getting old when he chases after women, and having caught them, forgets why.

1761   Whenever there's an office collection, he's the first to put his hand . . . in a sling.

1762   She wears tight-fitting slacks to prove that she's made of stern stuff.

1763   The agent told us the house had concealed lighting. I'm not sure if he's right or not—we haven't found where it's concealed yet.

1764   And remember that old Chinese proverb: he who cooks an old maid for dinner cannot expect a hot dish.

1765   She's got a baby's complexion; and the baby was glad to get rid of it.

1766   Our coalman was late last night. He'd been delivering 8 cwt. of nutty slack to his psychiatrist.

1767   At a party the other evening the choirboy was wearing some Government surplice.

1768   I've just taken out some new insurance. It's a double-indemnity life policy. I asked the agent what double-indemnity meant and he explained that when you die, the policy also covers you against fire.

1769   I'd like to tell you about Willie. You'd like Willie. I sometimes wish I did.

1770   Her husband was very hospitable. I'd hardly been there five minutes before he'd put the kettle on. When it boiled he poured boiling water down my neck.

1771   She worked in a large department store and when the manager told her he was going to take her out of dresses and put her in lingerie she gave in her notice.

1772   I went to the back of the car and looked in the boot. You'll never guess what I found in that boot. A sock.

1773   My father never could stand things that weren't perfect. If he disliked anything he'd create something awful. That's how I got here.

1774   He wasn't earning much money so he got a job at a film studio trying to pick up a little extra. Her name was Sally.

1775   I think the legal system is ridiculous. The other day I heard about a case where six men and six women were on the jury. They retired to a locked room for six hours and when they came out they all shouted "Not Guilty".

1776   We know a famous judge who celebrated the end of a long and bitter legal case by sending his wig out for a perm.

1777   We went to one of those small intimate night-clubs, and we sat down at a small table for two. A waiter came up and said: "I'm sorry, sir, you can't sit there." I said: "Why not? My money's as good as anyone else's." So the waiter said: "Quite so, sir, but that isn't a table—it's our dance floor."

1778   An American was bragging about the size of things in the States. He claimed that their buildings were much higher than ours. Some of them, he said, are well over a mile high. Even their bungalows have three storeys. And a hole in the road is often twelve inches high.

1779   I wouldn't say Ernie is exactly short-sighted. It's true that when he plays billiards he uses a cue fitted with a telescopic lens, but that's nothing.

1780   The other day I got invited to see the production of one of those BBC radio programmes in the studio. After watching that audience for half an hour I'm beginning to believe in life after death.

1781   A German stud farm advertised for an English trainer who "could speak German and who understood horses". I might have gone after the job—I can speak German all right, but I wasn't sure what accent the horses might use.

1782   A friend of mine's been seeing a lot of my wife. The other day I said to him: "Now see here, Fred—this is my last warning; stop fooling around with my wife or I'm going to let you have her."

1783   You can tell what sort of a life she led. When she was explaining some of her experiences to Dr. Kinsey he blushed.

1784   One night she got hold of all my clothes and tossed them on to the floor. And I was still in them.

1785   The best film you'll ever get on a TV set is a film of dust.

1786   The latest American sedan is so big it has a Minicar in the trunk for a dinghy.

1787 I've got a new job now, selling rimless spectacles to self-conscious private eyes.

1788 We quarrelled, but I think my wife is anxious to smooth things over. She came at me with a flat-iron last night.

1789 He's made a fortune out of the pools. Manufacturing wellington boots.

1790 I'm afraid I've lost my job at the bank. I'm six feet tall and £5,000 short.

1791 I looked at the pickled onions and I said to the waiter: "Do you call these *pickled*? You should see my old man."

1792 He's so cross-eyed he went to the south-east to join the North-west Mounted Police.

1793 As the Vikings approached the English shore, the peasants lit beacons with old faggots. Many a housewife got burned up that way.

1794 You should see some of the fashions they wear in Chelsea. I've seen better-dressed wounds.

1795 I went through that New Town the other day. How splendidly the whole place is laid out. It's so dead it had to be laid out.

1796 A small town is where everybody knows what everybody else is doing and the local newspaper tells you who was caught doing it.

1797 You can tell how crooked he is; even when he was a kid, his parents used to take him out in a folding-pram, without unfolding it.

1798 I went by air to Toronto. It was such a bumpy passage that even the automatic pilot baled out.

1799 Sonia bought a new dress out of a window. It was marked 50 per cent. off—and that's how she wears it.

1800 The volcano song: "Larva come back to me."

1801 The north of Scotland is the rainiest part of the British Isles. In one village up there it's so wet that even on a summer morning the dew has an undercurrent.

1802   I spent hours this week learning to do the cha-cha. Riding a racing bike with a loose saddle.

1803   When I went to South Africa last year I travelled First Class and my wife travelled Baggage Class labelled "Not Wanted On Voyage!"

1804   In the spring my fancy always turned to thoughts of love. I love beer.

1805   I see from a recent article in the magazine *Feathered Friends* that Peter Scott is anxious to find out where all the wild geese come from. I can tell him. Eggs.

1806   What I want to know is, whenever there's a new state of emergency why is it we never emerge from it until the next one?

1807   I don't like the way things are going in this country as far as the police are concerned; they're becoming tyrannical and officious, even when you only park your car so that it blocks their canteen. I always try to treat them as equals, but they should remember that the police in this country are paid by the taxpayers—and one day *I* might be one.

1808   I'm never going to take my wife to the zoo again. Last time we went the monkeys were teasing ME.

1809   I was watching my girl's mother take off her gloves. Have you ever opened a packet of frozen fish-fingers?

1810   I know a family of really fat people. The mother, father and two daughters add up to fifty-two stone in weight. Last week I went there for a drink and I noticed they'd had the trough redecorated in the dining-room. They never bother to lay a table for elevenses—Pop hands everyone a nose-bag. I can remember the day they went shopping in Selfridges. An elevator got trapped around them.

1811   At the Royal Mint the other day a gang of workmen were starching pound notes. That's one way of strengthening sterling.

1812   I just don't believe all the press stories about big bank raids in central London. Where could the crooks possibly park the getaway car?

1813   Have you seen some of these newly imported American paperback books? They're easy to recognise—there's a girl on the cover and no cover on the girl. These American imports are the reason why Britain is in the red and why the chancellor has warned us all to spend less money on luxuries like bread.

1814 I've just cured my wife of the habit of smoking in bed. I hid her pipe.

1815 I reckon my kids are very lucky now they're in their teens. They're able to have a room of their own each, while I'm stuck in the same old room with their mother.

1816 My wife objects to being called fat. Ever since commercial TV took a hold she prefers to be the "large economy size".

1817 That film industry party the other night was a tremendous affair. I got there half an hour late. There were so many famous people there I was the only person in the room I'd never heard of.

1818 The Russian newspaper *Pravda* recently ran a competition for the best political joke. The prize was won by a miner from Vrustlitovst—twenty years in Siberia.

1819 I had to go into hospital for an operation and while I was there the doctor took my wife out.

1820 You've seen these advertisements about Hire Purchase Air Trips, and Holidays on the Never-Never? Outside the local register office there's a big sign which says: "Marry now. Pay later."

1821 I caused quite a stir on New Year's Eve. The neighbours invited me to a Pyjama Party. And I only wear the jacket.

1822 A wonderful thing happened in Central London last week. They tore down a block of offices and built a theatre.

1823 I was crossing the race-course about two furlongs from the post when I broke a shoe-lace and bent to repair it. Before I could straighten up a jockey jumped on my back and dug his spurs into me. I was never so embarrassed in my life. I only came in third.

1824 He's the sort of long-haired, cultured bloke who always whistles after girls; but they are a few bars from Pushkopf's Sonata in F Sharp major.

1825 Western Films: Everyone loves our TV. Every night we get a roomful of in-laws who've come to watch the outlaws.

1826 Annie had such a twisted smile that her lipstick always looked smudged even when it was on straight.

1827 When he first became a doctor, he was so poor, his stethoscope was on a party line.

1828   They have the perfect system in Africa; the natives live in huts built in trees. If they don't pay the rent, the landlord just chops the tree down.

1829   On our way back from the Middle East we caught a vulture and brought it back home with us. Two weeks ago it was offered a job with Inland Revenue.

1830   Every time I get home my wife's face lights up. I push her nose into a lamp-socket.

1831   Many stars are hundreds of millions of years old; my mother-in-law can probably remember when they first started.

HUMOROUS DEFINITIONS

HUMOROUS DEFINITIONS

1832 ATOM: Male pussy.

1833 AUTOMATIC SHIFT: When a man moves closer to a girl passenger in his car.

1834 ACCOLADE: Cheap Egyptian mineral drink.

1835 ABYSS: An Abbot's wife.

1836 AUTOBIOGRAPHY: Log book for your motor vehicle.

1837 ATONIC: A lacer you add to gin.

1838 ASSASSIN: Half a sassenach.

1839 APEX: A female of the gorilla species.

1840 ACETONE: The whinny made by a mule.

1841 ADVERTISEMENT: Something which makes you think you've longed for it for years but never heard of it.

1842 ALIMONY: A mistake made by two people for which one keeps paying.

1843 ABSENTEE: A missing golfing accessory.

1844 ANTIDOTE: A funny story you have heard before.

1845 APOCALYPSE: A small pocket-sized lipstick.

1846 ARTIST'S MODEL: A girl who shows the painter where to draw the line.

1847 ANTI-FREEZE: A close relative without woollen underwear.

1848 ABACUS: A naughty word.

1849 ANTELOPE: When a female insect crawls down a tiny ladder and runs away to get married.

1850 ASBESTOS: As good as anyone else.

1851 AIRLESS: A modern song.

1852 ACROSTIC: Bad-tempered alarm clock.

1853 ANTIBODY: Uncle's fat wife.

1854 ARCADE: An instrument to assist the deaf to hear.

1855 AU PAIR: A living bra.

1856 AZURE: The first act of a Shakespearian play. The rest is called "Like It".

1857 ADAMANT: The very first insect.

1858 ADIEU: A Hebrew.

1859 ADORN: What comes after a darkest hour.

1860 AFFILIATE: When a stallion gets engaged.

1861 AIRCRAFT: The art of a coiffure stylist.

1862 ALIGN: What soldiers shoot when they are on leave.

1863 AISLE: A solemn place which will alter hymn to a husband.

1864 APIARY: A wrestling ring.

1865 AROMATIC: An automatic longbow.

1866 ARTFUL: A painting exhibition.

1867 AWE-STRUCK: Being hit with a paddle.

1868 AFFINITY: Plaice and chips at 4.30 p.m.

1869 ARCHERY: The job of an architect whose speciality is viaducts.

1870 AVAIL: The thing that stops a woman looking so ugly.

1871 ALPHABET: Not quite a complete wager.

1872 ABHOR: Someone who spends hours telling you about Switzerland if you ask him the time.

1873 ABOVE-BOARD: The upper berth on a sleeper to Scotland.

1874 ABUNDANCE: A local hop, usually staged in a barn.

1875 ACME: Pimples on the face, running towards the top.

1876 BURLESQUE SHOW: Where attendance falls off if nothing else does.

1877 BARETTE: A small cocktail cabinet in the lounge.

1878 BILLIOUS: Greatly in debt.

1879 BOYCOTT: A crib which is not good for baby girls.

1880 BLOW-OUT: Visiting eight public houses in succession.

1881 BARCAROLE: Small French loaf shaped like a noisy poodle.

1882 BALSAM: To weep copiously.

1883 BUTTRESS: A woman cream churner.

1884 BADMINTON: The reason why the lamb tasted awful.

1885 BAKELITE: Something a young bride cannot do with pastry.

1886 BANDINAGE: A bandage with an eye in it.

1887 BELSHAZZAR: A Romanoff indigestion mixture.

1888 BRAZIER: Garment worn by a nightwatchman's wife.

1889 BUCK TEETH: Cheap American dentures.

1890 BULLETIN: A can of pressed beef.

1891 BACKSTAYS: Reversible corset.

1892 BACTERIA: A modern self-service bookmaker's office.

1893 BALLYHOO: A directory of ballet dancers, sometimes called "Ballyhoo's Hoo".

1894 BACHELOR: A man who goes to work on a different train every day.

1895 BALANCE: Something which you lose if the bank is sitting on you.

1896 BARBARIAN: The man who cuts your hair.

1897 BAREFACED: Looking like a bear.

1898 BASQUE: Lying in the sun, like a man telling fibs to a blonde on the sands.

1899 BEACHCOMBER: A girl brushing her curls after a swim.

1900 BIZARRE: A market-place with stalls selling various commodities.

1901 BASHFUL: A pugilistic character.

1902 BEDROOM: What your wife takes up most of. Her two-thirds of the spring-interior.

1903 BELLICOSE: Extremely fat.

1904 BETEL-NUT: A crazy insect.

1905 BIRD-LIME: What the girl-friend puts in her lager.

1906 BLAZER: An arsonist.

1907 BLUBBER: A weeping and a whaling.

1908   BLUNDERBUSS: A vehicle which goes from London to Southend via Eastbourne.

1909   BOBTAIL: A shilling novelette.

1910   BOISTEROUS: A condition common to adolescent girls.

1911   BOLERO: A halter which halts all the men when there is a pretty girl in it.

1912   BORDEAUX: The loan you give to a person who is pestering you, to make him depart.

1913   BONANZA: A beautiful French reply.

1914   BOOKCASE: Litigation about alleged pornographic novels which ensures wide sales.

1915   BOSOM: Keeping abreast of the times.

1916   BOWIE-KNIFE: A bow-legged cutlass or sickle.

1917   BOUILLON: A restaurant soup which is made by dipping the end of an ox into hot water, and adding two noodles.

1918   BRIDLE: An invisible collar put around a man's neck by marriage.

1919   BRUSSELS-SPROUTS: A world-famous statue found in that city.

1920   BUOYAGE: A cruise on which a spinster embarks in search of a husband.

1921   BIG EXECUTIVE: A public hangman.

1922   BOXER: A fighter who stands up for the other fellow's rights.

1923   CARNATION: A tribe in which every adult is a vehicle owner.

1924   COUNTERPANE: The agony you endure when you ask the salesgirl how much it is and she tells you.

1925   CLOISTER: Very near to; in extreme proximity.

1926   CROCODILE: A toby jug.

1927   CHARCOAL: What the cleaning woman puts on the fire.

1928   CLANGOUR: Something frequently dropped.

1929   CISTERN: A container for toilet water.

1930   CLIMATE: The only thing you can do with a ladder.

1931   CONQUER: A cosh, or truncheon.

1932   CACHOU: A tissue; a sneeze.

1933 CANTATA: A prisoner's farewell to his jail.

1934 CARAMEL: A motorised camel.

1935 CARRION: A series of successful British movies, such as "Carrion Sergeant", "Carrion Nurse", "Carrion Smoking".

1936 CATASTROPHE: The winning tabby's reward at the show.

1937 CASINO: Where Grandma goes when you think she's working hard at home on the spinning-wheel.

1938 CIVIL SERVANT: One who starts work at 9.30 a.m. with a molehill of papers on the desk, and works until 3.30 making it into a mountain.

1939 CONSCIENCE: The thing that aches when everything else feels good.

1940 COURTSHIP: A matter of sofa and no further.

1941 COUNTERFEIT: Women's extremities crushed at a bargain sale.

1942 COWARD: A man who thinks with his legs.

1943 CABBAGE: The fare you pay a taxi driver.

1944 CHANCERY: A gambling den.

1945 CATACOMB: Toilet accessory for a tabby lover.

1946 CABALLERO: A leather jerkin worn by taxi drivers.

1947 CAR: A guided missile.

1948 CAR KEY: An unlocking device you search for, for hours and then find it in the ignition.

1949 CAUSTIC: An expensive Rolls Royce.

1950 CHANGELING: A damp baby.

1951 CHIMERA: Something you take pictures with.

1952 CHIT-CHAT: A talk with a garrulous young salesgirl.

1953 DIPLOMAT: An immunised man who can convince his wife that a fur coat would make her look fat.

1954 DIAMOND: A stepping stone to security for a single girl.

1955 DULCET: A very boring tennis game.

1956 DEBILITATE: Paying off some of the many creditors.

1957 DELIBERATE: To throw back into jail.

1958 DIATRIBE: An extinct race.

1959 DOGWOOD: Happy hunting-ground for canines, usually a forest.

1960 DRIVE-IN RESTAURANT: A hamburger stall surrounded by a car park.

1961 DIAGRAM: A broken record-player.

1962 DOLDRUMS: Percussion set played by a girl.

1963 DRAUGHTSMAN: Commissionaire outside a broken-down old hotel.

1964 DISCONSOLATE: Playing a gramophone at midnight.

1965 DETEST: The West Indians versus England at Edgbaston.

1966 DRAWING-ROOM: A dentist's den.

1967 DUCTILE: A mallard's hat.

1968 DURATION: An oration that goes on for ever.

1969 ELAPSE: A man sitting very close to his girl.

1970 ELECTRICIAN: A switch doctor.

1971 EMBROIL: To baste every twenty minutes in hot fat in an oven.

1972 EQUINOX: Peculiar noises at midnight in a haunted house.

1973 EARWIG: A fur muff for the ears.

1974 EROS: Brave people.

1975 EYEBROW: Having great culture and *savoir-faire*.

1976 FRIENDS: People who stick together until debt doth them part.

1977 FORTY: The age when women stop patting themselves on the back and start on their chins.

1978 FRUSTRATE: In the best class.

1979 FORTUNE: Barber-shop quartet.

1980 FARTHINGALE: A cheap hurricane.

1981 FILLING-STATION: A garage on a lonely highway where they fill your tank and empty your wallet.

1982 FORTITUDE: A banquet for two score of commercial travellers.

1983 FIELDFARE: Picnic.

1984 FLEXIBLE: Army regulations subject to amendment.

1985 FORCEMEAT: A girdle or corset.

1986 FRUSTRUM: Rum that has gone frowsty.

1987 FACTORY: A set of encyclopedias.

1988 FAGGOT: A female maggot.

1989 FASTIDIOUS: A girl who is fast and hideous.

1990 FUGUE: A dense fog.

1991 FAUCET: What you are compelled to do if the lock is jammed.

1992 FÊTE: A boring garden party which is worse than death.

1993 FIDDLESTICK: The hairy thing you play a violin with.

1994 FICTION: The story told by a completed Income Tax form.

1995 FIGMENT: Brief apparel worn by Eve in Eden, which stretched Adam's imagination; hence "figment of imagination".

1996 FIELDPIECE: Farmer's daughter.

1997 FLATULENCE: The opulence resulting from speculative building of apartment blocks in overcrowded areas.

1998 FLATTERY: A sack dress.

1999 FLEECE: Little sabre-toothed insects which hop all over you and get your wool.

2000 FOOTPAD: A doormat. See also, Husband.

2001 FRENCH LEAVE: Nothing.

2002 FRONTISPIECE: Cheesecake.

2003 FURBELOW: Hell.

2004 FUSILLADE: Wire for a bad fusebox.

2005 GOLF: A five-mile walk punctuated with bitter disappointments.

2006 GOLD-DIGGER: A sweet girl with the gift of the grab.

2007 GRASS-WIDOW: The former wife of an underworld squealer.

2008 GALLOP: A Pole.

2009 GALOSHES: Hungarian rhapsody cooked by a French chef.

2010 GENERALISSIMO: An officer in the Israelian Army, whose full name is Issy Mo Greenbaum.

2011 GAZEBO: A chap who is always peering at girls.

2012 GERMICIDE: Bacteria committing hara-kiri.

2013 GIMCRACK: A broken limb due to over-enthusiastic physical jerks.

2014 GANGRENE: Inexperienced mob.

2015 GONDOLIER: When a smug smile is wiped off the face.

2016 GRANARY: A home for senior female citizens.

2017 GALLERY: A hostel for young women.

2018 HUMBUG: A singing cockroach.

2019 HAWKEYE: A Scottish expression, spelled by Burns as Och Aye.

2020 HITCHING-POST: Marriage Register Office.

2021 HOLIDAY: A time when you do not have to go to work but just stay home and dig the garden, mow the lawn, and chop wood and put up shelves.

2022 HYACINTH: An American greeting for anyone named Cynthia.

2023 HABITUATE: An irritating mannerism which you dislike.

2024 HEALTH: Something that is always drunk to in order to create suffering the morning afterwards.

2025 HOBSON'S CHOICE: Any other woman.

2026 HERMIT: A lady's glove with the fingers cut away.

2027 HACKNEYED: The opposite of knock-kneed.

2028 HOTEL REGISTER: The local Smithy.

2029 HASHISH: Meal made from leftovers.

2030 HEXAGRAM: An urgent spirit message.

2031 HYPOCHONDRIAC: A person with an infinite capacity for faking pains.

2032 HASSOCK: A woollen garment for a foot, decorated with holes.

2033 HATLESS: The chap who wore the world on his head.

2034 HAREM: A palatial box of juicy sultanas.

2035 HOLLYWOOD: A district in California where actresses are made.

2036 HOUSEHOLD: A wrestling grip a mortgage gets round the neck.

2037 IRONY: The finishing department of a hand-laundry.

2038 IDOLISE: Eyes which refuse to look at anything.

2039 ILLICIT STILL: A banned photograph, usually printed in France.

2040 INTENSE: A camping holiday for scouts and guides.

2041 INKLING: A small ballpen.

2042 IAMBUS: Egotistical passenger-transporter.

2043 IMPALE: Ashen Red-Indian.

2044 IMPIOUS: Churchgoing elf.

2045 INCOME: What you have to make first because you can't make it last.

2046 ISOBAR: A lollipop with frost on it.

2047 IGLOO: The powder-room in an Eskimo's cottage.

2048 JEALOUSY: The friendship which one woman shares with another.

2049 JOHDPURS: The noises made by courting cats.

2050 JUGULAR: Shaped like a Ming vase.

2051 LIBRARIAN: An educated bookmaker.

2052 LITHE: What your girl-friend or boy-friend tells you.

2053 LOST CHORD: Probably something that Haydn would seek.

2054 LIMBO: A chap who always looks at girls' legs.

2055 LACTIC: An old grandfather clock which doesn't work.

2056 LATTICE: A green vegetable favoured by rabbits.

2057 LOW MILEAGE: About 100,000 on the clock.

2058 LIVING-ROOM: A lounge the average person wouldn't be seen dead in.

2059 LANDING-PARTY: An orgy on the mezzanine.

2060 LOGARITHM: Wooden dance music.

2061 LIVERY: Suffering with a hangover.

2062 LOBSTER: An impetuous tennis champion.

2063 LONGBOAT: A canoe that has been squeezed between two ocean liners.

2064 MODERN BRA: Young pretenders.

2065 MONOLOGUE: A discussion between husband and wife in which the woman plays the leading role.

2066 MALADY: A duchess.

2067 MAGPIE: A dessert concocted from old journals.

2068 MOTEL: A large packing-case consisting of inner-cases with pillows.

2069 MARGIN: Spiritual uplift for a tired mother.

2070 MACARONI: Inventor of the wireless. The first man to send a message through a length of spaghetti, without it touching the sides.

2071 MISFIRED: A jilted girl.

2072 MUSLIM COURAGE: The better part of Allah.

2073 McAROON: An Edinburgh biscuit.

2074 MINCE: Circular white sweets with holes in the middle.

2075 MADEIRA: The roaring twenties.

2076 MATRICIDE: Shooting yourself on the rug.

2077 MEDIOCRE: Browny-yellow with a touch of off-white to tempt an artist's palette.

2078 MELODRAMATIC: Sneaking a spot of whisky in the very top room.

2079 MERMAID: A girl who is half a woman and half a pilchard.

2080 METER: The local butcher.

2081 MILDEW: The damp that settles on a windmill.

2082 MOUNTEBANK: The place where a Canadian policeman keeps his money.

2083 MUSHROOM: The room where the love-seat is kept.

2084 MUSTARD: When the platoon is gathered together.

2085 NUDIST COLONY: An isolated area where hardly anything goes on.

2086 NEIGHBOURS: The folks who are always either knocking on the door to borrow or on the wall to complain.

2087 NIGHTINGALE: Stormy outing.

2088 NABOB: A hair-do, similar in appearance to a fetlock.

2089 NECTAR: A sweet thing out with a matelot.

2090 NONDESCRIPT: A television play.

2091 NORTH POLE: An inhabitant of Warsaw.

2092 NOTARY: A wallet, or purse.

2093 OPTIMIST: A hope addict.

2094 OBOE: A tramp.

2095 ODIOUS: Not very good poetry.

2096 OPERETTA: A girl who works at the telephone exchange.

2097 OBLIQUE: Desperately in need of a plumber.

2098 OYSTER: A lift or crane used in East London.

2099 OCTOPUS: A Lithuanian cat with eight feet.

2100 OVERTURE: A cow that chews the cud far too much.

2101 PASTEBOARD: The floor of a boxing ring.

2102 PAINFUL: A glasshouse.

2103 PALAVER: A sort of jersey.

2104 PHARMACY: The art of agriculture.

2105 POLONAISE: A sauce for putting on poloni sausage.

2106 PORNOGRAPH: A ticket issued by Uncle.

2107 POULTRY: A tree with all its branches shorn.

2108 POSSE: A Texan wildcat.

2109 POTTERY: Obesity.

2110 POPULACE: The admirable trimming on lingerie.

2111 PORCUPINE: Fretting for a slice of bacon.

2112 PORTABLE: A cheap piece of furniture in the dining-room.

2113 POMADE: A chambermaid.

2114 PRAWN: A small piece on the chessboard.

2115 PROPAGANDA: A real male bird.

2116 PULMOTOR: When you have a breakdown on the highway.

2117 PYLON: To make a heap.

2118 PYGMY: A hamlet.

2119 PUTTY: Miniature golf.

2120 PAVEMENT ARTIST: A man who paints pictures on his knees.

2121 PARKING SPACE: A vacant place usually filled by another car.

2122 PARLIAMENT: A bunch of gas-bags who are never pricked by conscience.

2123 POSTSCRIPT: The part of a letter from a woman which contains all the news.

2124   PANTRY: A storage place for feminine nicknacks.

2125   PARTITE: A stingy parent.

2126   PALEOLITHIC: Pale and dissipated.

2127   PARKING ZONE: A place where they re-model your car for half a crown.

2128   PEDESTRIAN: A motorist with two sons, each having a girl-friend.

2129   PLEASURE CRUISE: Battleship personnel on shore leave.

2130   PANTOGRAPH: Turnover chart on the wall of an underwear manufacturing company's sales manager's office.

2131   PARACHUTE: A double-barrelled shotgun.

2132   PLUMBAGO: A smooth prune's sciatica.

2133   POLITICAL ATLAS: A set of world maps which need revising weekly.

2134   PRE-SELECTIVE GEAR: Ready-to-wear articles purchasable in a store catering for modern youths.

2135   POLITICIAN: A man who thinks more about the next election than about the next generation.

2136   QUACKERY: A duckpond.

2137   QUAKER: A frightened lady.

2138   QUICKSAND: Why an hourglass is ten minutes fast.

2139   QUINCE: A litter of five children.

2140   QUATRAIN: A locomotive with four coaches.

2141   QUININE: Forty-five.

2142   RHUMBA: A method of waving goodbye with your whole body.

2143   RAGAMUFFIN: A biscuit made from old clothes.

2144   RANSOM: An Olympic gold medallist.

2145   RATTAN: Summer complexion.

2146   RHOMBOID: An American girl from Brooklyn, slightly odd.

2147   RAGTIME: Spring sales season.

2148   ROTUNDA: An author's pseudonym.

2149   REORIENTATE: Change back into a Chinaman.

2150   RACIAL DISPUTE: When the course judges call for a photo.

2151 REFLECTION: What a girl looks at but is not given to.

2152 REVELATION: An ecstatic feeling the driver of a sports car gets as the needle hovers around 150.

2153 ROMANTIC: What you get up to on holiday in Italy's capital.

2154 RUGGED: When you are sitting on the carpet.

2155 RANCOUR: A lowly placed infantryman.

2156 RAWHIDE: The material that covers a nudist.

2157 RAZOR: A knocker-up.

2158 REBELLIOUS: Having broken one's girdle.

2159 RECLUSE: An abandoned, damaged ship.

2160 RECITED: Had a second look.

2161 SAGE: A guy who knows his onions.

2162 SECRET: Something that is hushed up, from place to place.

2163 SULTAN'S PALACE: An edifice that covers a multitude of sons.

2164 SCRAPBOOK: A boxing promoter's diary.

2165 SALAAM: A small piece of salami.

2166 SHAMPOO: Imitation poo.

2167 SAVOURY: Trustee bank; or a ceramic pig with a slot in the spine.

2168 STALEMATE: Worked-out wife.

2169 SNUFF: Sufficient unto the day.

2170 SEA SHANTY: Mermaid's small bijou residence.

2171 SOMERSAULT: A seaside boatman.

2172 SQUALID: Fretful infant.

2173 SHAMROCK: An imitation mountain.

2174 SLACKS: Garments that tighten up on a woman.

2175 SMATTERING: Asking someone what the trouble is.

2176 SONATA: A song sung by Frank Sinatra.

2177 STABILISED: A horse confined to barracks.

2178 STOCKADE: A suspender.

2179 SYNONYMOUS: When the transgressor is unknown.

2180 SPELLBINDING: The cover of a dictionary.

2181   TRANSPARENT: Daddy in a trance.

2182   TURKISH BATH: A sponge-down that the Turkish delight in.

2183   TURKISH WASH: A swill in which a Turk can indulge without getting his fez wet.

2184   TAXIDERMIST: Inland Revenue Inspector, who skins you.

2185   TEMPEST: An ill-natured nuisance.

2186   TYRANT: Person unable to fix his bow.

2187   TIMEPIECE: A prisoner in Holloway.

2188   TELEVISION PLAY: Dirty pictures in a box.

2189   ULTRAMARINE: The best sailor in the navy.

2190   UNCHASTE: A plain-looking girl at a dance. Wallflower.

2191   UMLAUT: A Red-Indian beatnik.

2192   UNISON: An only boy.

2193   USED-CAR: A passenger vehicle that is not what it's jacked up to be.

2194   UPHOLSTER: To wear two six-guns, concealed.

2195   UNBRIDLED ORGY: A loose wild horse.

2196   UNIT: Derogatory expression applied to protagonist in an argument.

2197   VAGABOND: An unsuccessful stockbroker.

2198   VESTRY: A second-hand underwear store.

2199   VOTARY: Polling booth.

2200   WHISKY: Two pints of which make one cavort.

2201   WEDDING RING: A matrimonial tourniquet that stops a woman's circulation.

2202   W.R.E.N.S.: Girls who go down to the sea in slips.

2203   WINESAP: A man who prefers grapejuice to spirits.

2204   WARSAW: One of the tools of battle.

2205   WOODWORM: A do-it-yourself carpenter.

2206   WHISTLER: A man who could easily end up with a mother-in-law.

2207   WIRELESS: A human puppet.

2208   WOMAN: A person who, when the telephone rings, picks up the chair.

2209   YES-MAN: One who stoops to concur.

HUMOROUS PHILATELIC TERMS

2210   MINT STAMPS: On which the gum is flavoured with peppermint.

2211   APPROVAL BOOKS: The set which the shopkeeper submits to Income Tax Inspection, as compared with the real set.

2212   GOOD EARLIES: People who retire to bed at a decent hour.

2213   PART SHEETS: The sort which boarding-houses use for commercial travellers.

2214   DEALER'S STOCK: A whip used by dealers for persuading customers to buy

2215   OFF PAPER: An English custom for eating fish and chips.

2216   UNMOUNTED STAMPS: Stamps which have fallen off a horse.

2217   INVERTED SURCHARGE: Manner of compelling debtor to pay, by holding him upside down and shaking his pockets.

2218   HEAVY CANCELLATION: Overweight guest unable to arrive at hotel.

2219   1st. D.C.: The original electric power system.

2220   FRANK: Dealer admitting stamp is only worth its real value

2221   POSTCARD: French for art gallery.

2222   AIR LETTER: A letter full of 'gas', signifying nothing.

2223   SCARCE: Only about 6,000,000 in existence.

2224   BANK COVER: Dustsheet over an overdraft.

2225   POSTMARK: Greasy thumbprint left behind on envelope by postman.

2226   OVERPRINT: Politician with success written all over him in blue pencil.

2227   RAILWAY CANCELLATIONS: Two thirds of an A.B.C. timetable.

2228   MARGINAL PAIR: Couple who are nearly married.

2229   ADHESIVE: Blonde who cannot be shaken off.

2230   RARE: Underdone, as some dealers imagine after having sold stamp too cheaply by mistake.

2231   IMPRESSED: Customer listening to dealer's spiel.

2232   EXCELLENT STRIKE: Result of sit-down which effects wage increase.

2233   DEFECTIVE: Promoted constable, joining C.I.D.

2234   WELL-TIED-ON PIECE: W.R.E.N. lashed to the mast aboard the lugger.

2235   FOUR SHADES: Quartet of ghouls.

2236   CLOSE ALL ROUND: A Scottish collector.

2237   THIN: What a lisping girl is unafraid of.

2238   FINE STRIP OF THREE: Trio of chorus girls.

2239   HONG KONG: Motor hooter.

2240   24 ANNAS: And then the Sultan passed.

2241   MONACO TRIANGULARS: Nappies in Monte.

2242   RECONSTRUCTED PLATE: Repaired denture.

2243   CROWN WATERMARK: Near the top of the glass at the Crown tavern.

2244   DOUBLE PRINT: Single print seen by reveller checking his stamps after Stag Party.

2245   SUDAN: An American saloon car. (Earlier British model was the Sudan Chair.)

2246   BARELY SHAVED: Teddy Boy.

2247   PEN CANCELLED: Reprieve for American gangster.

2248   FIRST ISSUE: Blessed event. Later issues denoted by more vigorous adjective.

2249   VIRGIN ISLANDS: A place where the hand of man has never set foot.

2250   FINNISH: The other end of the beginning.

2251   LONG STAMPS: Policeman standing on corner in cold weather.

2252   CUT TO SHAPE: Modern method of dressmaking with curved scissors.

2253   WELL CENTRED: A phrase borrowed from International football.

2254   COMPLETE SET: Successful cement.

2255   FACE VALUE: Sometimes your fortune, often not.

2256   CONTROL NUMBER: Counting up to ten before hitting someone.

2257   PICTORIAL ISSUE: American paper's horror comic supplement, for father.

2258 COLD GHOST: Misprint. Should read Gold Coast. Now obsolete.

2259 LINE ENGRAVED: Henpecked husband after twenty years of martyrdom.

2260 HAITI: Where the Whites are haiti-taiti.

2261 TOP PRICE: The price paid for a low-slung-neckline gown.

2262 PEG FITTING ALBUM: An album in which you peg the stamps out on a line. Useful when the ink is still wet.

2263 MIXTURE: Something the doctor recommended for indigestion.

2264 METAL BAND PRINT: Sheet music for brass bands.

2265 PROVINCIALS: Country cousins.

2266 UNIQUE SPECIMEN: Stamp dealer with two heads.

2267 SMALL PAIR: Underdeveloped.

2268 RETOUCHED: The skin you like to touch.

2269 MOUNTED RANGE: An electric cooker being ridden by Grandma.

2270 SEPARATE SINGLE: Engaged couple's spare hotel room.

2271 CENSORED COVERS: Jackets of pornographic classical novels.

2272 BUNDLE OF SHEETS: Something lost by laundry.

2273 POSTAGE DUE: Stamp moisture.

2274 SIMILAR LOT: The crowd you met last week.

2275 OFFICIAL STAMP: The bearing of a Civil Servant.

2276 OBSOLETE: The decree you get after the Decree Nisi.

2277 PENNY BLACK: Cheap slave labour.

HUMOROUS BOOK TITLES

NOT RECOMMENDED FOR READING

2278 THE PICKLED HERRING by Della Katessen.

2279 THE LAST RETORT by Hugo Twell.

2280 THE BARBER OF SEVILLE by Aaron Flore.

2281 THE TWO KILLERS by Angus Eyatt Dorne.

2282 ONCE ABOARD THE LUGGER by Abel C. Mann.

2283 THE ARTIST AND THE MODEL by Adeline Toodraw.

2284 SCOTCH MUSCLES by Eva Caber.

2285 THE TRUSTEE BANKERS by Xavier Munney.

2286 NEGRO MAGISTRATES by Lady Lordowne.

2287 A LOST LOVE by Theodora Fledd.

2288 BRIEF ENCOUNTER by Felix Ited.

2289 THE DUBLIN SHEPHERD by Sean Flocke.

2290 THE DISUSED CHAPEL by Pugh Bustead.

2291 THE CONGO PARTY by Maud D. Merrier.

2292 SALVAGE MONEY by Rex Broughtin.

2293 THE TOY SHOP by Adolphus Ayle.

2294 MINK IS THE STOLE by Sheila Doritt.

2295 THE CARPET BAGGERS by Walter Wall.

2296 ALL FOR A FIVER by Bertha Quinns.

2297 SO TO CASANOVA by Caesar Titely.

2298 THE MATCH ON THE GRASS by Lorna Lite.

2299 WHICH WAY OUT? by Isadora Negsitt.

2300 TOPPERS AND TAILS by Hiram Frascott.

2301 THE ANGRY TIGER by Claudia Armoff.

2302 THE ICE MAN COMETH by Conan Waifer.

2303 THE UGLY GOURMET by Dinah Honor Rhone.

2304 STRAYS FROM THE FOLD by Gay Topen.

2305 CHAINS by Lincoln Weldham.

2306 THE GRETNA GREEN RUNAWAYS by Marius Ina Hurrey.

2307 THE TATTOOIST by Marcus Orlover.

2308 THE NYMPHS by Mandy Manders.

2309 WHO'S WHO? by Justin Quire.

2310 FLIP-TOP by Lydia Fagpacket

2311 THE SURGEON by Phoebe Foureye-Starte.

2312 OFF TO MARKET by Tobias A. Pigg

2313 THE UNEMPLOYED MAGICIAN by Trixie Cudden-Doo

2314 THE SECRET AGENTS by Webster Spynne

2315 TODAY AND TOMORROW by Alma Nack

2316 FASCISM by Dick Taters

2317 THE BEARDED LADY by Barbara Airoff

2318 SHE STOOPS TO CONQUER by Eileen Dover

2319 COCKTAILS FOR TWO by Bart Ender

2320 THE NEGRO SPIRE by Belinda Belfree

2321 THE DRUNKEN IRISHMEN by Carrie M. Holme

2322 THE WELSH COMEDIAN by Dai Larfin

2323 THE CAUTIOUS DEBUTANTE by Esme Socksaggin

2324 A LOSING WAGER by Henrietta Hatt

2325 THE MARRIED MAN by Helen Erth

2326 THE UGLY AMERICAN WOMAN by Ida Fayce

2327 A NIGHT IN PARIS by Cissy Bonne

2328 DISENGAGED by Lou M. T. Nowe

2329 THE FAST YANK by Maida Passe

2330 PASTE JEWELLERY by Fay Kearings

2331 THE GENIUS by Nora Mye

2332 AN ECONOMIC BREAKFAST by Roland Marge

2333 AN EXPENSIVE BREAKFAST by Hammond Tong

2334 JOCKEY'S KNOCK by Rhoda Loozer

2335 THE WRONG GIRDLE by Titus Kanbee

HUMOROUS SONG TITLES

2336 "If I had a Talking Picture of You." It'd be Certificate X.

2337 "In Room 504." That's where I spent my youth.

2338 "June is Bursting out all Over." So Mom's buying her a girdle.

2339 "Little Sir Echo." Radish and cucumber salad.

2340 "The Touch of Your Hand." I can still feel it on my wallet.

2341 "I Want the World to Know I Love You." But not my wife.

2342 "The Shrimp Boats Are A'Coming." At last I'll be able to sail.

2343 "Drink to Me only with Thine Eyes." I need all the Scotch myself.

2344 "I've Got You Under My Skin." Crowded in here, isn't it?

2345 "Cruising Down the River." And now I'm up the creek.

2346 "I'll Be Seizing You." In all the old familiar places?

2347 "Ain't Misbehavin'." For the next three hours, anyway.

2348 "Among My Souvenirs." An unidentified garter.

2349 "Carolina Moon." Full of Russians?

2350 "Happy Days Are Here Again." The divorce came through?

2351 "The Clouds Will Soon Roll By." And there'll be a hurricane.

2352 "I Can't Give You Anything but Love." The Scotsman's Pop-Song.

2353 "Have You Ever Been Lonely?" Try a deodorant, or chlorophyll.

2354 "All the King's Horses." Everything in the garden's lovely.

2355 "Nobody Loves a Fairy When She's Forty." But she's all right at 36–24–36.

2356 "The Sheikh of Araby." His passion was intense.

2357 "Rambling Rose." Someone took her for a ride.

2358 "SHAKE HANDS WITH A MILLIONAIRE." Then count your fingers.

2359 "AIN'T SHE SWEET." She must have been sugared up.

2360 "A BEDTIME STORY." No!

2361 "WHEN MY SUGAR WALKS DOWN THE STREET." The neighbours will just have to lump it.

2362 "LITTLE WHITE LIES." Account for the wife's dirty, black looks.

2363 "WHEN IT'S SLEEPY TIME DOWN SOUTH." It's Wakes Week in Blackpool.

2364 "MEET ME IN MY DREAMS TONIGHT." And you'll be sorry.

2365 "ON THE SUNNY SIDE OF THE STREET." It's raining there as well.

2366 "OH, MR. PORTER." Mind the baggage, she's not very well.

2367 "IF YOU WERE THE ONLY GIRL IN THE WORLD." You'd still be on your own.

2368 "IT HAPPENED IN MONTEREY." But it happens in other places too.

2369 "KISSES SWEETER THAN WINE." Depending on the vintage, of course.

2370 "I WANT TO GET YOU ON A SLOW BOAT TO CHINA." And tell you a lot of old junk.

2371 "THERE'S A RAINBOW ROUND MY SHOULDER." Then take that college scarf off.

2372 "WHEN I'M CLEANING WINDOWS." Who needs television?

2373 "MEMORIES OF YOU." Mostly in nightmares.

2374 "HAVING A HEAT WAVE." Mind you don't set your hair alight.

2375 "THIS CAN'T BE LOVE." No, it's probably dyspepsia.

2376 "I GET A KICK OUT OF YOU." Why don't you sell that mule?

2377 "I TALK TO THE TREES." And it interests my psychiatrist.

HUMOROUS ADVERBS

2378   "I wish I'd hedged that bet", said the bookmaker, hoarsely.

2379   "I really must do some reducing", she said, sternly.

2380   "Roll up your sleeve", said the doctor, in a serious vein.

2381   "Of course I know Fingal's Cave", said the cellist sharply.

2382   "It's a top floor apartment", said the estate agent, flatly.

2383   "Phew! Eighty crates of fish", said the lorry driver, truculently.

2384   "I must attend to my flock", said the vicar, sheepishly.

2385   "Gimme a Scotch on the rocks", said the drunk, drily.

2386   "Have you gathered all the peas?" asked the farmer, accusingly.

2387   "Bing Crosby might get a sore throat", said Bob, hopefully.

2388   "But I don't want a spaniel, I want a corgi", said the pet-fancier doggedly.

2389   "This is the very best indigestion mixture," insisted the chemist, acidly.

2390   "I don't understand it but I know what I know what I like," said Picasso, artfully.

2391   "I don't like taking my doctor's medicine," said the invalid, patiently.

2392   "Put another shilling in," sang the lamplighter, brightly.

2393   "What a rotten hand you've dealt me," said the bridge player, in passing.

2394   "But it *is* the latest design," said the dressmaker, cuttingly.

2395   "Stand closer together, madam," said the photographer to the fat lady, snappily.

2396   "My husband wants another gamekeeper," said the lady, chattily.

2397   "Your drip-dry shirts are all crumpled," said the laundry manageress, ironically.

2398 "It's a small place over the barn," said the farmer, loftily.

2399 "My horse won't stop," shouted the huntsman, woefully.

2400 "You mean you want another overdraft?" said the bank manager, incredibly.

2401 "I want to buy 10,000 sub-machine-guns and 50,000,000 rounds of ammunition," said the dictator, disarmingly.

2402 "My drill is going berserk," said the roadmender, shakily.

2403 "I've just got the job of doing the whole 20-storey block of offices," said the window cleaner, painfully.

2404 "Do you want the chicken without dressing?" asked the waiter, saucily.

2405 "This is an *imitation* diamond," said his fiancée, stonily.

2406 "The record is not the only thing I've broken," said the high-jump champion, limply.

2407 "Any advance on £1,000?" asked the auctioneer, morbidly.

2408 "I thoroughly enjoyed having the Bishop for dinner," said the cannibal, manfully.

2409 "I want to make jig-saw puzzles," said the carpenter, fretfully.

2410 "I played 'Othello' and Othello won," said the actor, playfully.

2411 "But I thought you weren't using real bullets," wailed the dying man, blankly.

2412 "Have you anything by *Hugo*?" asked Les, miserably.

2413 "Dash it all, that's not cricket," said the batsman, boldly.

2414 "Please may I leave the room?" asked the schoolboy, high-handedly.

2415 "You want the car on credit over ten years?" repeated the banker, with great interest.

2416 "Heck, still ten thousand trees in the forest," sighed the lumberjack, woodenly.

2417 "What magnificent muscles you have," said the girl, with feeling.

2418 "You should have turned right at the lights," said the examiner, testily.

2419 "I've got a nail in my shoe," said Spike, pointedly.

2420 "I've lost my Chinese necklace," she said, jadedly.

2421   "Hurrah for Scotland," said Angus, jocularly.

2422   "You have stolen my girl-friend," shouted Tom to Dick, ruthlessly.

2423   "How do you like my petticoat?" she asked shiftlessly.

2424   "I love every Tom, Dick and Harry," she said frankly.

2425   "I don't *have* to do this for a living," she said, tartly.

2426   "Dear Sirs, please send me your catalogue," he wrote, listlessly.

2427   "I'm writing my memoirs," said the pigbreeder, pensively.

2428   "It only took me an hour to learn to play the guitar," confessed the pop singer, pluckily.

2429   "There won't be anything for you from my estate," said his old uncle, wilfully.

2430   "I'm looking for a sugar-daddy," she admitted, sweetly.

2431   "You're through," said the telephone operator, with an engaging smile.

HUMOROUS HOROSCOPES

2432 JANUARY–FEBRUARY. *Aquarius the Water Carrier.* You were born under the sign of Aquarius, the water bearer, which means that you have a perpetual thirst. This month you are going to meet a lovely, big, shapely blonde dreamgirl. The only snag is that you will meet her in a dream and wake up before you've been introduced. Your health will be very good for a change this year, except for a touch of lumbago, splitting headaches and a sprained ankle, all due to you being a little run down. Don't worry about being run down; they will arrest the motorist. Your social prospects are quite good. You will be more popular than ever, especially with people of your own sex; until you stop buying them drinks. By nature you are romantic and imaginative, in fact you have a very strong imagination. You can even imagine that your wife is Venus de Milo. I predict for you some good fortune towards the end of next week. You will get a surprise from your wife or girl-friend. A new necktie. The surprise is because you are expecting a gold cigarette case. If you are *not* married, this could be your lucky year. In fact, it's a lucky year for anyone who is not married. Like all other Aquarian people, you like work. You could sit and watch it for weeks on end. You are a great worrier, always anxious and biting your nails. Watch this, because from too much nail-biting, your teeth get worn down to stumps, and when you find that you cannot bite your nails with your gums, you are liable to get frustrated. As a rule, you suffer from indigestion and the best preventative measure you can take is to give up eating.

FOR WOMEN. Your lucky colour is gold and your lucky jewel is the diamond. Normally you live happy contented lives as long as you can find a rich man, old enough to die quickly. Usually women born in this period are warm-hearted, except some nights when wearing low-cut evening gowns.

2433 FEBRUARY–MARCH. *Pisces the Fish.* You were born under Pisces, the fish, which accounts for your affinity for chips. Most men born in this period are in the Navy, and if you are not in the Navy you should check that you have your birthday correct. You are usually a lonely person, and your feelings are easily hurt, especially if someone punches you on the nose. You are not usually demonstrative in your affections, and any show of affection makes you embarrassed; you feel this way when you go to the cinema and watch romantic scenes, especially if they are taking place between the couple sitting two rows behind you. Even more so if you recognise one of them as your wife. You're the sort of person who would fight to the bitter end for the friends around you, but unfortunately you have no friends. People born in this period are generally highly strung, so be careful not to commit too many murders. You are generous to a fault; the fault being that you never give anything away. You have a scientific turn of mind and can tell when a three-minute egg is boiled without even watching the clock. Nine out of ten people born under Pisces usually work in the Civil Service; the rest die natural deaths. You are inclined to be an extrovert; you love crowds of people around you, being gregarious. Especially if you are a pickpocket. If you were born rich, you will have money, otherwise you will find that money comes only from working hard, or marrying it.

2434   MARCH–APRIL. *Aries the Ram.* People born under Aries the Ram are often sheep in wolves' clothing. Men are generally very well educated —they know the *history* of every horse running on every track—they know the *geography* of almost every blonde and redhead within an area of fifty miles, and when it comes to *mathematics*, they can work out the odds of 11 to 10 on for every donkey at the track, without the aid of logarithms. You dislike being dependent upon other people, except for the essentials of life such as food, money, clothes and luxury. You are inclined to smoke excessively and for this reason you should prevent yourself getting all burned up. Aries produces many famous people—writers, artists, musicians —but you are probably the exception. You are always a good loser, which is all to the good because very early in life you will lose your hair and teeth. You have an excellent personality, so that the loss of your looks doesn't matter much; nobody likes you anyway. It is possible that when you were born your mother was very surprised. She had been expecting a baby. You are very good at languages—there is no word used in golf which you cannot say fluently. You are the type who easily loses his head, but in your case this inflicts no great harm. You are very popular with girls and have girl-friends in every corner of the world. The trouble is getting them to come out of their corners. You will find something in life worth living for. Beer, if you are a man, and gin, if you are a woman.

2435   APRIL–MAY. *Taurus the Bull.* You were born under Taurus the Bull, and he probably stepped on you which accounts for your flat appearance. People born under the sign of the bull are generally as strong as lions, and some lions smell very strongly. You resent criticism and the only way to argue against it is by logic, reasoning and inherent cleverness; but you are not equipped to do this. You are usually unhappy in your domestic life and find it difficult to meet members of the opposite sex who understand you. Which is why you are often heard telling some blonde about it. You crave affection and sympathy which makes you an ideal person for the army. You would make a good sergeant-major. You like flattery and praise, and are just the kind of person to encourage the opposite. You are full of mental energy, always working on big new schemes, but nobody will put money into them, and your girl-friends are too smart to fall for the line. As you are inclined to lack caution, never visit a married woman on the fifteenth floor of an apartment house without taking a parachute. Women of this period are frank and outspoken, although it is difficult to find anyone to out-speak them. According to your sex, people of this period are brutal and tyrannical, or sweet and inoffensive; the women being the brutes and tyrants. You like to be looked up to, which is a pity, because you are generally short in stature. Your greatest happiness comes from working hard and overcoming obstacles, so don't expect much happiness.

2436 MAY–JUNE. *Gemini the Twins*. People born under Gemini are prone to sleeping troubles. They keep waking up every two or three days. They also have a great ability to commit things to memory from books, which is unfortunate because most of them cannot read. They are never happier than when entertaining friends, especially friends of the other sex. They are wonderful directors—if you are a married man and your wife is a Gemini, she will direct you where to go. They consider no sacrifice is too great for their partners, and so make no sacrifices. People of Gemini are usually lonely. This is due to their constant use of garlic. Most Geminis are mean in disposition. If they have measles, they hesitate before giving it to anyone else. If you are a bachelor you are going on a long journey. How long depends on where she lives and what time the last bus leaves. This is a wonderful period for making plans; just sit around and make plenty of plans. It's better than hurrying around doing nothing. You believe in the policy of give and take. Whatever anyone is giving, you take. You will have difficulty in making decisions next week, so better stick to beer. You should marry *early*. If the parson isn't up at seven in the morning, take your business elsewhere. If you are already married, it's too late.

2437 JUNE–JULY. *Cancer the Crab*. People born under this sign are generally crabby in nature. They also like a life of wine, women and song; therefore for economy purposes choose a woman who likes champagne and sings when she's drunk. Of all people in the world, Crabs are most difficult to understand, because most of them are foreigners. June people make excellent explorers, which is why girls are careful when out with one late at night. They are ambitious for high positions and many become social climbers, or hotel window-cleaners. Many of these people are restless, and always want the things they haven't got, such as good looks and money. They make good lawyers and good doctors . . . busy. Usually they are successful with money matters and often work in banks or on the Stock Exchange or else spend their time studying the horses and working out five-time accumulators. Women born in this period are often thick-skinned. They know how to get, and wear, thick-skinned mink coats. You are likely to have lots and lots of children, so marry a Marriage Guidance councillor. As you are fond of a little drink eat plenty of salt herring. The men of this period are the caveman type. Girls give them one kiss and they cave in. You are generally good hunters which is just as well because you have to hunt hard for women, food and money. You would go to the other end of the earth for the one you love, provided he or she paid the fare.

2438 JULY–AUGUST. *Leo the Lion*. People born under Leo the Lion are fearless and strong. They don't know the meaning of the word fear. They have to look it up in a dictionary. And they are so strong that they can bend girders with their bare hands; providing Gerda doesn't mind being bent. They usually have flat feet. You will find them in different flats most nights. When these people get married they realise what true happiness is, but then it is too late. They have many ups and downs in early life, especially if they work down a mine or run an elevator. The Leo men like women who are beautiful and blonde and generally marry ugly old widows who are bald. They have many home interests; and that's where they often end up—in a Home. The younger generation of Leo men often keep shops. The older ones keep women. They are very prudent and sometimes shy, which is why they join Nudist Colonies using assumed names. You are due for a big change in a month or two. Your undervest and your pants. You are of a sunny disposition but sometimes give way to attacks of bitter rage during which you are not yourself. Whoever you are is better. If you should see a black cat this week, the black cat will have seven years bad luck.

2439 AUGUST–SEPTEMBER. *Virgo the Virgin* and *Libra the Balance*. People born under these signs are as honest as the day is long. But at night it's different. They love money and worship gold, especially bright blondes. They make good leaders (like Napoleon) and can lead their men through fire and death, if they can get them to follow. The women of this period are good and sweet, up to the age of twelve, after which it's anybody's guess. The girls are big-hearted, and put themselves out for men. Most of the men of this period are frank and earnest, except Tom, Dick and Harry. They make a large number of enemies by being fond of free speech— speaking freely about their friends after they've left the house. The men have great will-power, and the women have great *won't* power. Great soldiers, leaders of finance and high public figures are born in this period, so naturally YOU will feel self-conscious and inferior. You seek to avoid bouts of melancholy by drinking hard liquor, which only makes you more melancholy and drives you to more drink, which in turn makes you happy. You are usually very healthy and considered a good insurance risk, but against this you are inclined to make *other* people sick. Smoking is not good for you, so give up that pipe, especially if you are a woman. You have the makings of a very charming and intelligent person, if only you can find someone to put you together.

2440   OCTOBER. *Scorpio the Scorpion.* You were born under the sign of the Scorpion, which means that you are poison to some women. You are slightly psychic and can look into the future and what you see there worries you because it reminds you of your past. You would make a very successful millionaire, if only you had a million to start with. You are a good speculator. You can look at a woman and speculate very quickly. But your advances are often repulsed because, to put it bluntly, you are repulsive. Up to the age of about twenty, Scorpions are usually pure-minded, virtuous and religious, but after that they swing to the opposite side of the street as character begins to form. They make excellent writers, especially of love letters and begging letters. Men who put their feelings into writing should not let the lady know who the sender is. In danger and sudden crisis, Scorpio people are very well equipped. They can run like hell. You can adapt yourself to any form of social life, which is just as well because you are in for a lot of changes of fortune. Sometimes you will be very poor but at other times you will be entirely impoverished. The best advice I can give you is to marry a wealthy partner and worship the ground she owns. You are a great humanitarian and love people, especially if you are a cannibal. You have exceptional eyesight and can tell the time just by looking at a clock. As you are a passionate type, you will have to earn a lot of money because it costs money to keep two homes going.

2441   NOVEMBER–DECEMBER. *Sagittarius the Archer* and *Capricornus the Goat.* Born in this period you are either an archer or an old goat. You are so generous that you could not bear to see a beggar starving before your very eyes. You would shoot him. The sign of the Archer is half a horse and half a man; this is because you are never certain which you are. You look like a man and work like a horse, or you run like a horse and drink like a fish. If you are a woman you look like a horse and run from a man. All of which is very confusing. Women of this period are very quick at making up their minds and very slow at making up their faces. Men of this period are slow at making up their minds and once they have done it, you see the results of unskilled labour. You are easily fatigued, so always seek sedentary work, preferably some job you can do lying in bed, like reading palms or meters. People of this period are the salt of the earth, but the women are not so easily poured. You have very high ideals and prefer to live up to your income which gives you a very mean existence indeed. You like sports and you break a lot of records, due to your inherent clumsiness and carelessness. You have a lot to look forward to next week. Monday, Tuesday, Wednesday, Thursday, Friday and Saturday and Sunday. You believe in prayer and often pray for your fellow-beings. Most times your prayers are not answered. You are trustworthy and kind in nature. Quite often you go to the zoo to feed the little rabbits. You feed them to the tigers. You are at your best in the world of entertainment. If you are married, you entertain the neighbours quite a lot, especially if the walls are thin. You are the type who will never stand for any nonsense. You prefer to sit down. You are going to be married soon, and not long after you will hear the tiny pitter-patter of little bills falling through your mailbox. You are musically inclined and like to sing in your bath which is why you are always looking for a fresh place to live.

TERSE VERSE

TERSE VERSE

2442   TAKE SIX EGGS
Mrs. Beeton wrote a book
Telling housewives how to cook;
But judging by the meals I've eaten
My wife's cooking can't be Beeton.

2443   ONLY HUMAN
Don't worry if your job's a joke,
And your successes few;
Remember that the mighty oak
Was once a nut like you.

2444   OUCH
No one knows, complains Miss Cox,
The pain that it engenders,
Keeping up my bobby-sox
With ordin'ry suspenders.

2445   ZOO TIME
The elephant is very large,
They ought to have him shrunk;
And pack his great big carcase
Into his little trunk.

2446   JUNIOR MISS
East is East and West is West,
But whatever the wise man thinks,
Completely universal is
The inscrutable smile of a minx.

2447   HOMELESS
The estate agent did his best
Because I was emphatic;
Now he lives east and I live west
In a small partitioned attic.

2448   WORKERS, UNITE
I'm a great do-it-yourself man,
And the system has its points;
But I've twinges in me hinges,
And judders in me joints.

2449   SEA-FRONT
She didn't give him many dates;
She thought he was a meanie,
So in order to see more of her
He bought her a bikini.

2450   MODUS OPERANDUS
With women, he has an infallible system;
He just makes no effort at all to resystem.

2451   WILLIE
Little Willie, late one night, lit a stick of dynamite,
Don't you think he had a cheek? It's been raining Willie for a week.

2452   BAR ROOM
What is so rare as a day in June
If it isn't free beer in a Scottish saloon?

2453   FASHION
Women, lovely women; how fair they are and sweet . . .
They wear more clothes when they go to bed than they do when they're
    out in the street.

2454   NURSERY RHYME
Little Jack Horner, he sat in his corner,
Not a solitary soul said "Hullo".
Then down came a spider who'd drunk too much cider,
And told Jack about his B.O.

2455   THE DEB.
A débutante at a country ball
Believed pride went before a fall,
So now when she trips the light fantastic.
She always wears good strong elastic!

2456   NOT LIKELY
Early to bed and early to rise,
While the best of the girls
Get the rest of the guys?

2457 UNDER THE CLOCK
It's very aggravating
To be kept waiting
By a girl who in the past
Has earned a reputation for being fast.

2458 BLACKBOARD JUNGLE
It seems to be the current rule
For sex to be discussed at school;
So now precocious little inkstained creatures
Are busy educating teachers.

2459 TRAVELLING LIGHT
Minnie paid a guinea for
A little floral pinnyfore;
Surprising what a lot it hides.
Since she wears nothing else besides.

2460 MEET THE WIFE
He used to call her Aphrodite,
Until he saw her in her nightie;
Face unpainted, hair all frizz—
So now he simply calls her Liz.

2461 IN CONFERENCE
The delegate was pretty smug;
He slapped his brief and cried: "Hey, presto!"
—Then missed his footing, slipped and fell,
And wrecked his entire manifesto.

2462 À LA MODE
Girls who wear flannel
The whole year through
Itch
To get married
But seldom do.

2463 THE WATER'S FINE
At one time girls went out to swim
Looking like old Mother Hubbard;
Today they don't look quite so grim.
They look more like her cupboard.

2464   O.S. 7

It's easy to grin when your ship has come in,
Some men laugh in the face of defeat.
But the guy I like best is the one who can jest
When his pants are too tight round the seat.

2465   OLD RHYME TIME

Little Jack Horner sat in his corner
Eating a home-made pie;
He stuck in his thumb, but instead of a plum,
He squirted fruit juice in his eye.

2466   TO THE FOUR WINDS

When eager lips are pressed so tight
And tender arms enfold her,
It's easy to know wrong from right,
Just as her Momma told her.

2467   HAVE A BITE

They make an awful lot of fuss about the hippopotamus,
They scurry from that beastie at the double;
Whereas the very humble flea who isn't very much to see,
Can often be a bigger load of trouble.

2468   GUESS WHO?

Who comforts me in dire despair?
Who softly grooms my thinning hair?
Who darns my socks? Who cooks my meals?
Who takes my shoes in for new heels?
Who keeps my suits and coats like new?
Who praises everything I do?
Who scrubs my back? Who makes my bed?
Who urges me to keep my head?
Who can this paragon of virtue be?
I'll tell you frankly folks—it's me.

2469   REFERENCES REQUIRED

She was courted by a millionaire;
The romance didn't last.
He never gave her presents—
But he gave her a wonderful past.

2470 GOING STEADY
  She was a pretty little girl
  And he an ardent male.
  He praised her shapely beauty
  In English, French,
  And Braille.

2471 STRICTLY FROM HUNGER
  Mary had a little lamb,
  A lobster and some prunes,
  A glass of wine, a piece of pie,
  A plate of macaroons;
  She also had two big cream puffs,
  A portion of cod's roe;
  And when they carried Mary out
  Her face was white as snow.

2472 RECOGNITION
  You can always tell a French girl,
  You can always tell a Swiss,
  You can tell a girl's from Sweden,
  By the way she learned to kiss;
  You can tell a señorita,
  You can tell a girl who's Dutch,
  You can also tell an English girl—
  But you can't tell that one much.

2473 THE NEIGHBOURS
  His wife has a musical nature
  She can yodel, and whistle and hum;
  She goes out as fit as a fiddle
  And comes home as tight as a drum.

2474 PROHIBITED
  Say it with flowers or say it with sweets;
  Say it with kisses or theatre seats;
  Say it with diamonds or even with mink,
  But never get careless and say it with ink.

2475 DARKEST AFRICA
  Deep in the heart of wild cannibal country
  I dated a maiden as brown as burnt cork;
  She waited for me in the shade of a Mango
  With a bottle of sauce, and a knife and a fork.

2476 BUCOLIC

A farmer who called his cow Zephyr,
Thought her quite a contented young heifer,
But when he drew near
She kicked off his ear
And now he's decidedly deafer.

2477 TESTAMENT

She went out with many men
And took all that they gave her;
But she married a man with a will of his own
—Made out in her favour.

2478 AIRY FAIRY

The Bearded Lady from the Fair
Used stuff to shift unsightly hair;
Exceeding wildest dreams by far
She's now a famous movie star;
Her smiles are broad, her cup is full,
Although her friends all call her Yul.

2479 NUPTIALS

There was a little man and he had a little gun
And his bullets were made of lead;
He stood close by with a fatherly eye
While me and the girl was wed.

2480 M.Sc., D.Litt., M.A., N.I.T.

Excesses have unhinged him
The professor's gone quite queer;
He brews his own tobacco
And grows his own mild beer.

2481 USELESS INFORMATION

Flies and fleas
When plied
With insecticide
Develop D.D.T.s.

2482 DEBASEMENT

At women's summer bargain sales,
The same eternal fight prevails;
Why can't they buy their lingerie
Without inflicting ingerie?

2483   Jeepers Peepers
I'll bet a fiver
That Lady Godiva
Would have given Tom's stare back,
If she hadn't been riding bare-back.

2484   Fashion
Some dresses worn by women,
Are like fences at the zoo;
They safeguard lovely property
But don't obstruct the view.

2485   Loneliness of the Long-distance Stayer
Most men have girls who at their best
Are scheming little madams;
I'd just as soon be on my own,
Or with Sweet Fanny Adams.

2486   Right Gear
With some of the clothes
Today's youngsters have got,
You can't tell which is her
And which is not.

2487   Two-way Stretch
There's just one point
I want to raise;
When a girdle gives,
What stays?

2488   Decision
She married the butcher instead of the brewer,
But butcher it was who caught her;
And she gave the reason to those who knew her—
Blood is thicker than water.

2489   Feline Philosophy
Take a tip from the placid, contented cat,
On the best things in life a tabby grows fat;
But although he will gorge all the fish he can eat
He's far too darned clever to wet his own feet.

2490   NOBLESSE OBLIGE
  When she rang Earl Posselthwaite
  She used to call him rather late;
  But now they're wed, she's a different girlie—
  She always calls His Lordship early.

2491   DOWN THE HATCH
  A small Iceland igloo's an iglet,
  A little idea's a hunch;
  A small home-raised hog is a piglet
  But two pints make an Englishman's lunch.

2492   DING DONG
  You can't gather fruit from Scotch thistles,
  And water won't go in a sieve,
  You can't plant the peas from tin-whistles,
  And the gutter is no place to live;
  No sow's ear will give you silk purses,
  You can't turn base metals to gold;
  An old car might suffer reverses,
  But a belle always does as she's told.

2493   MONKY TRICKS
  There was an old monk in Siberia
  Who developed a bit of hysteria.
  He escaped from his cell,
  With a roar and a yell,
  And ran off with the Mother Superior.

2494   UNMANNED
  They said that Anne
  Couldn't get a man;
  For she was a beginner.
  But now Anne has her breakfast
  With the man who came to dinner.

2495   FLORA DORA
  If you say it with flowers,
  To a blonde—send a bouquet;
  For ordinary brunettes
  A bunch of violets is
  Perfectly ouquet.

2496 ART
 There was a young model from Tottam,
 Who loved many men—then forgot 'em.
 But an artist in Bude painted her in the nude . . .
 And signed his name right on the bottom.

2497 SIGNPOSTS
 A blonde girl from Burton-on-Trent,
 Had a nose that was awfully bent;
 One day, we suppose, she just followed her nose . . .
 That's why nobody knows where she went.

2498 GOOD MORNING
 He used to see her every night;
 In glamour bathed; a radiant sight.
 But now he sees her every a.m.
 No wonder his thoughts stray to mayhem!

2499 ZOO'S WHO
 The zoo curator
 Selected an alligator;
 He might just as well have picked a
 Boa constrictor.
 Although personally, I'm fonder
 Of the anaconda.

2500 ON SHOW
 She was sweet and chic and svelte
 She always made her presence felt:
 She pulled men up right in their tracks,
 That window model, made of wax!

2501 C'EST LE VIE
 French postcards of French coastguards
 Rank two for a franc.
 But the charms of mesdames
 Rate *quatre-cinq*.

2502 CHILDHOOD
 When I was three
 There used to be
 A nurse to take me out;
 The years have fled
 And now, instead,
 It's the other way about.

2503 YOICKS!
A horsey damsel from Reading,
Wore her old riding clothes to her wedding
The groom sighed, "Such pranks"
As he flippered her flanks
And that stopped the habit from spreading.

2504 ODE OF A GIRL ON A SHELF
"I wish I were a number
In the telephone book paged:
Then sometimes I would get a ring
And call myself engaged."

2505 COCKTAILS FOR TWO
There was a young beauty from Kent,
Just over the age of consent;
When men asked her to dine, bought her cocktails and wine,
Well, she knew what it meant but she went.

2506 OH!
The girl who wants to triumph
Should try oomph.

2507 SHOWGIRL
She used to be a Follies girl,
Gorgeous, gay and jolly.
But now she's left the chorus
To become an old man's folly.

2508 UNPOPULAR
Fred thinks that he's very unique,
And he fancies himself as a sheik,
But the girls they don't fall for this fellow at all
'Cos he only makes ten quid a week.

2509 ON THE BEACH
Her bathing suit
Is very brief;
It's just a knotted
Handkerchief.

2510 GYPSY'S WARNING
Girls who act proper
Never come a cropper;
It's the other sort
Who get caught.

2511 GOOD RECEPTION
She is apprenticed
To a local dentist;
If he any nonsense ventures
She bites him with the nearest dentures.

2512 DIET NO MORE
Men hate women
Who have been slimmin'!
They rarely wed
The underfed.
It's the buxom
What hooks 'em.

2513 HINTS FOR STUMPED AUTHORS
If your villain's name is Jasper
And he's not feeling very good;
If he's dying for a gasper
And his head's as thick as wood. . . .
   Bring Jasper in
   And give him an aspirin.

2514 PHYSIOGNOMY
A woman's face no age betrays
However *tempus fugit*;
Because she has evolved new ways
To powder, paint and rouge it.

2515 MUSIC SOOTHES THE SAVAGE BREAST
Though woman's an inveterate chatterer
She'll listen quietly to Sinatra;
So young men scorning to take risks
Should lay in scores of Frankie's discs.
And if that isn't quite the thing,
Try Bing.

2516 FROZEN WAISTS
The Eskimo
May be slow
And surrounded by snow,
But in a trice
He can make a paradise
Out of a few blocks of ice.

2517 SURREALIST

Picture if you can a winkle,
Perched upon a green-striped cow;
Picture, too, a troubled wrinkle
On a three-wheeled sampan's prow;
Picture two arm amputations
Gory in their bed of sand,
With flags of fourteen foreign nations
Tuning up a rubber band.
Picture waving fields of demons
Being threshed by rigid barley;
And there you have, not delirium tremens
But a painting by Salvador Dali.

2518 FISHY

When it comes to size and length
There's no doubt that the angler
Displays great feats of mental strength
Just like a senior wrangler.

2519 HERBACEOUS

Over fuchsias, pentstemons, verbenas, lobelias and calceolarias,
The experts go crazy,
Nevertheless, give me the humble daisy—
It's not much different in its smell
And it's far, far easier to spell.

2520 ROAD HOG

He took the bend at ninety per:
And the garage lost a customer.

JOKES AND JESTS

JOKES AND JESTS

2521 An old lady on her way home on a very dark night bumped into an old man, and both fell to the ground. The old man couldn't apologise enough. "That's all right," said the old lady. "But will you please tell me which way I was facing before I was knocked down?"

2522 A youthful air force pilot landed his fighter after a mission north of the 38th Parallel and went in to make his report to his commanding officer. "Were you nervous?" inquired the C.O. "Who? Me?" asked the pilot, "No, sir, I was cool as a cucumber through the whole show." "Swell," replied the C.O. "I just thought you might have been a little jittery when you radioed that 15,000 enemy jets were coming in at eight feet."

2523 The commanding general of a line division was inspecting one sunny afternoon when three sniper bullets from a nearby hill whizzed over his head causing him to jump into a bunker that was occupied by a be-whiskered sergeant. "Locate that sniper!" snapped the general. "We know exactly where he is, sir," the sergeant replied calmly. "Why the devil don't you shoot him then?" demanded the general. The sergeant shifted his tobacco to the other side of his mouth and explained: "Well, sir, that fellow has been sniping at this hill for six weeks now and hasn't hit anybody yet. We're afraid if we kill him, they might go ahead and replace him with one who can shoot."

2524 A patient was pleading with a doctor that he really didn't need an operation. "There's nothing wrong with me," he argued, "except that my appendix itches." "Good," replied the doctor, "we'll take it right out." "Just because it itches?" the patient gasped. "Certainly," the doctor boomed back. "Have to take it out before we can scratch it."

2525 A certain storekeeper reported a fire in his establishment the very day he signed a new fire insurance policy. The company suspected fraud, but had no proof. The only thing the manager could do was to write the policy-holder the following note: "Sir, You took out an insurance policy from us at 10 a.m. and your fire did not break out until 3.30 p.m. Will you kindly explain the delay?"

2526　Lazarus Smith had never been late for work in all the forty years he had worked for Mr. Cohen. But one morning he drifted in at eleven-thirty. Cohen frowned at him and asked him where he had been. Smith answered: "While I was rushing my breakfast I had a giddy turn and fell through my apartment window—twelve floors up from the street." Cohen considered this for a moment or two and then shrugged and said gruffly: "And this took you three hours?"

2527　A salesman called at a house where there was a great big alsatian on guard. The woman of the house came to the door and shouted: "How dare you! Molesting my poor little dog. Take your ankle out of his mouth at once."

2528　Just outside the Hotel Metropole, there was a beggar selling matches. The notice on his chest said he was blind. A man gave him threepence for a box and he said: "One of these pennies is counterfeit." The man said: "I thought you were blind." He said: "This isn't my own pitch. I'm just keeping it for a pal—he's gone to the pictures."

2529　A beggar knocked unsuspectingly at the door of the village police-man. The door opened and, with head bent, the beggar started telling the tale. "I didn't eat yesterday," he whined, "and I haven't eaten today." He raised his eyes and noticed blue-uniformed legs. "And," he ended, "I don't care a hang if I don't eat tomorrow either!"

2530　A welfare worker was interviewing a new inmate at the prison. "Did you say they put you in for borrowing money? That's no crime." The prisoner shrugged: "I know, I got a bad break. The man I was trying to borrow it from was asleep, but he woke up before I was finished."

2531　The drama critic started to leave in the middle of the second act. "Don't go now," said the manager, "I promise there's a terrific kick in the next act." "Fine," was the retort, "Give it to the author."

2532　After performing some hair-raising acrobatics, the pilot turned to his companion and said: "I bet half the people down there thought we were going to crash." "Half the people up here thought so, too," came the reply.

2533　A teacher received a letter from the mother of one of her pupils: "Dear Miss, Please don't give Johnny any more homework. That sum about how long it would take a man to walk fifty times round Trafalgar Square caused his father to lose a day's work. And after he'd walked it you marked the sum wrong."

2534 In a crowded cinema a young woman brushed past a man about to take a seat. Before he recovered his balance the young woman and her husband had taken the only two seats available in that part of the cinema. "Sorry," said the husband; "we just beat you." "That's O.K." said the man who had been pushed out. "I hope you and your mother enjoy the show."

2535 A man was tried and sent to prison. When he arrived there the warder handed him a form to sign. The man said: "I'm sorry, I can't write." The warder said: "But if you can't write, how is it you got five years for forgery?" The man said: "I dunno. Maybe I have a rotten lawyer."

2536 *Kitchen hint.* The best way to eat spinach is to feed the spinach to a chicken until it's fat enough to cook—then eat the chicken.

2537 His wife was interviewing a new daily woman. Help was so hard to get that she tried to make the job seem attractive. She said to the char: "We've got no children, so you won't be annoyed by anyone." And the daily woman said: "Oh, I don't mind children lady, so don't go on restricting yourselves on my account."

2538 Fred was enthusing to me about the marvels of television. "Just imagine" he said, "you just turn a switch, and a gorgeous young girl appears before you, dressed in a clinging low-cut gown." I said: "Well you don't have to have television for that; in some of the hotels I've stayed in out East, you get the same effect by pressing a bell."

2539 Alfred and Mary were married five years. Alf had always been a lad for the girls, and his wife never finished suspecting him. For two years or more she used to examine his clothes every time he came home late from the office . . . sometimes as late as three o'clock in the morning. When she found blonde hairs on his lapels, she raised the roof. When she found brunette hairs on his shoulders, she threw kitchenware at him. Then, strangely, Alfie started coming home, just as late, without a single hair on his jacket or overcoat. Not a sign of a hair. This went on for three or four weeks. Mary was more suspicious than ever. She used to go over his clothes with an enlarging glass; used to run the vacuum cleaner over his suits, and then sift the dust. Not a hair. She got more and more worried, nearly had a nervous breakdown. Finally she buttonholed him one night as he was creeping upstairs at four in the morning, shoes in hand. "Alfie!" she roared. He stood still. "Alfie, come on, let's have it," she cried. "No more messing about. Who's the bald-headed woman you're messing around with?"

2540 Little Jackie went into the sweet shop clutching his penny. He turned the whole shop upside down and examined the various offerings, and had the harassed shopkeeper up and down the step ladder thirty times.

In the end the shopkeeper snapped: "Look, lad, what do you expect for a penny—the whole wide world with a fence around it?" Jack looked up and said: "Well, I dunno—let's see it."

2541 Summer is here . . . last week a shy young girl went to join a nudist colony. She listened bashfully to the secretary's lecture, and answered all his questions, blushing delicately. The secretary was satisfied with her answers and finally told her she would be elected to the Sunbathing Club. He told her to go along to Cabin 44, see the matron, and get stripped. Then he handed her her diploma and the Sunbathing Club Badge. The girl went off but reappeared five minutes later, shyly sticking her head around the door. The secretary said: "Well, what's the matter?" The girl said: "Er— please, if you don't mind—could I have another two badges?"

2542 Flying to Paris, a man pushed into the pilot's cabin and said: "Abandon the plane—it's going to break apart any minute." The pilot got angry and said: "Don't tell me how to fly this thing—I've been flying these planes for four years." The man said: "And I'm the guy who designed them." Then he quietened down and said: "Did you hear that a crazy lunatic escaped from an asylum in Birmingham this morning?" The pilot said: "No, I didn't hear about it. Do you think they'll catch him?" The man said confidently: "No. They wouldn't dream of looking for me up here."

2543 He said to the recruiting officer: "Look here, you can't possibly mean that you're turning me down for the army! I've just got engaged to three girls, told my boss what I think of him, and sold my car."

2544 A small lad of five was sitting at a table with his father and two of his uncles. Miserably he complained to his father: "Dad, why can't I go out and play like the other kids, with my tricycle? Why can't I join the gang and have time to ride my scooter and eat bubble-gum?" And his father snarled: "Aw, shut up and deal."

2545 A man who smoked 100 cigarettes a day went to the doctor with a racking cough and a sore throat. He could hardly speak. Pointing to his throat he said hoarsely: "Doc, cigarettes." The doctor said: "Smoking them?" And the man said: "No—asking for them."

2546 There was once a dear old maid who went to see a stomach specialist. For forty minutes the specialist rubbed, massaged, and manipulated her stomach and then said: "How's that, then?" The old maid said: "That's real fine, Doc, but the pain I came to see you about is in my left foot."

2547 When I went into my barber's for a haircut this morning I noticed how filthy his hands were as he worked. I protested about it and he just shrugged and said: "Can I help it if no one's been in for a shampoo yet?"

2548 The repertory company, producing a very poor play, had watched their audiences diminish gradually over the week. On Friday night, during the performance, the hero and heroine were on stage, sitting on a couch, and the hero went into his big romantic scene. . . . "Darling, at last we are alone!" he cooed. And suddenly the manager stamped out on to the stage, stared into the House and snapped: "Brother, you ain't kidding."

2549 A young married couple with their baby went to the cinema. The manager told them that they could take the child in if they kept it absolutely quiet. Fortunately the baby was sound asleep. Half-way through the picture, the husband turned to his wife and said: "What do you think of this film?" His wife whispered back: "It's rotten." The husband sighed and said: "Okay, pinch the baby."

2550 Husband returns home as usual at six o'clock. Wife says to him: "Alf, did you eat all the sandwiches I made for your lunch?" He said: "Oh sure." She said: "Did you like them?" "Yes, they were fine," he answered. "Why? What's the matter?" The wife said: "Oh, nothing . . . except that tomorrow you'll have to clean your brown shoes with fish paste."

2551 I once stayed at an old house in the depths of the country—a gloomy remote old mansion. It was a stormy night, pitch black. The man I was staying with showed me to my room up in an attic. The wind was howling and I could hear chains rattling. There was only a candle to light the place. As he showed me where the nail was for my clothes, he said: "Oh, and if you need anything in the night, just scream."

2552 His wife bought a new spring hat decorated with little flowers and bits of fruit. She shouldn't have left it lying around. He put it back on the window-sill and watered it twice before she told him it wasn't a window-box.

2553 A man swallowed his glass eye and went to the doctor. The doctor put a long tube down his throat and then put his eye to the eye-piece that was sticking out of the patient's mouth. All he saw was another eye blinking back at him.

2554 A friend of mine's been seeing a lot of my wife. The other day I said to him: "Now see here, Fred—this is my last warning: stop fooling around with my wife or I'm going to let you have her."

2555 Comment by rival when screen actor played dual role in picture: "He's achieved his ambition at last—to co-star with himself."

2556 A vacuum cleaner salesman was demonstrating the power of his machine to a sceptical customer. She insisted: "But are you sure that the cleaner will pick up every scrap of dirt?" The salesman said: "I'm quite sure. Yesterday I ran this model very lightly over a copy of *Lady Chatterly's Lover* and when I'd finished it was *Little Women*.

2557 Fred was afraid to return to his office after taking two days off for his wife's confinement. So she sent a note to his employer: "Dear Sir, Please excuse Fred not turning up for a couple of days as I've been in bed having a baby. It wasn't Fred's fault. Yours truly, Mrs. Blobb."

2558 We once knew an ex-editor who used to spend his spare time nostalgically chalking captions under the exhibits at the Tate Gallery.

2559 A couple of weeks back Joe went to see the animals at Whipsnade Zoo. While he was there he saw a middle-aged woman chasing a man, flourishing her umbrella savagely. The husband finally found one of the cage doors open and ducked into the lion-house and hid behind one of the lions. His wife chased up to the bars and screamed at him: "Come on out of there, you rotten coward!"

2560 Two sportsmen were walking home after the football match: "Of course I agree that your team were good losers, Archie, but think of all the practice they've had. . . ."

2561 There was a terrific explosion in a mine. A reporter happened to be rushing to the scene when he was stopped by an Irishman named Kelly. Kelly was very bothered about the catastrophe and asked the reporter what had happened. The reporter said: "It's a bad business. The mine caved in, too. I understand that the dead include 46 Englishmen, 15 Scotsmen and an Irishman named Murphy." Kelly shook his head and muttered: "Begorah, the phoor bhoy!"

2562 Maud bought herself a pair of those big brass rings for her ears; the other night she went running into the house from the street and hung herself on the hallstand.

2563 He said to his girl: "That's a lovely fur you're wearing." She said: "This isn't fur, Herbert. It's my old cloth coat, but the dog always sleeps on it."

2564 Ellen is going out with a dispensing chemist while her fiancé, who's a doctor, is abroad. The doctor writes to her regularly, and she needs the chemist to act as interpreter.

2565 He said to the dentist: "This will be the first tooth I've lost." The dentist said: "That's a strange coincidence. It'll also be the first one I ever took out."

2566 The agent was showing prospective tenants over the new house. He said: "With a couple of coats of enamel on those walls they'll be twice as thick."

2567 A man in Luton had a hard time trying to decide whether to marry the very beautiful girl from the chorus, or another woman who was nothing to look at but who had a magnificent singing voice. He decided on the soprano; the morning after the wedding he took a good hard look at his bride and nudged her and said: "For Pete's sake, *sing*."

2568 A party of people were travelling by train and discussing why British Rail were losing money. One old gentleman said it was due to faulty management. A lady in the corner thought it was due to too many people being employed. Another man thought it was due to the laziness of the staff. Another woman was just about to give her views when they heard the ticket inspector coming and they all dived under the seats.

2569 As the President of the Republic stepped ashore he was greeted by a salute of twenty-one guns. He stepped into the waiting limousine bleeding from twenty-one holes.

2570 They were out on the dance floor and his girl was wearing a very low-cut gown. She was quite hot and she said: "Gee, it's crowded, isn't it?" So he looked down at her dress and said: "Well, maybe it is, but it suits you."

2571 A man walked into a small village general store and asked for a pair of shears. The shopkeeper looked thoughtfully over his glasses and muttered: "Garden shears? That'd be hardware, wouldn't it? Now where the blazes did I put the hardware department?"

2572 Two stupid farmhands were watching a flight of birds. One of the birds dived down to about a thousand feet. The first farmhand muttered: "Well, what do you know? They're gulls!" The other said: "Garn—how can you tell what sex they are from this distance?"

2573 A woman went to hospital for observation. One physician examined her eyes; another one examined her throat; a third examined her respiration and a fourth X-rayed her stomach. This kind of wholesale investigation went on for several days during which she was examined by everyone on the medical staff. On the fourth day, a little man came into her room laden with a bucket of hot water, a mop and brush and some soap. "What are YOU going to do?" asked the patient anxiously. The little feller said: "Well, lady, my instructions were to wash down your transom."

2574   When an actress promised to ride down Broadway, New York, on a white horse to advertise a film about Lady Godiva, the streets were packed with innocent bystanders. It had been so long since any citizens had seen a horse.

2575   "She conked me on the head and knocked me insensible," said a witness in Police Court.
  She Conks to Stupor!

2576   Athletic Girl: "What can he do?"
  Chorus Girl: "How much does he have?"
  Literary Girl: "What does he read?"
  Society Girl: "Who are his family?"
  Religious Girl: "What church does he attend?"
  College Girl: "Where is he?"

2577   A little boy and girl who lived next door to a nudist colony found a knot-hole one day. The little girl took the first look. "What are they?" the little boy asked. "Men or women?" "I don't know," she replied. "They haven't any clothes on."

2578   Ed Hollins says: "Nowadays when I'm on tour I always stay at first-class hotels where they have full-length mirrors in the bedroom. In the old days I used to stay at cheap hotels where there were only half-length mirrors and eight times I went out without my pants on."

2579   One ghost met another in a haunted house and said to him: "Who was the ghoul-friend I saw you with last night?"

2580   Did you hear the story of the new recruit who walked up to an American officer in Piccadilly and fingered the gleaming rows of medals on his chest, saying: "Got any swaps, mate?"

2581   Jonesey is one of those people who simply must obey orders. He saw a notice in the park saying "Keep Off The Grass"—so he walked on the flower beds.

2582   Once upon a time there was a big grey donkey that got on a tram. The conductor had him thrown off—for tendering a pound note for a twopenny fare.

2583   There was a pretty young girl strap-hanging in the crowded car of an underground train. Sitting opposite her was a rather elderly gent who got up and offered her his seat. The girl hesitated for a moment, but when the train lurched round a corner she swayed and sat on his knees. The train swung along around the curves until the old gent muttered suddenly: "I'm afraid one of us will have to get up, Miss. I'm not as old as I thought."

2584 They were married and went to Torquay for their honeymoon. On their arrival in the honeymoon room of their hotel the bride looked in dismay at the twin beds. "What's the matter, darling?" asked hubby. She said miserably: "You told me we were going to have a room to ourselves."

2585 A woman fell down and hurt her leg very badly. Because she was getting on in years, her doctor strapped the leg tightly and warned her: "Now remember, Mrs. Arkwright, this leg is going to take a long time to mend—you're not to go dashing up and down the stairs." About a month later the doctor called again and found that the leg was quite mended. "Thank heavens for that," said the old lady. "I was getting quite tired of shinning up and down that drainpipe outside."

2586 An English officer, an Egyptian oil man and an American pilot were standing on the corner of a street in Tangier when a stunningly beautiful young Egyptian maiden passed by, wriggling her hips and winking her eye. The Egyptian cried: "By Allah!"; the Englishman removed his monocle and muttered: "Bah Jove!"; while the American chewed his gum harder and breathed: "By tomorrow night!"

2587 A variety artiste sauntered into an agent's office and announced that he was an illusionist with a marvellous act. The agent asked him what he could do and the illusionist said: "I can saw a woman in half." The agent said: "That's one of the most hackneyed tricks in the business. Every magician I know saws women in half." "Yeah," said the artiste. "Lengthways?"

2588 One night after a dance at the Palais, a long-haired beatnik was walking his girl home through the desolate murky streets of Soho. When they passed one of those dingy alleyways where there is always a threat of trouble they heard a gruff man's voice arguing with a woman, using some awful language. There came the sounds of a scuffle and then the dreadful discordant racket of dustbins being mown over as the man hit the woman and knocked her into a row of them. The lids jarred and the bins clanked and clanged like mad. The boy cocked an ear and whispered to his girl as they passed: "Listen—they're playing our song!"

2589 A very angry mother took her young son, Henry, to see a famous Harley Street surgeon. "Doctor," she exploded, "can a lad of thirteen perform an operation for appendicitis on himself?" The doctor laughed and shook his head wisely. The lady slapped her son across the face and shouted: "So now, who was right? You put it right back."

2590   A young air force lad, pilot of a jet 'plane, got ten days' leave when he married. On the tenth day of his honeymoon he sent a wire to his C.O. "It's wonderful here. Request ten days' extension of leave." The C.O. wired back: "It's wonderful anywhere. Return to your squadron."

2591   Two Negro soldiers were discussing fear. One said to the other: "Sambo, what was the most frightening experience in your life?" Sambo said: "Once when ah was callin' on a married gal her husband came home unexpected, and boy, was I scared stiff." The other Negro asked why and Sambo said: "Ah dunno for why, all ah know is dat her husband says to this gal, 'Mandy, what's dis white man doin' here?' "

2592   I told the doctor that I kept seeing spots in front of my eyes and he told me to stop going with freckled women. Then he told me to stick my tongue out. I said: "Why?" and he said: "I positively detest my nurse."

2593   A Moon-Man reaches earth in a rocket ship and lands outside an Espresso bar. Hearing the peculiar static noises from inside he jerkily enters and looks around. He walks across to the flashing juke-box and says to it: "Hi. What's a flashy dame like you going to do in a crummy joint like this?"

2594   Punter: "That horse looks very hot and tired. Did he win the last race?" Jockey: "Win it? He got this way walking to the starting-gate."

2595   Forty swans were gathered in conference. The leader spoke: "The farmer is planning a new feather-bed and we're expected to supply the down, and winter is coming on. So I vote that we have a whip round to buy the old boy a spring-interior mattress."

2596   THE ENGLISH PEOPLE
   English people never bother to learn foreign languages because they know that foreigners all have to learn English. The British people are so peace-loving that they have devoted the last thousand years to knocking the hell out of people who *don't* like peace. English parliaments always have two parties; the one in power and the Opposition. Nationals vote one party into power and then the other party is elected to set right the mess created by the first party; this is known as perpetual motion and takes place about twice a decade. England is a country surrounded by hot water. It's only a small island, but the British once had an Empire on which the sun never set and England has people upon whom the sun never shines. Englishmen are known by their bowler hats, tweed suits, umbrellas and moustaches. The women are different—they don't wear bowler hats. English food is wonderfully simple; we write all our menus in French and cook everything in water. There are nearly sixty million English people, with eighty million civil servants to look after them. Civil servants in England are recognised by

breast-pockets full of pens, pencils and teacups. Rain is one of the principal products of England. It's the only country in the world where the dew has rapids. Smokers and drinkers bring the Treasury £1,000,000,000 per year; if everyone stopped smoking and boozing, the Government would have to look for some other kind of work. English people are the most law-abiding in the world. Juvenile delinquency is practically unknown over the age of forty-two. Although places in Britain are rarely less than a few miles apart, it usually takes between a week and ten days to do forty miles by car on the highways. Traffic is so thick that if you once leave town to live elsewhere, you virtually emigrate. If all the cars in Britain were laid end to end— preferably in a scrap yard—there'd be enough tin to make enough cans of tomato soup to feed half the population of China for the next ten years— if only Chinese didn't detest tomato soup. Englishmen are notorious lovers; it only takes the average man ten years to ask the woman he loves for a kiss. Sometimes he proposes to a girl in maybe a year and a half—but not marriage. Englishwomen are mainly the horsey type, Spartans and outdoor Amazons. So Englishmen go out with foreign beauty contest winners and the horsey Englishwomen go out with themselves.

2597 Two road repair men arrived at the location one morning and couldn't start work because they'd forgotten their spades. So one of them rang through to the foreman and explained. "I'll send the spades along in the truck," said the foreman. "Until they arrive you'll just have to lean on each other."

2598 Bank cashier to new assistant. "Count this package of notes to make sure there are one hundred." The new employee started counting, finally getting up to 54, 55, 56. Then he threw the package in the drawer. "If it's right this far," he remarked to the man next to him, "it's probably right all the way."

2599 "Why did you decide to buy a cow?"
"On account of the price of milk going up all the time."
"You didn't like paying so much for milk at the door?"
"No, sir. That's why I decided to buy a cow and take things into my own hands.

2600 Have you ever been in a restaurant and found a fly in your soup? You'd be surprised how often it happens, and how different people in different parts of the world handle the situation. Now in America, when a man finds a fly in his soup he sends it back to the kitchen and has a row with the manager. In England, the fly is quietly and daintily removed and hidden in a handkerchief. In France the soup is eaten and the fly left on the side of the plate. On the Orient the fly is eaten first, and the soup used to wash it down. In China the fly is eaten with the soup. And in Scotland the fly is picked up, wrung out to dry and then the soup is eaten. But in Tangier, a man stares at the soup and says to the waiter: "What's this? Is this all I get? *One* fly?"

2601 A man who was very careful about his wife's health decided that she needed a tonic and bought her a large jar of iron tablets. One day a month later he found her in the kitchen wiping her hands every three seconds while washing dishes. She explained that if she left her hands in water too long, they rusted up.

2602 Once upon a time, there was a very mean guy who took his girl for a twenty-mile walk in the country, much against her inclination. When she got tired she insisted on their taking a bus home. The man didn't like the idea as the fare was 20 pence. She persuaded him, however. When she got home she told her mother about it. So the indignant Ma raced over to this fellow's house, pushed 10 pence into his grubby hand and snorted: "That's to cover the expenses you incurred in taking my daughter out." The guy shrugged and muttered in a weary voice: "Well, thanks, lady, but you really needn't have bothered to come all this way tonight—it would have done any time tomorrow. . . ."

2603 He drove his old car up on to the toll bridge and the gate-keeper slouched over and said: " 25 pence for the car and 10 pence for the passenger." He said: "The car's yours for 20 pence but I wouldn't take less than fifty pence for my wife."

2604 A tramp was standing by the roadside sticking his tongue out at passing cars. Sometimes he would stop sticking out his tongue and thumb his nose. A pal came up to him and said: "You'll never get a ride if you do things like that to passing drivers." The other tramp said: "Who cares? This is my lunch hour."

2605 Psychiatrist to patient: "I am going to sketch some pictures, and you have to tell me what you think you see." The psychiatrist proceeds to sketch a circle with a dot in the middle. The patient says: "That's Jayne Mansfield with her long, slender bare legs." The psychiatrist sketches a cube with a cross on one side. The patient says: "That's a picture of Diana Dors lying on a couch." The psychiatrist draws a rectangle with a triangle inside it. The patient says: "Oh yes, that's a picture of a young girl putting on her bobby sox." The psychiatrist gets up and says to the patient: "I'm afraid I can't do anything for you—you're a sex-maniac." The patient sneers. "Who? Me? It's *you* who's been drawing all the dirty pictures!"

2606 They caught the burglar whom they thought had robbed No. 17 Beach Street. He denied the offence, insisting that they couldn't hold him, they had nothing on him, they couldn't prove it, and indeed he had an alibi. On the night of the robbery at No. 17 Beach Street, he had been in Black-heath murdering his aunt for her money. The police checked on this and the alibi was cast-iron, so they had to let him go. After he'd left the station, the sergeant scratched his head thoughtfully and said to the constable: "I think we slipped up on something, but I can't just think what it was." So the constable blurted out: "Of course—when we searched him, I noticed that his driving licence expired a month ago." The sergeant said: "No that isn't it. He didn't have a car." "Oh," said the constable, "then whose was the big black car that he drove off in? The one that was parked outside?" The sergeant said: "Did you get the number?" The constable said: "Of course. It was RIP 546." "Dam," said the sergeant. "I think that's the Commissioner's."

2607 It was two o'clock in the morning. The writer looked haggard and worn. "Darling," said his wife, "are you coming to bed?" "No" muttered the busy author. "I've got the pretty girl in the clutches of the villain, and I want to get her out." "How old is the girl?" asked the wife. "Twenty-two," replied the writer. "Then put out the lights and get to bed," snapped the wife, "she's old enough to take care of herself."

2608 The organiser of a Youth Club should be someone who knows exactly what teenagers enjoy doing—and firm enough to stop it.

2609 "My gosh, Bill," groaned the managing director of the tabloid, "nothing scandalous has happened in twenty-four hours. What'll we do for the front page?" "Aw, don't get discouraged, Steve," the city editor comforted. "Something'll happen. I've still got faith in human nature."

2610 A motion-picture mogul recently bought a ranch and put up palatial barns, stables, and chicken houses. "And are the hens laying?" asked a friend. "They are," said the movie monarch, "but of course, in my position they don't have to."

2611 Grandma leans over the cot and says with tears in her eyes: "Oh, you luvverly little cherub you, you dark darlin', I could eat you." Kid sits up and says: "With no teeth?"

2612 There's a Hollywood actress who charges 40 dollars a head for atten-dance at her weddings. She claims they are professional performances. Now she's in New York on Broadway doing scenes from her divorces.

2613 An anxious wife went to a psychiatrist and implored him to do some-thing about her husband. She insisted that the poor fellow was psycho-pathic. The doctor asked her why she was so sure and she answered:

"Well, you ought to see the maniacal tantrums he gets into if he comes home unexpected and finds another man in his pyjamas."

2614 A policeman came across an inebriate gent late at night, going round and round a lamp-post, tapping on it with his knuckles. The cop said: "Now then. Come along. Get going . . . " And the drunk said: "Don't be daft, offisher . . . I'm walled in."

2615 She asked the police to help her look for her husband and when they lined up fourteen suspects at the station she said that none of them was quite suitable.

2616 When he confessed to her after the wedding that he was colour blind, she remarked: "Yo' sho' am, Albert. Yo' sho' am dat!"

2617 The average man, according to a professor of sociology, now lives twenty-five years longer than his seventeenth-century predecessors. He has to, in order to have time to pay his taxes.

2618 When they brought little Johnny home after his very first visit to church they asked him how he liked it. He said he thoroughly enjoyed the music and the singing, but that he didn't think much of the news.

2619 Two truck drivers had a slight collision as they were backing their big vehicles out of a parking lot beside a transport café. One shouted to the other: "You great big silly-looking moron, why the hell don't you look where you're going, you cross-eyed apology for a gorilla's love-child." The other one leaned out of his cab and grinned back: "I think you're cute, too, sugar."

2620 She was learning to dance at an academy and her teacher insisted that she should watch his feet carefully in order to follow properly. She was so anxious to please that she kept one step ahead of him all the time without waiting for his lead. Irritably he held her tightly and said: "Pardon me, my dear, but aren't you anticipating a little?" So she stammered: "Oh no. I'm not even married."

2621 Gus was telling us about his travels in the mysterious East, where there are many mystics. Once when he went sight-seeing he entered a strange-looking temple where incense burned in an urn. An old man stood on a dais supported by crutches. He was very unsteady on his crippled legs. He stood there praying and chanting in a strange lingo. After an hour of it, he suddenly threw away one of his crutches. Then he prayed for another hour after which he excitedly threw away his other crutch. We asked Gus: "Well, what happened then?" Gus said: "Poor feller fell flat on his face."

2622 The journalist got his first job as a cub reporter on a country weekly. The managing editor was very explicit that names must be obtained on all news items. So he handed in this item—"Last night during a severe storm, lightning killed three cows on a farm in Ashford. Their names were Bessie. Bluebell and Bunty."

2623 The bus was crowded when an old Irish woman got on, and had to stand. A polite lad stood up and said: "Would you like my seat for a while?" and she said: "No, I daren't sit down, I'm in a hurry."

2624 She was a BBC announcer's daughter so after praying for quite a long time before getting into bed one night she added: "And here again, dear God, are the headlines."

2625 She was anxious to become engaged, but her mother was more than a little dubious. "But darling," said her mother, "don't you think you ought to wait a little before you think of becoming engaged? You haven't known him long, you know." "Oh, he's not exactly a stranger," was her daughter's calm reply. "I know a girl who was engaged to him for months."

2626 An old Southern planter was discussing the hereafter with one of his servants. "Sam," he said, "if you die first, I want you to come back and tell me what it's like over there. If I die first I'll come back and tell you what it's like." "Dat suits me, massa," replied the old Negro, "but if you dies first, ah wants you to promise dat you'll come back in de day-time."

2627 Two women were sitting in a bistro in Paris during their holiday when they noticed a man at a corner table with his coat held open and his hands inside the jacket. His companion was watching him intently. One of the women called over the waiter and whispered to him, blushing as she did so. The waiter went over to the two men, and returned shortly afterwards. He said to the women: "I'm sorry mesdames, but he is not selling postcards. It is just a deaf and dumb man telling his friend some saucy jokes."

2628 They were at the pictures. During a very ardent and intense love scene, his girl nudged him in the side and whispered: "Why don't you ever make love to me like that?" So he said: "Don't be silly, dear, do you know how much they have to pay that feller for working that hard?"

2629 Alice was taken to the annual sports meeting at the Huntingdon Athletic Club ground. When asked if she would like to see an egg-and-spoon race she laughed and said: "You're kidding me. How could they?"

2630 They were married, came out of church and drove off in a limousine. Down High Street, the groom asked the chauffeur to stop; got out, and went into a billiards saloon. He was in there for three hours. Then his bride went in after him and found him playing snooker. She started to remonstrate and he stopped her, saying: "Oh, blimey, you nagging already?"

2631 An Irishman called on his friend Murphy and found him looking very worried. Murphy said: "I've been trying to commit suicide." So his visitor said: "Why don't you put the rope around your neck?" Murphy said: "Shure, and I had it there, Patrick, but the ruddy thing nearly choked me."

2632 Stella was told about the very famous oarsman at Oxford who always had the date of his racing successes engraved on his scull. "Gee," she gasped, "won't it show when he goes bald?"

2633 Phillips rang up the head office of a large firm in Birmingham and asked to speak to someone in the sales office. When he was put through he said: "This is Phillips. Who's that?" A gruff, impatient voice said: "I'm Holden, the secretary." Phillips said: "Well put her down for a minute, I want to talk business."

2634 Two elephants were out courting and decided to get married. The female elephant whispered to the other: "And perhaps soon we will hear the thunder of little feet . . ."

2635 MONEY, MONEY, MONEY
If a man runs after money, he's money mad. If he keeps it, he's a capitalist.
If he spends it, he's a spineless playboy.
If he doesn't get it, he lacks ambition.
If he gets it without working, he's a rotten parasite.
If he gets it after a lifetime of gruelling hard labour he's a stupid fool who got nothing out of life.
So what's a fellow to do?

2636 The new nurse was watching her first operation in the theatre and asked: "Who are they operating on?" She was told: "It's some poor chap who had a golf ball knocked down his throat." So the nurse said: "I suppose that poor worried-looking old man waiting outside is his father?" Came the answer: "No. It's that chap's ball, and he's waiting to get on with his game."

2637 In the waiting-room at the doctor's last night, the Doc put his head around the door and asked: "Who's been waiting longest?" The feller sitting in the corner stood up and said: "Me. I made you that blasted suit three years ago."

2638 An actor was once playing at a small theatre in a remote part of Wales. They had a cast of fourteen players. One night the Irishman who played the villain in the drama got annoyed about the poor audience and said: "Let's have a peek through the curtain. If we outnumber them tonight, I vote we start a fight."

2639 Dr. Arbutnott, a family doctor, is one of the best medicine men in the business. One night a fellow walked in on crutches, with his arm in a sling wearing an eye-patch and a blood-stained bandage round his throat. Gasping for breath and wheezing like a grampus the poor guy staggered into the consultation room. Ten minutes later it was my turn. The first thing I asked the doc was about the other chap. The doc said: "Oh him? I kicked him out. Does he think I can't tell a malingerer when I see one?"

2640 A financier always lectured his family about extravagance. He said one day: "You ought to save your money. If you only put away a thousand pounds each year, at the end of ten years you'd have a nest-egg of ten thousand pounds. You'd be on easy street if there was a depression!" One son said: "Yes, but what about if there wasn't a depression? I'd be stuck with ten thousand quid!"

2641 An angry, jealous man rushed up the stairs of the hotel, barged his way into one of the hotel apartments, pulled out a gun and fired it wildly at a man and a woman who were locked in a passionate embrace by the window. The woman fell to the floor dead. The intruder strode across the room, kicked the woman over with his foot, and then turned to the other man and said: "Whoops, sorry. Wrong apartment."

2642 It was dark in the parlour. Mom came down the stairs into the hall. Hearing voices, she peeped into the parlour, then jabbed on the lights. There on the sofa was her pretty young daughter, necking very passionately with a strange young man. Mom got very indignant and shouted: "Well, I never!" The daughter looked up and said: "You must have, Mom."

2643 The preacher was getting on nicely with the wedding ceremony. Reaching the point where the audience is invited to join in he asked: "Is there anyone here who believes this marriage should not be performed?" A thin voice replied hesitantly: "Yes, me." The preacher turned his head and whispered loudly: "You shut up . . . you're the groom."

2644 FRED: Kipling once said that a woman is just a rag, a bone and a hank of hair.
MUGGIN: Well then, what's all that other stuff?

2645 A man in Wigan was crazy about pigeons. He was always talking about his birds and his pigeon-loft. Drove everyone crazy. One night he went up to the loft to see the birds come winging home. Twenty-four pigeons showed up, and the twenty-fifth was missing. The pigeon-fancier got worried. About four hours later this late-homing pigeon showed up. The man said angrily: "And where the heck do you think you've been? You should have been back four hours ago." The pigeon shrugged its shoulders and said: "It was such a lovely day, I decided to walk."

2646 An Englishman was talking about his trip to Africa: "We were on Safari and we lost our way. My wife was worried sick because the place was infested with cannibals. For hours we tried to find the way out of the jungle . . . and then we bumped into a tall, dark, ugly tribesman from the Umbegini region. I spoke to him for ten minutes asking him the way to civilisation, but he just ignored me. Wrathfully I said to him: 'I've been stood here for ten minutes asking you a civil question. Do you mind answering me, you big oaf?' My wife butted in and said: 'How the hell can he answer you when you're standing on his lower lip?' "

2647 A fellow went to see a wonderful leg-show in London . . . where some of the most beautiful girls in show business were doing their stuff. Every time the girls were on stage, this fellow kept saying: "Uh! Phooey!" After a while, his neighbour said: "You want a lot for your money, don't you. Every time you see those lovely girls, you say Phooey." So the guy said: "I know. I keep thinking of my wife. . . ."

2648 A very good old actor never quite made the grade. He did his best in good and bad parts, but never hit the top. Then one day his big chance came. He was cast for the leading role in the play *Abraham Lincoln*. He played the part really well, but the audience didn't appreciate his performance. Yet he was so realistic that on his way home he got assassinated.

2649 "I've got terrible toothache. Do you know a good dentist?"
    "You don't want a dentist. I had awful toothache yesterday but my wife put her arms around me, kissed me, hugged me, and very soon all the pain went away. Why don't you try the same thing?"
    "Okay, where will I find your wife?"

2650 Charlie drinks a lot, so it's no wonder he had to go to the doctor again yesterday. The doctor examined him and told him to wait in the reception room for a report. Half an hour later the doctor came out to my brother, looking very anxious. "Well, what's the verdict?" asked Charlie in a scared voice. The Doc said: "According to the analysis, I'm afraid you've got a small percentage of blood in your alcoholic system."

2651 Bert's bought himself a second-hand car for taking the wife and kids out this spring. It's quite a wreck. Yesterday the car broke down in the High Street, and there was Bert angrily swinging the starting handle, for about twenty minutes. He got so fed up with it, he threw his hat on the ground and swore, then did some more swinging. And a woman walked over to him, threw 20 pence into his hat and said: "I can't hear the tune because I'm stone deaf, but you have all my sympathy, young man, and I'm glad you like music."

2652   Angela said to Mavis: "I wonder what the men talk about when they're alone or at the club," and Mavis said: "I suppose they talk about the same things as we do," and after a moment's thought Angela said: "The rotten beasts!"

2653   The efficiency expert will tell you that if a farmer's boy can pick six boxes of cherries in an hour, and a girl five boxes, the two of them together will pick eleven boxes. But any farmer knows that the two of them together won't pick any.

2654   He went to the newspaper office to put an ad. in the paper offering £5,000 reward for the return of his wife's cat. The man behind the counter said: "That's a lot of reward isn't it?" He said: "It doesn't matter. I drowned the cat."

2655   Angus was the father of eleven children. The other evening he heard the front-door bell and went to answer it. A tall, dark man stood on the threshold, holding a black bag in his hand. Angus said thickly: "Well, come on in—and I hope you're only going to tune the piano."

2656   You just can't beat the marvels of nature. Less than three months ago Bert bought a couple of rabbits and put them together in a little cage outside in the back yard. And do you know what's happened in less than eight weeks? He's still got two rabbits. They're brothers.

2657   Sam had to go and see Charlie at his new house yesterday. There was a notice on the gate which read: "Beware of the bad-tempered dog." Sam was standing by the front door patting this dog on the head when Charlie came out and bit him.

2658   When their first child was born he turned to his wife in relief and said: "Thank heavens, Maria . . . now we can call your mother 'Grandma' instead of 'Hey you'."

2659   After three weeks during which her husband had been lying in bed, slowly dying, the doctor came down one evening from the bedroom and said: "Mrs. Totty, I've got some news for you. Your husband is making good recovery at last." Mrs. Totty burst into tears. The doctor said: "Now,

now, go on and cry if you like. Tears of joy, I suppose?" She muttered weepily: "Joy, nothing, Doc. Yesterday I sold all his perishing clothes to help pay for the funeral."

2660   A drunk fell into the village water trough and the local constable had to wade in to get him out late at night. As he grasped the drunk by the shoulders, he said to the rozzer: "Hey, I c'n shave meshelf . . . you shave the wimmin an' chillen."

2661   Little Willie had never been to a concert before. The morning after his father asked him how he had enjoyed it and Willie said: "It was a real shocker . . . there was a man standing up in front of the band waving a stick at a big fat woman on the stage, and she was so scared she was screaming her head off!"

2662   Friend of a celebrated "glamour" queen turned to her at a party and muttered: "I see your husband is wearing another new suit." She answered in a whisper: "Not another new suit, darling—it's another new husband."

2663   A Texan oil millionaire decided to send his only son to school in England, and chose a very expensive and exclusive county college. Three months later the Texan came over on vacation to England and looked in at the school and spoke to the headmaster. "How is my lad comin' along, Prof?" he asked. The Professor answered eagerly: "Dang me if he ain't the smartest critter I ever seen."

2664   A woman and her five children were prowling along the beach at Rhyl one sunny morning and the woman was obviously worried about something so a passing boatman asked her what she had lost. She told him that she was trying to find the place in the sand where her children had buried their father. The boatman asked: "Can't you remember where you were all sitting?" and she said: "Don't be daft. Can you remember where YOU were sitting this time last summer?"

2665   An American millionaire wanted to buy his son at college an expensive graduation present. At an antique store he was offered by the sales manager a violin. The sales manager told him: "Now this violin is a Stradivarius and is priced at ninety thousand dollars—it was manufactured in 1730." The rich American said: "Is the firm that made it still in business?" The manager said: "Hardly, sir." So the American shouted: "What you trying to do? Give me a bum fiddle? How the hell would we get spare parts?"

2666   When the young footballer told his father that Wolverhampton Wanderers were prepared to buy him for £10,000, the old man said they could have his mother for 50p.

2667 In a recent radio broadcast they wanted the effect of water lapping against boards for a shipwreck scene. They tried rattling dried peas on oiled paper, dropping pins on taut silk, and shaking broken glass on sandpaper, without success. Then someone thought of dropping water from a can on to some boards.

2668 Two skeletons are in a cupboard in a doctor's surgery. One says to the other: "Gosh, it's hot and stuffy in here—I can hardly breathe."

2669 BBC News announcer: "And here is a news item. No dangerous drugs were lost from doctors' cars today."

2670 A dumb blonde who knew nothing about the game was encouraged to accompany two men around the links. One of the players had a really hard time. He got into a deep rut and had trouble getting the ball out. Then he got into a sand trap and almost failed to get out. At last he got a good shot and the ball trickled directly into the cup. He glanced up at the blonde, hoping to have impressed her at last. She stared at the ball and said sympathetically: "Hey, now you're in a REAL fix."

2671 St. Peter, customs officer of the Pearly Gates, was bored. There'd been a run of the same sort of people for weeks, and he wished for a change. Suddenly there was a knock on the gate and he called cautiously: "Yes, who's there?" A very suave and cultured voice answered bossily: "It is I." St. Peter groaned and shouted back: "Oh, go to hell. We've all the Eton and Harrow men we can stand for the time being."

2672 The coroner was questioning the young doctor, who had qualified only a few weeks before, and whose first patient had died under tragic circumstances. The young doctor explained what had happened, in a stuttering voice. "You see, sir," he said, "this man came to me with a very bad cut on his head. The blood was pouring from it. I didn't know what to do for a moment and then I remembered my manual . . . so I put a tourniquet on his neck."

2673 Pat walked into a restaurant one Friday evening feeling hungry after a hard day's work. Without looking at the menu he said to the waiter: "Have you any shark." The waiter said: "No, we haven't." Pat said: "Have you any filleted octopus?" In surprise the waiter said: "No." Pat persisted: "Well, have you any swordfish?" In annoyance the waiter said: "No." "Ah well," muttered Pat, "bring me a large steak and chips. It ain't *my* fault if you ain't serving fish."

2674 Mother had taken her little lad of eight to a theatre, not knowing that the show was very French and very spectacular in its variety of scenes featuring statuesque blondes. Suddenly little Willie said to his Mom: "Ma, are there any Indians in this show?" His mother said: "No." "Oh," said Willie, staring at the backs of the tired business men who crammed the front rows, "I was only wondering who scalped all them men sitting in front."

2675   The farmer's wife, expecting a baby, needed a doctor in the middle of the night. The farmer called for help from his new hired hand who had been hitting the cider barrel hard until going to bed at twelve midnight. Roused from his sleep he heard the farmer yell at him: "Sam, go down and harness my horse, I gotta ride into the village right away." Twenty minutes later the farmer went in search of Sam and found him trying to harness one of the cows. "Blimey," he told his boss, "I can't get the collar over this danged creature—his perishing ears are frozen!"

2676   The engineer came from the Post Office to fix my 'phone and the first thing he said was: "I don't like the look of your dial." I told him that he'd come to mend the telephone and not give me a screen test.

2677   Short of cash, he decided to sell an antique heirloom that had been handed down to him. The dealer offered him only £1. He said: "Don't be ridiculous. It's very old. It belonged to my grandmother." And the dealer said: "The only one interested in what your grandmother had was your grandfather."

2678   He was once playing in a concert at Carnegie Hall when a string broke. He had to finish the oratorio holding up his trousers with one hand.

2679   At her fourth marriage ceremony, the film-star bride said to her new husband: "All right, Gerald. I'll take your arm. I know the way better than you."

2680   An elderly spinster was re-visiting the town where she had worked as a midwife years before. Meeting a middle-aged farmer she said: "Bert, I can remember back to the time when I used to put the nappies on you." Bert was stone deaf but realised the woman wanted to be friendly, so he nodded and said: "Yes, indeed, ma'am—things have changed . . . you'd hardly recognise the old place now."

2681   He came downstairs on Saturday afternoon wearing a plaid suit, a bright red and yellow shirt, a green tie, with a rosette in the buttonhole and a big rattle in his right hand. His wife said: "Oh, and where are *you* going?"

2682   A little robin went away for a few months and when he got back to the nest he found his mate sitting on four eggs—three robins' and one which was a foreigner. He glared suspiciously at his mate. "It's all right my dear," she said, "I only did it for a lark."

2683 After the wedding some clever idiot tied an old pair of boots to the car in which the couple were going away. And I was still wearing them at the time.

2684 She said to her husband the other day: "Have you got a good memory for faces?" He said yes—he did have a good memory for faces. She said: "That's just as well—I've just broken your shaving mirror."

2685 Jones and his wife went to one of those small intimate night-clubs and sat down at a small table for two. A waiter came up and said: "I'm sorry, sir, you can't sit there." Jones said: "Why not? My money's as good as anyone else's." So the waiter said: "Quite so, sir, but that isn't a table—it's our dance floor."

2686 A traveller stayed overnight at a farmhouse on the road north and the woman showed him the bed and said: "Dick Turpin slept here." He took a good look at the bed and said: "Lady, by the shape of that bed I think his horse slept with him."

2687 Did you hear about the cannibal chief's wife who called in the witch-doctor for advice. Her husband didn't have much appetite. They'd had a beautiful blonde for dinner the day before, and he'd done nothing but play with his food.

2688 A lovely young girl was trying on a pair of high-heeled shoes. She said: "Oooh! Ouch! Yes, these will do. How much are they?"

2689 When the new baby arrived, little four-year-old Pete wanted to know all the answers, so his mother explained that the baby had come from a gooseberry bush. The next day the baby was missing and Pete told his Ma that it had cried so much he had taken it home.

2690 Young Teddy was told that the reason for his father's complete baldness was a lot of anxiety and domestic trouble. When a new baby was born into the household, Teddy got a look at it, and then demanded to know what the baby was worrying about.

2691 Two Russian spies met at the crossroads at midnight. One turned to the other and said: "What time do you make it?" The other one said: "I'm not sure. My time-bomb is a little fast."

2692 A few Labour Members' wives spend a fortune having their jewels cleaned. Tory MPs' wives can't afford to have their jewellery cleaned: when it gets dirty they have to throw it away.

2693   My pal Bill writes fiction. He's not an author—he writes fiction when he's filling in his income tax returns.

2694   She saw a gadget for the kitchen the other day. On the card it said that it would cut her housework in half. She bought two.

2695   A titled gent who already had six daughters and was terribly anxious to have a son, a male heir, heard with joy that his wife had finally produced a boy. Two weeks or so later a friend asked him: "Does the little rascal look like his mother or like you?" The Earl replied: "I don't know—we haven't looked at his face yet."

2696   A Scot decided to take a correspondence course in body-building. He had to take it by correspondence because he lived in a remote part of the Highlands. For six months he kept getting text-books, exercise leaflets and loads of apparatus and weight-lifting equipment by every post. It didn't help him one bit. But you should have seen the way the postman developed.

2697   A Scotsman was travelling in the Holy Land, and when he came to the Sea of Galilee he saw a boatman standing beside a board which advertised trips in a pleasure boat. Wishing to see the sights, the Scotsman asked the boatman how much he charged. He was told the fee would be the equivalent of five pounds.   The Scotsman said indignantly: " Five pounds ? D'you know that in Glasgow I can hire a boat for a week for that much money?" The boatman shrugged and said: "But these are the waters upon which Our Lord walked." The Scotsman turned away and said: "Nae wonder He walked."

2698   Two teenagers scared their parents by running away to Gretna Green. Dragged back home, the girl, who was sixteen, and the boy, who was seventeen, prevailed upon their respective parents to allow them to get married. To avoid further trouble the parents agreed. At the wedding the youth stood at the altar with his young bride, and when he repeated to the Minister: "With all my worldly goods I thee endow," the groom's father whispered to his wife, "Now she's got his stamp collection."

2699   One solitary lonely chick was taking a gander around the electric incubator full of unhatched eggs. He said to himself: "It sure looks like I'm gonna be an only child—Ma's blown a fuse."

2700   A man was awakened in the early hours of the morning by a grating noise downstairs in the street. Looking down he saw a drunk trying to open his front door. He shouted: "Scram, you old fool. You're trying to open the wrong door." The drunk looked up and retorted: "Nutsh. How d'you know you ain't leanin' outa the wrong window?"

2701 Mick's wife went to the hairdresser to have an expensive new perm. For several hours that night she kept looking at him and patting her head, to draw his attention, but he took no notice. Finally, around midnight, as they were going to bed, she grumbled: "Aren't you going to say anything about my hair. This perm cost me five. guineas." So he said: "You mean it cost ME five guineas and I must admit it's a very nice job. In fact, with hair like that you ought to have a better looking face."

2702 OTHER PEOPLE'S TROUBLES
Some records in a Welfare Office, dealing with the domestic troubles of the common people:

"I have not yet received my allotment money. I have seven children. Can you tell me why this is?"

"You promised to help me. I have had nothing to wear for several months, but I am regularlyvisited by the Minister."

And here are some others:

"This is my ninth baby and I want to know what you are going to do about it. If you do not send me an allotment soon I shall tell my husband."

"I see that you have changed my little boy into a little girl on the application form. Will this make any difference?"

"I am married to a foreign gentleman who has been laying bricks since he came out of the army, but he can't get no work just now. We have twelve children and another is on the way. My husband also does plumbing and steam-pipe fitting."

"You inform me that an examination shows that my husband is illiterate. If this is so, who are those people up in Stockport what he palms off as his parents?"

2703 A well-known American movie actress died in an accident and her numerous friends got together to hire the country's highest paid poet to compose an epitaph for her. When the stone was laid, across the top in Old English letters were the words: "At last she sleeps alone."

2704 A young American couple had parked their car in a quiet, dark lane and when a motor-cycle cop pounced upon them, they knew nothing about it until the cop's torch lit up the inside of the car. "Okay," said the cop, eyeing the couple accusingly. "What are you doin' here?" The young man shrugged and said: "Guess we ain't doin' nothing, officer." The cop looked at the girl and then turned to the man and said: "Yeah? In that case, you come out here and hold the torch."

2705 The beautiful model got down from the dais when the artist suggested she might like to have a look at the finished picture. She looked at the canvas, blushed and said: "Oh! Mr. Spinto—you've been looking."

2706   The insurance salesman was telling Sam: "And in this policy, suppose your studio gets burned down to the ground, we build you another one exactly like it." Sam said: "Thank God you told me that—I was just going to insure my wife."

2707   "How did you find the weather while you were away?"
  "It was just outside the front door."

2708   The surgeon was operating on a glamorous showgirl when the assistant surgeon pushed him aside and said: "Do you mind if I cut in?"

2709   "I know a fellow who thinks in millions."
  "A banker?"
  "No. Bacteriologist."

2710   "Does your radio set still make those awful noises?"
  "Yes. But so would you if you were just coming out of the ether."

2711   "Does your sister still make up jokes?"
  "Yes, she's still working at the beauty parlour."

2712   "I see that Jones has started to make quite a good living with his pen."
  "I didn't know he'd become a writer."
  "He hasn't—he's breeding pigs."

2713   A young blonde went with her kid sister to see the new young doctor in the village; when it was her turn to go in she warned the kid: "Look, if I'm not out in ten minutes, break down the door!"

2714   A woman on a tube train thought she recognised her husband in the crush, pushed towards him and gave him a big hug and a kiss. It turned out to be a complete and unknown stranger. Embarrassed she said: "I'm terribly sorry, but your head looks just like my husband's, behind."

2715   Husband anxiously inserts an advertisement in the newspaper addressed to his runaway wife: "Alice, please do not come home and all will be forgiven."

2716   He was getting down on his knees to propose to her when a 50 p piece   fell out of his pocket and rolled away beneath the sofa. In the twenty minutes it took him to find it she lost interest in him.

2717   A vicar proposes to campaign against those extra-long movie kisses. He says he was at the cinema the other night and the goings-on in the back row were terrible.

2718 A lawyer and his wife were walking down the street when a luscious blonde waved to the lawyer, and threw him a kiss. His annoyed wife asked him who the girl was and he said: "She's just a woman I met last week, professionally of course." Starchily, the wife asked: "Whose profession? Yours or hers?"

2719 Out west they like their women weak and their liquor strong. In the frozen north they like their women hard and their drinks soft. In town they like their liquor straight and their women curved. In Huddersfield they don't bother with liquor at all.

2720 Our house is positively full of insects and flies and things. Only this morning I had to go out and get the moths another suit—they'd finished my blue serge hacking jacket.

2721 She said: "I've been here in this new district for three years, and I still don't know a soul, or have a neighbour to talk to—yet our cat's already had five sets of kittens."

2722 A young oaf up from the country went to the town fair and took his girl through the tunnel of love. They came out the other end soaking wet. A waiting friend said: "Blimey did the boat sink?" The oaf said: "You mean there's a boat?"

2723 I took a plane trip to France last week-end. One chap sitting in the plane was trembling, biting his nails and turned bright green. It worried me a bit—he was the pilot.

2724 Two gay young dogs were drinking in a small town. Before them were bottles in great variety and at intervals they took time out to stare at an old crone who sat at a nearby table. A bystander, intrigued, finally asked them the reason why they ceased drinking to study the crone. To which one replied: "As soon as she begins to look beautiful we're going to call it a night."

2725 THE WAR BETWEEN THE SEXES
He filled all her perfume atomisers with gin. . . . He hid a dictaphone under the love-seat. . . . He played poker with her house money, lost and then beat her for being extravagant. . . . She hid his false teeth to keep him from going out at nights. . . . She used his razor to shave the dog. . . . When he read the paper at breakfast she'd set fire to it. . . . He handed her one of those "Even Your Best Friend Won't Tell You" ads, signed "A Friend"— and she recognised his handwriting. . . . He wore one of her hats to a masquerade and won first prize for the funniest costume. . . .

2726   A film critic writes about a new "Western": "In one scene the sheriff says to the blonde: 'I've got you covered!' That's when I lost interest."

2727   A playwright decided to leave Hollywood and gave notice to that effect to his employer. The producer sent for him to try to dissuade him from this radical step. "You can't make any money writing for the stage," the producer said. "Take your last play—how much money did that make?" "Seventy-five thousand dollars," the playwright said, with some pride. "See?" said the producer.

2728   "Have a pinch?"
   "No, thanks. I detest snuff."
   "What d'you mean, snuff? This is arsenic."

2729   He was trying to impress upon her the endurance of his love and exclaimed that he could never pay as much attention to any other woman, not in a thousand years. Just then a blonde walked into the bar and as his eyes ran up and down her he exclaimed: "My—how time flies."

2730   The young lady had to fill in a form about her travel experiences. She wrote that she'd been a year in Germany but was not a Nazi, and that she'd spent another twelve months in Russia, but was not a Communist. And she added that she owned some property in the Virgin Islands.

2731   Report of a launching: "And then Lady Smallpiece broke a bottle of champagne over her stern as she went gracefully down the slipway."

2732   The barber was late for work one morning. While shaving he had talked himself into a shampoo, massage and hot towels.

2733   He was proudly showing his friend the bear-rug, explaining that he'd shot it in Alaska and that it had been a matter of himself or the bear, when his wife interrupted by observing cynically: "I sometimes wish the bear had shot first."

2734   A TV personality was asked by the makers of a brand of cigarettes if he would advertise the cigarettes for a fee of £2,000. The TV star answered: "For *that* money I'd even smoke the wretched things."

2735   Napoleon came home tired, weary, wet and wounded. Pausing on the doorstep he was surprised to see a pair of rubber gum boots leaning against the wall. He shouted to Josephine through the open window: "Josie—Josie—what are these rubber boots doing out here?" And Josephine called back: "It's all right, Nappy, they're only Wellington's."

2736 A sweet old lady went to see a psychiatrist. "Doctor," she explained, "my grandchildren think I am funny because I like pancakes." "Why, there is nothing wrong with that, I like pancakes myself," said the doctor. "Come over to my house, I've got five trunks full of them."

2737 Bill Prince, an airline agent in South Africa, had been reproved times without number for doing things without orders from headquarters. One day his boss received this telegram: "Tiger on runway eating pilot. Wire instructions."

2738 Would-be Army recruit is filling in his application form:
Have you always led an active life? Yes.
How many in your family? Eight girls and seven boys.

2739 The family purchased a television set. Everyone in the family except Grandma was very enthusiastic about it. She steadfastly refused to have anything to do with it until one night when the family was out the eighty-year-old lady turned it on. Next morning she enthusiastically described a programme in which some men were chasing a big black bug with sticks. A check with the newspaper disclosed that an ice-hockey game was transmitted.

2740 They were considering marriage. Being afraid of the high cost of living they each got out a ballpen and figured up to see if they could afford to take the plunge. After he had the estimate of what married life would cost, he decided that they had better wait. Then, after carefully studying the girl's figure, he threw away his pen and rang the vicar.

2741 Through self-denial and hoarding of hard-earned dollars the frugal Scotsman was finally able to buy a hotel where instantly he introduced his system of economy. Everything in the place was put under lock and key. He installed one clock in the lobby and over it posted a sign reading: "This clock for the use of the hotel guests only."

2742 In the dock was a pin-brained hoodlum, being tried for a brutal murder. The judge said sternly: "Do you mean to imply that you battered that poor old woman to death with a wrench, after strangling her, just for a paltry three pounds, ten pence?" And the crook said: "Well you know how it is, Judge—a few quid here and a few quid there, it soon mounts up."

2743 A visitor from Mars landed on Blackpool pier alongside a man playing a fruit machine. At the time the machine was paying out the jackpot —spluttering tinkling coins into the tray. The Martian looked at the fruit machine and said to it: "You really should do something about that rotten cough, son."

2744   Two beatniks lived in a grimy basement cell in Bayswater with damp walls, bare floors and boxwood furniture. One of them came home from a punchup one afternoon and saw a colour print of Spain stuck on a window where the other beatnik had put it to keep out the rain. "Blimey," said the other one, "we've had the decorators in!"

2745   A fellow went into the chemists and bought some Phensic, which was wrapped up and handed over against the payment. He was walking up the street when the chemist came running after him. "Stop," shouted the chemist, "there's been a mistake! I'm glad I caught you. Instead of Phensic, I gave you arsenic!" The man said: "Oh. Is there any difference?" The chemist said: "Difference. Of course. That'll be another fivepence."

2746   Russian vodka is far stronger than French champagne. They launched a new Russian ship the other day by throwing vodka at it, and it broke eight steel plates.

2747   The purser told the young lady on her first Mediterranean cruise that if she felt seasick she should hold tightly on to something; an hour later he saw her on the bridge clutching the captain.

2748   When he was trying to get out of the Navy he pretended to be nuts; said he was Horatio Nelson. They sent him to the M.O., who handed him to the psychiatrist. He told the psychiatrist he was Nelson. The doctor shut the door, came back to the sailor and whispered: "Gosh, I've always wanted to meet you again—tell me, where *did* I go wrong at Austerlitz?"

2749   A frustrated spinster rushed into the local police station and cried: "I want to complain about being molested." The sergeant said: "Have you any proof?" and she said: "Well, you're going to search me for fingerprints, aren't you?"

2750   A man was told by his doctor that he must stop drinking. To overcome the craving, the doctor told him to eat something every time he felt like taking a drink. He tried it and found that it worked rather well. One night, however, he was in his hotel room and, upon hearing a strange sound in the next room, climbed on a chair and looked through the transom. He saw a man just about to hang himself from the ceiling. He rushed from the room, ran down the stairs three steps at a time and grabbed hold of a waiter. "S-s-say," he stammered, "there's a f-f-f-fellow in the room next to mine. He's hanging himself. For heaven's sake, give me a plate of ham and eggs!"

2751   He thinks that electricity was invented by Voltaire.
He thinks that Robinson Crusoe was a world-famous tenor.
He thinks that a Norwegian fjord is a Scandinavian motor-car.

He thinks that Mata Hari was the rambling rose of the wildwoods.
He thinks Karl Marx was the brother of Chico and Harpo.
He thinks Crêpe Suzette is stuff they make lingerie from.
He thinks that a concubine is a merger of commercial concerns.
He thinks that myxomatosis is wiping out Rabbis.
He thinks Columbine is the wife of the guy who discovered the USA.
He thinks a monsoon is a small Frenchman.
He thinks that in the Stone Age everyone was petrified.
He thinks Kosher is Jewish bacon.
He thinks that where there's life there's opium.
He thinks a psalmist is someone who reads hands.
He thinks a polygon is a dead parrot.

2752 A famous surgeon was asked out to dinner. The hostess felt that because of his professional training he would be the logical person to carve the chicken, so she asked him to perform that little task. All did not go well, however, and the bird slipped off the platter and landed squarely in the lap of the hostess. She was extremely embarrassed, but attempted to pass it off with a bit of pleasant banter.

"Gracious, doctor," she burbled, "I don't know whether I would trust you to operate on me or not!"

The surgeon pulled himself up to his full height. "You, madam," he said, "are no chicken!"

2753 A husband and his wife are arguing about discussing the facts of life with their offspring. After twenty minutes of controversial nattering the husband finally makes his decision: "Look, Martha, we'd better tell him NOW—he'll be four tomorrow."

2754 A wealthy man, noted during his lifetime for his selfishness and meanness, died and arrived outside the pearly gates. He was disconcerted to find that before entering he was required to explain why he should deserve admission. So he told St. Peter that once on a cold, wet winter's day he had given twopence to an old lady who was starving, and on another occasion he had given a penny to a little boy whose parents had been killed in a revolution. St. Peter transmitted this information to Gabriel and inquired: "What shall I do with this applicant?" and Gabriel said: "Give him his threepence back and tell him to go to hell."

2755 A chap was arrested for breaking into the stately home of the Duke of Bedford and stealing fourteen paintings. He might not have been caught, but he was such a polite character, he'd gone downstairs and signed the distinguished-visitor's book during the robbery.

2756 Two mosquitoes happen to make a forced landing in a nudist camp. One says to the other: "Heck, this is a nudist holiday centre, what do we do now?" The other one said: "I know *what* to do, Mac, but I don't know where to begin."

2757   Bumptious rookie (son of Major-General Hoptwitch) on being reprimanded by his C.O.: "Look here, Major, do you know who my father is?" The Major: "No. Don't you?"

2758   Hollywood is still the crisis area for marital breakdowns. Giving a bedtime performance to her latest adopted baby girl a four-times married sex kitten recounts the story of the three little bears thus: "Once upon a time there were three little bears, Mama Bear, Daddy Bear and a baby bear by a previous marriage."

2759   Last night he went home unexpectedly and found his wife being embraced and kissed by a strange man. The moment he opened the door she glanced over his shoulder and said: "Ai ai, now it'll be all over the neighbourhood—here comes Blabbermouth."

2760   He bought a bubble car but can't join the Automobile Association because when he fitted a badge on the front, the car tilted forward.

2761   THIS WEEK'S MOVIE TRAILER
    You screamed when you saw *Wagon Trail*, you shrieked when you saw *Son of the Comanches*, you yelled when you saw *Sunset Rustlers*, you went positively berserk and stamped your feet when you saw *High Noon* . . . and now, a word from the manager: "Why do you make such an unholy row when you come to the pictures?"

2762   The inebriated patriot decided he would donate some blood to the Red Cross blood bank, but in haste he staggered into a barber shop by mistake. When the white-coated man came towards him with an open razor and said: "Open your collar, please," the patriot was cold sober before he was a block away from the shop.

2763   Little Johnny was very naughty. Later, after he had been reprimanded, his father asked: "Now, son, tell me why I punished you." Johnny threw up his hands and exclaimed: "That does it! First you pound the devil out of me and now you don't know why you did it."

2764   After years of seeking gold in a Western mining district, a prospector managed to raise a thousand bucks from the few nuggets he'd discovered. With the money he decided to buy a horse and buggy and travel East back to civilisation to buy a small business. Accompanied by his big, ugly daughter, he set off on board the buggy, across the desert. Mom was to follow by stage coach. Half-way across the burning desert, a bandit held them up, searched them thoroughly and then rode off in the buggy with his own hoss tied to the rear. The shock left old Pete speechless for some minutes and as the bandit disappeared in the distance he moaned to his daughter: "Gosh, Stella, I spent eight years making that thousand dollars, spent five hundred on that hoss and buggy, and I was gonna buy me a little business with the other five hundred. And now that blamed hornery coyote has ruined me. I've lost my horse, lost my buggy and lost my five hundred dollars. . . ." The girl said: "No, Poppa. Wait. I saved the five hundred dollars." "What!" cried Pete. "You saved the money? Where is it?" His daughter said: "While that lout was searching us I stuffed the five hundred dollars into my mouth. Here they are!" The old prospector grabbed the money and looked up at his daughter and said: "Goshdarn it, Stella. If the old woman had been along we could have saved the horse and buggy, too."

2765 A visitor from Mars landed outside the Palladium Theatre just as the chorus girls were coming out of the stage door to go home. He went up to one of the blondes and said: "Take me to your leader—but there's no hurry."

2766 An overworked business executive goes to the doctor who gives him a thorough working over and diagnoses that the chap is overdoing things mentally and needs more exercise. He says: "I advise you to stop driving to work, and to buy a hoop and bowl that to and from the office every day. It will make a new man of you." Whereupon the executive bought the hoop and bowled it to and from the office every day, garaging it during business hours at his usual garage. One evening after work he walked into the garage to pick up his hoop and couldn't find it. The garage manager was finally approached, and investigated. He concluded: "Yes, I'm sorry; due to a terrible mistake we have let someone else take your hoop. But don't worry, tomorrow we will replace it for you free of charge." The executive got so mad he went hopping around, clenching his fists and shouting: "Tomorrow? What do you mean tomorrow? How the hell am I going to get home *tonight*?"

2767 Jack's wife was on the telephone when he walked in last night. She usually keeps calls going for about an hour once she gets started, so he was surprised that she rang off after about twenty minutes. Jack said: "Who was that? You were quick." And she said: "Oh, yes, but it was a wrong number."

2768 Did you hear about the shop steward who happened to be the only man in the deep fall-out shelter when a 500 megaton nuclear bomb hit Britain. Emerging with his Union Card intact he looked around him at the devastation and said to himself: "I know. I'll call a strike."

2769 You remember Basher Jarvis, of course? Years ago he used to be the middle-weight champion of the world. Now he's so punch drunk he's the only fighter we know who has to be carried into the ring as well as out.

2770 His wife had become a card fanatic. Night after night she went out to gambling dens to play poker, pontoon, chemmy and anything else that offered a flutter. One night he was in bed, around four in the morning, and his wife decided not to disturb him by getting ready for bed in the bedroom, so she undressed in the lounge and walked upstairs, entering the bedroom in the nude, carrying her handbag. The husband opened a bleary eye and gazed at her and said: "Heck, this time you really DID have some rotten hands."

2771 A homeless, penniless young man went to the estate agent and asked him about finding a house, and he said: "Very well, just tell me what sort of price you can reckon on paying, then we'll all have a good laugh and go on from there. . . ."

2772 Into a theatrical agent's office one morning walked a middle-aged man, late for his appointment. The agent said: "I'm busy right now, you should have been here an hour ago. Anyway, as long as you're here you might as well tell me about your act. What do you do?" The chap said: "Well, mostly I do bird imitations. . . ." Before he could get any further the agent said: "Oh, hell, I can't waste time on you. Bird imitation acts are more common than pop singers. Just leave your name and number." So the man said: "My name is Cliff Hanger, and here's my number." With which he took a numbered ring off his left leg, gave it to the agent, laid an egg, and flew out of the window.

2773 A girl was washed up on the beach, half drowned. The first-aid man put a mirror to her mouth to see if she was still breathing—and the girl took out her lipstick and started making up her lips.

2774 A wealthy young widow inherits her husband's fortune and takes herself off to the biggest hotel on the Riviera. She rents the presidential suite and treats the staff as if she owns the place. One afternoon, just before lunch, she goes up to the penthouse floor to sunbathe, and seeing a wonderful glass patio, she decides to stretch out there in the sun, high above the town, alone with her thoughts. She strips off slowly, indulging in some relaxing exercises. Four minutes afterwards the hotel manager comes hastening on to the roof, leaps towards her, and rolls her naked body over the glass on to the surround. "How dare you!" shrieks the widow. "I'll have you dismissed for this. Is it impossible to get a little privacy around here for sunbathing?" The manager says: "Madam, if you want privacy, please refrain from basking in the sun on the skylight of the dining-room at lunchtime."

2775 A girl beatnik meets a boy beatnik outside the coffee house. "Oh Mike," she exclaims, "I went to a smashing wedding this afternoon. You remember my friend Eileen—she's sixteen but she looks thirty—and what a gorgeous bride she made—her black sweater trimmed with destination-badges and black boots to match . . ."

2776 After leaving his initial hospital appointment, a new doctor began specialising in treating schizophrenics. This went on for some time, then one day an associate asked him "Why have you always specialised in treating patients with split personalities? It must get very boring." And the specialist replied: "So tell me any other kind of a practice where you can send each individual private patient two bills every month?"

2777 He accidentally ran out of petrol down a dark lane, and was apologising to the girl about it when she opened her handbag and drew out an enormous flask. So, he thought, she wants to get merry first. "Is that gin, or whisky?" he asked happily. "Neither," the girl said, opening the door. "It's Esso Extra."

2778 A stage magician and illusionist used to have for his assistant a very beautiful redhead with the most magnificent figure who looked a wow in spangled tights. After her came several other equally delightful and attractive assistants. In the end he got fed up with having to change his girl assistant every few months when each one got married to a rich husband from the audience. So he decided to use a middle-aged dumpy woman to help him. Immediately his work fell off, bookings didn't come, and he was almost unable to get any jobs at all. So he went to his agent and asked him why he wasn't getting any Variety or Club work any more. "That's easily explained," grunted the agent—"you've changed your girl. Incidentally, I've often wondered but never asked you. What sort of an act do you do?"

2779 Phyllis went on a camping holiday by herself after an argument with her boy friend. She wanted to be alone to think, so she chose a small isolated little fishing resort a few miles up the coast from Portsmouth. The first day she did some washing and hung it up beside her tent on a line erected from two posts—a green baby-doll nightie, two black brassières, a pair of panties, some nylon stockings, a nylon lace petticoat, a silk slip and a pair of satin drawers, as well as her blue playsuit and a bikini. There they were blowing in the breeze overlooking the cliffs when a naval gun-boat pulled in-shore and landed fourteen Marines by liberty-boat. They scampered up the cliff-face and rushed towards the girl. The captain demanded: "All right! What's the trouble?" It seems that the washing spelled out the message: "Send reinforcements."

2780 There was a robbery last week at the bank in the main street of Preston. Detectives were on the scene, trying to find out about the stolen getaway car. But an ice-cream van had driven down the road just after the robbery and the trail was already cold.

2781   A man named Stokes put in an emergency call to a Brooklyn model agency and ordered a girl who had to be exactly five stone nine in weight, six feet two inches tall in her bare feet. When the girl arrived, Stokes instructed her to go into the studio and strip off; and to give him a shout when she was ready. Half a minute later the eager young lady shouted through the door: "I'm all ready, honey!" Stokes told her to open the door, which she promptly did. Stokes was standing outside carrying a small infant in his arms and he said to the kiddie: "So okay then, Louella, take a good look at this girl and see what'll happen to you if you don't eat up all your Sugar-Coated Crispie Crackers, like I told you . . ."

2782   A bunch of screen critics and censors were doing the cutting on another of those Italian sex movies in which the main actress's gowns were not credited to any particular costumier because the most she wore for the biggest part of the film was half a bikini. One of the censors insisted on seeing this film about a dozen times before he would agree to one part of it. This was a part where the star was undressing outside her car, parked by a river, so that she could dive in for a swim; but just as she's about to take off her last garment, an express train shoots over the level-crossing, blotting the star from view. The other censors said to the awkward member: "Look, Sir Wilfred, why do we have to keep going over and over that clip?" Sir Wilfred pulled a face and said: "Well, I know them Italian Railways. Sooner or later that express is going to be a couple of minutes late . . ."

2783   A famous painter used to get a lot of visitors to look over his excellent portraits and paintings, especially the nudes for which he was world-renowned. One day an aristocrat from the country visited the studio to examine the works, and he paused for a long time, staring at the picture of a very shapely blonde posing in the nude beside a statue in the grounds of a Scottish castle. The visitor began to grow very angry and perturbed. He attacked the painter: "You swine! You fiend! You beatnik," he yelled. "That's a picture of my wife standing there. How dare you! How dare you make my wife pose for you in the—the castle grounds. Don't try and lie to me. That's her. I'd know her anywhere, anyhow, in anything. She posed for you, didn't she?" The painter, somewhat scared said: "Of course not, your Lordship. I assure you that I painted that from memory!"

2784   He went to the local barber shop for a haircut and explained to the barber that he wanted it done specially because he was going to Italy on holiday with his wife for ten days. The barber said: "Italy's a fine country, I hope you have a good time there." A fortnight later the man went back to have his hair repaired by the same barber and the first thing he said was:

"How did your Italian trip go off?" The tourist said: "Splendid. In Rome I visited the Vatican and had an audience with the Pope. He even said a few words to me." The barber said: "That was a very high honour—to see the Pope. What did he say to you?" The tourist replied: "He shook hands with me and stared at me and said: 'Who the heck cut your hair like that?'"

2785 A painter learning the art of life-studies was advised by a leading Academician to take up sketching, whereupon he forthwith applied to a stage agency for a model. Getting this girl into the right poses proved difficult and the artist spent several hours shifting her position, her head and her limbs to try and get right the composition and lighting. This energetic preparation brought him so close to the attractive female that he became overwhelmed and lost all sense of decorum. Finally he grasped her in his arms and gave her an ardent kiss. The model wasn't much bothered as she had been in the business a long time and knew she was irresistible, but she asked: "Do you do that to all your models, Mr. Totteringham?" And he said: "Not really. The only other thing I've ever done so far is a bowl of fruit."

2786 Little Doris was off school one morning and her mother happened to be having a bath. The front-door bell rang and little Doris answered it; a man stood there and said: "Hello, little girl, can I see your mother, please?" And little Doris let him.

2787 A young man dropped into a pawnshop and noticing the large amount of guitars and revolvers in the window remarked: "Do you ever sell any of them?" "Oh yes," answered the proprietor. "Every time I sell a guitar, it isn't long until one of the neighbours comes in and buys a gun!"

2788 Little Angela was crying bitterly to her mother because her father had drowned the three new kittens. Apparently Dad had promised her *she* could do it.

2789 Patrick, just arrived from the old country, entered a sea-food restaurant. "Bring me the bist meal ye have," he told the waiter. "I would be-knowin' what ye English folk eat." The waiter brought a steaming bowl of clam chowder. Pat eyed it with some suspicion, but ate it. The next course was a cucumber-and-crab salad. Pat ate it in silence. Finally the waiter brought in the main dish, a fine boiled lobster. Pat stared at it, jumped to his feet and cried: "I drunk your dishwater, an' I et your garbage, but I'll be dommed if I'll touch yor big red bug!"

2790 A Scotsman on his sickbed fumbled for his medicine. Unable to find it in the semi-darkened room he called for his wife, who, after frantically searching discovered a half bottle of ink standing on the bed-table where the medicine should have been. Frightened, she gasped: "You must have taken a dose of ink instead!" "Well don't stand there," shouted her husband, "bring me all the blotting paper there is in the house."

2791 A party of Trade Unionist officials visited a London factory where automation had been installed throughout. The party came down from the fourth floor by express automatic lift. They had lunch in the automated canteen. On the way out past the office block, through the glass picture window they suddenly saw a pretty young typist jump into the air and shriek wildly. One of the older officials nudged a companion and said: "Thank heavens there's still one thing left that's done by hand."

2792 The entire family, including Grandpa who was ninety-three, decided to spend their holiday at a nudist camp. When Grandpa was informed that all of them would strut in the sun and play games, in nothing but their birthday suits, Grandpa wasn't keen. "D'you mean I'll have to take off all my clothes," he yapped. "Sure," said his son. "That's the whole idea of a sunbathing holiday at a nature camp." Grandpa said: "And will I have to shave off my beard, too? It's taken me forty years to grow it down to my knees like this." The son said: "No. You'd better keep your beard as it is. Then we'll have someone to run down to the village ever Saturday for the fish and chips."

2793 He protested, when she spurned him: "I don't understand you, *last* night you said there was something about me that thrilled you to the core." "Yes," she said, "but you spent it all."

2794 I bet most of you think you understand English perfectly because you're British people. Oh yes? A woman, for instance, goes into a dress shop, tries on a dress and the manageress says: "But, Modom, all the new gowns cling that way." Translated into English, what she is saying is, "You are a 39 hip, but we only have a 34 in stock." Or your wife has been a little lacking in efficiency and on Sunday night you remind her that your socks need washing. "Yes, dear, I'll see to it first thing in the morning," she says. Translated into English, she is saying: "I'll have them done by next Friday, or Saturday." In a hat shop, your wife is told: "Modom, it gives you height." Translation: "You're a dumpy old thing, and that feather in the hat suits you fine."

2795 A suspenseful incident on the beach last summer. A woman goes swimming in the sea while her husband is taking a nap. An hour later he wakes up. No wife. He searches the beach anxiously and comes to a sand-dune behind which he sees the lifeguard with a girl in his arms. "Please," cries the husband, trying to pull the lifeguard from the girl, who's half hidden in the sand. "I've lost my wife. She's out there in the sea somewhere, drowning. You must save her!" The lifeguard says: "Aw, don't get so hysterical." The husband cries: "But she's drowning! You're a lifeguard, aren't you? Then save her! Save her!" Suddenly the girl drags herself out of the sand-dune and says to the man: "Herbert, don't be so silly. I'm not drowning at all." With relief in his anguished voice the husband says: "Stella! You're there! Thank God you're safe!"

2796 The Chinese are worried about the enormous increase in the population under Communism. Statistics have shown that in Shanghai alone a woman gives birth to a baby every two and a half minutes. The secret police have orders to find her and shoot her on sight.

2797 A city was staging a mock air raid and the Boy Scouts had been called on to act as wounded persons to be picked up and cared for by members of the civil defence organisation. The first-aid people got behind schedule considerably and one little Scout lay awaiting his rescuers for over an hour. When they finally arrived at the spot, they found a note in a childish scrawl. "I bled to death," it said, "and went home."

2798 Ladies—don't spend so much time over the housework. Next Monday, why not leave all your clothes at the Launderette, and go out and have a good time?

2799 The local reporter called one evening on a very rich old farmer to learn the farmer's story of how he had become so wealthy. "It's a long story," wheezed the old man, "and while I'm telling it, we might as well save the candle." With that he blew it out. "You needn't go on," interrupted the reporter, "I understand."

2800 Acquaintances of a bashful young man were astonished when they learned that he'd become engaged to a girl during the same night on which he'd met her at a dance. "Yes, it's true," the shy individual acknowledged to these friends. "I danced with her four times and by then I couldn't think of anything else to say."

2801 SCENE ON UNDERGROUND DURING RUSH HOUR
"Excuse me, Miss, would you like to share my strap?"
"No, thank you. I already have one."
"No, Miss, that's my necktie you're pulling on."

2802 The new recruit, more than a little dim, was crossing the parade ground after being allotted his hut. He chanced to cross the path of a gruffy old colonel who had just had a wigging from the top brass. "Hey!" shouted the colonel when the rookie didn't salute. "Didn't you notice the uniform I'm wearing?" The rookie stopped, felt the cloth of the colonel's tunic and said: "Eeh! That's a smashing job. Look at the tatty old baggy rubbish they gave me!"

2803   All this crooked horse-racing that's going on! There isn't one race these days that's strictly honest. At Doncaster recently, when the tapes went up, four horses who were so tired they'd been leaning on them, fell down in a drugged stupor.

2804   His wife lies dying on the floor of the living-room. The man leans over her, anxious to hear what his wife is trying to say. She speaks: "Henry, before I die, I must tell you something . . . I must confess. . . ." He says: "Hush, honey, don't strain yourself." She says: "But I've got to talk. Erh-erh-erh . . . Henry—forgive me . . . I've been unfaithful to you—frequently. . . ." Her husband says: "Forget it. Why do you think I fed you the poison?"

2805   He was kissing her at the party when she said: "Am I the first girl you ever had?" He stared at her thoughtfully and answered: "Could be—where *were* you in 1964?"

2806   A few words on Civil Defence. If you are caught in a nuclear attack: dig a hole six feet square, lie down in it with anyone you can find for company, and pull twigs, branches, grass, rubble and earth over you. This won't do any good, but it makes the place look tidier.

2807   Three men were discussing very intellectually the subject of feminine beauty. "I think the most fascinating thing about a woman is the curve of her sweet lips," said one of them. The second man said: "No, no. A woman's attraction starts with the shining lights of her soft blonde hair." The third man said: "You're both wrong. It's really the brilliant glow of her limpid eyes." A fourth man joined the group and they decided to ask his opinion. He said: "Frankly, I think the same as you fellows, but I don't lie about it."

2808   They were sitting together in the parlour, a little scared. It was quite cosy, soft lights enveloped them and sweet music softly played in the background. Mom and Dad were out. The young man was nervous. Suddenly, the girl said, "Arnold, shall we pretend we're married." Arnold said: "Ooooh yes!" "Well, be a dear and pop into the kitchen and make me a corned-beef sandwich—I'm starving," she said.

2809   Four men were stranded on a desert island after a shipwreck. They found an empty bottle on the beach, wrote their names and rough bearings on a piece of paper and flung the bottle into the waves. Ten months went by and then, one day, as they all watched eagerly, a 'plane flew overhead and dropped them a package. Inside it was a letter from the outdoor department of a pub in Balham, enclosing three pence.

2810 Two heavy-weights were proud to be featured in a television outside broadcast. Half-way through the third round, as they went into a clinch, one whispered to the other: " 'Ere, Lefty, you ain't 'alf muckin' up my TV make-up; lay off."

2811 Missionary in darkest Africa meets cannibal chief in darkest night. The cannibal immediately goes down on his knees and utters a prayer. Missionary says: "How wonderful it is to find that our teachings have spread so far." The cannibal chief grunts: "Stop interrupting me while I'm saying grace before meat."

2812 Two old goats were out on the pasture when they found two old reels of film dumped in a corner. They proceeded to eat the old movie reels. Then one goat said: "Good, don't you think?" The other goat said: "I dunno—I think the book was better."

2813 You know, a lot of people don't believe in psychiatry. I didn't myself until last week. You see, I'd developed a nasty habit of walking about with my shirt-tail hanging out and I used to fasten two carrots to it. A friend stopped me one day and said: "Why do you always walk about with your tail hanging out and two decaying carrots tied to it?" I confessed to him. I said: "I don't know why I do it. And it makes me feel awfully foolish; I'm so embarrassed." My friend said: "You ought to go and see a psychiatrist." So I went. Two days afterwards I met my friend and told him I'd been to his psychiatrist and that I was cured. He said: "But you're STILL walking about with your shirt-tail out and two carrots tied to it!" So I said: "Yes—but it doesn't embarrass me at all now."

2814 Have you ever wondered how girls are chosen for the harems of the mysterious East? Well, a team of eunuchs go out with a fire truck, and every time they pass a girl they play the hose over her. If she sizzles, she's sent to the sultan.

2815 He told the psychiatrist that for three nights running he had dreamt he was playing cricket at Lords. The psycho asked him: "Don't you EVER dream about girls?" He said: "What? And lose my turn to bat!"

2816 His wife said to him: "Where shall we go this year?" He said: "I know—let's go to a sunbathing camp for a change." She said: "Oh, no. How can we go to a nudist camp? I've got something to wear!"

2817 For a whole month he was buying his girl friend a dozen red roses every night. Then one night he asked for white roses. I said: "Why are you getting her white roses this time?" And he said: "Last night she surrendered."

2818 Teacher asks little Gerald what he saw when he spent his first day in the country. Gerald told her: "I saw a lot of little piggy banks robbing a very big piggy bank. . . ."

2819 A wealthy oil man from Texas was driving furiously along the M.1 highway when he suddenly saw in front of him a long procession of animals and caravans, etc., from Chipperfields' circus. He swung away and narrowly missed the six big elephants but could not miss the smaller baby elephant which was right at the end of the line. The car hit the baby elephant squarely, killing it instantly. When the circus manager came up the Texan readily agreed that it was all his fault and offered to pay up immediately. But when he got the bill he protested noisily. There isn't one single elephant in the whole wide world that's worth £7,500," he exclaimed, "let alone a baby elephant!" The manager said: "It wasn't only the baby elephant—you jerked the big ends out of six big elephants."

2820 The farmer had a mule and one day this here mule kicked the farmer's mother-in-law to death. The crowd at the funeral was so enormous that the minister said to the farmer: "The old lady must have been extremely popular in the village for so many farmers to leave all their work and pay homage to her in this way." Said the farmer: "They ain't here for the funeral, Reverend. They're here to offer for the mule."

2821 The plumber called to fix the pipe. The lady of the house happened to be out but he was admitted by a very attractive maid who showed him where the leak was. As he was rather handsome and she was rather forward, they soon got on friendly terms, and were making passionate love. The plumber then completed his job and as he was leaving the maid said: "Shall we meet again, tonight?" Said the plumber indignantly: "Blimey, you don't think I do that sort of thing on my *own* time, do you?"

2822 He told the wealthy widow that if she married him he would lay the earth at her feet. So they married, he insured her for ten thousand pounds —then he shot her, carried her into the garden, dug a hole and laid the earth at her feet.

2823 They was hard days for the hillbillies when the mule was invented. It threw four hundred women out of work.

2824 Two army lads were close pals. One day Alf told Bill that he had a date with a girl—eighteen, tall, well-built, blonde, passionate and friendly. Bill said to Alf: "Gosh, has she got a sister?" "Sure," nodded Alf. "Can I come along then?" asked Bill. Alf said: "Sure." So for the whole night there was Bill stuck with the blonde's sister—doing the homework for a seven-year-old schoolkid.

2825 Lovely shapely Rosa told her Mama that she was marrying a man for his enormous fortune. Mama said philosophically: "But, darling, money isn't everything. Are you sure this man will love you when you are old as much as he loves you now that you are young and desirable?" Said Rose: "By that time he won't be around, Mama. He's already eighty-three."

2826 He said soulfully: "I'd like to get you on a slow boat to China." She said: "But why China, Herbert?" And he said: "I know a smashing joint on Yink To Street in Hangcow where you can get the best noodle soup in the world."

2827 ALF: I'm training for a stage career. I'm going to be best next to Jayne Mansfield.
      BILL: You mean best next to Olivier. Jayne Mansfield is a woman.
      ALF: Look, you get next to who *you* like and I'll look after myself.

2828 A tourist in Brittany went to the bakehouse early one morning to get a cottage loaf. The French baker couldn't understand what the young Englishman wanted, so the tourist outlined a cottage loaf with his hands. Five minutes later the baker comes back with his very pretty shapely niece.

2829 Jones was home early for once, cold sober. They went to bed early. About two-thirty in the morning Jones felt his wife nudging him anxiously and saying: "George, I'm sure I heard noises downstairs and somebody bumping up the stairs." George said wearily, "What time is it?" She said: "Going on for 3 a.m." So George turned over, yawned and said, "Go back to sleep. It's only me."

2830 They're so superstitious in Athens. They reckon that if you break a mirror you get seven years bad luck. One Greek we met there broke a mirror and HE didn't have seven years bad luck. He got run over and killed the same afternoon.

2831 Blake went up to Carstairs in the pub and grabbed his arm. "Listen, you," he said severely, "have you been going around telling everyone that I'm a loose-living playboy who can't keep his hands off women and who spends all his time and money giving girls a good time, and that no woman is safe within a yard of me?" Carstairs gulped and said: "Well . . . yes . . ." "Oh," said Blake, "well thanks, chum. It helps quite a lot, but you might add, the next time you're telling girls about me, that I also run a red MG sports."

2832 The stern father delayed the young man when he brought home the daughter of the house. Said Pop: "Marylin is young and innocent. If you're going to be friends with her, I rely upon you to show her the difference between right and wrong." The young man said with a frown: "But surely you yourself have brought her up to know what's right?" Pop admitted that he had. "Okay," said the young man, "and I've taken care of the other side, so everything's fine."

2833 He went to a psychiatrist who treated him for an hour. The psycho diagnosed the trouble as a "split personality"—saying that the patient was really two different people struggling for supremacy within himself. At the end of the session the psychiatrist handed him a bill for ten guineas. Giving the doctor a cheque for five guineas the patient said: "You can get the other half from the other guy. Why should I worry about his troubles."

2834 Joe Brown was telling his friend Jim how he and his wife spent their twenty-fifth wedding anniversary. "It was wonderful," he said. "We left town on the same train, went to the same hotel, ate dinner in the same restaurant at the same table, and were served by the same waiter, and I got the receptionist to give us the very same room that we booked twenty-five years ago. Everything was exactly the same as it was then . . . only this time it was *me* who went into the bathroom and cried."

2835 An absent-minded professor got himself married to an absent-minded librarian-girl. One evening they were spending a quiet time at home when somebody knocked very loudly at their door. "Oh heavens!" shrieked the wife, "it must be my husband!" And the absent-minded professor jumped through the window.

2836 He once did an act at a night-club . . . ten minutes of patter during which there wasn't even a titter . . . then he sat down at his table and for twenty minutes the audience laughed like mad . . . he was trying to shake ketchup over his chips. . . .

2837 Zeke was standing outside the barn leaning on his mule when his Ma came out to dust his jacket and she said: "Zeke, you're standin' with yer foot on a live coal." Zeke yawned and drawled: "Ya don' say, Maw . . . which foot?"

2838 Zeke had two idiot sons. The rest were normal imbeciles. One day he bumped into a youngster while he was riding the foothills on his mule. To the youngster he said: "Yure face is familiar, buck; where I seen you afore?" The youngster says: "Hey, paw, it's me, Ebenzer. You remember me, don'cha?" And Zeke said: "Wall, now I come to think of it, yup. It were yore red hair as threw me. How come a kid of mine got red hair." His son said: "Heck, Paw, didn'ya know Ma has red hair?"

2839 Two hillbillies were sitting under a tree working hard on their think-ing. Suddenly Zeke said to Abendigo: "Abby, I got a feelin' there's Indians around." Abby said: "You have? Why?" Zeke said: "There's an arrer stickin' through yore head."

2840 Hillbilly Zachariah was in town and he bought the first ice-cream cornet he'd ever tasted. When he finished the ice-cream he went back into the shop with the cone in his hand and gave it to the woman behind the counter, saying: "And thank you, ma'am, for the use of your vase."

2841 A tramp walks up to a wealthy-looking man in Piccadilly and asks him for twenty pounds and fivepence for a cup of coffee. The old gent says: "Twenty pounds and fivepence for a cup of coffee? You could get a good cup of coffee for fivepence." The tramp said: "I know, but coffee makes me sexy."

2842 The station announcer was saying in her prettiest voice over the relay system: "The train now standing at Platform Four is for Chiselfield, Braseknock, Tipperford West, Ponterbury and I wish you'd take your hands off me, Mr. Harding!"

2843 Visitors to one of those stately homes in the country—Goldmine Hall in Surrey—were walking along the main gallery which consisted of oil paintings of ancestors. A door leading off to the left was marked: "Strictly Private. No Admission." A beatnik pulled the notice down and tossed it over the gallery. The group of visitors turned left through the private door and found the lady of the house taking a bath in a very ornate marble pool, stark naked. The lady shouted out haughtily to the visitors: "The 2s. 6d. admission fee does not entitle you to view my private quarters." So a bluff old Yorkshireman waved his catalogue at her and responded: "In that case, ma'am, you'd better sit down and pull them there bubbles over you."

2844 The purser on a large luxury liner was given a message to deliver to a gorgeous unattached young blonde who had, the night before, been introduced to the captain. "The captain's compliments," said the purser, "and would you care to join the captain for breakfast in his cabin?" The girl was very pleased and accepted the invitation. Arriving outside the captain's cabin she was met by a steward who handed her a nightdress and a serviette. It wasn't until she got inside that she found out the captain always had breakfast in bed.

2845 One day a bearded and be-turbaned foreigner from Persia stopped a policeman in Piccadilly and told him he was looking for a marriage bureau. The policeman directed him to an office across the way. Ten minutes later the Persian sultan came out and the policeman asked him if everything was right. The sultan said: "Not all right. You send me to retailer. Now, please, you direct me to wholesaler."

2846   He was so ill his wife called in four specialists. They stood just a little way off from his bed whispering earnestly in consultation for about twenty minutes after examining him. He was getting really worried . . . then finally one of them limped over to him and said confidently: "All right then, Mr. Knut, we've agreed at last. Each of us will charge twenty-five guineas."

2847   A man went up to his pal and said: "I'm going to have it out with you. I walked past my house last night and looked through my front room window and saw you kissing and cuddling my wife." His pal said: "Oh, no, you didn't . . . I was in the local from 6 till 10-30 p.m." The man said: "Oh. What a nuisance . . . I've clobbered my missus for nothing."

2849   The tailor couldn't sleep because trade was bad. His doctor advised him to try counting sheep. A week later he called at the doc's again. "Is your insomnia better?" The tailor said: "Is it better? I count about 500,000 sheep. Then I shear them. Then I spin wool. Then I make up 500,000 suits. Then I have to spend the rest of the night wondering where the hell I am going to get 500,000 linings!"

2850   A well-built and pretty young woman had a bad cold, but she didn't want to lose the chance of going to the big party. So she took one handkerchief in her bag and put another one down her bosom. During dinner she had a spasm of coughing, and having used one handkerchief searched for the other one and couldn't find it. After poking and probing around for a long time she turned to her neighbour, a bishop, who was eyeing her in embarrassment, and said: "I—I'm sure I had two when I came here."

2851   The customer in the pub complained that his beer was cloudy. The publican snorted angrily: "What are you complaining about? You've only got a glass of it—I've got a ruddy cellar full."

2852   I was blackberrying the other day when I found a pound note in the bush. I was putting it into my pocket when a young fellow came up to me. He was wearing running shorts and a jersey. "Hey," he said, "I saw you. Put that back." I said: "Nothing doing—I found the pound note, and finding's is keepings." The young guy said: "Don't be a fool—I'm secretary of the Civil Service Sports Club—we're having a paper chase and you're spoiling the trail."

2853   The navigator of a big liner suddenly turned to his captain on the bridge and said: "Sir, I think there is something wrong with our compass." The captain said: "Indeed, Fotheringay? What gives you that notion?" The navigator said: "Well sir, a Number 18 bus just passed us."

2854   My wife went into the milliners for a new hat. She said to the elegant salesgirl: "Just a plain hat. No trimmings and no veil." The girl said: "But Modom—you have just the face for a veil."

2855   Mr. Enwhistle marched into a doctor's surgery for the first time and said to the doctor: "I want to thank you for your treatment. I have benefitted greatly from it." The doctor was puzzled and said: "But I don't know you, and you're not one of my patients." The young man said: "I know. But my uncle was—and I've just inherited his estate, thanks to you."

2856   An Irish clergyman was visiting London and got himself accidentally invited to a cocktail party at which all the young women were wearing the most remarkably low-cut gowns. He was gingerly sipping a glass of water when the hostess came up to him and said: "I don't suppose you've seen anything like this before, have you?" The clergyman shook his head and answered: "Not since I was weaned, anyway."

2857   The girl-friend got annoyed because her boy came to the house nearly every night of the week and did nothing but play poker with her father. "Are you getting tired of me?" she asked him. "You spend all your time playing cards with Dad." "Well," he answered, "we've got to get enough money to get married on, haven't we, darling?"

2858   We'd been drinking steadily all night and I found that I'd only got a five-pound note left. So when I ordered the next round of drinks I handed the fiver to the waiter and added apologetically: "And you'd better get yourself something, too." Later he brought the drinks—an hour later. And 5 pence change. "What's this?" I said. "You told me to get myself something, didn't you? I got a new jersey."

2859   Mrs. Smith had two grown-up sons. One went into politics and the other is a nice, hard-working boy.

2860   The lunatic was visited by the doctor who asked how he was. "I'm not so bad today. In fact I'm thinking of changing the cabinet. As Prime Minister it's about time I stirred things up." The doctor said: "So you're the P.M. now? Yesterday you were Lord Nelson." "Of course," said the lunatic, "but that was by my first wife."

2861   The biggest difference between the news on television and the news in a paper is that you can't wrap up fish and chips in a TV set.

2862   Over in the corner, at the meeting, was a man from the East and we got talking. This man said: "Back home I have seven wives—three blondes and four dark." I said: "I suppose that's the custom out there. Is your brother married?" Said the other man: "Oh no, he's practically a bachelor. Only two wives."

2863   After the mailbag robbery the chief was sitting around the table with his men, counting the loot. Suddenly, after the third count, he asked angrily: "Say, what happened to that batch of tenners. It was here when we made the first count." The crooks all looked at each other suspiciously. "Damn it!" exploded the chief, "I had a suspicion one of you guys was dishonest!"

2864 The impoverished young man was waiting anxiously for his rich old uncle to die, because he was scheduled to inherit Uncle Albert's fortune. Meanwhile Uncle Albert was ninety-six and as fit as a horse. So the young man went to his uncle's doctor and said: "I'm a bit worried about my uncle." "What's the trouble?" asked the doctor. The young man said: "I was wondering if you could tell me how long he's likely to suffer from this terrible longevity of his?"

2865 The traffic cop stopped a gorgeous blonde who had been speeding along a country lane. After questioning her for ten minutes, he said: "So, no licence numbers, no driving licence so I can't take the number of that, and no insurance certificate, so I can't take the number of that. . . ." The blonde said archly: "Would you like my 'phone number?"

2866 A New York policeman came upon an unkempt young man leaning against the wall of the First National Bank. "On your way, Mac," he said. The young man refused to move. "What's the big idea leaning there?" the cop asked. "I'm holding the bank up," came the reply. "Huh, a hold-up guy, eh?" sneered the cop. "Get moving." So the young man moved away and the bank fell down.

2867 He was so engrossed in the amateur boxing on TV that his wife began to feel lonely. "George," she said, "if you could have your time over again, would you still marry me?" Without looking away from the screen George answered vaguely: "Not tonight, dear."

2868 A friend of mine was complaining about having his brother-in-law living with him, because the man was so terribly lazy. He asked me: "Lazy as he is, do you think they'd take him into the Army?" I said: "I don't know . . . how tall is he?" My friend answered: "Dunno. Never seen him standing up."

2869 The guide was showing a party of North Country people around Warwick Castle. He said: "For hundreds of years this place has been left as it stands—not a stone has been touched, not a single thing repaired." One of the visitors said: "Gosh—we must have the same landlord."

2870 In the French Chamber of Deputies a deputy was arguing for equal rights for women. He cried passionately: "It's a crying shame that the wonderful women of France who are famous throughout the world for their chic and their beauty and intelligence should not have equal rights. In the modern world there is practically no difference between French men and French women." A visitor up in the gallery frowned and turned to his companion and said: "That guy must go out with foreigners."

2871   A young Midlander took on an older London man as a partner in his business. Within a month the Londoner had twisted him out of his share in the business, taken over his motor-car and run away with his buxom young wife. The younger man at last caught up with the runaway couple in a hotel in Cornwall. Dashing into the room he cried: "Some day, Fred, you're going to go too far."

2872   A wife who mistrusted her husband always slept with the light on. When a woman friend asked her why she explained that her husband was deaf and dumb, and that he talked in his sleep.

2873   He started a chicken farm and had no luck. Every bird died. At last he decided to get expert advice so he wrote to the Agricultural Board explaining that he had found another eighteen birds lying on their backs with their legs in the air, and their feathers discoloured, and asked the experts if they could tell him what the trouble was. Three months later he received a telegram from the Agricultural Board which read: "Your chickens are dead."

2874   The little hand-broom turned to his parents and asked: "How did I get here?" His mother answered: "Your daddy and me swept together."

2875   He went to Scotland on a sleeper, but he didn't get a wink of sleep all night. In the bunk above him there was a worried midget who spent the whole night pacing up and down.

2876   He took his wife, Stella, to Baker Street and showed her the plaque on the wall outside Sherlock Holmes's house. She said: "But that plaque says Sherlock Holmes lived there!" "That's quite right." So Stella said: "It must have been jolly uncomfortable living half-way up a wall, like that."

2877   When they arrived at the hotel for their honeymoon he gallantly picked her up from the taxi and carried her into the hotel. A week later when they were leaving, she carried him back over the threshold and put him in the taxi.

2878   An American on tour noticed a lazy Indian lounging at the flap of his wigwam. He said: "Why don't you go and get yourself a job, son?" The Indian asked: "What for?" The American said: "You could earn money. Lots of money. Maybe fifty dollars a week. And if you worked really hard you'd maybe even get to have a bank account. Think how marvellous that would be. You'd be someone. You'd be able to save your money, and one day you could retire and then you wouldn't ever have to work any more. . . ." The Indian shrugged. "Not working now," he said.

2879   The husband came into the house, and sat down and said to his wife: "The fellows at the club were saying today that Wilkins, the milkman, has kissed every woman in our street except one." His wife was thoughtful for a moment and then said in a rather bemused voice: "I wonder who that can be?"

2880   Two Englishmen went on a journey round the world on the same liner. They travelled separately and didn't know each other. Five months later as they were heading back across the Atlantic on the final stages of the trip they accidentally bumped into each other and although they had sat side by side on deck-chairs for months this was the first time they had spoken. The larger one who caused the collision said: "Sorry, old chap." The other one said: "That's all right. Nice day for the crossing, isn't it?"

2881   "If you're offered a second piece of cake, Willie, be a little man, and refuse it, just as nicely as your father does." Willie returned exultantly from the party. Fondly his mother asked him: "Did you refuse the second slice of cake, as I told you?" "Oh yes, Mother—just as Father does. I just said: 'Take that awful stuff out of my sight!'"

2882   The sentry challenged the uniformed figure that had just entered the camp. "Major Phelps," came the reply. "Sorry, sir," said the sentry. "I can't let you proceed without the password." "Drat it, man, I've forgotten it," snapped the major, "but you know me well enough." "Can't help it, sir," persisted the sentry, "must have the password." "Don't stand there arguing all night, Bill," came the voice from the guard tent. "Shoot him."

2883   A ham actor who was resting got work with a travelling carnival. His job was to hold his head through a piece of canvas while people threw balls at him. "Man, it was tough," he related to a friend afterwards. "I guess those balls really hurt when they hit," sympathised the friend. "No," said the actor, "it wasn't that that bothered me so much. What really got me was the people throwing darts at me from behind."

2884   A man was sitting at the bar in a saloon with a big yellow dog curled up under the stool. About that time another fellow came in with a very tough-looking bulldog. The character with the bulldog said: "You'd better get your yellow mutt out of here before my bulldog hurts it." "Don't worry about my yellow mutt," said the first one, "he can take care of himself." Says the second one: "Suppose we take them out in the alley and see who's so tough." So out in the alley they went, and in pretty short order the bulldog was out of commission. "Well, I'll have to admit your dog can really fight, but he's one of the funniest-looking mongrels I've ever seen." "Oh, you think so?" said the other. "You should have seen him before I shaved off his mane and tail!"

2885 They had five children named Alice, Jack, Tom, Mary and the baby who was called Ho Ching Hu Flung Wong. They called the baby Ho Ching Hu Flung Wong because they'd read somewhere that every fifth child born in the world was Chinese.

2886 A man who loved his wife dearly had her ashes placed in a beautiful golden urn which he kept on his mantelpiece. Tidy friends who visited him got into the habit of flicking their cigarette ash into the urn. Some months later the man's brother turned up from the West Country and idly glanced into the urn. In surprise he said to his brother: "Gosh, Alf. Your missus ain't half putting on weight."

2887 Husband and wife were sitting at home one evening and the husband did not take his customary time off to go to the pub. The telephone rang and the husband answered it. He rang off and turned to his wife, protesting: "It's about time people learned to use the 'phone properly. Fancy thinking this was the Coast Guard Station." His wife said: "What do you mean?" The husband said: "Some silly idiot asked me if the coast was clear."

2888 A man walks into the bar and says to the bartender: "My usual please." The bartender dutifully begins to prepare a dish of stewed prunes, but he then laces them with a liberal measure of whisky. A bystander watches with interest as the customer eagerly disposes of the dish of prunes, but makes a rather distasteful face every time he swallows. Curious, the bystander says: "What's the matter? If you don't like that stuff, why order it?" The man replies: "I hate prunes, but that juice, mister—it's out of this world."

2889 A very plump, brassy blonde with a large bosom staggered into an Espresso bar, shuffled to a stool and leaned over the counter saying: "Gimme a strong coffee. Gee, have I got a hangover!" And the man serving her looked down and said: "You sure have, honey."

2890 Their new home is unique. It's situated in a lovely locality—just a short walk from the new atomic-bomb rocket-missile research station and headquarters of the germ-warfare tactical planning service . . . right out in the country . . . birds come and perch on the window-sills—vultures and buzzards.

2891 There was a terrific accident at the corner of Piccadilly. The policeman said to the woman driver who had caused the mishap: "Why didn't you signal that you were turning?" So she said: "Don't be so stupid—everybody knows that I turn down here."

2892 An agent was giving an audition to some new acts. A woman came in and said: "I've got a fine act for you. My husband stands on the stage with his hair alight, eating hot coals—and he stands right on top of a burning brazier while he does it. Now that's a real fire-eater for you. . . ." The agent was impressed and asked how much the act would cost. The woman said: "Fifty quid a week." The agent bridled. "What—for a solo turn?" "Solo turn nothing, what about me and my daughter?" demanded the woman. The agent said: "Oh, what do you do in the act?" The woman said: "Be your age—we hold my husband in position—he doesn't *like doing* the act."

2893 Figuring that he could easily find out if his girl was visiting another fellow, who was a farmer's son, Bill crawled into the farm one night and set fire to the hayrick, hoping that the flames would attract the farmer and the girl outside to see what was wrong. While the hayrick burned, Bill kept a watchful eye on the farmhouse door, but nobody came out. Later that night he wandered moodily into the local pub to buy himself a drink —and found his girl there with the farmer's son—both of them with scorched hair.

2894 A big, brassy, overpainted girl, with a very voluptuous figure and big blue eyes arrived at the psychiatrist's office for treatment. The psychiatrist pointed to his couch and said briefly: "All right, Miss Hammerbrock, lie down and let's get started." She said wearily: "Say, Doc, do you mind if I stand? I've been working all day."

2895 Once upon a time there was a pretty young dancer who worked in a London club doing a strip routine. Every evening she would stop at the flower stall and buy just three carnations . . . the three carnations which she wore as a costume on the stage. Then one dark night she went up to the flower-woman and bought only TWO carnations. The flower-woman said: "What's up, dearie? Not working tonight?" "Oh, yes, indeed," answered the dancing girl, "but tonight is GALA NIGHT."

2896 In the old days parliamentary candidates used to go around the constituencies kissing babies as a vote-catching stunt. Our Member used to kiss all the baby girls when he campaigned twenty years ago. He's doing it again now—and some of those babies are twenty-one.

2897 Candidate, orating from election platform: "We must get rid of Communism, Bolshevism, Anarchism, Radicalism. . . ." From the front of the hall comes the plaintive voice of Wilfred Pickles. "Ai, and what about rheumatism?"

2898 Mrs. Braddock came home and told her husband: "Everything is going fine. We're going to sweep the country." And he said: "Not with our blinkin' broom you ain't."

2899 The candidate was a grocer in a small village. In his election speech he declared: "And I think we can trust the people of this country. . . ." Whereupon a meek little voice from the front of the platform said: "Blimey —he don't even trust his customers."

2900 A farmer had eight sons and when they were old enough to vote there came an election. Seven of the boys voted for one party, and the eighth boy, Cyril, voted for the other party. The farmer said angrily: "Dammit, why the hell did I let Cyril learn to read?"

2901 The candidate declared: "What I want is housing reform, land reform, school reform, law reform. . . ." A woman shouted out: "And what about chloroform?"

2902 For four hours he listened to his candidate talking on the platform and then he went out for a breath of fresh air. Outside a friend asked him what was going on, so he told him that their candidate was still talking. His friend asked: "What about?" and he answered: "I don't know. He didn't say."

2903 "What we want in the House is a working majority," declared the speaker. But a voice protested loudly: "Better still, what about a majority working?"

2904 A man went to a psychiatrist with rhubarb in his ear-holes, a goldfish bowl over his head, a snake round his neck, a TV aerial strapped to his back. He wore gloves on his feet. He sat down, looked seriously at the psycho and said: "Doc, I want to talk to you about my wife. . . ."

2905 You have to be smart in this world. For instance, if you hear of a lovely young widow who's so rich she buys evening gowns at £1,000 each, dresses at £350 each, and skirts at £120 each—well, don't marry her because she'll have spent all her money in a couple of years. Marry her dressmaker.

2906 A drunken man went into the park. He sat down on a bench in something of a coma and after a while a couple of pigeons came down and started pecking crumbs off the ground. The drunk dug into his pocket and pulled out a stale sandwich. He broke it up and scattered crumbs for the pigeons. When they'd scoffed the lot he said to them: "Would you like some more?" The pigeons ignored him, and he kept asking them in a louder voice and they still ignored him. So he burst into tears and I heard him say to himself: "How do you like *that*! Deaf and dumb pigeons!"

2907 "I didn't know you were an artist."
"I'll say. My work is world renowned. One of these days I'll be immoral."
"You mean immortal."
"I know what I'll be . . ."

2908 "I want you to help me with a little job."
"Okay. Let's get crackling then."
"You mean let's get cracking."
"You get what you want and I'll get what I want."

2909 "My barber's a very honest man. Last Thursday he clipped a piece out of my ear while shaving me."
"And he's paying you compensation?"
"No, but he found the piece while they were sweeping the floor, and he sent it back to me this morning by registered mail."

2910 "I know a man who speaks Latin, Sanscrit, Ancient Greek, and Pictish."
"But those are all dead languages."
"So's this feller I'm talking about."

2911 "I love the dimple in her chin. I love the dimple in her chin. I love the dimple in her chin . . ."
"All right, I heard you, you don't have to keep repeating it."
"I do—she's got three chins."

2912 There was once a spiv who had the bright idea of buying a million cigarettes and insuring them for £5,000 against fire. He smoked all the fags and then put in his claim for £5,000 insurance, and the insurance company had to pay out. The spiv was just making plans for an extended vacation in Miami when police pounced on him and arrested him for arson. At the trial, the spiv still came out on top—he produced an alibi for the day on which he was said to have set fire to the fags: he proved that he was in Exeter, stealing a horse. When asked by the judge if he had any evidence to prove this convenient alibi the spiv said: "Evidence? I've got loads of it."

2913 "Pull up the couch and sit by me."
"But I have just eaten a garlic sausage."
"Then pull up a window."

2914 A television writer dashed into the office of the Head of the BBC and cried: "I've got it! At last! A most wonderful NEW idea for television." And the head of the BBC said angrily: "Are you mad? Get out of here."

2915 The conjuror had fluffed eight tricks in a row. Starting his ninth trick he went to the footlights and asked: "Has anyone in the audience got an egg?" and a voice shouted back: "You know darn *well* nobody out here has got an egg!"

2916 When the world was first made, all the men were in Scotland and all the women were in Ireland. That's why the Scots have become such good boat builders.

2917 Did you hear about the fellow who won £50,000 on the pools? He paid in the cheque and it was returned to the promotors marked "Insufficient Funds. Not you—US."

2918 Tessie O'Shea was playing a theatre with Norman Wisdom years ago and she asked him how much he weighed. Norman said: "I weigh about nine stone two" and Tessie said: "Just imagine that! I ate more than that for lunch."

2919 There is such a shortage of Cadillacs in Texas that salesroom managers are limiting sales of Cadillacs to two to any one customer.

2920 There was a strike in the sewing-room at the prison when the Governor offered the prison workers time and a half.

2921 Russian archaeolgists discovered the skeleton remains of a pre-historic figure and when interviewed by the Secret Police their leader told them that the remains belonged to a Neanderthal man. At first this was disbelieved and the Secret Police took the remains to headquarters. Two days later the remains were returned to the scientist and the Chief of the Police agreed that the remains were of a Neanderthal man. The scientist asked how the police had verified it. The police said: "He confessed."

2922 The manager of a cinema decided, as an advertising stunt, to give away free antiseptic adhesive plasters to every patron to publicise the forthcoming showing of the film I *Was A Nurse*. He wired his friend who owned a large chemist shop: "Please send me 40,000 adhesive plasters—urgent." Back came a telegram from the chemist: "What the hell happened to you?"

2923 A War Office censor took a beautiful young blonde typist out to dinner at a classy restaurant. The next day she was asked by a friend if she'd had a good time. "Good time, hell," she answered. "The cheap skate censored two-thirds of the best part of the menu."

2924 Publishers of a very ordinary cookery book were having no luck with sales until their advertising manager started to boost sales with adverts which read: "What every young girl should know before she embarks on marriage . . . Get this new book." The edition was sold out in a fortnight, to customers buying through the mails—book sent in a plain envelope.

2925 Said the filly to her young little colt who was misbehaving! "If your father could see you now he'd turn over in his gravy."

2926 After several days absence from the Garden of Eden, Adam returned to find the lonely Eve sulking and suspicious of his actions. "Really now, darling," said Adam, "how could you possibly be jealous of me? Don't you realise that I'm the first man and you're the first woman—the only two humans in existance? There just aren't any others!" "Yes, I know," replied Eve, "still . . ." Adam was finally able to soothe his wife and soon they both drifted off to sleep. In the midst of the wee dark hours of morning, Eve arose from her sleep, pulled the bearskin covering off Adam and then carefully counted his ribs!

2927 Little Johnny was having trouble with his arithmetic problems and the teacher in a desperate effort to illustrate the problem said: "If I lay two eggs here and three over there, how many will I have?" Johnny stared at her for a moment, then slowly shook his head and said: "I don't believe you can do it."

2928 Once upon a time there was a prosperous couple who hired a maid from abroad because maids were scarce. A few months later, the maid told her employers that she was in trouble. The mistress of the house didn't want to lose her maid so she said: "Well, never mind, Gerda. My husband and I will adopt your child and you can still stay and work for us." That was fine. But the next year, the maid again spoke to her employers and told them she was in trouble. The mistress shrugged and said: "Well, never mind, your other child will be company for the first one, so we will adopt it, and you can still go on working for us." A few months later, the maid appeared before her employers and told them she was leaving. The mistress said: "But, Gerda, why? Haven't we been good to you?" "Yes," said the maid, "but when I first started working for you, you didn't have such a large family."

2929 A party in New York was given by one of the big movie directors. Jayne Mansfield was invited and when she showed up she was wearing a most gorgeous evening gown—there was so little of it that she might just as well have left it in the box. Naturally every man in the place started to stare rudely at her, and after a time she got annoyed about it. Slinking into the middle of the dance-floor with one hand on her hip she said: "What's the matter with you guys? The way you're staring at me, anyone would think I'd got two heads or something."

2930   It's a strange thing, somnambulism, isn't it? There once was a fellow who walked in his sleep. He met a girl, and found out that she walked in her sleep, too. So they got married. They're still walking out together—at two or three in the morning.

2931   There was a pretty redhead in court and the judge asked her what gear she was in when the accident happened to her car. So she said that she was in a pale green two-piece with high-heeled green shoes and a chartreuse picture hat.

2932   Two men were sweeping up the wastepaper in Downing Street during a gale. Suddenly one of the men shifted his broom and a piece of tissue paper blew right through into the Prime Minister's study. The man got worried and rushed into the house to apologise. Two minutes later he came out again, turned to his colleague, shrugged and said: "I was too late—he'd already signed it."

2933   A woodpecker was pecking a nest for himself in the trunk of a tall pine tree when there was a sudden electric storm and a flash of lightning hit the tree and felled it instantly. The woodpecker looked stupidly around him and turned to his wife and said: "I guess I don't know my own strength."

2934   A beautiful blonde went to the dentist the other day and after the dentist had run his eyes over her, he had a look at her teeth. He said to her eventually: "You need treatment, but I'm afraid I've run out of gas." She sneered: "Don't tell me you dentists pull that corny line, too."

2935   Little Johnnie came home from school and told me that his teacher had made him stand with his face to the wall. So I gave him a good belting for being delinquent in class, and then I asked him what he'd done to be punished by his teacher. He said he hadn't been punished—she'd wanted to fix one of her garters.

2936   A beautiful girl was just leaving the house after a party when her dress caught in the door and the lower part was torn right off. The vicar noticed this and cried out to the rest of the guests: "Anyone who looks will be struck blind." There was a deathly silence and then one old gent who was collecting his crutches from the hatstand muttered: "Ah well, I was a bit dim in that eye, anyway."

2937 Angus was the father of eleven children and had only been married sixteen years. When the eldest girl Sally, was trying on her confirmation dress one day her mother said: "I think that dress makes you look absolutely beautiful." The kid's face lit up, and then her mother teased her and said: "Of course, darling, I'm prejudiced." Sally's face fell and she said: "Oh no, Mother. Not again!"

2938 An American was visiting this country and most anxious to impress his hosts that he was a wealthy and influential man. One evening he came into the drawing-room and found his hosts, Lord and Lady Steveringham, playing a delicate duet on their grand piano. The American listened for a while and then said smugly: "That's nice. Very nice. But back home, me and my wife, we have a piano EACH."

2939 He applied for a job as a lifeguard on the beach. They asked him if he could swim and he said: "Well, actually, no, but boy, you should see me wade!"

2940 Fifi de la Rue was undecided about the dress she was buying. But she bought it when the salesgirl told her she couldn't go wrong with it. Shows you what that salesgirl knew!

2941 Sir Roger de Coverlet's family motto was "Trois Têtes Sont Indispensibles!" which freely translated means "Three heads are better than one." As he dressed for the jousting tournament he put on his breastplate, then his helmet, then his other helmet, then his other helmet. . . .

2942 Raleigh threw down a cloak for the queen to step upon. Raleigh's girl-friend, the Lady Leonora, looked daggers at him. Which is how Raleigh became the first cloak-and-dagger boy. No wonder his girl-friend looked daggers when Raleigh put the cloak in the mud. It was *her* cloak.

2943 Unfortunately the leading players in the courtroom were all stone deaf—but wouldn't admit it. The magistrate adjusted his hearing-aid and the first man said: "Your honour, this man owes me a tailoring bill of £50 and refuses to pay me." The other man jumped up in denial and shouted: "It's a dirty lie! My dog didn't bite him—he never touched him." So the magistrate said: "I understand your feelings, but in my opinion you are both old enough to support your ageing mother and I shall make an order for you both to pay her £5 a week." At this, an elderly lady at the back of the court jumped up and shouted: "Goody, goody!" The magistrate waved a finger at her and said: "All right. Sit down. Your case is being considered by another court under the new Unmarried Mothers' Protection Bill."

2944 Ye Olden Daze!
They threw him into the dark dungeon and trussed him in chains. All night long he lay there, chain smoking.

2945 The White Knight lost his breastplate, so he had to borrow one from his wife. Every time someone tapped him on the chest there was a hollow ring.

2946 He wanted her to go walking in Sherwood Forest but she told him she couldn't go because she was being presented at court that day. "You mean you're a debutante?" he asked. "No," she replied. "I've been summoned for speeding in my sedan chair."

2947 They called him Richard the Conkerer. While all the others were away fighting the Saracens, he was at home playing conkers with the kids.

2948 Then one day he stained the family escutcheon. He always was an untidy eater.

2949 The Black Knight drew his sword. The White Knight drew a fish out of his scabbard. It was a swordfish.

2950 She went to the door and looked out at the weather. Turning to her Lord and Master she said: "M'Lord, it's a terribly dirty night outside." "Well don't just stand there," said his lordship, "show him in."

2951 He had nothing to defend himself with except his pointed beard.

2952 She had a face that had lunched off a thousand chips.

2953 He was so influential they decided to throw a big Ball in his honour. A cannon ball.

2954 He told Sir Brian that he had fought with King Henry at Agincourt. It was over Anne Boleyn, and the king had won.

2955 Sir Roland Bolingbroke walked into the castle. He was soaking wet. He said to his host, Lord Pomeroy: "Y'know, there's a great big whacking puddle right outside your front door." His lordship said: "Idiot, that's the moat."

2956 He put on his armour, and then his helmet. But his face was still uncovered. The government wouldn't grant him a visor.

2957 Admiral Smallbone gave his guest a glass of port. There was a woman in it. The Admiral kept a woman in every port.

2958 The two friends met again after an evening booze-up. Said Fred: "You silly old chump—you were so damn stinko last night, you went and sold some mug Buckingham Palace for £5." Said Sid: "Oh, my God! Did I? What should I do?" Fred said: "Gimme my fiver back—I tried to take possession this morning and there's a guardsman billeted in the garden shed."

2959   A pretty young schoolteacher was shepherding the class across the busy road when the traffic lights turned to green to let the traffic across— but the teacher kept the kids going over. The first car braked beside the teacher and the irate man leaned out of the window and hollered: "Dammit, girl, don't you know when to stop?" The girl said haughtily: "They're not *all* my children, you know."

2960   After a very difficult Caesarian operation that had taken ten hours, everybody was exhausted. The anaesthetist said to the surgeon: "What was it, boy or girl?" The surgeon muttered: "I don't know." "Neither do I," said the obstetrician, mopping his brow. Then one of the newest student nurses standing by whispered shyly: "Let me see the baby—*I* know how to tell."

2961   The doctor had two patients from different ends of the town, both chronic insomniacs. To help them sleep he gave the patients some sleeping tablets. One got green pills, the other red pills. One day they met and got into conversation about their sleeplessness. At the end of this talk, one of the men felt so annoyed he rushed to the doctor and said: "How is it that when I take *my* pills, I go to sleep and dream that I'm a stevedore unloading a dirty tramp ship in Glasgow and getting smothered in oil, grease and pulpy banana, while *Mr Brown* takes *his* pills and sleeps and dreams that he's lying on a soft, sandy beach in Tahiti, surrounded with half-dressed beautiful native girls, all caressing him, kissing him and giving him a good time?" The doctor shrugged and said: "Be reasonable. You're on National Health. Mr. Brown is a *private* patient."

2962   A fat gentleman found it necessary to go to the toilet during a very bumpy air trip across the Atlantic; He was still in there as they neared New York, and suddenly the hostess banged on the door and shouted: "Emergency, Mr. Frobisher—we have to make a crash landing, our under-carriage has jammed." Frobisher yelled back: "What a strange coincidence, so has mine."

2963   "My wife's so absent-minded she got arrested yesterday for weighing herself on a weighing machine at a railway station."
    "Don't be silly. Lots of people weigh themselves on station platforms."
    "What—stripped?"

2964   "It says on that card there that if customers have any complaints they should tell the manager."
    "That's right, sir."

"Well, I thought I'd just let you know I suffer pretty badly from rheumatics and pains in the head."

2965 "This wretched clock I bought from you is out of order. This afternoon at three o'clock it struck six."

"Naturally, sir. It's a special model. It always strikes again in case you don't hear it the first time."

2966 "You know perfectly well, dear, that breakfast cereals are packed solid with calories and nourishment."

"Well to hell with it—I'm sick of nourishment. What I want is some food."

2967 "Is your husband double-jointed, Mrs. Harris?"

"No, I don't think so, Mrs. Clarke."

"Oh, then when he tripped over my dog he must have broken his leg."

2968 "I must say, Alice, my dear, you handle the car just like a veteran."

"How do you know how I handle veterans?"

2969 "What are you crying for, Agatha?"

"Oh, Mother! Fred's left home again! We had a row."

"Never mind. He'll come back again."

"Not this time—he took his dartboard."

2970 "George, I don't like the way our daughter Anne keeps getting picked up by strange men."

"In that case you shouldn't leave her lying around."

2971 "I met my wife at a night-club."

"How romantic."

"Romantic, nothing. I thought she was at home looking after the kids."

2972 "Betty wasn't very eager to marry me, so I told her about my rich Uncle Joe."

"I bet she jumped at the chance of marrying you after that!"

"No, she didn't. She's my Auntie now."

2973 "There's a salesman waiting outside, sir. He's got a big blonde woman with him."

"Get rid of him, Miss Phelps. Tell him I've already got one."

2974 CONVERSATION ON THE TELEPHONE:

"Hullo. Hullo. Is that Jake?"

"Yes, this is Jake."

"It doesn't sound like Jake to me."

"Well it is. I'm Jake all right."

"Are you sure you're Jake?"

"Positive."

"Good. Look, Jake, could you lend me a fiver for a couple of weeks?"

"I'll tell him as soon as he comes in. G'bye."

2975   Three members of a terribly mediocre beat-group were preparing to open their show in Liverpool, when the lead guitarist said: "Who's playing bass guitar?" and one chap said: "I am." The leader said: "Who's playing the drums?" and another chap said: "I am." The leader looked again and said: "And I'm playing this guitar. So who the hell is driving the getaway car?"

2976   While he was sauntering along the beach he saw a lovely blonde sunning herself in company with the lifeguard. He shouted to him: "You're supposed to be the lifeguard—there's a woman out in the sea, screaming for help." The lifeguard looked out to sea and said mildly: "Oh, *that* one. I've pulled her out of the sea four times this week already—her husband keeps throwing her back in."

2977   Father Tomkins walked into the cathedral and saw a figure kneeling by the altar. He went forward and inquired: "Who are you, and what are you doing here?" The figure replied: "Peace be upon you, I am God." The priest hurried to the nearest 'phone booth and put through a call to the Pope, stating what had occurred and asking: "What on earth am I to do?" and the Pope replied: "You'd better go back—and *do* try and look busy."

2978   American scientists have now found a new additive for toothpaste to prevent tooth decay. In a recent experiment on American children, the new toothpaste was used by 450 infants, and proved that in 443 cases it prevented tooth decay. We have only just found out that those 443 kids were wearing dentures.

2979   The cinema business is doing so badly, one of the few remaining small-time cinema owners has started a new publicity stunt. Outside the cinema is a placard stating: "Special Offer—Old Age Pensioners Admitted Free to Matinees—If Accompanied by Both Parents."

2980   A large firm sent its commercial travellers on a holiday cruise to ferment good staff relationships. During the voyage one of the men died and the captain ordered the first mate to sew the man in Cabin 26 into a sack and give him a sea burial. An hour later the mate reported that he had duly buried the man from No. 46 at sea. The captain roared: "I said 26, you big nit! Was the man in 46 dead?" The mate saluted and answered: "Well, he said he *wasn't*, sir, but you know these commercial travellers— they're such bloody liars."

2981   Two Scotsmen stood outside a liquor shop each waiting for the other to take the first step. Finally one said: "Well, Sandy, what are we going to hae?" Sandy paused, looked about him thoughtfully, and replied: "Rain, I think."

2982   Two salesmen travelling together had car trouble on a lonely country road, and it was necessary to stay at a farm-house all night. The farmer, they discovered, had died, leaving a beautiful young widow. She welcomed them in and said that they could use the spare room upstairs. The next morning she prepared breakfast and they went on their way. Months later they were discussing that particular night and one asked the other: "You didn't by any chance sneak downstairs that night, did you?" "Yes," he replied, "I did." "Well, you didn't by any chance use my name, did you?" "Yes, I did, I'm sorry." "That's O.K. I just got a letter from her solicitor. She died last week and left me her farm."

2983   Bill kept hens. One night he had two stolen. The next night he stayed up in the hen coop with his friend Alf to wait for the thieves. After they had been waiting a while a storm blew up and the shed started swaying in the breeze. After an hour's waiting, Alf got fed up, and said: "I'm going home. They aren't coming tonight." He stepped out of the shed and found himself on a truck moving slowly along a country road. The thieves were taking the shed too.

2984   I spent last Easter at a big house-party in Somerset. My host was one of those very wealthy old-English-gentlemen types. One morning I walked into the bathroom and got the surprise of my life—his wife was in there having a bath. So I went straight down to the drawing-room where he was drinking his breakfast and I said: "I'm dreadfully sorry, I just walked by accident into the bathroom and unfortunately your wife was in the bath." He looked up from his tankard and said: "You mean you actually saw my wife in the bath?" I said: "Yes. I'm dreadfully sorry." So he said: "Skinny little thing, isn't she?"

2985   Would you like a good tip? Why not try smiling a little more? Smile and spread a little happiness around. Smile on your way to work; smile at your friends—your relations. Smile at strangers in the street and at parties. Sooner or later, believe me, somebody is going to come up to you and say: "So all right, smartie, what's so funny?"

2986   DIARY OF THREE MEN STRANDED IN A HUNTING LODGE IN SWITZERLAND
"December 22nd.—Snowing hard. Can't hunt bear today. December 23rd.—Still snowing. Everyone hungry. Cannot hunt bear. December 24th. —Drat this snow and ice. Starving. Can't hunt bear. December 25th.—

Christmas, no food, nothing. Snow piling in drifts. Cannot hunt bear. December 26th.—Got fed up with this waiting to hunt bears. Shot and mounted Grandpa."

2987 He told his girl that he'd got spring fever and that music was in his soul and she said: "I didn't know you were musical. Do you know Fingal's Cave?" He said: "Of course! Do you want me to play it for you?" and she said: "No. Go and hide in it."

2988 In olden days there lived a wag who was the court jester. One night he crept into a dark room and slapped the king on his bottom. The king turned round, lit a candle and swore at his jester, who said: "So sorry, Sire, I thought it was the queen."

2989 Rustic yokel is meandering across lane and meadow sprinkling some orange-coloured powder from a large can. A passing American tourist stops and asks him what the hell he thinks he's doing. The yokel explains: "It's like this. Another tourist sold me this tin of powder and I'm sprinkling it all over the ground like he said. It only cost me fourteen pounds." The tourist, intrigued, said: "But what purpose does this powder serve?" Yokel: "The man said it's guaranteed to keep the lions away." The tourist cried in astonishment: "Lions? Lions! Look, man, there are no lions around these parts—no lions for thousands and thousands of miles." The yokel nodded amiably and, continuing to sprinkle the powder, said: "Good stuff, ain't it?"

2990 Two drunks were driving up a main street unsteadily, crashed into a store window and knocked everything flying. A fashion-model dummy leaned through the broken plate glass. The driver hiccuped angrily to his companion and drawled: "Shee . . . what did I tell you—a loushy woman driver. . . ."

2991 Two Irishmen were climbing the Alps. At one dangerous spot the heavier man fell down a crevasse and hung suspended by the rope held by his companion. He shouted up: "Help. I'm slipping. Pull on the rope." The other man answered: "Shure I will. Just wait while I spit on me hands."

2992 "Did you say that blondes were dumb?"
  "Yes, I certainly did."
  "Well yesterday I asked a lovely blonde how to spell M-I-N-K."
  "So?"
  "She spelled it Y-E-S."

2993 He said to the waitress: "Well, and what have you got?" She said: "Devilled kidneys, calves brains, pigs feet, chicken liver. . . ." He said: "Look, miss, I'm not interested in your health—bring me a menu . . ."

2994 Two prominent specialists had been asked to visit a local G.P.'s patient, a pretty young girl whose illness was a mystery. They called unexpectedly one afternoon. They both gave her a good examination and then one of them said to her: "Your main trouble is over-anxiety about the state of local affairs. You don't want to take such a great interest in civic matters and municipal politics. Relax." With which advice they left. Outside the house, the other specialist, looking very puzzled and impressed asked his colleague: "How on earth did you even know that the girl was interested in local politics?" The other answered: "That's easy. During the consultation I accidentally dropped my thermometer, and when I stooped to pick it up I saw the mayor hiding under the bed."

2995 Two big cannibal chieftains had dined unwisely and too well off a large tureen of parson soup. As they were retiring for the night one said to the other: "I feel quite sick. I'm sure that missionary was too rich." His brother chief replied: "Well you know what I always say, Ballomga—you can't keep a good man down."

2996 After they'd only been married a couple of months his wife was in the kitchen one evening cooking dinner when she called: "Hey. The stove's gone out." So he shouted back: "Well get a perishing match and light it again." She answered: "I can't, silly. It went out through the roof."

2997 So he went to the doctor and told him: "Look, Doc, there's something wrong with me. I inhale every cigarette I smoke and I smoke thirty-five a day." The doctor said: "That's nothing to worry about. Nearly every one I know inhales these days." He said: "Maybe they do, but I never EXHALE."

2998 A commercial traveller knocked on the door of a farmhouse, deep in the country, late at night, during a very intense and drenching storm. A middle-aged man answered the door and the traveller said: "I'm sorry to bother you, but my car's broken down miles from anywhere and I'm stranded." So the man said: "Well, I can put you up for the night if you have no objection to sharing a room with my young son." The commercial traveller gasped: "Good grief! I'm in the wrong joke!"

2999 He was sitting in his agent's office the other day when a man burst in—a friend of the agent. He cried: "I've just met a new client who sings like Caruso, acts like Olivier, dances like Fred Astaire and fights like Brando!" The agent cried: "Solly, I'll take fifty per cent. of this guy with you—we'll make a fortune out of an act like that! What's the feller's name?" So Solly shouted: "What feller? THIS IS A GIRL!"

3000 They are now making a new kind of record, a wax platter which is automatically sliced from a cube of black material. These new discs are for squares.

3001   FIRST RUSSIAN WIFE: My husband is in oil. He's in Vladivostock at the moment.
SECOND RUSSIAN WIFE: My husband is in salt. Siberia.

3002   An irrepressible toper accidentally left a full bottle of whisky on the local bus. Anxiously he raced around to the Lost Property Office of the bus company to inquire about the bottle. They gave him the Irishman who had found it.

3003   There was an advertisement on a Commercial Television programme for a certain beer. It consisted of a lovely, full-figured blonde dispensing glasses of the product across the counter, and various exchanges of enthusiasm for the perfection of the brew. An hour after the wonderful advertisement the brewery began receiving wild telephone calls from the drinkers asking questions about the ad.—such as what was the 'phone number of the blonde.

3004   When he was applying for a new job, the boss interviewed him and asked him a lot of personal questions, ending with: "I have to know all about you because this job is important and calls for a responsible person. Tell me, do you drink heavily?" And he said: "Thanks. I'll have a double brandy."

3005   The doctor told him to induce sleep by counting sheep, but he explained that he couldn't do that because he was a vegetarian. The doctor said: "So all right, count carrots."

3006   Ernie got on to a bus and had to go upstairs because he was smoking his pipe. He sat next to a young Indian girl visiting from the Sioux country. The girl watched Ernie smoking for some time, fascinated by the smoke curling into the air. Then she smacked his face hard.

3007   Last night Bertie took his girl to a Hungarian restaurant where they had Hungarian goulash that was made from real Hungarians. They called the waiter and asked for some wine and he said, "Don't speak when you have someone in your mouth."

3008   The prisoner whispered to his girl from behind the bars: "Listen, ducks, get a file and some wire-cutters and smuggle them in to me in a cake." A month later she visited her boy-friend again in prison and he said, "What went wrong?" So she said: "I got the file and the cutters, but tell me—how do you bake a cake?"

3009   He offered to take his girl to the theatre, and waited while she got ready. She came downstairs in a very revealing off-the-shoulder evening gown. Said he: "Look, I said get ready for the opera, not for an operation."

3010   "It's a nice day. I think I'll take our little Johnnie to the Zoo."
   "Oh, don't bother. If they want him, let them come and collect him themselves."

3011   "My wife has developed a habit of bathing in milk."
   "That's quite a popular trend these days."
   "Maybe. But I've had to shift all my pigeons from the spare room so that she can keep her cow there."

3012   "Will you marry me, darling? I'm not as good-looking as Phil Travers, I know. I haven't got a big car like Phil Travers. I haven't got lots of money like Phil Travers has got. But I love you. Do you love me, Alice?"
   "Of course I love you, Bill. But tell me, who's this Phil Travers you keep talking about?"

3013   "Dick, this is an awful café. I can't even eat the steak."
   "Oh, it's not such bad steak, dear. Just chew it."
   "Chew it? How can I? It's already bent my fork."

3014   A friend of mine was advised by his doctor to give up smoking. "When you feel like a cigarette, try a bar of chocolate," said the Doc. My friend tried it, but he couldn't get the chocolate to light.

3015   " 'Ere, mister, how about a luvverly bunch o' violets for the woman you love?"
   "Sorry. I mustn't do things like that. I'm married."

3016   She accidentally knocked against his expensive radiogram. He shouted: "You are listening to a stereogram that cost over three hundred pounds!" She said: "You'd be better off with a ten-guinea hearing-aid."

3017   His wife was admiring a new cocktail dress in the store window. "I can't see it," he told her. "There," she said, pointing, "just behind the price ticket."

3018   Two moths were perspiring in a tight girdle. "Stuffy in here, isn't it?" one remarked.

3019   Two beatniks got into a fight. One threatened the other: "I'll knock all your flipping teeth out—except two. I'll leave them in, and hope you get toothache."

3020 Pat had a terrible dream one night. He dreamt he was cast away on a remote Pacific island with six lovely redheads, eight gorgeous brunettes and four luscious blondes. But in the dream he was a girl, too.

3021 A man who won four medals during the Middle East campaign has just written his life story. It's appearing in a Sunday newspaper. He really wanted it published in a kid's comic so that his old sergeant could read it.

3022 As he was leaving the night-club he was presented with the bill, which read: "Oysters £3.00 , Pearl £6.00 "Arguing with the head waiter he said: "Look, the oysters, yes. I had oysters. But there wasn't a pearl in any of them." The head waiter replied: "Pearl is the hostess you bought all the drinks for."

3023 "Well now, how are those shooting-pains today?"
  "Not so bad, doctor."
  "There. I told you they'd go."
  "Maybe they've just gone to reload."

3024 "I'd get married if I had enough money."
  "Would you? If I had enough money to get married, I'd buy myself a racehorse."

3025 The colonel was invited to a reunion dinner. He expected to have a lot of fun talking over old times. Instead one old soldier talked about his weak heart, another about his liver, another about kidney trouble and a fourth kept moaning about his spleen. When the colonel got home his wife said: "Did you enjoy the reunion, darling?" "Reunion!" he bawled, "I haven't been to a reunion. I've been to an organ recital."

3026 The Inland Revenue Social and Dramatic Club made a bit of a *faux pas* when they decided on the production for last Christmas—they chose *Ali Baba and the Forty Thieves*.

3027 "I began life as a poor bare-footed lad."
  "So what? Do you think I was born wearing gumboots?"

3028 Never get wedded to a redhead
  Even though she's sweet;
  You may grow fonder
  Of someone blonder,
  Who hasn't got such big feet.

3029 There's a stockbroker in Luton who does all his business over the 'phone. In fact, he lies in bed, surrounded by bowls of fruit, cigarettes, bottles of liquor, dishes of chocolates; and does nothing but make telephone calls. Yet sometimes he says to his wife: "You know, Joan, there must be an easier way to make a living!"

3030 Newspaper report: "At the wedding of Miss Tapton to Mr. Hawker at Newport yesterday, the bridesmaids looked extremely chic in subtle combinations of pink and white."

3031 "Bill, Bill, I think I can hear a mouse squeaking under the bed."
"Well, crawl under and oil it."

3032 A prisoner in jail for life banged on his cell bars with a tin mug and when the warder rushed up, the convict said: "I just wanted to know the time." The warder said: "It's 1965."

3033 "Hullo, Agnes. Is that you, Agnes? Look, Agnes, will you marry me?"
"Of course I will, darling. Who's speaking?"

3034 "Do you play cricket?"
"Yes, dear. I've played for my school and my country."
"Hard or soft ball?"

3035 The Joneses bought a new house on the coast. The estate agent told them that on a clear day they would be able to see a hundred miles out into the Atlantic from their cliff-top patio. He didn't tell them that on a windy day they'd be in it.

3036 She said: "Before we were married you promised me a new car, prosperity, a house of my own, and sun right round the year. . . . Well, where is it?" So he said: "Well, what are you complaining about? During the last election, the Government promised me a new car, a house of my own . . . and am *I* beefing?"

3037 They are superstitious in Russia, especially in Siberia. When they spill salt there, it's usually in 2-cwt. slabs. Not easy to toss over the shoulder.

3038 Salvador Dali talking to Picasso: "Excuse me a moment, friend, could I have a word in your eye-ball?"

3039 Patrick went on a day trip to Boulogne to try those long french loaves. His wife ate one in two minutes. Got the whole loaf in her mouth in one go. And sideways, at that.

3040 The Advertising Manager of a small resort has a new slogan. "Come to Shellsea, the Manchester of the South; the only place by the sea where they daren't try to sell 'Wish you were here' cards."

3041 Then there's the pedestrian who got knocked down in the street and had to go to hospital for an emergency operation, to have the bubble car removed from his stomach.

3042 Her people were just ordinary working folk. They saved up a whole fortnight to have a holiday on the Mediterranean Coast. They'd have gone sooner, but the husband wanted to change his yacht for something less ostentatious.

3043 This girl was so natural and easygoing, she brought with her the scent of the countryside . . . fertiliser.

3044 Her father said: "You must understand that my daughter is accustomed to being well supported. How are your finances?" The suitor said: "Not too good, but dammit I can afford to buy her a girdle now and then!"

3045 He bought one of those bubble-cars. Couldn't find it in the garage this morning—his young son was pulling it around the kitchen on a length of string.

3046 A chap put a counterfeit coin in the fortune telling machine at the fair and it shot out a card that read: "You are Honest, Reliable, and Trustworthy."

3047 She lay in bed all night strumming her catarrh.

3048 A fat woman went to weigh herself on one of those machines which speak your weight for a penny. As she stood on the footplate the machine panted: "That will be another twopence, please."

3049 The doctor told her never to touch any white meat; that's why she has to get undressed wearing gloves.

3050 When I was very small my father used to take me out in a red velvet jacket and fancy short knickerbocker pants . . . honest, he did look a scream.

3051 A patient had an awful row with his dentist and he got good and mad. In the end he roared: "Look, if you ain't satisfied you can have your damn teeth back."

3052 A psychiatrist bought his young daughter a doll. She doesn't play with it. She lays it down on the couch and asks it questions.

3053 When Horace applied for a new job, the manager was a snooty type who asked him a lot of questions about his background and education.

Finally he said: "Tell me, do you have a family tree?" Horace said: "Rather, but of course it really belongs to our dog."

3054 It was one of the biggest ships ever built. There was room for four hundred people under the tables in the bar. You could order whatever you liked for dinner in the Tourist Class . . . but you still got biscuits and cold tea.

3055 Gigolo: "I wish I had 50 pence for every time I've kissed a woman."
Lady: "Because you've kissed so many?"
Gigolo: "No, because I've only been charging 10 pence."

3056 "How's that married daughter of yours getting along up in London?" inquired Mrs. Smithers. "Oh, she's doing fine," replied Mrs. Brown. "She's got the prettiest little flat imaginable, lovely furniture, a nice car—and she's never had so many frocks. The only thing is, she can't stand her husband—but there's always *something*, isn't there?"

3057 An office manager was telling how a girl came in to apply for a job, and when asked if she had any particular qualifications or unusual talents, stated that she had won several prizes in crossword puzzles and slogan-writing contests. "That sounds good," the manager told her, "but we want somebody who will be smart during office hours." "Oh," she explained, brightly, "this was during office hours."

3058 A man wanted to make a telephone call from a call box, but it was occupied by a lady looking through the directories. After waiting for twenty minutes the man opened the door and asked if he could help her find the number she was looking for. "But I am not looking for a number," replied the lady, sweetly. "I am looking for a nice name for my new baby."

3059 Eleven-year-old: "I've walked to school with her three times, carried her books and bought her two lollipops. Now do you think I ought to kiss her?"
Ten-year-old: "No—you've done enough for that doll already."

3060 A newspaper reporter rushes up to the first man to return from a trip to the Moon. He asks: "Is there any life on the Moon?" Spaceman says: "Well, there's a bit Saturday nights, but the rest of the week's damn dull."

3061 The day after UgUg the caveman invented the bow and arrow it started to rain heavily, the wind blew like mad, thunder thundered and lightning lightened. UgUg's sister complained: "There, you see? We never had terrible weather like this until you invented the ultimate deterrent."

3062   There were about forty blank car stickers plastered on a new Jaguar 3-litre saloon, each marked: "This space reserved for places I ain't been to yet."

3063   A London banker bought one of those fast new electric toothbrushes for his girl-friend. The first time she used it, it slipped and scrubbed her tongue to a point. Now she can get pickles out of a jar without using a fork.

3064   "Are you getting engaged to Sybil?"
   "I'm not sure. I've still got an option on Mavis."

3065   Hire purchase and credit have eaten into the soul of commerce. If you go into a shop and buy something, should you try to pay cash down it completely disrupts their accounting department.

3066   She hitched a ride with a man in a big Cadillac, heading north from London. "How far are you going?" she asked him and he said, "That depends on you."

3067   A man bought a marvellous, expensive hi-fi stereo-radiogram recently. The effect is wonderful. Quite often you can almost feel twenty or thirty men in the room with their instruments. They're repair men from the radio shop, fixing the set.

3068   Alf was surprised one morning when his wife called him from Wigan. It's 200 miles away, so you can figure out how loud she talks; she wasn't even on the 'phone.

3069   "Mary has said she will be my wife."
   "Well it's your own fault for hanging around the house every night."

3070   Dolly asked Priscilla why she had given up her previous boy-friend and she said: "I saw him diving at the swimming baths one day, and he looked different without his wallet."

3071   His girl got blind drunk at the Xmas Eve party. When Father Christmas called he found her two stockings hanging over the bedrail, with the girl still in them.

3072   An acquaintance rang my doorbell late on Wednesday night and asked to stay with me. He said he'd heard so much good about our town, the strip shows, the pretty girls, the riotous bingo games, the lovely barmaids in all the pubs, that he'd decided to spend a few days visiting me. I said: "That's okay. But what's that book you're carrying?" He said: "Oh, it's my Bible . . . if this town's as good as they say it is, I might be staying over Sunday."

3073 When he was thirteen his father started to explain the facts of life to him. "Son, never chase after girls. Girls is poison. And, just like buses, if you miss one, there'll be another one along in five or so minutes. I tell you, laddie, girls is ten a penny." So he said to his father: "I wish you'd told me years ago. Think of all the pennies I've been frittering away on jelly babies."

3074 He thought she was in love with him because every night they met she used to ask him for a lock of his long curly hair. This went on for months until she suddenly said that things were over between them. "But, Phoebe," he said. "I thought you loved me. Think of all those mementoes you kept of me. All those locks of my hair." "Oh, those," she said, surprised. "I only wanted them because Mom's been stuffing a mattress."

3075 His wife said irately: "Well, where were you all last night?" The husband said: "If it comes to that, where were you all night?" The wife said: "Oh, you needn't sound so suspicious. As a matter of fact I was with my old school friend, Norma." The husband said: "What a terrible liar you are! You weren't anywhere near Norma's last night. That's where I was."

3076 A spinster was disturbed in the dead of night by a man who climbed through her bedroom window, mask on his face, jemmy in his hand, swag-bag in his teeth. She faced the burglar with steady courage and said: "Well, don't just stand there—attack me."

3077 It's too bad about poor old Tony Harrison. He went all the way to Algiers to join the Foreign Legion because he wanted to forget his wife, and the sergeant of his platoon looked just like her.

3078 "I kissed a girl in the moonlight but she wouldn't kiss me back."
"Why should she? What's so special about your back?"

3079 The price of meat gets higher and higher. Last week-end his wife said: "I can't afford to buy English meat. I'm going to get this week's joint from France." So she did. But the price of meat is higher in Paris. Have you ever tried carving a frog's leg?

3080 Stan's girl friend went to a doctor. He asked her which doctor she went to and she said: "Oh, Doctor Johnson-Smith." He said: "Dr. Johnson-Smith is a doctor of *music*." She said: "Really? But he never mentioned it when I stripped." Stan said: "Why did you have to strip? I've told you, he's a doctor of music." And she said: "He was interested in my glocken-spiel."

3081 He was invited to sing at the Metropolitan Opera House in America. He was so excited, when he stepped off the plane they had to call an ambulance. He stepped off it ten minutes before it landed.

3082 He was giving a strange girl a long kiss last night and she kept saying: "Hurry up, I want to slap your face."

3083 What a bore I met last night. I was introduced to him and casually said: "Hullo, how are you?" Then he spent two and a half hours telling me how he was.

3084 After a lorry nearly ran a motorist off the road he bawled at the big lout of a driver: "Where the hell are your road manners?" and the truck driver yelled back: "Look mate, when you've got a five-ton truck, you don't *need* road manners."

3085 An artist kept going to the supply shop and buying tubes and tubes of pink paint. Finally the shop manager said jokingly: "You've bought nearly four gallons of that pink paint. What are you doing? Painting your kitchen?" And the artist said: "No—nudes. And all of them are *so* fat."

3086 His girl was driving and suddenly there was a bump. She said: "I've just run over a big black cat with a band of white fur round its neck!" Silly young fool. It was the vicar.

3087 Mr. Johnson went into show business because commercial work was unprofitable. At his last job the chairman called him into the office and said: "You're alert, intelligent, aggressive, smart and ambitious." He said: "Thanks, what do I get? Promotion or a raise?" And the boss said: "You get fired. I don't want anyone stepping into my shoes."

3088 Mr. Hicks told his wife he was fed up and was going out to cut his throat. She said: "Don't do it. You've got so much to live for! . . . You haven't finished paying for the car, the house or the fridge . . ."

3089 Patient: "My tongue is continually furred."
Doctor: "Tell your wife to stop dishing you up so much frozen food, then your tongue won't need such a thick fur."

3090 "Dear Aunt Sally of *Woman's Sphere*, I want to be hugged and squeezed tight, I want to be embraced with fervour, I want to be grasped and thrilled in a possessive hold. How can I get a husband? Signed Matilda Morris."
"Dear Matilda, you don't want a husband; get a corset, it's cheaper."

3091   A defiant beatnik broke into the Lucifer Galleries and daubed different coloured paints over an art treasure worth £10,000. The curator craftily moved it to the Abstract Section—and sold it to an American collector for £15,000.

3092   When I was in the navy we were warned that we would have to pay for any damage to government property. They made me a captain within six months and gave me a ship. Out in the North Sea one day, a large wave hit us, and the ship began to sink. I figured out what it was going to cost me to repay the Admiralty—and that's how I perished with the ship. It was cheaper.

3093   "I've been playing truant from my Correspondence School"
      "How can you play truant from a Correspondence School?"
      "I send back empty envelopes."

3094   Sid has been out of work for four years, living on National Assistance. One day he visited the Labour Exchange, but he was only sheltering from the rain till the pictures started. He got married a fortnight ago. Most newly-wed men look for a home close to a school. Not Sid. He found one close to a pub. He was in there one day when the landlord served him with his usual pint and Sid was mad. He said: "This beer is cloudy". The landlord said: "What do you expect for 20 pence—thunder and lightning?"

3095   Danny had a tooth out the other day. The dentist lined everything up and then said: "This might hurt a little. Just grip something tight." That's when his receptionist screamed.

3096   Fred's been given a part in a new Bible picture. He acts a Christian who has to be thrown to the lions. At rehearsal yesterday they pushed him into a den full of forty roaring sabre-toothed lions and the producer yelled at him: "For Pete's sake try and look frightened!"

3097   The Russian soldier went to the dentist with violent toothache. The dentist said: "Open your mouth wide." The soldier said: "What? And get shot!"

3098   A woman took back her mottled blue and yellow summer dress to the store and said: "I thought you promised me that the colours wouldn't run when I washed it?" The manager examined the dress and said: "Madam, we didn't say they wouldn't *walk* a little."

3099   The prices at the cinema are getting ridiculously high. I took my girl to a West End cinema last night. Two seats in the back row— £2.50 each! It was one of those Cinerama Vistacolour Stretchscreen epics, where the action goes on all around you. The film was a Biblical Extravaganza and in the scene where the Romans are throwing Christians to the lions, the lions were all round us. One of them sat down on the empty seat next to me for a rest. I said to him: "You're doing a fine job. And it isn't often you see a lion sitting in this cinema," and the lion said: "I should think not at £2.50 a time!"

3100   "When you married me you said you had a great big white ocean-going yacht."

"Stop complaining, and row."

3101   They went for a trip in a boat and his wife is so fat the boatman charged double fare for her. That was bad enough but she fell overboard and sent the tide in an hour early.

3102   To the waitress: "A pot of tea and bring me lots and lots of hot water."

"Why? Are you having a baby?"

3103   It was a wonderful hotel. As he checked in, a blonde showed him where the dining-room was, sent a lad up with the luggage and smiled sweetly at him. Then she said: "And if you fancy anything in the night, Mr. Smith—just forget it."

3104   The day two young priests were ordained one turned to the other and said in a very friendly manner: "So, Albert, why don't you and I go out tonight and celibate?"

3105   The sergeant said: "How come you're such a titch?" Private Scott replied: "Well it's like this, I used to be in the parachute regiment, and one day my chute didn't open, and whenever I get cramp in my ankles I have to have my stomach massaged."

3106   A photographer was assigned by the Government to take pictures of the Navy on manoeuvres. The results were marvellous. Three commanders in an opium den, four midshipmen at a gambling saloon, and the rest of the men in dark doorways.

3107   Have you ever been in those cosy intimate little crowded restaurants where the lights are very low and the atmosphere is stuffy and there's always a hum of conversation? In a little place like that last night Oscar was just ordering chicken noodle soup when the porter shouted: "Mind the doors, please."

3108   A tramp was standing by the roadside sticking his tongue out at passing cars. Sometimes he would stop sticking out his tongue and thumb his nose. A pal came up to him and said: "You'll never get a ride if you do things like that to passing drivers." The other tramp said: "Who cares? I'm on strike."

3109 Slim has been a hotel thief for five years. Two policemen caught him yesterday, at last. In his back yard they found fourteen hotels.

3110 A new, young policeman walks along the road and sees lady parked down a dead-end street. Goes to her. "Lady, you can't park here." Lady says: "Nonsense, officer, this is a cul-de-sac." Cop says: "I don't care if it's a Rolls-Royce, you still can't leave it HERE."

3111 The surgeon looked down at the patient. His face was smothered with scars, bits of plaster and soap suds. He said: "Now don't worry, I've done this operation so often it's second nature to me now, like shaving."

3112 Scene in maternity ward; one baby belonging to thin woman and the other, a girl, to a big showgirl. Girl to boy: "Trust me to find a good restaurant."

3113 The patient lay on the psychiatrist's couch for twenty minutes and it didn't do a thing for him. The psychiatrist asked: "Well, haven't you got anything at all to say?" The patient said: "Sure. Your ceiling needs redecorating."

3114 They went on a cruise last year. The ship was a converted oil-tanker. The only snag was you had to pack your luggage in barrels.

3115 "In the First Aid Manual it distinctly says: 'Remove all tight clothing and make the patient comfortable. . . .' "
"Yes, Reggie, I know, but I'm not a patient. . . ."

3116 A TV producer in Germany wanted to screen pictures of British workers in the transport industry. Unable to find suitable film clips in the British Film Library, the producer decided to run film clips of German workers . . . in slow motion.

3117 She was very short-sighted, but so vain that she wouldn't wear glasses, and because she didn't wear glasses she married a fellow who had been engaged eighteen times before. So off she went on her honeymoon and a fortnight later I called around to see how she was enjoying married life. I said to her: "And how's Henry?" and she said: "He's fine, and he doesn't mind me being short-sighted, either." So I said: "Maybe he doesn't, but I bet he's going to mind you bringing this other fellow back from your honeymoon."

3118   A small lad was doing his homework and he asked his mother: "Say, Mom, have you any idea where the Alps are?" She said: "Don't bother *me*, ask your father; he's been tidying up again."

3119   He called upstairs to his wife: "Sarah, how long are you going to be, we'll miss the train. Go on, be specific, give me a date. . . ."

3120   "My wife's going for a check-up."
   "You mean to the doctor?"
   "No, to the beauty salon."

3121   Cyril got in after midnight and his mother said: "Where have you been till this hour?" and he said: "I've been out on the town with a boy I know." His mother said: "You mean with a girl you know." He said: "Look, boy, girl, what difference?" "If you don't know the difference, I guess it's all right," sighed his mother.

3122   Some local councils are running their own theatres these days. But it doesn't make any difference even though the seats are free. Even people who don't pay their rates won't go to see a show there. There's no need for commissionaires any more. One commissionaire who was idling about outside his theatre one night got arrested for loitering. Things are so bad at that particular theatre that they can't even afford to have the roof repaired, and it's in a shocking state. Any day now it's going to be the only open-air indoor theatre in the town.

3123   He got so fed up with the constant nagging of his wife that he told her he was going out once and for all to drown himself in the near-by river. "Alf," she said, "would you do me a favour? Leave your clothes on the bank. They might fit my second husband."

3124   There was news in the paper tonight about that accident that happened to a local magistrate. "The chief magistrate's injury is not serious and he hopes to resume sitting shortly."

3125   Julia got home very late and started to tell her mother: "Ma, it was like this . . ." Mother said: "I know how it is, who's the chap?"

3126   His wife said: "Do you HAVE to come home at this hour, blind drunk?" and he said: "Unfoshunately yesh—the joints ish all shut up."

3127   Bill went to the dentist about his teeth and the dentist said: "Your teeth are in a dreadful mess. It's all the tinned food you're living on." Bill said: "You mean canned food is bad for me?" The dentist said: "Well it wouldn't hurt if you bought yourself a tin-opener, instead of biting the lids off."

3128 The hostess was charming. Just before dinner she asked Doris: "What would you like? Aperitif?" Doris said: "No thanks, I've brought my own teef with me."

3129 They've invented the last word in alarm clocks. It rings five minutes before getting-up time; right on getting-up time; and again five minutes after. If you're not out of bed by then, it 'phones your boss and makes an excuse for you being late.

3130 A very palsied man stood stripping in front of the young doctor. The doctor asked him to stretch out his arm and extend his fingers. The man's vibration now increased so that he trembled and shook. "Good God," said the doctor, "you have got it bad! Chronic DTs. You must drink an awful lot!" "Drink?" protested the patient. "Look, I can't drink at all. I spill most of it down my shirt." The doctor said: "Then it's something else. Are you promiscuous?" The man said: "No, I'm a Methodist." "Look," said the doctor, "if it isn't drink and it isn't sex, what is it? You're shaking like a palm tree. What's your job?" "Oh," said the man, "I'm a pneumatic drill operator."

3131 In the interval the screen showed an advert stating: "You'll love it! You'll like it! It lasts fifteen minutes!" The spotlight slipped and hit a courting couple in the back row, and a queue formed half-way up the aisle.

3132 She went to the doctor, who examined her. He put his stethoscope to her chest and every time she breathed in her heart seemed to give a little squeak. He wrote out a prescription for her—lubricating oil for her suspenders.

3133 "My girl went to the fancy dress ball as a flower girl."
"Did she? Mine went as a flour bag."

3134 The visitor was leaving the art museum after an hour's visit. "Well," said the curator proudly, "what do you think of our galleries?" "The pictures are good enough," replied the critic, "but there aren't any jokes under them."

3135 "Last night I kissed a girl against her will."
"Was she annoyed?"
"No, she enjoyed it. But Will was furious."

3136 "My wife is the happiest woman in town at the moment," said one husband to another. The other said: "Is she? And have you found out who it is she's playing around with?"

3137   The busy film executive asked his secretary where his pencil was and she told him it was behind his ear. He snapped: "Come, come, I'm a busy man—which ear?"

3138   "My husband is the only man who has ever kissed me."
"Are you boasting or complaining?"

3139   "I'm not sure whether I'm in love or not."
"It's probably just inflation."

3140   "What kinds of sports do you like?"
"I'm not fussy—blondes, redheads, brunettes. . . ."

3141   "At least Florence dresses like a lady."
"I wouldn't know; I've never seen her dressing."

3142   A magician doing the celebrated trick of sawing a woman in half always used a lot of inane patter. The girl was extremely lovely and her shape was encased in a very clinging little swim-suit. As he began the trick the magician said to the audience: "After the show, this young lady's brain will be presented to the medical world, and the rest of her will not be wasted, it will be thrown to the dogs." Immediately every man in the front row started to bark.

3143   A society lady found herself seated next to an eminent bishop at a dinner party. Hoping to stir up the conversation, she placed the fruit bowl in front of him and said: "Do you like bananas?" The bishop, who was very deaf, cupped a hand to his ear and asked: "What did you say?" "I asked you if you liked bananas." The bishop pondered for a moment and then said: "Well, if you want my honest opinion, I prefer the old-fashioned nightshirt."

3144   Scene in the C.O.'s Office
"So you want leave so that you can get married and go on a honeymoon? How long do you want?"
"Well, how long do you suggest, sir?"
"No good asking me. I haven't seen the girl."

3145   There was a notice in the office which read: "Owing to the fact that clerical staff is difficult to obtain, will all departmental managers please take advantage of their typists early in the day?"

3146   Pop idol Frenzied Freddie's latest disc is terrific. It sounds just as good without a stylus.

3147 The hen went up to the pig and said: "Boy, are you in trouble," and the pig said: "Why?" The hen said: "The farmer is having bacon and eggs for breakfast."

3148 Woman Customer: "I refuse to accept these photographs! My husband looks like a baboon!"
Photographer: "I can't help it, madam. You chose him. I didn't."

3149 "Why did you put me in the same room with that fellow?" asked the indignant patient. "The hospital is crowded," the doctor explained. "He's being troublesome, then?" "Troublesome? He's crazy! Keeps looking around and saying 'No lions, no tigers, no elephants,' and all the time the room is full of 'em."

3150 A stockbroker who had undergone a medical examination for a life insurance policy, received a telegram: "Regret to inform you that your tests show you have pneumonia, heart disease and stomach ulcer." An hour later, however, a second telegram arrived: "Sorry," it said, "first telegram mistake. Confused your examination with another applicant." The patient sent back a telegram in reply: "Too late. Have already committed suicide."

3151 A young woman on the Underground looked up from her book and gasped in surprise. Perched on the shoulders of the man opposite her were a pair of pigeons! The man sat calmly reading his newspaper apparently oblivious to the birds. The girl restrained her curiosity until the train reached her station, then she could wait no longer. "What in the world are those pigeons doing on your shoulders?" she asked. The man looked up, shrugged his shoulders and replied: "Darned if I know. They got on with me at Baker Street."

3152 "Who's the new workman?" asked the visitor.
"Boss's son," said the foreman laconically.
"Oh," observed the visitor with enthusiasm. "Very commendable! Starting at the bottom and working up?"
"No," was the reply. "Started at the top and got shoved down!"

3153 A colony of ostriches—ninety-nine birds in all—had their heads buried neatly in the sand when ostrich number 100 came galloping on to the scene. He looked about in a puzzled way and inquired, "Where on earth is everybody?"

3154 The rogue was making his fortune, and one week-end he had a few pals down to his country place for a bit of relaxation. "I'd like to show you lads a couple of interesting little things," he said, leading them into the drawing-room. "You see these two pictures? I picked 'em up comparatively cheaply. They're masterpieces—old masters—this one's by Constable. The other one's even more valuable. It's by Leonardo da Vinci." "But look," said one of his buddies, "they're both signed 'Ruby' not Constable or Leonardo." "Ah, yes, but I've put everything in my wife's name."

3155   It was pouring with rain when two men who had quarrelled went outside to settle their differences. They fought until one got the other on his back and held him there. "Will you give up?" he asked, and the reply was, "No." After a time the question was repeated, but again the reply was "No." "Then," said the other, "will *you* get on top for a while and let me get under? I'm getting soaked."

3156   Brown was visiting a girl who lived in the country; as they walked through the fields they noticed a cow and a calf rubbing noses in bovine love. He spoke up: "The sight of that makes me want to do the same thing." "Go ahead," she invited. "It's all right, it's father's cow."

3157   The great big beautiful car drew up to the curb where the cute little girl was waiting for a bus, and a gentleman stuck his head out of the window and said: "Hello, I'm driving west." "How wonderful," said the girl. "Bring me back some cider."

3158   A little girl ran to her mother in great excitement—she had come across a pressed maple leaf between the pages of the big family Bible. "Look what I found, Mother," she gasped. "I bet it belonged to Eve."

3159   As the liner docked in New York, the G.I. bride caught sight of her husband holding an armful of beautiful flowers. She dashed down and cried: "How sweet of you, Elmer, to meet me with that lovely bouquet." "Cut it out," said Elmer, "peel off your coat and help sell them."

3160   Two German cyclists were going home along a dark road when one of them accidentally ran over his mother and killed her. Turning to his friend who was holding the two bicycles, the culprit said: "Look, Hans— no Mum."

3161   They are reviving all the old American Western pictures and selling them to British television; last week I saw a Western movie that was so old the Lone Ranger was riding a brontosaurus.

3162   Our neighbours have just had their nineteenth child. It was brought by a duck . . . well, it wasn't really a duck, it was the stork with his legs worn down.

3163   Two houses being built on a new estate collapsed suddenly. Only after an exhaustive inquiry was the cause discovered—seemingly the builders had taken down the scaffolding before putting up the wallpaper.

3164 I spent five months training my dog to be a watchdog; training him to be tough and reliable. Then my wife started to teach him to carry newspapers and her shopping basket. The first time we had burglars what do you think happened? The animal went upstairs and held the torch for the burglars.

3165 He fell in love with a girl and said to her father: "Your daughter is no longer a child and I'd like to marry her." The father said: "Nonsense, when my daughter gets married a proper preacher will do the job." So the fellow said: "You misunderstand me; I want her for my wife!" And Daddy said: "Silly man, what would your wife want with my daughter running around your house?" So the fellow tried again, and said: "Look, what I mean is I'd like your daughter to change her name to mine." And Pop said: "Oh, I don't know, she'd feel silly being called Horace." So after that Horace gave up; he was frightened that the daughter might have inherited her father's brains.

3166 Sam went to the doctor to complain about his insomnia. He told the doc he was sure something was wrong because he kept waking up every two or three days. . . .

3167 A well-known comedian accidentally fell off a ship near Eddystone lighthouse. He almost drowned to death swimming round in circles to keep in the spotlight. . . .

3168 A film star was called to jump seventy feet from a high cliff into some water; before playing this shot he had a look at the water. Angrily he turned to the producer and said: "Are you mad? I have to jump all that way down and you've only given me about eighteen inches of water!" The producer said: "Look, mister, we're paying you forty thousand dollars a week. Do you think we want you to drown before the picture's finished?"

3169 They took a place in town. To the north was the gasworks, to the south was a glue factory, and to the west there was a rubber works. The rent was cheap and they could always tell which way the wind was blowing.

3170 Our advertising manager got the sack. Outside the theatre he had stuck big placards advertising the show: "All Next Week. 'When Irish Eyes Are Smiling'. With a huge cast . . ."

3171 A strip-tease blonde was doing so well at a London night club that she insisted on a raise from £500 to £1,000 a week. The manager snorted: "£1,000 a week? Listen, baby, the president of the biggest oil-distributing company in the country doesn't get £1,000 a week, and he's an experienced old man of 72." The blonde said: "So all right. Get him to come and strip for you."

3172 A fellow took his girl to see the latest Stereocynphonic Cinerama Videoscope at the local pictures. Half-way through the show he felt thirsty and asked an usherette where he could get a drink. She told him: "Go down front, turn right, up the steps, past the red curtains, through the door, turn left and you'll see a door. Go through there, past two palms and into the little room next to the fountain—you'll find a tap." So off he went, trying to remember the instructions, and he got lost, but he did find a stream of water where he quenched his thirst. Struggling back to his seat he apologised to his girl and asked her what had been happening in the picture while he'd been away. She said: "You ought to know—you were in it!"

3173 Once upon a time a Red Indian chief was taking a holiday on the coast of France when a mermaid suddenly popped up in the water and seated herself on the groyne beside him. The young blood gazed at her for a long time and then said in bewilderment: "How!"

3174 A hospital patient had two charts over his bed: one showing how he was getting along with his treatment and another showing how he was getting along with his nurse.

3175 Two men in an art gallery were studying a fine portrait of a Spanish woman. Said the highbrow: "Gosh, it's terrific. Who's the artist?" The other character said: "Never mind the artist—who's the doll?"

3176 We planned to go around the world in eighty hours, by air. We started off by road and about two days later I said to my companion: "How far have we got?" He said: "We'll soon be there now." I said: "Where? Egypt?" He said: "No. The airport."

3177 Have you seen the stupid advertisements which some newspapers print?
Young woman wants washing and cleaning. Rates pretty low.
Wanted, girls; to sew on men's trousers.
Front room to let suitable for two ladies, use of kitchen or two gentlemen.
Wanted, people who suffer from Neuritis, Debility and Rheumatic troubles. Can be destroyed in three days.
Bargains in all departments. Three-day Baby Sale. Save yourself lots of trouble. All accessories reduced.
A better outlook. Widows made to order. State size and other specifications.
Mahogany table wanted by lady with Hepplewhite legs and round shape.

3178 A lugubrious workman was toiling away on top of a partly completed building project when his pal shouted up to him from the street: "Hey, Joe, come on down here. Your wife's just phoned to say you've won seventy-five thousand pounds on the pools." There was a long silence followed by some sort of a commotion above and the messenger, staring upwards yelled: "Hey, Joe, come on! What's keeping you?" Joe shouted back: "Just give me one more minute to finish this off." His pal shouted: "You don't need to finish anything. You're rich." "Look," yelled back Joe, "this I got to finish—it's the foreman."

3179 When he returned from the railway station after seeing his wife off on a six-week trip to Scotland his secretary observed that his hands were dirty. He said: "Yes, I know—I got them all sooty when I was patting the engine."

3180 The wife told the court that although she had broken her umbrella over her husband's head, it was an accident. If she'd known the umbrella would break she would have used one of his golf clubs.

3181 AUNT MAUD'S ADVICE CORNER.
If you want to remember, tie a little string around your finger. If you want to forget . . . tie a long rope round your neck . . .

3182 Before he bought his farm, Harold used to be a motor mechanic. One day he was trying to milk a cow and something went wrong, so he got underneath the cow to see what the trouble was.

3183 And then there's Stanley, the laziest guy you ever met. He's so used to having people do things for him that he even married a widow with four children.

3184 The other day my M.P. stood up in the House and asked a question. The opposition speaker dealt with the question for forty minutes, raising every argument he could think of. It really was a splendid speech, especially considering my M.P. had only asked him the time.

3185 The government is always asking us to do something for posterity. It's about time posterity did something for us.

3186 Have you noticed that almost every high-ranking civil servant is writing a book this year? It would be a lot better for the country if some of them *read* a book for a change,

3187 "I switched on at lunchtime and a horrible noise came from the radio."
"What was it? Static?"
"No—Mid-day Music Hall."

3188   When he was parking his very old and decrepit motor-car a policeman came up and asked him if he had reported the accident.

3189   I went to see a soccer match when I was down south. A chap next to me said: "Do their forwards ever score?" I said: "Don't ask me. I've only been following 'em for three seasons."

3190   Air Hostess (shooting a line to handsome passenger): "And then when we touched down at Istanbul, a most terrible thing happened. A great big fat Turk grabbed me around the waist and dragged me behind the tennis courts . . ."

Man, (in soft English drawl) "I say, how intriguing! And who won the first set?"

3191   First parachutist to one directly underneath as they spin down towards earth: "I say, the pilot said pull the cord . . . I've done that and nothing's happened . . ."

Second parachutist: "Oh yes it has—you pulled the wrong cord and you're unravelling my string underpants."

3192   Air Hostess to passenger: "Why, Mr. Deakins, your face is green and you're trembling all over and your forehead is wet with perspiration! . . . do you suffer from air sickness?"

Deakins: "I know . . . I guess I just can't stand air travel."

Air Hostess: "But, goodness, what are you going to be like when we take off?"

3193   "How far is it from here to Nairobi, then?"

"Oh, I guess it must be about 4,000 miles as the crow flies."

"Heck, do we have to follow a crow all the way?"

3194   Pilot of Charter Plane (setting machine down on airstrip): "Well, there you are, chaps. Safe and sound at San Francisco International Airport —and jolly good time, too."

Passenger (weakly): "But we were supposed to be going to Tangier."

Pilot: "I knew I shouldn't have listened to that chap who showed us the way from Benghazi."

Passenger: "Why not?"

Pilot: "I can't understand Arabic."

3195   Then there was the tall baldheaded soccer player who accidentally headed the ball into his own net. A spectator shrieked: "Hey, Bill—you oughta've chalked yer cue!"

3196   "What does Gladys's new evening dress look like?"

"In a lot of places it looks like Gladys."

3197 "Dick talks a lot of tripe."
"Yes, practically everything he says would make a pop song title."

3198 "What's that big statue outside New York harbour?"
"That's the famous Statue of Liberace."

3199 "Her husband didn't leave her much when he died."
"No, but he left her quite a lot when he was living."

3200 "You were in prison for some years, weren't you? Did you like it?"
"Not much. Just because I once hit a warder with a shovel the governor wouldn't let me attend choir practice."

3201 Two drunken Irishmen were lost in the countryside one dark and dismal night. Groping around for some directions, they found themselves in what appeared to be a graveyard. Mike Murphy was embracing a big tombstone as the other one, Patrick, struck a match to look. "This old girl lived to be a ripe old age, begorah," he said. Mike said: "Can you read her name on the stone?" "Shure," said Pat, peering, "some colleen named Vi Miles from Dublin!"

3202 "When I turned Harry down he went drinking."
"Well he had to celebrate some way."

3203 "He reckons he comes from a good family."
"Bet he's tired—it must've been a hell of a long walk."

3204 He took his wife to the fairground in the evening and as they were standing outside the booth of "The Fattest Lady on Earth" a rough, muscular man nudged the husband threateningly, nodding towards the wife, and said: "Get that dame away from here! We're losing half our business!"

3205 They were on holiday at Southend and Mr. Hopkins was asleep in a deck-chair. His wife nudged him in the ribs and awakened him. She said: "Did you see that! A great big lifeguard walking over the sand carrying a blonde!" Her husband shouted: "What do you expect him to carry at his age? A bucket and spade?"

3206 A chap who couldn't afford to buy a new house spent all his free nights building one for himself. Now it's finished and it's wonderful in the daytime, but all night he has to keep the front and back doors open to let the traffic through to the main highway.

3207 A fellow went to South America exploring and he was shot by a Peruvian Indian with a poison-tipped arrow. That was thirty years ago, and he's just died. From incipient woodworm.

3208   Little Tommy was very fond of his small poodle dog called Paddy. Coming home from school one day his mother tearfully told the kid: "Tommy—you must be brave. I've got bad news for you. Poor Paddy was run over this morning." The child shrugged and asked: "Say, Mom, what's for dinner?" His mother frowned and said: "Didn't you hear me, Tommy? Your lovely little Paddy is dead." Tommy burst into tears and was unconsolable; through his weeping he said: "I thought you said Daddy."

3209   He used to be a butler to Lady Abercrombie. One evening her ladyship was giving a party to some high society friends at the embassy. The butler received a message from the kitchen about the dinner, which her ladyship always used to cook herself. As he sidled alongside her as she sipped her drink he whispered: "Madame, pardon me but your dumplings are boiling over." Her ladyship said: "I know—my shoulder straps broke."

3210   The Army of today offers great improvements upon the Army of yesterday. Most of the spring-loaded muskets have been replaced with automatic longbows, and there is some talk of introducing ammunition, too. The average soldier of today is 5 ft. 8 in. tall, married and has 1¾ children. This is why he needs married *quarters*.

3211   Two St. Bernard dogs were on duty high in the snow-covered Alps with their brandy barrels around their throats. It got rather cold so one of them said to the other: "We don't seem to be finding many customers today and I'm thirsty. How about sampling this stuff ourselves." Forthwith they chewed open the barrels and drank the brandy. One smacked his lips and said to the other: "Y'know something. This stuff's good. No wonder those chaps climb up here to get lost."

3212   A newspaper reporter invited a prominent celebrity to dinner to get a story. Arriving at the house the visitor was alarmed to find that the reporter's big Alsatian dog kept staring at him and growling. He asked: "Is that dog going to bite me?" The reporter whispered back: "No. He'll be all right. But for Pete's sake don't let him know you're an M.P."

3213   The son of a wealthy American had just inherited a fortune from his grandmother, and come down from Harvard. Visiting Britain on vacation, the family put up in a suite at the Ritz. One morning the father was shaving and he called to his son who was just going out: "Hi there, Brad, would you slip out and buy me a newspaper?" The son called back: "Sure will, Pa." An hour later the son came back. Dad was having breakfast. Dad said: "Well, Brad, did you get me that newspaper?" Sonny answered: "Well, I sure tried. They wouldn't sell the Express and I tried Amalgamated Press. The only thing I could buy was some out-of-town thing called *Tooting Gazette*—and you can move in tomorrow."

3214 The managing director of a large retail store specialising in electrical goods was awakened at two o'clock in the morning by a telephone call. The man said: "I called to tell you how much I appreciate your goods and your service. It isn't many stores these days that give such excellent terms and swift attention. I bought a washing machine from you three months ago and it's just about the most splendid bit of apparatus I've ever seen. If you want me to do an advertisement for you, just let me know. My name is Wilkins." The store owner was still half asleep and he muttered, "Mr. Wilkins, do you realise it's the middle of the night? Did you have to wake me up to tell me about something you bought from us months ago?" Wilkins said: "Well, yes. It's just been delivered."

3215 A fellow walked into the bar towing behind him a ragged-hair old pogie with matted mane, bent ears, flat feet and a twisted tail. Ordering his drink he noticed the barman looking askance at the dog. "He's okay," said the customer. "As a matter of fact he's an excellent police dog." The barman was astonished. "That scruffy old mongrel—a police dog?" he scoffed. The customer leaned forward and whispered: "Yes, right now he's in plain-clothes. Secret Service stuff."

3216 Fred is so dim; when Annigoni the Italian painter said he'd been commissioned to paint Lord Ingleberry's wife, Fred asked him if he had to strip her down before starting work.

3217 They were in the garden on a sunny day, taking life easy; the wife got up and shouted very loudly to her husband: "Come along now, Philip, and have your chicken Maryland with new potatoes and troscotto sauce, lemon meringue pie with peach melba and creamed raspberries, with a nice glass of brandy to follow." Her voice echoed against the wooden fence and shook it. Hubby said: "Are you kidding?" She said: "No, I'm just impressing the Joneses, next door. The old cat's got her ear to the fence."

3218 The postman called at a house where an artist had just moved in with his family. The artist was renowned throughout the world for his impressionist and surrealistic daubs; and the hallway was lined with some of the framed pictures. The postman's knock was answered by two small children, one a girl of six named Eva. The postman, trying to show neighbourliness to the new tenants, admired the paintings as he sorted the mail, and muttered as he patted Eva's head: "I see you paint, too, little girl."

3219 Dad was annoyed with the mischief created by Willie's pet terrier. Angrily one evening he remonstrated with his little son and demanded that the dog be got rid of. Next day when he came home he asked Willie: "Well, did you get rid of that perishing dog?" Willie said: "I sure did. I traded him with Oscar from next door for five new puppies."

3220 A truck driver accidentally drove his enormous tipper too far across the edge of a gulley. The weight of the load of rubble on board lifted and the front of the truck went up in the air. His mate said anxiously: "Blimey, Cyril, what are we going to do now?" Cyril studied the situation from all angles before answering: "Well, there'll never be a better opportunity. Get out and grease the front springs and axle."

3221 Albert and his wife decided to visit their friends, a married couple who had recently bought a farm in a remote part of Cornwall. Although they were unexpected, when they reached their destination and knocked on the door at midnight, their friends were delighted to see them. "Stick your car in the barn," said the husband. "You're both very welcome to spend the night here." At four o'clock in the morning, the farm activity started briskly with roosters crowing, tractor engines revving, gates squeaking, dogs barking and the water-pump shrieking. The visitors yawned and got out of bed. The man said to his wife: "Well, it sure didn't take very long to stay all night did it?"

3222 Stan had four dogs. Three of them are worth £4 each but the third is worth £5.00 —yesterday he chewed a pound note.

3223 Coming home late at night, much the worse for strong liquor, he was bedraggled and unsteady, both eyes as bloodshot as Spanish oranges. He explained to his wife that on his way home a man had accosted him, struck him, knocked him over, and forced some terrible strong-smelling liquid between his lips. And she didn't believe him.

3224 John and Frank were talking about the latest best-selling novel. Frank being an author himself, complained that John couldn't possibly appreciate the merits of the book having never written anything for publication in his life. John said: "That's not strictly right. I've never laid an egg but I'm a better judge of a pancake than a hen."

3225 A Hollywood actress celebrated for her revealing charms and numerous former husbands was standing once again before the clergyman, her latest acquisition alongside her, looking ruffled but hopeful. The vicar was very nervous as he had never before conducted a wedding ceremony for a beautiful star. As he fumbled and jittered about with the prayer book, the actress whispered anxiously: "Page seventy-six, you fool."

3226 She said: "The man I marry has got to be versatile, he's got to be able to sing and dance, tell good stories, cheer me up when I'm feeling blue, excite me when I feel the need for it, never smoke or drink, never stay out at night, and he must keep quiet when I say so." Her boy-friend said mildly: "You're not looking for a husband, darling—you need a television set."

3227 Walking up and down the waiting-room at the maternity hospital was a beatnik-type young man, looking worried as he strolled to and fro. He wore a long matted beard, long sideboards, a turtle-neck sweater, baggy trousers, winkle-picker shoes, and looked like something that had been out in a hurricane and hadn't eaten for a fortnight. Eventually the matron of the hospital came into the room and said to him: "Congratulations, Mr. Swinney, your wife has just given birth to a baby."

3228 The pompous old duchess was staying at an expensive hotel in a market town. She beckoned the waiter to her table and said: "I'd like two dozen oysters, grey-blue, not too large, fairly evenly shaped, not too salty and not too fat and make sure they're from Norfolk. I'm in a hurry, and I want them with the chill off." The waiter said: "Yes, m'lady—and do you want them with pearls or without?"

3229 A visitor to a town of four churches asked the vicar of one dying place of worship how things were going. Vicar replied sadly: "Things are far from well with my church, but thank the Lord, the others are doing little better."

3230 A dear old lady was seen to bow every time the preacher mentioned Satan. Later the preacher accosted her and demanded to know why she bowed every time he mentioned Satan. "Well," she said, "politeness costs nothing and one never knows. . . ."

3231 Business is bad because so many people are do-it-yourself fans. Everybody is painting his own house, repairing his own furniture, or painting his wife's nails. To help the do-it-yourself fan make a professional job, brushes have given way to sprays, lambswool rollers and even drip-dry paint that covers everything in one coat—even your overdraft. One fellow is making a fortune out of the do-it-yourself racket. He goes around repairing do-it-yourself paint jobs.

3232 Most of the time he was in the army they had him on K.P. and he mashed about ten thousand tons of potatoes in twelve months. Wore out eight pairs of combat boots doing it.

3233 At the circus he's a fire-eater who puts flaring torches in his mouth and blows flames twenty feet long. But after every meal he's tortured with heartburn.

3234 Customer: Have you a suit to fit my size?
Tailor: The shoulders, yes; but not the stomach.

3235 A tourist was buying a bauble from a jewel merchant in India and he was assured that his rupees were being spent for a rare gem that was worth 100 times the purchase price. The tourist was reaching for his wallet when the merchant, who obviously couldn't read English, made the mistake of proudly exhibiting a letter of recommendation from his last customer. It read: "To Whom It May Concern: This thief took me for over a month's salary. He sold me a sapphire and I sent it to my girl. She sent it back and said: 'I drink gin out of better glass than this!' "

3236   Some fellow told about watching the kids who were playing Wild West. One had made a bar out of a packing-box and scrawled a sign on it. "This is the Wild West and this is the Last Chance Saloon." Another kid swaggered up, pounded on the bar and said: "I'll have a rye." A third, much younger and apparently less sophisticated, swaggered up alongside him and squeaked: "I'll have a whole wheat."

3237   A farmer hired a hand and set him chopping wood. In the middle of the morning the farmer went down to see how the hand was coming along. To his astonishment he found the wood all chopped. Next day the farmer told the man to stack the wood in the shed. This involved a lot of toting and the farmer figured the job would keep the man busy. But by noon he had done it. On the third day the farmer, thinking he had given the man a light job for a change, told him to sort out the potatoes in the bin. "Put the good ones in one pile, the doubtful in another, and throw out the rotten ones," said the farmer. An hour or so later, he went back to see how the job was coming. He found the hired man passed out cold, with virtually nothing done. After throwing water in the man's face and bringing him around, the farmer demanded an explanation. "Hell," the man said wearily, "it's making them decisions that's killing me."

3238   A nondescript hold-up man waylays a gent on the street. "Spare a quid or two, guv'nor, for a poor chap what ain't got nothin' in the world except this 'ere gun?"

3239   Woman: It's my nerves. I need something for my nerves.
Quack: How about this, then? £1.00   a bottle.
Woman: I'll give you 50p for it.
Quack: There's nothing wrong with your nerve, lady.

3240   Salesmanship is a science, an art, a vocation. But selling is hard or easy depending upon the nature of the product; its capacity for filling a demand; its effectiveness; its cost. Some things are easy to sell—like labour-saving devices or money-saving devices. Recently a professor of commercial psychology at Northern Shires University compiled a list of the fifteen things most *difficult* to sell:
In Russia: Life Insurance. (Prohibitive premiums)
In Ghana: Flesh-coloured stockings made in Britain.

In Hungary: Escapist novels. (Banned)
Comprehensive Insurance Cover to Strip-Tease dancers.
A Contemporary World Atlas (it's out of date every week).
In Ireland: Scotch Whisky.
To Orthodox Greek Padres. An electric razor.
To cannibals: Cooking oil. (All whites are boiled in detergents.)
To a Bedouin Arab: Real estate.
To an American showgirl: Reading lamps (they can't read).
To Esquimeaux: Frozen Fish Fingers.
In Alabama: Golliwogs.
The ultimate corrosive: (There's no way to package it.)
To a TV producer: A new idea.

3241 A doctor and a lawyer were arguing over their respective professions. "I don't say that all lawyers are crooks," said the doctor, "but you'll have to admit the profession doesn't make angels of men." "You're right." answered the lawyer. "You doctors certainly have an advantage over us there."

3242 A salesman joined the team of a firm selling a very new and improved form of wound dressing,—Antibiotic Stretchplast, which was just medically impregnated plaster. The stuff sold for £1 a thousand. The salesman complained: "But on commission it will take me a year to make a decent month's salary!" "Not at all," said the manager. "This stuff sticks like hell. The only thing that will shift it is our special Stretchplast Remover, which is £3.50 a small bottle."

3243 Harper worked for a small family business that was rapidly expanding, and being their head salesman he was nagged and nagged by his wife to demand more money from his boss. Plucking up courage one morning he went to the boss's office and said: "I've been with you for ten years, and my sales record shows an annual increase of over 50 per cent. and my wife told me to ask you for a raise." The boss picked up the telephone and called a number and spoke to his wife at home. Then he put down the 'phone, shrugged and said to Harper: "These wives! Mine says *no*."

3244 The three business men had finished their meal and the bill was presented. "I'll pay," said Mr. Smart. "With income tax at 90p in the pound it will cost me only half."

"No, I'll pay," said Mr. Clever. "It will come out of E.P.T. and will cost me nothing."

"Certainly not," said Mr. Best, "I'll pay. We work on a cost-plus basis, and this will show me a profit."

3245 A despondent salesman, known to his colleagues as a congenitally lazy individual, was so discouraged by his sales record for July that he sought an interview with the area manager. He arrived impeccably dressed, closely shaven, white cuffs gleaming with smooth starch and clipped with diamond-studded links. He told the manager: "I don't understand it; I dress better than the others, I speak better English than the others, I'm more educated than the others. I mix with a better class of people, and I know our product inside out. Yet my figures are four thousand pounds below the average for the month. Where am I going wrong?" The manager said: "Your appearance and good manners are excellent, Mr. Young, but if I were you, I'd get rid of that thick solid gold wristwatch with the thick solid gold expanding bracelet and buy yourself a cheap but accurate alarm clock."

3246 Every salesman on the force received an office memo from the area manager reading: "Recently there has been too much comment circulating about the basic salaries of individual salesmen in this district. Your salary is a very personal affair and should not be disclosed to anyone else." One salesman wrote a note back to the manager in protest: "Dear Mr. Smith, re your memo, I assure you I am not guilty of the indiscretion you accuse me of. I'm just as much ashamed of what I'm getting as you are."

3247 Judge: "You are sentenced to four years' hard labour and then deportation. Have you anything to say?"
Accused: "Yes, I would like to do the deportation part of the sentence first."

3248 Woman: Is this stuff guaranteed?
Quack: Of course, it's guaranteed.
Woman: What if it poisons you and you die?
Quack: It can't. I never take it.
Woman: I mean if *I* take it and it poisons me and I die.
Quack: That's when the guarantee comes into effect. We give your husband half the money back for the rest of the bottle.

3249 Elderly bespectacled spinster books room at lush resort hotel. The porter shows her up to her room: "Heavens," she complains, studying her surroundings, "this is horrible. Hardly enough room to turn round, and the bed's as hard as nails. . . ." The porter says: "This is the lift, madam, fasten your safety belt, we're taking off."

3250 A Polish refugee goes to the eye hospital for a test. Seated in front of the chart, the doctor asks him to go through the lines one at a time. As he gets to the bottom line which reads C S V E N C Z W he hesitates. The doctor says: "Don't look so worried. If you can't read it, just try your best." The refugee says: "Read it? But I *know* the feller personally."

3251 The two travellers had wandered far from civilisation and had fallen into the hands of a savage chief. The day following their capture the chief ordered them to go out and gather fruit. The first returned, bearing a plentiful supply of grapes. The chief commanded him to swallow them whole. The traveller burst into laughter, and the chief demanded to know the reason. "Sorry," he said, "I was just thinking of my pal. He's bringing coconuts."

3252 The manager and assistant manager of a new branch are instructed to hire a departmental secretary. They advertise and screen applicants' letters down until the final selection is three. Interviews are arranged. Mr. Brown and Mr. Smith, the interviewers, take the appointments together. The first girl, dark little brunette with sparkling eyes, has a marvellous figure, nice long legs; thirty certificates for proficiency and is willing to learn. She goes out to wait while the next girl is interviewed. No. 2 is a ravishing big blonde, well built, wearing a swollen sweater and slacks which outline her beautiful body; she has twenty-five certificates for proficiency and a personal recommendation from Mr. Pitman, plus a medal from Mr. Gregg. Having interviewed her, both the assistant manager and the manager are perspiring. She goes out to wait while they interview the third applicant. No. 3 comes in. She is tall, thin, spindly-legged, flat-chested, wears horn-rimmed spectacles, a straight black skirt, frilled blouse, and bites her nails. She has only had four typing lessons and her shorthand is so bad that she can write quicker with a paintbrush. She has no personality and is very cross and ill-mannered, with no time whatever for the male sex in managerial positions. She goes out to wait while the interviewers add up the score. Mr. Brown, the manager, says to Mr. Smith: "Well? What's the verdict?" Smith says: "I reckon it's a toss-up between the blonde and the brunette, unless we can have a secretary each. But you're the manager, so what you say goes." The manager shrugs and says: "Okay. That's settled then." Smith asks: "Which one are you taking?" Brown says: "That last one." The assistant manager stares at him as if he's mad. "Look," he says, "are you crazy or something? That dry-haired, shapeless, untrained atrocity?" Brown says: "She's got the best qualifications of the lot—she's the boss's niece."

3253 High sales figures are not necessarily the only way to the top of the ladder. Michael Mercer worked for the Eureka Amalgamated Spinwasher Corporation, and although he was a smart, handsome, eligible young man, his heart was not in his work at all. So one morning the area manager called him to his office and pointed to the wall-map which showed the locations of all the sales force throughout the country. Intent upon giving the young man something to worry about, the area manager indicated various pins in the map, each marked with a small banner showing whom it represented. "This is Phelps up in Manchester. He did ten thousand above quota last year. This is Yates, in Nottingham—won the firm's free holiday for topping fifteen thousand in three months. This is Phillipson—just promoted to area manager in the North-East. And this, Mercer, is you," proceeded the manager, lightly fingering the pin in the chart. "Just to indicate how precarious your position is with the firm, I'm going to lightly loosen your pin a little, Mr. Mercer, and I hope you get the point, if you'll pardon the pun." Mercer smiled amiably and stretched out his hand, removed his pin from the map and stuck it into his lapel. "It's good to see you're so efficient, yet so charming, Mr. Woods," Mercer said. "Keep it up. I won't be working Sussex after this week. I'm getting married to the managing director's daughter on Thursday. I'll bear you in mind if we need a replacement for Sussex."

3254 Two men finished their drinks at the tavern, said good-bye to their friends and began the forty-mile drive to the city. After a while one of them observed: "We're gettin' closer to town." "What makes you think so?" countered the other. "Well," reasoned the first, "we're hittin' more people."

3255 The Judge looked sternly down and inquired reasonably: "What exactly is the charge against this man?"

"He's charged with cruelty to his wife. She says he spent a whole afternoon throwing oak leaves at her . . ." reported the prosecuting solicitor.

"Well," mused the Judge, "I don't think that's particularly serious: there's nothing much wrong with a husband playfully throwing oak leaves at his own wife."

"Maybe not," said the solicitor, "but these were from the dining-room table."

3256 The farmer bought an expensive, gleaming new black Super-Magna limousine out of his profits. It was equipped with all the latest modern gadgets, such as heater, demister, triple horns, cocktail cabinet, twin fog-lamps, radio, rimbellishers and a speaking-tube from the back to the driver's seat. After he had had the car in use for a couple of weeks, the manufacturers wrote, as they did to all users of that particular model, asking what feature of the car the farmer was most impressed with. He replied: "The window you can wind up between the front and rear seats."

A representative called to ask why.

"Well," the farmer told him, "it's loike this 'ere. When I'm takin' them theyer pigs to market, it stops 'em breathin' darn me neck, see."

3257 She was involved in a divorce action and when it came to the tricky bit about the hotel she replied to the lawyer's question by saying: "And in any case, it wasn't really my fault. He deceived me."

"In what way," asked the lawyer, "did he deceive you?"

"Well," she said, "he told the reception clerk I was his wife."

3258 A former undergraduate returned to his old college as a highly successful doctor. He was to lecture to the medical students in the evening but spent the day joyfully exploring the college and noting what changes had taken place. Eventually he came to his old room and knocked. There was a slight pause and then a rather harassed young man threw open the door. The doctor explained about it being his old room and was reluctantly invited in. Glancing around he said: "Ah, the same old fireplace. The same old wardrobe over there! Nothing is changed." He glanced out of the window and said: "Yes, and the same old view from the same old window."

Just then the wardrobe door creaked open and before the undergrad could push it to again, a slim young woman was visible among the hanging coats.

Red-faced the undergrad said: "Oh, doctor, this is my sister, Edna."

The doctor smiled a greeting and murmured: "Even the same old story."

3259 The timid little guy walked uncertainly into the Loan Office and observed: "I'd like to borrow fifty pounds. I'm thinking of getting married."

The usurer remarked: "Fifty pounds isn't much to get married on."

"The fifty," explained the potential client, "is for getting my head examined.

3260 They were holding their Annual General Meeting in the lavishly appointed walnut-and-maple Board Room and every Director was smoking a huge cigar. The Chairman informed them: "As I see it, gentlemen, the success of this corporation is so vital to the country's export programme that it is our solemn duty to cook the books for Tax purposes."

3261 Kelly returned from America with a brilliant idea. He had made over twenty thousand pounds in six months. Bill asked him how he did it.

"Well," he said, "I merely adapted an idea from the juke box."

Bill said: "But that's ridiculous. There's nothing new about juke boxes, and the competition must be terrific."

"It is," he admitted. "The competition is wonderful. Everybody is selling juke boxes. That's why I'm making a fortune. You see, I sell a small gadget which fixes on top of the disc-mounting."

"What kind of gadget?" Bill asked him.

"Another slot. You put sixpence in it, and it stops the juke box playing."

3262 At a recent Stationery Exhibition at a large hotel in London there was an engagingly beautiful young girl wearing a very chic cocktail gown with a V-front that was almost two parallel lines. She would go up to a buyer and whisper seductively: "How about slipping up to my room for half an hour?" They all succumbed. In her room there was a very large display of the latest stationery cabinets. She was the Manufacturer's Sales Manageress.

3263 "In order to pay for my upbringing, my mother did fancy-work," explained the actor who was now on the way to fame and wished to boast of his hard struggles. "And to educate me, my mother did fancy-work . . ."

"Look," inquired a reporter, "you had a father, didn't you? What about him?"

The actor said blandly: "Oh him. He just *didn't* fancy work."

3264 The boss of a small Independent film-producing company decided to make a super-colossal epic in technicolor based on the Battle of Agincourt. His partner exclaimed: "Sol, it's a wonderful idea, but, heck, the cost! We'll need at least five thousand extras—English and French! The wage-bill will be enormous. . . ."

"That's all right," replied the boss. "I already thought of that. For the shooting of the final battle scene we'll dip the arrows in poison.

3265 It was well known at the club that Mr. Grimwald had a memory like that of a plumber's mate. His wife was notorious for the things she did to help him remember important meetings, appointments and so forth. One evening he appeared in the clubroom with a piece of crimson ribbon tied round his finger. He explained to his questioners: "My wife put the ribbon there to remind me to post a letter for her."

"And did you remember?"

"Sure," said Grimwald. "But she forgot to give it to me."

3266 A man jumped into a first-class railway carriage just as the train started. Breathlessly he collapsed into a seat. Then he looked across the carriage and saw a man sitting there, with a dog right beside him. The dog was a St. Bernard with big, sad eyes, and his muzzle was completely wrapped around with sticking plaster.

"What's the idea of the plaster round his muzzle?" he asked the dog's owner. "Does he bite or something?"

"No," snapped the owner. "But he keeps telling shaggy dog stories."

3267 Once upon a time there was a very dear old lady who loved animals so much she used to spend the winter knitting woollen pullovers for the sheep to wear after they were shorn.

3268 "The workmen are demanding shorter hours," explained the foreman to the boss.

"That's all right, humour 'em," said the boss. "Knock ten minutes off their fifteen-minute morning break and trim down their lunch-hour to three-quarters."

3269 Because of the increase in thefts from the expansive building site, special police were drafted to watch all the gates. One evening a workman walked through the north gate pushing a wheelbarrow piled high with straw. The policeman accosted him and carefully probed through the straw with a stick, seeking stolen materials. But there was nothing there except the worthless straw.

The following evening, as the whistle blew, the same workman again marched through the gate pushing a wheelbarrow laden with straw. Again the policeman poked and probed with his stick, found nothing suspicious, and let the man through. This routine went on for six weeks. The project was completed and the men were paid off. The policeman at the north gate was retiring, so the workman invited him across the road for a drink. After a few glasses of beer, the ex-policeman said: "Y'know, I always thought there was something suspicious about you—going out of my gate every night with that straw. I think I owe you an apology."

"That's all right," the workman assured him. "As a matter of fact the straw was just a ruse. Every night for the last six weeks I took home a brand-new wheelbarrow."

3270   The miserable able-seamen stood on the carpet before the commander, accused of being absent without leave. They were three very rugged, very tough-looking sailors, broad and husky, and each had a couple of days' growth of wild and wiry black beard.

The commander snorted: "Well, what have you got to say for yourselves?"

The younger of the three burly men said: "It was my fault, sir. I went and got meself married."

The commander turned to the other two and snapped: "And did you two make equal fools of yourselves, or have you some other stupid excuse?"

"Nah, we wasn't married," replied one of them. "We was just Nobby's bridesmaids."

3271   Smith was telling some friends about the girl he loved. Then he confessed: "I wanted to marry her but her family objected."

"You mean her father and mother didn't like you?"

"Oh *they* didn't mind me, it was her husband and three children who spoiled things."

3272   A couple of happy Irishmen went to the county fair and each bought a horse. So that they could distinguish between the two horses, O'Leary suggested that O'Brien should cut off his horse's tail. This was done, but overnight a local wag named Mulligan broke into the stables and clipped the tail off the other horse. Next morning O'Brien and O'Leary bothered about this, so they decided to shave off the mane of O'Leary's horse. This was done. But overnight, the wag Mulligan again broke into the stables and this time he shaved the mane off O'Brien's horse. In the morning O'Leary and O'Brien noticed that both horses were without manes. O'Brien said to O'Leary, "Look, Mike, I've had enough of this. You have the white horse and I'll take the grey mare."

3273 A pompous official of the Ministry of Agriculture called upon a Midland farmer who also happened to be the oldest inhabitant of the district. Asserting his bureaucratic authority he told the farmer that all the livestock on the farm would have to be branded forthwith. Two months later the official called again. Inquiring as to progress with the branding, he was told by the farmer: "Things is goin' fine but I might tell ye we'm had a basinful of trouble with them thar bees over yonder."

3274 An impresario toured the whole of Scotland searching for a Scottish singer for a new musical show. Finally he returned without success to London.

"Do you mean to say there wasn't one singer in all Scotland?" asked his partner.

"Not one," grumbled the impresario. "I guess they're all somewhere else, singing about it."

3275 The American farmer was telling his grandchildren about his early struggles. "Usedta git up at half-four in the mornings and work on the big hunk of territory all day, sometimes till eleven or twelve at night, working by torchlight, day after day for years and years. . . ."

"Gee, Gramps," said one of the impressed kids, "and is that why we're all so rich now?"

"Waal," said Grandpa, "not exactly. Y'see one day when I was jest about to sell up an' go back to the city, comes along a guy with some kind of gadget and finds oil on me land."

3276 A pretty young college girl was being escorted around the big industrial plant to gather information for an article for her college mag. When she saw the whirling turbines she said: "Gosh, that sure makes me think of men." The foreman said nothing and took her to see a vast machine which was a threshing mass of intricate cogs and pistons. She said: "Gee, that sure makes me think of fellers."

"Look, Miss," said the foreman, "I'm showing you our plant and all you can say is it makes you think of men. Why should all this make you think of men?"

"I never think about anything else," she explained.

3277 As the outside representative for a northern firm of toilet-requisite manufacturers, Herbert Forstairs had often stayed at a certain hotel in Brighton when working on the South Coast. Having recently married he not unnaturally thought of the same hotel as a good place for the honeymoon. On the first evening there he ordered a chicken dinner for the two and there was some delay with service.

He beckoned the waiter, whom he knew quite well, and asked briskly: "Where the deuce is my chicken?"

"Sorry, Mr. Forstairs," replied the waiter, "if you mean the blonde with the beauty spot on her shoulder, she was fired a couple of weeks after you were last down here."

3278 Mrs. Rosencrun was perplexed at the sight of her neighbour, Mr. Goldmintz sitting for hours on end on the doorstep, resting his chin in his hands and staring thoughtfully at the ground. She watched him continue this caper for many hours on several different days until her curiosity could no longer be checked. She accosted Mrs. Goldmintz and said: "What's wid Isaac your husband—sitting there brooding so long?"

"Him? He ain't brooding," replied Mrs. Goldmintz. "Training he is—practising for the chess tournament next Friday."

3279 Old McTavish had a terrific row with his wife and in a fit of temper, slouched out of the house and slammed the door so hard that a picture fell on to the hall floor.

He stayed away for fifteen years and then, one day, stricken with remorse, he walked back into the house and stood in the doorway leading to the living-room. His wife turned and stared at him.

"And where the heck have you been?" she asked crushingly.

"Out," he said, with smarting brevity.

"Well, pick that picture up," she commanded, "and let's have none of your tantrums."

3280 An able-bodied seaman was so conceited he joined the Navy to let the world see him.

3281 The following discussion was overheard at a table in a saloon bar where two middle-aged men were chatting.

"Sam, did you hear about what happened to Mac?"

"No, Fred. What?"

"Dropped dead, he did. Outside a pub."

"Gosh. Going in or coming out?"

"Going in."

"What lousy luck!"

3282 Mr. and Mrs. Morris were staying at an hotel on the South Coast. They had been there a couple of days and had got to know one or two people. Over dinner one evening Morris turned to another guest and said: "I've been here some days now, and what beats me is why they call this place The Palms Hotel. There isn't a palm within miles."

The other guest said: "Wait till the morning you're leaving and the staff lines up by the door."

3283 The chief gate-keeper at the City football ground rang through to one of the directors and said: "The referee has just arrived with two friends who haven't got passes. Can they come in?"

"No," snapped the director. "There's something fishy about them. It's a confidence trick."

"How do you know?" said the gate-keeper, "you haven't even seen them."

"No," admitted the director over the phone, "but did you ever know *any* referee who had two friends?"

3284 Cynical husband, explaining about his wife being late: "She won't be very long now. I left her in front of the mirror, clocking on."

3285 Two American visitors were being guided around the stately home of the Dukes of Crumbleigh; one of the visitors was the inevitable dim blonde. In the museum room facing the extensive lawns there were several human skulls exhibited in a glass case. "Who's skull is that?" asked the blonde, pausing to stare at one of the exhibits in fascinated surprise. The old butler, a family retainer who intensely resented the idea of throwing the mansion open to inquisitive proletarians replied: "The Second Duke, Madam. He died of an infected lance wound in 1567." "And the smaller one next to it, Mac?" inquired the blonde. The butler sniffed and said: "*Also* the Second Duke's, Madam. When he was a child."

3286 Secretary: "My fiancé lost all his money speculating on the Stock Exchange."

Boss: "I bet you feel sorry for him."

Secretary: "Oh yes. He must miss me an awful lot."

3287 A very worried-looking little man consulted a doctor who examined him microscopically and then announced that there seemed to be nothing organically wrong.

"But," complained the patient, "I'm worried sick. All I do all day is worry and worry."

"What you need is a little change," the doctor suggested.

"I need more than a little change," the patient corrected, "It's big money I need. I'm practically bankrupt."

3288 He said to the dentist: "I want all my teeth out. Can you help me?"

"Certainly," said the dentist.

"Okay," said the patient, handing him a pawn ticket. "Just pay the fifty pence and get them out of hock for me."

3289 Two prisoners were escorted to the rock-pile where a warder supervised the distribution of picks. Then he snapped: "Right. There's the rock. Split it." The warder went away. One of the men started work, slamming away furiously at the rock while the other one just stood around watching him and toying with his finger-nails. For twenty minutes the pick-wielder attacked the big stone, and then he turned and said sarcastically: "Hi—come on! Didn't you hear the screw say we had to split this goddamned rock?" "Aw," grunted the other. "I don't want no part of it. You can have my split."

3290   As he was passing the bend of a narrow but deep river in the heart of Warwickshire where he was on holiday, an Irishman named O'Cohen saw a man throw himself into the water. He dived in and pulled the man out. The stranger immediately thrust O'Cohen aside and threw himself back into the river. Unable to stand by and see a man commit suicide, the Irishman went to the rescue again, and once more hauled the man out of the water. As soon as his saviour had turned his back, however, the would-be suicide hanged himself from a tree nearby. At the inquest shortly afterwards the coroner demanded to know why O'Cohen had not cut the poor man down. "Shure," argued O'Cohen, "and I was after thinkin' the onfortunate character had pegged himself out to dry the same as meself."

3291   Frank met a friend in the bar and apologised for not turning up for an appointment they had had the previous afternoon. "You see," Frank explained, "I had to go with my wife to an auction. She wanted me to get something for her." "Oh? And how much did she fetch?" he was asked.

3292   Bentham had been an insurance agent all his life, and knowing something about risks had hesitated long before deciding to get married. But Camelia was the sort of girl he couldn't resist. He simply had to marry her, and he was so anxious to tie the knot speedily that they arranged a Register Office wedding. Unfortunately the happy couple arrived at the Registry just as they were closing on Saturday morning. "Sorry," said the Registrar. "Can't do anything for you till after the week-end." "Aw heck," groaned the insurance agent. "Look, how about this: give us a cover note until Monday."

3293   Towards the end of the party, when it was growing late, the hostess remembered that one of her guests was reputed to have a soprano voice. So she asked her to sing. "But isn't it getting too late?" the soprano suggested wearily, "I wouldn't like to give your neighbours cause for complaint." "Oh, never mind them," replied the hostess, "Anyway, their wretched dog barks nearly all night."

3294   The proprietress of a flourishing model gown house in London was entertaining some business acquaintances at *Le Chat Noir*, a French restaurant-club in the West End. When the time came for settling up, she beckoned

a waiter over and whispered confidentially into his ear: "*Et maintenant,
l'addition s'il vous plait, garcon.*" "Oh yus," the waiter whispered back. "Yer
can't miss it, lady—fird door on the right, dahnstairs."

3295   The well-dressed patient in the private sanatorium was given the
usual periodical examinations by a visiting psychiatrist. On that particular
day the psychiatrist remarked an improvement in the man's condition and
informed him that he might not have to remain in the hospital much longer.
He promised to examine him again on the following Monday and if the
improvement was maintained, the patient would be discharged. Twenty
minutes later, as the doctor was leaving the asylum and walking across the
drive to his large new car, an accurately-aimed chamber pot struck him
behind the ear. He turned angrily and was surprised to see the same patient
grinning down at him from a seventh-storey window, shouting: "Hi there!—
you!—don't forget Monday."

3296   This story is told about the large Birmingham firm of manufacturers
with branches throughout the world. One morning an air-mail letter
arrived from the Sahara branch and the assistant manager rushed into the
Director's office waving the message urgently. He shouted: "Our Sahara
branch is in trouble again—the staff have no water." The pompous Director
snapped: "That's nothing new—they are always complaining about being
short of water. Only last month we sent them a new tank." "Well it's serious
this time," insisted the manager, "the stamp on their letter is stuck on
with a staple."

3297   Mr. Dick Fisher had spent eighteen years touring the world in search
of adventure. One fine day he returned to his home town after this long
absence, eager for the sight of old friends and familiar faces, His eyes lit
up when he recognised the station-master as someone he had known quite
well in his younger days. Grasping his bag he chased along the platform,
caught the station-master by the arm and cried: Hello! Hello!" The station-
master turned, smiled, looked at the bag and then said cheerfully: "Well,
hello Dick! Going away?"

3298   Due to the shortage of eggs Harold hadn't had a decent breakfast
for months. One day his wife came home from having tea with a former
schoolfriend who was married to a builder; the builder kept a few hens and
had given her a couple of eggs.

   With a flourish she set the table for breakfast next morning, and when
Harold sat down she put an egg in front of him. He attacked it hungrily,
but found it rather solid.

   "This egg's as hard as a brick!" he complained.

   "Well!" his wife breathed in distress. "That's the last time I get eggs
from a bricklayer."

3299 Two young men who worked for the local undertaker were passing a notice outside the Town Hall when they read that there was a big gala dance taking place there that night. One turned to the other and said: "Say, Syd, how about me and you going to this dance?"

"I'm game," Syd answered, "if we can dig up a couple of girls."

A cynical friend of theirs who was also passing at the same time overheard this conversation and said to them: "While you've got your spades out get me one, too."

3300 This is the story of a brilliant advocate who had a reputation for turning the tables on his legal adversaries. He was appealing for damages for a client who had been run down by a very expensive limousine.

"Gentlemen," he said, "the driver of the car has argued that at the time of the mishap he was only travelling at three miles an hour. Imagine it, gentlemen. The unbearable agony of my unfortunate client as the car drove with pitiless slowness over his tortured and racked body . . ."

3301 There was a family crisis. The pretty teenage daughter of the house was clamouring for permission to wear a low-cut off-the-shoulder cocktail gown to her first big dance and Mother reasoned that for a seventeen-year-old the dress was much too sophisticated. The controversy raged for hours until Father arrived home. Then Pop put in his two-cents' worth of sense. "Listen," he grunted, "let her try the durned frock on and if it stays up she's old enough to wear it."

3302 Just after midnight, two cats were sleeping in their basket in the kitchen of their mistress's apartment on the first floor when they were awakened by the noise of a couple of drunks outside in the street, singing a duet out of key. The two cats slinkily raised themselves from the basket, sloped over to the window, opened it and threw a bucket of water over the drunks.

3303 Up to the farmhouse door mooched a tramp. When he knocked on the door a good-looking woman answered.

She snapped at him: "Young man, you look well enough and strong enough to be working down a mine, yet here you are wasting your life and begging for tea and cake."

"Yes, lady, it looks that way," he answered. "And take yourself now. You look beautiful enough to be in moving pictures, yet here you are wasting your time working on a farm."

"Just a minute," she said with a blush. "I'll see if the kettle's boiled."

3304 The landlord was interviewing a young couple in connection with the flat he had just offered to them. The tour of inspection over, the landlord started to ask them the inevitable questions:

"Any children?"

"No," said the husband.

"Any animals? Cats, dogs?"

"No," said the wife.

"Do you have a radio, or television?"

"No, sir," they said in unison.

"Very well. I think you'll do," the landlord said reluctantly. "Just sign this lease."

The husband leaned across the table, and began to sign his name on the document. The landlord suddenly snatched the paper away and cried wrathfully: "Smartie, huh? Why didn't you tell me your pen scratched?"

3305   Prodnose inquired of Saunders: "What would you do if you were lost on a distant desert isle, and felt lonely?"

"I guess I'd take a pack of cards along, and play patience," Saunders answered, "then while I was playing you can bet some busybody would come up behind me and say, 'Why don't you put that red queen on that black jack?'"

3306   Here is a rustic tale about an old farmer who, after many struggles and setbacks succeeded in raising and marketing a dozen fat pigs. After the sale he sat down with a pencil and notebook and laboriously figured out how he stood in relation to expenditure. The final assessment indicated a total dead loss of £25, He leaned back thoughtfully, sucked the end of his pencil and sighed fitfully: "Aye, aye . . . anyway, they wus grand company."

3307   A friend with a quaint sense of humour sent Pat O'Reilly a birthday present: it was a cuckoo clock and it was sent through the post. A conscientious P.O. clerk heard the package ticking and forthwith immersed it in a tank of water, convinced that he had prevented a violent explosion. In due course the error was discovered and the parcel was sent on its way with an apology from the Postmaster-General. And now Pat is the only Irishman in London who has a cuckoo clock with a cuckoo that pops out every hour and gargles.

3308   In Hungary three dispirited political prisoners were shackled in a dank, gloomy cell discussing the mystery of their arrests. The first one exclaimed: "I was arrested because I said I was in favour of Shloboskovitch." The second one remarked: "That's very odd: I was arrested because I was overheard to say that I hated Shloboskovitch's guts!"

There was a slight pause and when the third prisoner was asked to comment he said drily: "I am Shloboskovitch."

3309 An Arab tribesman was leading a caravan across the Sahara when he sighted a solitary figure struggling gamely through the soft sand: a man wearing a pair of swimming trunks.

"Where are you going?" the Arab asked.

"I'm going for a swim," explained the stranger, whom the Arab now recognised as a Foreign Legionnaire rookie.

"Swim?" repeated the Arab. "But there is no sea for hundreds and hundreds of miles!"

"So I've noticed," the legionaire admitted. "They told me back at the barracks that the tide goes out a long way."

3310 "What you need," the doctor told his patient, Fisby, "is something to give you strength. Try drinking stout."

Fisby bought a barrel of stout and wedged it up on the floor in his bedroom. A couple of weeks later he rang the doctor.

"Well, how's the treatment going?" asked the Doc.

"Fine," said Fisby. "When I first got the barrel I couldn't even lift it single-handed, and now after two pints a day I've got so much strength I can carry it all round the room."

3311 Very disgruntled, the customer walked into the showroom of the second-hand car dealer and said to the head salesman: "Say, can you remember selling me a car last week?"

"Yes. I remember you," the salesman admitted.

"Good," said the customer. "Would you mind going over that sales-talk routine once more? I'm getting a bit discouraged."

3312 In a certain section of town, night-watchmen were attacked fairly regularly by cosh-gangs raiding warehouses. Things got so bad that the watchmen all chipped in with contributions to a fund for hiring watchmen to watch them.

3313 The diminutive lift-attendant grew sick and tired of constantly being asked the time, so he bought a cheap clock and hung it on the wall of the cage. Thereafter he was pestered by folks who kept asking him, "Is that clock fast?" In disgust he took down the clock and threw it away. And now he gets awfully tired of folks asking him what happened to the little old clock that used to hang up in the lift.

3314 At the New Year festivities sweet young Felicity Manders nudged the handsome young man beside her and giggled: "I know—let's all play Jockey's Knock?"

The young man inquired: "What's Jockey's Knock?"

She told him: "It's just the same as Postman's Knock, with a bit more horseplay."

3315 The Council received a petition from a number of local people deploring the shortage of houses in the borough. It was signed by twenty-nine burglars.

3316 The absent-minded atomics professor was so busy on a new formula that he missed dinner at home two nights running. His wife, worried about his health made a point of ringing him at the research station the next night and reminded him to be home for dinner at eight.

"Very well, dear," said the professor absently. "I'll be there. What's the address?"

3317 The amateur dance band was at rehearsal. Suddenly the conductor moved across to the window and leaned out to listen. He was the eldest son of the house where they practised, and the outfit rehearsed three evenings a week. As he pulled his head back inside the room he remarked happily: "Gee! We must be getting better."

"Why?" asked the weedy-looking clarinetist.

"Because the neighbours are bawling 'Turn that damned radio down!' "

3318 The dumb blonde was being escorted around the Homes and Gardens Exhibition by a reporter. They came to the landscape section where there was a very elegant sundial on a marble pedestal. The blonde eyed this curiously for several moments and then asked the reporter what it was supposed to be. He patiently explained that it was a sundial and that the sun's shadow indicated the time of day.

"My, my," the blonde exclaimed. "Always somethin' new, ain't there! I bet this will make the electric clock a back-number in no time at all!"

3319 Two men had shops in different parts of the town. Both were watchmakers and jewellers. Harry met Micky in a pub one Saturday evening.

Said Harry: " 'Lo, Mick. How you feeling?"

"Run down," said Mick. "How's business, Harry?"

"Wound up," said Harry.

3320 The psychiatrist told his patient: "I'm afraid you'll have to give up smoking."

"Injurious, huh?" asked the patient.

"Very," replied the psychiatrist. "You've set my couch alight three times this month."

3321 A young, recently married couple chose to stay on holiday at a small, obscure, country hotel. On the first evening there the wife went up to bed leaving her young husband watching television in the lounge. When he finally got around to retiring, the landing was in darkness and he had difficulty in finding his way around the building. After a half-hour of fumbling about in the dark he thought he had found the right door. He knocked and whispered: "Honey! Honey!" There was no reply. He whispered again, urgently. Then a gruff voice growled from the other side: "Look, don't be an idiot. This is the bathroom, not a beehive."

3322 A burglar crawled in through a window he had carefully broken, and then spent half an hour exhaustively searching the lower floor for loot without success. There was no money, no silver; not even the dregs of any liquor in the cheap glass decanter in the sideboard. Gradually he grew more and more despondent. Finally he mooched upstairs and looked in all the bedrooms until he found one room where a couple were in bed. He shook the man until he woke him.

"Say," asked the burglar, "are you the owner of this house?"

"Yes," said the astonished householder.

"Well, what d'you mean by wasting my ruddy time?" the burglar demanded warmly.

3323 Into the consulting room walked Dr. Lullerton's best patient.

"Well, hello there, Mr. Graham. I haven't seen you for *months*!"

"No," said Graham. "I've been very ill."

3324 An English missionary in Africa was captured by cannibals. As they were preparing him for the evening meal he called the chief over to his stake and asked to borrow a knife. With the sharp blade he cut a slice off his thigh and offered it to the cannibal chief as a sample. The chief chewed it for a moment and then spat it out in disgust. Not relishing the white man for dinner, the chief gave orders for him to be released and history records that the man lived happily among the tribe of cannibals until he died at the age of ninety-six. It was only then that the cannibals discovered that their white friend had a cork leg.

3325 At the little village general store there was a so-called sub post office. One day a very pompous official walked into the store and introduced himself as a Post Office Inspector. He criticised the storekeeper for inefficiency, incompetence and indolence, and threatened to report him to the postal authorities. The old storekeeper dug under the counter and pulled out a tin box. Removing five penny stamps and a handful of coins he thrust the lot at the Inspector and growled: "Look, take your perishing post office and get to hell out of my shop!"

3326 Foster was a very wealthy man and a heavy sleeper. Awakened one night as he lay asleep in the four-poster bed in the vast bedroom of his country mansion he was surprised to find his valet shaking him by the shoulder.

"Yes, Maltravers? What time is it?"

"Midnight, sir," said the valet in a hushed whisper. "I'm sorry to wake you, but I can hear strange noises coming from the library downstairs. I'm afraid there are burglars."

Foster casually eased himself out of bed. "Very well, Maltravers," he drawled. "Get me a decent 12-bore gun and lay out my hunting gear."

3327 The lieutenant of the submarine was being briefed by his commander. "And now, Clingsby, I shall hand you this envelope which contains your sealed orders and your destination. Let me impress upon you once more that your mission is so vitally secret that this envelope containing your orders is not to be opened until you get there."

3328 A radio review in the paper said that for once the BBC had put a programme on television which was so realistic it had brought tears to the eyes of millions of viewers. Reading this, a non-viewer inquired of a neighbour what the title of the play was and if he could pop round to see it if it was repeated.

"No play," explained the TV owner. "It was just the announcer showing how to make an onion salad."

3329 A couple of drunks were discussing the different merits of the beauties of English and Swiss landscapes. One of the drunks, Chumley, was avidly patriotic. He remarked: "I don't know that there's anything remarkable about Switzerland's scenery. After all, take away all those lakes and the mountains, and what have you got?"

3330 "And at the hotel where you stayed," asked Mrs. Pomeroy, "did they have hot and cold water?"

"Indeed they did," Mr. Taggerty assured her. "The hot water was served up in the dining-room as soup and the cold water was dished out in the bar as beer."

3331 "Why did you break it off with Herbert?" Alice asked pretty Nelly Kelly.

"The cheapskate," hooted Nelly. "Last night he said he'd brought me a present. It was a string for me to start collecting pearls on."

3332 Mr. Rasen couldn't sleep; he paced the bedroom floor for hour after hour, until finally his wife could stand no more. Easing herself up in bed she said to him: "Look, Edgar, for crying out loud come to bed."

"Stella, I'm worried sick. You know we won't be able to meet the quarterly rent account tomorrow! How can I sleep with a load like that on my mind."

Mrs. Rasen leaned over to the bedside table and picked the telephone off the cradle. She dialled a number: "Hello, is that Mr. Fusdick? This is

Mrs. Rasen. I just called to tell you we won't be able to pay your rent tomorrow. Sure, I know it's two o'clock in the morning. That's why I rang. Good night." Replacing the receiver she waved commandingly at her husband, saying: "All right now. Come to bed. Let Fusdick pace the floor."

3333 Once upon a time there was a rating who was cast adrift on a small raft in the Pacific after his ship had been sunk. He had nothing but the ragged shirt and trousers he wore and a newspaper, and he was some two thousand miles from land. Glancing through the paper he looked up his horoscope. It read: "You are going on a long journey. Do not enter into any financial deals today. This week you will have difficulty in making friends."

3334 An Athletic Club is said to be planning a big Festival in honour of Adam because he was the first man to start a race.

3335 "I have some good news for you, Mrs. Tidesdale," said the doctor after examining his patient.
   "It's *Miss* Tidesdale, Doctor," corrected the sweet young lady.
   The doctor adjusted his smile and said: "In that case I've got some bad news for you."

3336 A disgruntled cannibal housewife was discussing the tribe's menfolk with a woman friend. She said: "I don't know what's come over my husband lately. I just don't know what to make of him at all." The friend said: "I must lend you my new recipe book."

3337 The wealthy stockbroker was aghast when his daughter's fiancé announced to him that he intended to break the engagement.
   The young man exploded: "She's thoroughly spoilt."
   The elder man said sternly: "Now see here, Basil, Greta might have been brought up in the lap of luxury and given everything of the best, but I won't have you going around saying she's spoilt."
   The young man replied: "That's not what I meant."

3338 Every day a man working on a large construction job in a remote part of the country was seen to sit down at lunch-time and consume a large pile of kipper sandwiches. He always ate them as though they were tasteless and difficult to swallow. A curious fellow workman said to him one lunch-time: "Why do you pull such faces when you eat your lunch?"
   "Because these sandwiches are kipper sandwiches. It's always kippers. I detest kippers."
   "In that case why don't you tell your wife to make you some different sandwiches for a change?"
   The kipperphobe stared back and growled: "What wife? I ain't married. I make these myself."

3339   In Texas they tell the tale of the lunatic who decided to end it all by suicide. Unfortunately he used a piece of rope that was too long and broke both his legs.

3340   A little rabbit was very nearly run down by a fast roadster. As it jumped miraculously out of danger and the speeding car whizzed into the distance the little rabbit pulled a man's foot out of his pocket and said, soulfully: "Gosh! It works."

3341   The beautiful Hollywood actress had recently announced her fifth marriage. Interviewed by a gossip-columnist she informed him: "You can quote me as saying that it really was the happiest week-end of my life."

3342   She rushed into the hospital and demanded to see the House Surgeon. The receptionist informed her that Mr. Thompkin was in the operating theatre.
    "That's the whole point," said the pretty girl. "He's supposed to be operating on Mike Longley this morning. Now Mike happens to be my fiancé, and I'm hanged if I'm going to have a complete stranger opening my male."

3343   The author of a Chicago gangster's biography writes that the gangster's living-room was curtained in shot silk. Well, he had to practise somewhere.

3344   Mrs. Shnutzbaum said: "How's your husband, Mrs. Nussman? I heard he was in hospital."
    "Is right," nodded Mrs. Shnutzbaum. "Poor Sam is suffering from fallen arches."
    "Hm, hm, bad feet, eh?"
    "Not bad feet. A railway bridge fell on him."

3345   Jackie Yates was telling some acquaintances about a certain music publisher from Denmark Street who had just bought an enormous mansion out in the country.
    "It's got everything," Jackie said. "He's even installed a set of musical chimes for a door-bell. The only trouble is that before you can get into the darned house you have to buy the sheet-music."

3346   Two ghosts met on the battlements of a historic castle. Said the first: "Know something? You give me the eerie ache."
    "Zat so?" said the other. "In that case I'm sorry I spook."

3347   She came home from the big dance, full of bright-eyed enthusiasm for the young stockbroker who had danced nearly all night with her. His father was a big shot on the Stock Exchange. Thinking it was time she was told the facts of life, her mother took her on one side and explained about the Bears and the Bulls.

3348 Mrs. Rushby told her maid: "Alice, when you are serving my dinner guests tonight, please don't wear any of your fancy jewellery."

"Well, Mum," said Alice, "none of it's the least bit valuable, but thanks for warning me."

3349 A man walked into the bookstore and sheepishly asked if they had *The Sexual Activities of the Human Female*. The assistant admitted that it was in stock and mentioned the price.

"Good Heavens!" protested the customer. "If it's as expensive as that I can't buy it. Sooner or later they're bound to film it. I'll wait."

3350 She came out of the fitting-room wearing the new gown she was trying on. Her husband regarded her with renewed interest.

"Like this one, darling?" she asked hopefully.

He said: "Is that the dress or just a sample of the material?"

3351 A woman is one of those people who always holds her hand out— except when she's driving round a corner.

3352 "Blindfold yourself when you write this down, Miss Glump," the Ministry Official said to his Secretary. "It's a top secret memorandum."

3353 "Good gracious!" exclaimed the dear lady who had run from the farmhouse to help the man who was floating down from the storm-swept sky. "You're a silly young man to be parachuting from your airyplane on a foul night like this!" she shouted into the wind. "Lady," he answered breathlessly. "I'm not coming down by parachute, I'm going up with a tent!"

3354 There had been a fire at a girls' college and when the fire station superintendent was reading the report he found reason to query the length of time the men had been absent. He called the captain into his office and asked him why it had taken them four hours to put out a small fire. "Well," said the captain. "It took the firemen two hours to put the fire out, then it took the girls two hours to put the firemen out."

3355 The pianist at the party turned around suddenly and said to a girl who had attracted him earlier: "Do you *like* good music, Miss Featherby?"

"Yes, I do rather," she said, "but don't mind me. Go on playing."

3356   Two years before, red-headed Stella Marriss had been a chorus girl in a third-rate musical. Now she was leading lady in a West End production, owned a couple of Rolls-Royce cars and four mink coats. A man who had known Stella in the early days and who had been abroad for two years saw her new show. Afterwards he was having a drink with a blonde and he said: "What beats me is how she did it." The blonde said: "Well, you've heard of the ladder of success, I suppose? Stella took the elevator."

3357   Pravda's leading article recently was devoted to the wonderful new Russian invention, the radio-electronic infra-stabilising spectro-magnetic nuclimeter. Russian agents are working overtime in Britain trying to find out what it is.

3358   They were a very ordinary family and extremely gratified that their only son was doing so well at medical college. One day they received a letter from him and Father read it. He turned to his wife and informed her: "You know what, Sarah? Now our Markie is starting to specialise in obstetrics." "Well, if I know our Markie," replied Mrs. Noodleson, proudly, "he'll find a cure for it, too."

3359   A lyric writer named Wezerl didn't feel too good in the morning so he went to the doctor and got a prescription for some medicine. At lunch-time he went across the street for a snack, and accidentally left the prescription on the piano. His collaborator found the piece of paper, sat down and wrote a score for it, and that's how the "Snoozy-Woozie Blues" came to be top of the Hit Parade.

3360   Bergfield's wife was trying everything to get her weight down. Pills, exercises, special corsets, dieting. The lot. After three months of obsessional chatter about slimming from his wife, who seemed to be getting fatter all the time, Bergfield shook his head sadly one morning and told her: "Becky, give it a rest. No matter how much you reduce, you'll never be a bargain."

3361   An elderly Texan oil-millionaire arrived in England at a very early date to be certain of seeing as much as possible of the Spring Exhibitions. Just the same he quickly discovered that London was packed tight with tourists and there wasn't even an empty bathroom to be booked at the better hotels. Eventually he tried for reservations at a small hotel in Soho. "We're short of staff," the reception clerk told him as he signed the register. "You won't mind making your own bed, I suppose." "Heck, no," the Texan said, only too thankful to have found somewhere to stay. "Good," said the receptionist, and handed him some wood, a hammer and a bag of nails.

3362   Two men-about-town were sitting at a table in a very exclusive night-club, watching the cabaret. A tall, slender, wonderfully-proportioned girl, wearing the ultimate in plunging-neckline gowns was singing a popular hit tune. She took eight bows before they let her go. "Gee," said one of the men, "didn't she have a beautiful voice!" "Did she?" said the other. "I wasn't looking at it."

3363 After the races, two sporting types were going home from New-market. One of them said: "What do you think about Dave Saunders's new restaurant in Soho? I was in there the other night. Place was nearly empty." The other fellow said: "If you ask me, Dave's flogging a dead horse." "And the way business is," his companion said, "it ought to last him three or four months."

3364 Three cats were going home from a symphony concert when they passed a shop window filled with sporting accessories and games. The tabby paused and pointed to the section of the window displaying tennis equipment. "Gee, look," he said. "My old man's in that racket."

3365 The managing director of a very large store was making his first personal visit, to review the staff. Steered by the store's general manager he arrived eventually in the pot and china department, where the general manager beckoned to Mr. Stifinger.

"This is Mr. Stifinger," the boss was told by way of introduction. "He's been manager of this china department for forty years. Last week he broke his first cup."

"Uhuh," nodded the managing director. "It's to be hoped that he'll be more careful in future."

3366 Two neighbours who both had television became worried when their sets started to go wrong. The 'H' aerials were on opposite chimneys on a mutual roof, eight storeys above. One feller said: "I'm going up there to check the aerials. Maybe something happened to 'em." Ten minutes later he came back and reported the cause of the interference. Two teams of cats were playing rugger on the roof.

3367 The young husband, unexpectedly delayed, telephoned through to his wife in Birmingham to say how sorry he was, and how much he was missing her. She asked: "But Willy, where are you calling from?" "I'm at St. Albans," he told her "Oh!" she said. "What are you doing at his place?"

3368 Fenwick was bemoaning the onset of senile decay. Talking to a drinking friend over a pint of beer he alleged: "There was a time when I could hold my girl-friends tight. Now I can't even do it sober."

3369 Jonesey opened his mail one morning and found a cryptic note in one of the envelopes. It read:

"See here, Jonesey, if you don't leave my girl-friend alone, I'm going to kick your spine up through your hat and fly your legs from it."

Extremely perturbed about this threat, Jonesey thought he'd better inform the police. The desk-sergeant grinned amiably and suggested: "Well, Mr. Jones, it's as simple as this. Just leave the girl alone."

Jonesey protested: "But don't you understand—look, the note ain't signed. How do I know *who* sent it?"

3370 Old Dinglefield had never been much of a mathematician although he was a good businessman. His chief accountant was laid up with influenza one week and Dinglefield was struggling with an account which merited some discount. After worrying away for twenty minutes he called his pretty secretary over and said: "Miss Hampton, what would you take off to make five per cent. of £546?"

"Mr. Dinglefield!" she exploded. "How dare you!"

3371 Emily Westhaven had just left the Centre where she was finishing a long First Aid course. As she walked along a side street she was shocked to see a man lying flat on his face in the middle of the road, obviously in pain. The fact that no other passer-by took any notice of the unfortunate man's predicament appalled the good lady, who walked straight into the road and bent down by the man, hurriedly applying artificial respiration.

The man wriggled a great deal and finally managed to turn his head. " 'Ere, nark it, lady," he protested. "I don't know what *your* game is, but I'm trying to get this dratted pipe down this 'ere manhole."

3372 A traveller knocked at the door of the suburban house and after a few moments a beautiful young blonde answered. He regarded her with interest and said: "Could I please have a few words with Mr. Sillbottom?"

"I'm sorry," she purred, "but my husband is out."

"That's too bad," he said. "I wanted to see him on business."

"Well, he won't be back for a fortnight or so," she told him.

He gave the blonde a long, appraising look and then said:

"That's all right. I'll wait."

3373 The door-keeper at a famous and exclusive London club was hastening down the twelve steps from the entrance to the road in readiness to open the door of a limousine that was pulling into the kerb. Missing his footing, he fell headlong on his face in the gutter. The secretary rushed out into the street and hauled him to his feet, saying angrily:

"That's enough of that, Cassidy. Do you want folks to think you're a member!"

3374 Professor Hackenpuck was visiting some friends across the other side of town. After a good dinner and a friendly game of cards, the professor elected to leave. But his host looked through the window and observed that a terrific gale was blowing up.

"It's not fit for a dog to be out," he told the professor, "I think you'd better stay here tonight."

Shortly afterwards the professor disappeared and the host and hostess were completely baffled. They started to make preparations for retiring when the professor suddenly reappeared through the back door, soaking wet.

"Oh, there you are," said the host in relief.

"Sorry I was so long," smiled the drenched professor. "I just slipped home for my pyjamas."

3375 The inebriate tourist was introduced to another member of the party at the night-club.

"This is Bill."

"Bill? Another Bill?" exclaimed the tourist. "I don't know—every Tom, Dick and Harry in this country seems to be named Bill."

3376 Bill Riorden was a very sick man, unlikely to leave his bed, and his friends took it in turns to visit him and buck him up.

Spencer was a bit worried because the other fellows had already agreed to handle the funeral arrangements on behalf of Riorden's wife, and Spencer had a mean streak in him. He drew Deakin to one side and whispered: "Say, Deakin, I don't know that we need three carriages. Let's just have one carriage and the hearse."

Deakin whispered back: "Well, okay."

Spencer said: "And another thing, we could also save dough if we didn't bother with wreaths and flowers. Bill won't know any different."

Just then the third visitor shuffled over and whispered: "Take it easy, fellers—he might hear you. I heard every word."

Spencer whispered to him, "Do you agree about it?" O'Feenly nodded and said: "Yes. I've been thinking we might economise further by not putting those announcements in the newspapers."

Just then poor Riorden painfully pulled himself up in bed and threw them all a dirty look. "Listen," he breathed hoarsely, "if you'll throw my trousers over, I'll walk there with a placard on my back."

3377 A couple of fattened turkeys were chatting together by the fence. One said to the other: "Gerald, do *you* believe in Santa Claus?"

3378 Fazakeley was running to the railway station when he bumped into Tyler. Tyler said: "What's the rush?"

Fazakeley panted: "My wife went away for a holiday last week."

Tyler, who knew that Fazakeley had a very beautiful young wife, looked perplexed. "So?" he inquired.

"I had a letter from her this morning, and I'm on my way to Scarborough."

"She wrote and asked you to join her?" Tyler said.

"No. She just wrote that she's having a wonderful time. The trouble is for once she didn't ask me for any money."

3379 A small, gawky young lad asked the manager of his local football team if there was any chance of him being signed on for the team. The genial manager said gently: "Phil, you're only a youngster. You ain't old enough to play for the Rangers yet. Tell you what—come back and see me in a few years' time, son, and we'll talk about it again."

Two weeks later little Phil was back in the manager's office. Again he asked to be signed on.

"Look, Phil," grumbled the manager, "I already told you. Come back when you're a bit older."

"I am older," Phil said earnestly. "I watched our team playing on Saturday, and believe me, they put years on me."

3380 She came downstairs, wearing her newest gown. Her face was expertly made up, for the express purpose of intriguing her husband, who had recently become a mite inattentive.

He stared at her and lowered his glass of whisky.

"Lydia!" he breathed. "You look like a million."

She was just going to kiss him when he took a deep draught and added: "Every day of it."

3381 All their married life he had been relentlessly henpecked, and had suffered in silence, being of a timid disposition. One evening he had a few too many with some friends at the local and came home drunk as a lush, and raring to assert himself for once. He stormed at his astonished wife for two hours and finished up breathlessly: "And another thing, in future I want my name on my dish, the same as the perishing dog!"

3382 A class was asked to write an essay on the life of Benjamin Franklin. After much pencil-chewing a little boy briefed the man's life down to its basic details and turned in the following script: "Benjamin Franklin was born in Boston. He travelled to Philadelphia, met a lady on the street, she laughed at him, he married her and discovered electricity."

3383 A young lad in a hygiene group wrote the following essay on anatomy: "Your head is kind of round and your brains are in it and your hair on it. Your face is in the front of your head where you eat and make faces. Your neck is what keeps your head out of your collar. It's hard to keep clean. Your shoulders are sort of shelves where you hook your braces on them. Your stummick is something that if you don't eat often enough it hurts, and spinach don't help it none. Your spine is a long bone in your back that keeps you from folding up. Your back is always behind you no matter how quick you turn round. Your arms you got to have to pitch better and so you can reach the butter. Your fingers stick out of your hand so you can throw a curve and add up rithmatick. Your legs is what if you have not got two of you cannot get to first base. Your feet are what you run on, your toes are what always get stubbed. And that's all there is of you except what's inside and I never saw that."

3384 The traveller was telling some friends about his visit to Russia.

"Of course things are a little crowded in the cities. The place where I stayed, I had to share my room with some singers."

"You mean duettists?"

"No. I mean the Vladivostock Girls' Choir."

3385 A really prize effort is this essay by a ten-year-old Scot on birds and beasts:

"The bird I am going to write about is the owl. The owl cannot see at all by day, and at night it is as blind as a bat. I do not know much about the owl, so I will go on to the beast which I am going to choose.

"It is the cow. The cow is a mammal. It has six sides: right, left, and upper and below. At the back it has a tail on which hangs a brush. With this the cow sends the flies away so that they will not fall in the milk. The head is for the purpose of growing horns, and so that the mouth can be somewhere. The horns are to butt with. The mouth is to moo with. Under the cow hangs the milk. It is arranged for milking. When people milk, the milk comes, and there is never an end to the supply. How the cow does it I have not yet realised. The cow has a fine sense of smell; one can smell it far away. This is the reason for the fresh air in the country. The man cow is the ox. It is not a mammal. The cow does not eat much, but what it eats it eats twice so that it gets enough. When it is hungry it moos, and when it says nothing it is because its inside is full up of grass. . . ."

3386 A young curate named Skoggs was being interviewed by his bishop, to whom he had applied for permission to get married. "I think it is always advisable for a man of the cloth to take unto himself a helpmate," observed his lordship. "But, tell me, Skoggs, whom do you propose to marry, and have I ever met her?"

"No, I don't think you ever met her," Skoggs replied.

"Is she a woman of standing?" asked the bishop.

"Well," Skoggs said awkwardly, "she's only a carpenter's daughter, but . . ."

"That will do Skoggs," snapped the bishop indignantly. "I've heard that before, and I was not amused."

3387 Sydney and Rose Nutzbaum were invited to a very exclusive dinner where the upper-crust aristocrats were flaunting their largest diamonds and their lowest-cut chicery. It so happened that Rose Nutzbaum was seated next to a young man from the Diplomatic Corps. She kept up a very animated conversation with this guest throughout the meal and so unnerved him that he accidentally splattered her beautiful gown with casseroled chicken when his knife and fork slipped out of his hands.

He turned to her, red-faced and contrite, apologising profusely: "My dear Madam, what a deplorable thing to do. I can't tell you how sorry I am. It's unutterably stupid of me and I humbly beg your gracious pardon; truly I wouldn't have had this happen for anything in the world. . . ." And so on, for several moments. His wordy discomfiture troubled Mrs. Nutzbaum who felt more guilty than the clumsy guest. She assured him, blushing freely, that everything was quite all right, and she mopped away the fragments of chicken and the stains with her napkin.

For the ninth time the D.C. gentleman husked: "I really am frightfully sorry. . . ."

This was too much for Rosie Nutzbaum. Smiling understandingly, she grasped a dish of creamed potatoes from the table and upended the lot over the young man's head, saying: "Lookit, son, now we're quits. Stop worrying so much."

3388   Vanessa was having trouble making the drinks at her cocktail party. Suddenly she spotted a well-known playwright among the guests and beckoned him over.

"Thank God you're here, Tony," she sighed with relief. "I'm sure *you* know how to make a peach cordial."

"Easy," nodded Tony. "Just promise her a mink coat."

3389   The salesman was demonstrating the glittering, sleek, new green and cream 100-h.p. convertible priced at £8,000. It had every conceivable refinement and was smothered with electric gadgets. Showing a prospective buyer the different instruments, he came to the roof.

"You press this button and the roof opens," he explained. "You press this other button and the roof closes. You press this button and part of the roof slides back half-way."

The prospective customer asked: "What about if any of the buttons don't work?"

"Ah," said the salesman, "this car is fitted with an automatic sense of humour. If the buttons fail, you press this red-tipped switch here and get a horse-laff from the radio."

3390   A tramp knocked on the door of the doctor's house and the door was opened by a very refreshingly lovely young lady.

"Pardon me," said the tramp in his most servile manner, "but do you think the doctor might have any old underwear to give to a poor, cold, starving tramp?"

"Very probably," she said, "but I don't think the things would suit you very well. I happen to be the doctor."

3391 "That's my daughter over there," said the banker proudly, indicating the pretty young brunette talking to the hostess. "She's got her mother's eyes, her mother's chin and her mother's lips."

"Uhuh," said his bored listener. "And tell me, since you seem to know everyone here, who is that odd-looking woman over by the mantelpiece? The one with the vacant expression on her face."

"That's my wife," said the banker.

3392 Dibbins had dined well, taken a few drinks on board, and in a mood of surfeited complacency was on his way home. He got off the train and walked to the barrier. As he passed through he remarked to the ticket-collector who punched his ticket: "How long have you been doing this sort of thing?"

"This? Oh, about eighteen years now," the ticket-collector answered cheerfully.

Dibbins nodded, studied his ticket with interest and then said appreciatively: "You do it rather well, you know."

3393 The well-known mountaineer and explorer was lying ill in bed when two girls came to see him. They were both a bit on the dim side. One of them gazed around the sickroom and eventually her eyes lighted upon the wall behind the bed. She turned and whispered to the other visitor: "Gee, Myrtle, he's awful sick. Just look at that chart! I never saw such ups and downs."

"Hush, Ivy," whispered back the other. "That's not his chart. It's a painting of the Alps."

3394 Nurse to Doctor: "I'm sorry, doctor, but this patient is so utterly disgusted with this one-horse town he refuses even to have a *local* anaesthetic."

3395 A case for legal separation was concluding.

Judge: "I have taken all the factors into consideration and I am going to award your wife £5 a week."

Defendant: "That's mighty nice of you, your honour, and if I can get around to it I might slip her a quid myself now and again."

3396 Smelling something burning strongly he got up and mooched into the kitchen. There was a cloud of thick black smoke coming from the oven and the kitchen was filled with an acrid, suffocating smell of charred flesh. His wife was standing at the open window, clutching a book.

"Agnes," he said quietly. "Hadn't you better take whatever it is out of the oven?"

She said: "I'm waiting to. It says in the recipe book thirty minutes. There's still four minutes to go."

3397 A woman rang up the Lost Property Office in Glasgow and informed the clerk that she had lost a large octopus on the night train from London.

"Yes, madam," remarked the imperturbable clerk. "And what colour was it?"

3398 Sidney Rosenthal was spending a holiday in San Angel in Mexico and couldn't speak one word of the language. It was a very pleasant hotel, however, and he was enjoying himself. One morning, as he sat down to breakfast, a chap sitting opposite him said: "*Buenos dias,*" and bowed. Rosenthal thought he was introducing himself, so he bowed back and said: "Rosenthal."

The following morning the same man bowed again and said: "*Buenos dias.*"

Said Rosenthal: "Rosenthal."

The waiter who was serving them happened to know a little English and after breakfast he spoke to Rosenthal.

"Señor, the other guest, when he say to you every morning, '*Buenos dias,*' this is not his name, you understand; he is only saying to you 'Good morning.'"

Rosenthal was grateful for this explanation, and on the following morning as he sat down to breakfast he bowed and said to the Mexican: "*Buenos dias.*"

The Mexican looked up, pleased to think that his friend had taken the trouble to learn the language and retorted: "Rosenthal."

3399 Her husband was making big money, and to show his wife the kind of man he was, he fitted out the kitchen with every conceivable modern piece of equipment: electric washer, deep freeze, electronic cooker, garbage disposal filter, automatic air conditioner, tapped ice-water, dishwashing- and drying-machine, and a dozen other pieces of apparatus.

A few days afterwards his wife said to him at dinner: "Basil, with all those labour-saving devices I thought it was no longer necessary to have the two maids helping me, so I fired them."

"Good of you to be so economical, Ethel," said Basil.

Just then two men walked in and sat down to dinner—two strangers, both wearing overalls. Basil stared at them curiously, and then glanced at his wife. Ethel said: "Oh, Basil, there's something else I have to tell you. I hired these two men today."

"What for?"

"One's an electrician and the other's a mechanic. It's a full-time job keeping those gadgets working properly in the kitchen."

3400 Jones, a youthful fifty-two, had been retired for some years and seemed to live quite comfortably with his wife and grown-up sons in their own cosy house in the suburbs. Richards now worked for the same firm and remembered Jones from when he had been his superior. When they met in the pub one evening Richards said: "You know, I've often wondered how you managed to retire at fifty and live so comfortably. It takes me all my time to save a pound."

Jones said: "Well, you see, young feller, *I* retired on my savings, but that was before we had the Welfare State which takes income tax, health contributions, society payments, union fees, party contributions, pension funds, unemployment contributions and purchase tax out of your pay envelope."

3401   The demonstrator was working hard to interest the newly-wed Mrs. Joslyn in an automatic washing machine. After giving her the routine sales-talk according to the firm's high-pressure manual he added: "And as for operating—this thing is so simple, a child could easily work it."

Blushing slightly she said: "Very well, I'll talk to my husband."

3402   The parents of eighteen or nineteen children took their latest arrival to be christened, having decided upon the name "Fred". The following day the harassed husband visited the priest and asked if it would be possible to change the baby's name from Fred to Sydney.

"But why do you wish to change the infant's name so soon?" demanded the priest.

"Last night," explained the husband, "we suddenly remembered we already have a Fred."

3403   A very harassed sickly-looking young man sat down in the doctor's surgery. The doctor shrewdly looked him over and said: "What's the trouble?"

"I don't know. I feel weak. Exhausted. I haven't any strength. I don't eat well and I can't sleep. I worry too much and I look like losing my job if I don't show a little more life."

"I see," muttered the doctor, drumming his fingers on the desk-blotter. "What kind of work do you do?"

"Well," said the patient, "you know those cartoon advertisements in the papers—those things that advertise Scroggs' Super-Pep Tonic Wine? Well, I'm the fellow who draws 'em."

3404   The patient walked into the consulting room. He was a tall, lethargic-looking character, very nondescript and slovenly.

"What's your trouble?" asked the Doc.

"I'm just tired. Tired all the time," yawned the patient.

"Are you ill?"

"No, not ill. Just tired. Weary as Willie."

"What's the matter, don't you like going to work?" demanded the doctor, sensing a ruse to obtain a certificate of incapacity.

"Oh, I don't mind going to work," said the man. "For that matter I don't mind coming home either. But the bit in between! Gee, Doc, that's killin' me!"

3405   After the recent argument with his battleaxe of a wife, Simpkin said he was going to commit suicide. His wife, who had heard that story before, ignored the threat. An hour later, after he had stormed out of the house, she put on her coat and went into town to do some shopping. In High Street a crowd of people had collected beneath a very high building: some fourteen floors above, a figure was to be seen standing on a window-ledge, poised as if ready to jump into the street. The crowd was hushed, expectant, horrified. Mrs. Simpkin drew in a sharp breath. Then she screamed frantically: "That's my husband! Save him! Somebody save him!"

A policeman in the crowd looked round sharply and gave the woman a long, hard stare. "Is it really your husband?"

"Yes, yes."

"Oh," said the policeman, still staring at her. "That's as well to know. We thought for a moment that he'd gone crazy and didn't know what he was doing."

3406   She was describing the man she had been out with.
"He's tall and in the dark he was handsome."

3407   A shabby-looking character was slouching through the open market when he passed a stall on which were a number of second-hand leather goods and oddments. The stock included an old fibre valise. The stall-holder noticed the unkempt stranger's interest in his stall and, pointing to the suit-case, asked: "Want ter buy that, cheap?"

"What would I want wiv a fing like that?" replied the stranger.

"Put your clothes in it," suggested the stall-holder.

"Wot? An' have ter walk arahnd in the nude?" sneered the other man.

3408   Mulligan was a bookmaker of sorts, and was experiencing a run of bad luck because of the favourites winning. He was having a drink in the local one evening when a pal entered. Mulligan pounced on him and started to unburden himself. Sympathetically the friend said: "Well, Patrick Mulligan me boy, it beats me why you don't give up the business, for after all you can't go on losing money like that, day after day."

"Give up me business!" exploded the Irishman. "Give up me business indade! Shure and how can a man give up his living?"

3409   Into the garage drove the owner of a large sleek new American sedan; the back had been badly damaged and there were sundry dents in the rear guards; the bumpers were twisted and one wheel was buckled.

The mechanic said: "Gee. Looks bad. What happened?"

The dismayed owner said: "A fellow in an old Ford hit me."

"Uhuh," said the mechanic. "How often?"

3410 A famous violinist was a guest of honour at a party in Richmond and during the evening he entertained the rest of the guests by doing a few simple conjuring tricks. Just before the party broke up, a woman who had watched him with considerable interest went up to him and said: "Everyone here seems to be talking about you! Look, I'm giving a party for my son's twenty-first next week; I wonder if you'd be good enough to perform there."

The violinist said: "Well, my agents arrange these things for me. You'd better see them."

The woman approached the agents and the details were fixed up. On the night of the big affair, the virtuoso arrived and immediately set about organising for his performance. The hostess was as pleased as punch after he had rendered his first concerto. She went up to him while the applause was still echoing round the room and said: "My goodness, you *are* versatile! I didn't realise you played the violin, too!"

3411 A prisoner named Wimpleby was on trial for the alleged theft of £1,500. A lawyer named Fisk was defending him, and had never worked so hard or so sincerely to get a client's name cleared. When the case was over and Wimpleby had been acquitted, he went up to Fisk and said: "You did a great job of work. How much is it going to cost me?"

Fisk said earnestly: "Look, old man, I did it purely in the interests of justice. I was completely convinced of your innocence. I'm glad you got off, and it won't cost you a penny."

Wimpleby protested: "Come now, Fisk, don't be like that. I've got my scruples, too, and I reckon you're entitled to some kind of a percentage of that fifteen hundred I made."

3412 The post-war period will go down in history as the time when even cheap things were expensive.

3413 Lord Gamerbilge can trace his family tree right back to the time when it was his ancestors' address.

3414 All the garages were primed by the large petrol combines to show every courtesy to motorists. Old Mackay pulled up on the drive of a garage outside London. Before the wheels stopped rolling a white-overalled assistant jumped out from behind a pump.

"Good morning, sir. I trust you are well. Can I wipe down your windscreen?"

"If you like," said Mackay.

"Your bodywork is a little dull," said the mechanic. "Do you mind if I just give it a brisk rub over and shine it up?"

"Help yourself," said Mackay. When this was done the mechanic said:
"There's some dust and litter in the back of the car, sir; I'll just run our vacuum cleaner over it and tidy up."

"Thanks," said Mackay. This was done and then the garage-hand inquired:
"And now, sir, how many gallons?"

"Oh, I don't want any petrol," said Mackay, "I was just wondering if I could use your phone."

3415 The prisoner was a rather small man but had nevertheless been charged with creating a disturbance at a well-known club.

The Clerk turned to him as he stood in the dock and said: "Prisoner at the bar, do you want to challenge the jury?"

"Well," he answered, eyeing the jury box thoughtfully, "not all of them, but I wouldn't mind going a couple of rounds with the plump feller in the corner."

3416 Not long up from the country, a young son-of-the-soil got himself a job at one of the big city theatres, running messages for the cast of a large musical show. There were thirty gorgeous girls in the production and on a number of occasions he had to deliver messages to their dressing-room.

At the end of the first week he was handed an envelope by the stage-manager.

"Where do I deliver this?" asked the former country boy.

The stage-manager said: "You don't deliver it anywhere. That's your wages for this week."

The rustic looked puzzled. Then his eyebrows shot up and he exclaimed in wonder: "You mean I get paid as well?"

3417 An American was puzzling over the statement made to him by a friend in England who told him that deep-freeze refrigeration was still fairly new to English households and that only 53 per cent. of people had refrigerators.

He said: "But darn it, fella, if you ain't yet got around to using the deep-freeze system, how come your young ladies got the way they are?"

3418 She was anxious to give her cultured Continental host a good impression: he was rich, a confirmed bachelor preyed upon by matchmaking socialite matrons.

"You know," she said, over the hors d'oeuvres, "I simply adore Keats."

"Dot's ferry good, my dear. It's always nice to meet a girl vot lofs leetle cheeldren."

3419 Mrs. Snapp asked her butcher: "Do you happen to suffer from rheumatism?"

"No," said the butcher. "Why?"

"It's a complaint," jeered Mrs. Snapp, "which causes one to imagine one's joints are larger than they look."

3420 A young man, immaculately dressed in a morning suit and top hat, walked into a high-class milliners in Bond Street and sat down on one of the deep-sprung davenports, digging his heels into the lush pile of the thick burgundy carpet. He sat there for about an hour, watching numerous women coming in, trying on hats, and going out again.

After ignoring him for quite some time, the manageress walked over to him and said: "M'sieu is waiting for someone?"

"Oh no, no."

"You wish to buy a hat for your girl-friend; your wife, perhaps?"

"No, I'm not buying anything," said he. "As a matter of fact I feel a bit low this afternoon. I just came in for a few laughs."

3421 She wept when he threatened to leave her and get a divorce.

"You're leaving me without any reason whatever!"

He sneered back: "I'm leaving you exactly as I found you."

3422 Describing a particularly attractive girl he had seen on the beach at Bournemouth Leon Murko says: "She was the kind of girl you wanted to whistle at but couldn't because your tongue was hanging out."

3423 The waiter on the night train to Edinburgh knew the rich, elderly gentleman in the diner quite well as a regular traveller. That evening, when he asked him what kind of soup he wanted, the wealthy businessman said: "For a change I'll have split-pea soup." "We're serving whole-pea soup." the waiter said gently. "It's all the same." "Split-pea soup," insisted the diner with finality. "All right. You're a regular diner on this train. You're a big tipper," said the waiter. "I'm going back there and personally split some whole peas for you. How's that?" "Fine. That's what I call service." An hour later the diner got his soup. He took a mouthful and spat it out. The waiter said: "What's the matter?" "Idiot," snapped the diner. "You've split 'em the left to right instead of down the middle."

3424 He had recently left the university and his first job was selling encyclopaedias on the instalment plan, door-to-door. Successes were entirely absent and somewhat dubiously he went up to the door of a suburban house which was next on the firm's list. A stubble-chinned man answered his knock. The salesman went into his lengthy spiel about the value of the encyclopaedia: it was a mine of information on politics, history, economics, mathematics; it was filled with vital statistics and articles about geography, physics, chemistry, nuclear fission and abnormal psychology. Ending his sales-talk he added: "What's more, there are ten volumes, beautifully bound in morocco leather with hand-tooled spines, and each volume contains 1,500 pages, which makes it three inches thick."

The haggard-looking householder stroked his chin for a moment and then said: "Half a mo." He went inside and closed the door. About five minutes later he came back and said: "I'll take Volumes One and Two." The salesman was puzzled and asked him: "Why don't you want the whole set?" "Because," said the householder, "the broken leg of our table is only six *inches* short."

3425   Old Shaunessy was explaining to a reporter why it was that his wedded bliss had endured for fifty years. "Well, y'see, after the first ten years I did think about getting a divorce, but I gave her another chance. After twenty years I did think once or twice of committing suicide, but I plucked up courage. After thirty years I had a notion I'd commit murder, but the feeling passed off. After we'd been married thirty-eight years I figured on leaving her and starting a new life in Canada, but the fare was too much. Six years ago I had a mind to kick her out of the house, but she locked herself in the coalplace. Then a couple of weeks ago I got to thinking—"What the hell—we only live once, and so after not talking to each other for forty-nine years we went to the pictures."

3426   Throughout its trials the new ship kept lurching and reeling and rolling and bucking and swaying until the captain could hardly stand up straight. Clutching the rail of the bridge he scowled at the first mate and grunted: "I was agin Lady Howsis launching this craft wi' whusky all along!"

3427   Nine-year-old Egbert was on trial for shooting his mother and father. Appealing to the jury for leniency, the defending counsel drew out his handkerchief and wiped the tears from his red-rimmed eyes, saying: "And I put it to you, ladies and gentlemen of the jury, surely in your hearts you can find compassion for this misguided little feller. After all, what is he, but a poor friendless orphan?"

3428   Smidgley decided he'd had enough of the world and was going to end it all. To make absolutely sure he would perish he planned his suicide attempt with strategic precision. He rigged up a gallows just off shore so that, if he failed to hang, he would drown when the tide came in. And to make things more certain, before he fastened the noose round his neck he took a dose of poison and also stabbed himself in the chest.

But the best-laid plans of men often misfire. When the tide came in it floated him and the noose was loosened around his neck so that it dropped over his chest and staunched the flow of blood from the dagger wound. And at the same time he was bound securely to the post when the wet rope contracted, and was thus held securely above the water as the tide flowed in. He didn't drown but swallowed a mouthful or two of the ocean, and the salt water acted as an emetic which prevented the poison from being effective.

Worse than anything, however, was the fact that this immersion in salt water completely cured his rheumatism so that thereafter he never felt so healthy in all his life.

3429 Unfortunate slip-up by a firm advertising Maternity Fashions. "When ordering please state whether Junior Miss, W.X. or O.S. size."

3430 The two shops were almost opposite one another. Kelly and Cohen were in the middle of a large-scale price-cutting war. They watched one another's business like hawks. One day Cohen put up a notice: "Cohen— General Dealer." After lunch there was a notice over Kelly's shop. "Kelly— Field-Marshal Dealers." Next day Kelly put up another sign, over his toilet goods display: "*Mens sana in corpore sano.*" Not to be outbid, Cohen countered with a sign: "Mens and *ladies* sana in corpore sano."

3431 Summerfield is the sort of man who always lets his friends pick up the dinner bill when dining out. This is because the poor chap has an impediment in his reach.

3432 Farbicker thought that he might just as well mow the lawn since he had a few hours off that afternoon so he ambled around to his neighbour's front door and rang the bell. Sipley came to the door and Farbicker said: "I'm going to mow my lawn this afternoon so I came to borrow your mower." Said Sipley in annoyance: "That's too bad: Griffiths had it last and he hasn't returned it yet." Farbicker sucked his tongue and thought for a moment. Then he shrugged and said: "Oh, well, may as well take the afternoon easy then. Lend me your golf clubs."

3433 The first lunatic took the ladder away and the second one who was whitewashing a ceiling came clattering down to the floor with a mighty thud. "You must be mad," he complained angrily. "You knew I was up that ladder!" "Yes, but I thought you'd got a firm grip on your brush," said the other.

3434 A fellow walked up to an alluring young blonde on the street corner and said politely: "I'm sorry to bother you but I'm a stranger in town and I don't know my way around. Could you tell me where you live?"

3435 The producer was auditioning acts for a new show. Into his sanctum eventually stepped a bright young man, bringing with him a dog. The dog carried a violin.

Said the newcomer: "Got a smashing act here. My name's Turner and this here dog of mine plays the violin."

The producer sniffed and said: "Well let's hear something."

Turner nodded to the dog, who sat down, put the violin to his jaw and proceeded to play. The producer listened with casual interest. Then, as the dog finished playing he said: "Not bad. Let's hear him again."

Turner said to the dog: "Bruno, play some more for the gentleman." Bruno put the violin to his jaw, picked up the bow, and played again. The producer was shaking his head a little.

He said: "He's just played that tune once. Let's hear something different."

Turner stared at the producer and remarked sadly: "But that's the only thing he can play."

"The act's out then," the producer decided. "We already have a tenor who's going to sing 'Trees'."

3436   Mick and Bruce were in the cocktail bar with a couple of girls when they noticed a solitary drinker in the corner, hunched over his table. The table was littered with his empty glasses and he was working his way stolidly through another double.

Mick said: "That's Tony, isn't it? What's hit him?"

Bruce said: "Well, what do you do when you have troubles."

"Me? I drown 'em, I guess," admitted Mick.

Said Bruce: "Well, Tony over there takes his out and just gives them swimming lessons."

3437   Thelma was lying on the couch in a dishevelled condition and looking utterly weary. Her room-mate came in from the theatre after a hard "twice-nightly" show, but didn't look anything like as tired. "What's the matter, Thelma?" she asked. Thelma said: "Battle fatigue. I was out with an infantry sergeant tonight."

3438   The Judge was giving his young son some advice about dealing with girls.

"Some time ago," said the judge reminiscently, "I had a case in my court. A very lovely young chorus girl was suing for breach of promise. It cost the unfortunate banker who was involved a lot of money. I awarded the girl £10,000 damages."

"Dear me," said the son, impressed.

"A year later," went on the judge, "the same girl was again in my court. She had been knocked down by a motor-car and had suffered a fractured skull. I awarded her £50 damages."

"Thank you, Father, for your advice," the son said, "but if you were trying to point a moral, it evades me."

The judge shrugged. "It's simple enough," he remarked. "The moral is this: never toy with a girl's affections. Slap her on the bonce. It's cheaper."

3439   He was trying assiduously to sell the woman of the house a new electric carpet-sweeper. Having dealt with the wonders of the mechanism, he turned gently to the financial details. "Look, lady, you just pay a small deposit and then you make no more payments for six months."

"Who's been telling you about us?" demanded the housewife indignantly.

3440 There's the sad little tale of the impoverished medical student who battled his way to a degree and was ready to go into business. Too poor to buy himself a brass plate he stole a sign from a big store in Regent Street, and stuck it over the door of his surgery.

It read: "Complaints Office."

3441 As the politician was mounting the rostrum where he was scheduled to deliver a speech to his constituents, one of the ushers whispered to him and pointed to a grim-looking young rebel who was sitting in the front row of the hall.

"Mr. Chichley," warned the usher, "watch out for that young feller down there. He belongs to the opposition, and he'll not only be calling you a liar but quoting from some of your earlier speeches to prove it."

3442 She was one of those sultry blondes who couldn't tolerate rivals. Speaking of a certain enemy of about the same age she told a boy-friend: "I'm not sure exactly how old she is, but a cup of tea refreshes her." And of another rival she expressed this sentiment: "If ever Alice becomes a mother I'm going to ask her for one of the kittens."

3443 The psychiatrist inquired of the middle-aged patient: "Now tell me, have you had any dreams lately?"

"No."

"Tough luck," said the psychiatrist. "I've had some corkers."

3444 The broad-beamed duchess was giving a soirée in an effort to further the career of her protégé Leon Lennon, who was reputed to have a wonderful tenor voice. Extra chairs had been drafted into the lounge from the hall and dining-room. A number of people had gatecrashed because, although they were totally disinterested in the protégé, they were cognizant of the duchess's lavish hospitality, and consequently there were more guests than chairs.

A new footman had been hired for the occasion and he realised the predicament. Buttonholing the duchess he said: "Your Grace, I'm afraid there is something wrong with your seating arrangement."

The duchess gave him a frigid glare and retorted: "Phelps, you were hired as a footman not as a medical adviser."

3445 Cary Lloyd was employed by a company using radio time to advertise their breakfast cereal in which was incorporated a mild tonic and a gentle laxative. It was Lloyd who broke into the normal programme with the advertising spiel. One day he received a formal notice telling him he was doing his last broadcast for the company. When the time came for him to pitch in with his sales talk he said: "Folks! Do you wake up in the morning feeling tired and listless? Do you lack stamina and endurance? Is your head always thick and are your eyes always bloodshot? Do you crawl to work feeling weary and sluggish? You do? Well don't expect any sympathy from me. I'm just as decrepit as you are."

3446   The notorious writer of very spicy novels was telling a party of friends about his most recent product.

"It's a terrific book," he claimed. "I'm having it bound in morocco."

"Why?" sneered a critic, "is it too hot to handle in this country?"

3447   The harassed woman had spent over a month wrangling with solicitors, estate agents, insurance men, Inland Revenue officials and Building Society representatives. Her wealthy husband had died and left her a fortune, but his financial affairs were in an extremely complicated state. One afternoon she ambled wearily into a café for a hurried snack and chanced to sit down opposite an old girl-friend.

"Why, Agnes," exclaimed the other woman, "you look worn out."

"I know," said the widow. "You've no idea the amount of worry and trouble I've had over Rupert's will. What with all his business to attend to and everything, I sometimes wish he'd never died."

3448   They were honeymooning at one of those small, under-staffed hotels where service and comfort were totally lacking. The young wife decided to take a bath straight away because they had had a long, dusty journey. Her husband waited dinner for her, and it was three hours before she showed up.

"Angela, for Pete's sake," he complained. "Does it take you three hours to have a bath?"

"Not usually," she said, "but there were no curtains in the bathroom and I had to keep getting out to breathe on the windows."

3449   In the office of the Lubrick Sales Company there was a huge map on which salesmen were indicated by coloured pins stuck into their territory. Salesman Marks was being disciplined for poor sales figures. Said the manager: "I'm not going to fire you this time, Marks, but just to illustrate to you how precarious your position is with the company I'm going to loosen your pin a little."

3450   The skunk stopped for a moment in his headlong dash and observed that the direction of the wind had altered. Said he: "Ah—it all comes back to me now."

3451   There was a picture of a wonderfully-muscled man in a pose at the side of the advertisement for a body-building course. Then the copy went on: "Here is a good test for your stomach muscles. Clasp your hands above your head, feet together on the ground. Now bend slightly to the right at the waist, and sit down to the left of your feet. By sheer force of your muscles bend backwards and touch the tip of your left foot with your right ear. Stay with this exercise and let us know how you make out. We'll be glad to hear from you."

The day after the ad. appeared the advertisers received from a reader a succinct telegram which simply stated: "Hernia."

3452 She was a sweet, lovable creature, on the surface, and she said to him, with stars in her eyes: "Benny, when we're married I want to share all your worries and all your troubles and help to lighten your burdens and . . ."

Benny said: "Forget it, sweetheart, I don't have any worries and troubles."

"We're not married yet," she pointed out.

3453 In the Maverick Saloon in Texas trouble started when one cowhand called another one a yellow-abdomened rattlesnake. Guns were blazing away and hot lead was flying furiously from all quarters. Then a very timid-looking baggage-office clerk walked right into the saloon and ordered a glass of lemonade. The barman had ducked behind the counter but he managed to fix a drink for the mild-mannered customer, mostly out of admiration for his nerve. When the shooting died down the bartender said:

"Gee, you sure showed courage, mister."

"Aw, it was nothing," said the clerk. "I was safe enough. I owe most of those quick-triggered cowhands some dough."

3454 He was telling his girl-friend that he had worked for two years at the Thorpe Research Institute for Brain Disorders.

"What were you specialising in?" she asked him.

"Oh, I wasn't studying anything there," he answered. "They were studying me."

3455 A party of sailors on board a cruiser off Jamaica thought they would like to take a dip but they had a suspicion the waters were infested with sharks. To check this feeling they rowed ashore and asked a native if there were any sharks in that particular bay. The native replied: "No sharks: sorry master." Relieved by this news the sailors forthwith went out again in the boat and enjoyed themselves for half an hour or so swimming in the bay. Later, as they came back ashore to lie on the beach they asked the same native boy *why* there were no sharks there. "Sharks no like all them barracudas out there," the boy explained.

3456 This rustic story happens to be quite true. A farmer went on his first trip to the metropolis and when he returned to his village he told all his friends about the wonderful hotel and all the marvels of the city; he and his wife had had a real good time, he said, "but the biggest trouble was the light burning all night in our bedroom."

Someone inquired politely: "Well, dange it, Jarge, whoi didn't ye blow un out?"

The farmer snorted: "Blow un out? How could oi? Dratted thing was kep in a glass case."

3457   The Skipper and the Chief Engineer of the good ship *Asparagus* were always arguing about who had the most important job on board the vessel. To settle the argument one day the skipper said: "Tell you what, let's change places for a few hours—that's the best way to find out."

So they switched jobs for a while.

Six hours later the Captain, down in the engine-room, whistled up to the Chief Engineer who was on the bridge and admitted flatly: "Okay, I give in. I can't even get the durned engines to start."

"That's nothing to worry about," said the Chief Engineer, "we've been stuck on a sandbank for five hours."

3458   Dentist to new receptionist who has just replaced the receiver: "Miss Ethering, in future would you please bear in mind that it is customary to tell patients that their dentures are ready and not that their choppers are now off the mould."

3459   In the office of the Travel Bureau an elderly man named Blopp was having a slight altercation with a clerk.

"Look, Mr. Blopp, I keep telling you it's impossible for you to buy a return ticket to Vienna which is charged at full-fare going out and half-fare coming back. You must pay full-fare both ways."

"Nonsense," insisted Blopp. "I'm going to Vienna for monkey-gland treatment, ain't I?"

3460   Brando Mundo, the famous Hollywood star, was proposing to Lila Lottie, the beautiful Hollywood starlet.

Brando: "Marry me, Lottie. I love you."

Lottie: "No, Brando."

Brando: "Aw, gee. Go on. Just this once."

3461   A young man was surprised when his proposal of marriage was turned down by a pretty girl he adored. Seeking an explanation in the absence of any reason given by the girl, the suitor consulted her mother.

"Well," said the mother, "you insulted the poor girl."

"I did? That's ridiculous. I only said nice things to her. I even said she was as pretty as a picture," protested the young man.

"Exactly," nodded the girl's mother. "You see, Priscilla used to work for a surrealist."

3462 The young man stood cap in hand waiting to see Mr. Wesell. At last Wesell came into the room.

"Yes?" he demanded, bluntly.

"You don't seem to remember me. I'm the feller who eloped with your daughter, June, six months ago."

"Well?" snapped Wesell. "What's on your mind?" What have you got to say to me?"

"Congratulations," said the young man dolefully.

3463 The village doctor was the proud father of the two most beautiful local girls, both teenagers. One day the two pretty girls chanced to pass a couple of young boys who were waiting for a bus, and one of them was a stranger. He turned to the other boy and asked:

"Did you see those two girls? I wonder who they are?"

The other lad said: "Aw, they're the doctor's kids. He always keeps the best for himself."

3464 The pretty young salesgirl was fired. As she was putting her hat and coat on in the cloakroom, one of the other store salesgirls asked sympathetically: "What's the trouble?"

"I slapped the manager's face," the other girl admitted. "He's a nasty old crab."

"That's odd," the sympathiser said with a frown. "Why, only the other day I heard the manager say that you were one of the best salesgirls in the store, and he was going to promote you."

"Just the same," said the sacked girl, "he told me that he was going to take me out of shoes and put me in pyjamas."

3465 A professional punter, notorious for picking losers, was accidentally run down by a horse-box on the course and killed. Shortly afterwards two of his friends found out about it and went to the mortuary to identify him. As they entered they saw a mound covered by a white sheet on a marble slab. One of them raised the sheet, but the mound was not the punter. The other man lifted the sheet on the second mound, but that wasn't the punter either. So they lifted the sheet over the third marble slab, and there, right enough, was their friend. "Anyway," said one of the visitors quietly, "he was placed."

3466 A young, but socially conscious, undergraduate visiting the Metropolis for the first time stepped across to the coffee stall by the river and asked for a cup of tea. Then he saw some hamburger rolls on a plate and said: "I'll have one of those, too, but please give me the one on the bottom of the plate. I'm always for the under-dog."

3467 A thirsty man walked into a pub and found himself alone with the proprietor who was standing behind the bar but leaning forward with his head cupped in his hands and looking exceptionally jaded.

"I'll have a small whisky," said the customer.

"Help yourself," said the publican. The customer frowned, but since the publican made no attempt to move, he went round and poured himself a whisky. Then he tossed a pound note on to the bar and said: "Give me my change."

The publican still wouldn't move. "Help yourself," he said miserably.

"What the heck's the matter with you?" asked the customer irritably. "You look as sour as a man who's won sixty thousand quid on the football pools and forgotten to post his coupon!"

"That," the publican scowled dejectedly, "is exactly what has happened."

"Good grief," expostulated the customer. "If anything like that happened to me, I'd cut my darned throat."

The publican said: "Why do you think I'm holding my head on like this?"

3468 Guide: "We are now passing Piccalilli."
Tourist: "You mean Piccadilly. Piccalilli is mustard."
Guide: "So's Piccadilly."

3469 Then there's the one about the idiot who was accompanying some other tourists on a cruise to the Middle East: having been told they were all going up the Nile he wore climbing shoes.

3470 He got up late and fell out of bed on the wrong side. The hot water ran cold in the taps and his razor was blunt. At breakfast his toast was burnt and the tea tasted like dishwater. He had to run for the bus and even then he missed it, in consequence of which he was fifteen minutes late at the sheds. Because the train he was driving was also fifteen minutes late out of the station, he had to boost the speed up to 100 miles an hour. Just as they were rounding the bend beyond the first junction box, he saw another express coming towards him on the same line. Turning to his fireman he muttered: "Say, 'Arold, did you ever have one of them days when nothing seems to go right?"

3471 The mistress was interviewing a prospective maid. After questioning her about her earlier jobs she requested some references.

"Well, I'm sorry, madam," said the applicant as she fumbled in her handbag, "I'm afraid I've lost the reference the Duchess of Tidbank gave me, but these 'ere spoons with her crest on them will prove I worked there."

3472 Kelly, who liked a drink, was staggering home with two bottles of whisky in his overcoat pockets when he was knocked down by a cyclist. The cyclist pedalled back to the victim, in the darkness, alighted, and ran to the scene of the mishap. Kelly was moaning on the ground, staring at his right hand which had been lying in a pool of blood from his injured arm. "Saints be praised!" ejaculated Kelly in relief as the cyclist's light fell upon his hand. "For a moment I was afraid this was *whisky*!"

3473 The timid little man visited the psychiatrist and told him about his awful dream.

"Every night I dream that I am trying to book seats for the Folies Bergère, and the girl in the ticket kiosk keeps telling me that the entire theatre is booked out, and all I want is a couple of seats in the stalls. . . ."

The psychiatrist calmed him down and said: "Well, your problem is quite easily solved. When you have the dream again, ask the box-office girl for two seats in the gallery. There might be some room there."

The patient went away satisfied, but returned the next day, still complaining.

"I had that same dream again last night," he groaned, "and I managed to get two seats in the gallery, but I forgot to take my glasses and I couldn't see a thing."

"That's too bad," said the psychiatrist. "You'd better remember to take your spectacles with you tonight, and you might also hire some opera glasses. They'll help."

So away went the patient, only to return again three days later.

"Everything all right now?" asked the psychiatrist.

"Nothing's right," moaned the timid little man. "I had trouble getting in when I dreamed the same dream on Saturday but I had some wonderful luck on Monday. I got two seats in the front stalls."

"Then what are you complaining about?" the doctor inquired.

"They changed the show over the week-end," said the patient. "In my dream last night there was ballet at the theatre—and I hate ballet."

"That's too bad," the psychiatrist sympathised. "But if you're still anxious to dream about seeing the Folies Bergère, why don't you dream about going to see it at another theatre?"

"Don't be daft," said the patient. "It's been moved into the West End, and how do you think I can afford to pay the prices they ask there."

3474 Officer (to liner passenger who is leaning far over the rail just below the bridge): "I'm very sorry, sir, but you can't do that there."

Passenger (going greener): "Wanna bet?"

3475 The owner of a furniture store was talking to his bank manager about the depression which had suddenly struck his business. "I tell you things are so bad that even the people who don't pay have stopped buying."

3476 A sign at the entrance to the women's wear department of the large store read: "Ladies Ready-To-Wear Clothing." Underneath this some wag had scribbled: "But not all of 'em."

3477   A Northern manufacturer walked one day into a restaurant in London and was surprised when he was served by a waiter whom he recognised as a former friend named Jarvis. Jarvis had been an up-and-coming actor at the time when Denham Studios were going strong. The Northener said in astonishment: "Didn't you used to play big lead parts? I thought you were a famous actor. Why on earth are you doing this kind of thing?" The waiter flicked crumbs off the table and replied: "I suddenly got a mad, impulsive desire to eat."

3478   As usual he was late for the office and bustling around furiously. As he was going out of the door with his umbrella, case and morning paper, his wife handed him his hat and something extra—a bottle. He stared at it and saw that it was a hair-restoring preparation. "That was very thoughtful of you, Martha," he told her, "but I'm not going bald."
   She said severely: "It's for your secretary. Her hair's coming out on your shoulder."

3479   A radio comedian was bemoaning his bad luck: "You know," he said, "I got such terrible luck that if I bought a suit with two pairs of trousers, I'd go and rip the jacket."

3480   A well-known chain-store executive was telling his girl-friend about a particularly terrible nephew who was scheduled to spend Christmas with him. "I guess I'm in for some trouble," he prophesied, "that kid has driven so many adults nuts that psychiatrists use him as an agent."

3481   Suddenly the captain of a large liner looked out over the side of the bridge and observed that the fog had cleared. He also noticed that the ship was sailing blissfully down the main street of a coastboard city. He rang the navigator and said, quietly: "Hargreaves—just check that you're using the right charts, will you?"

3482   The people in the ground-floor flat kept protesting to their landlord about the noise a young married couple above them created every night at bedtime. After several complaints the landlord felt he must warn the young couple not to keep disturbing the tenants below. When he went to the flat a young man answered the door and invited him in. The landlord explained the reason for his visit, and then the young man said apologetically: "The trouble is I married a strip-tease artist and every night when she gets ready for bed I have to clap and stamp on the floor."

3483   The middle-aged couple were just starting off on their train journey to the coast for a holiday. As the train pulled out, the husband asked his wife: "Quite comfortable my dear?"
   "Yes thanks."

"Not feeling the vibrations of the engine?"

"No dear."

"The draught from that window isn't bothering you?"

"No dear."

"Right—I'll change places with you."

3484   The newly-rich hostess was trying to impress some influential guests at her first big party. Noting that a certain spinster, a town councillor, seemed hungry she asked: "Miss Craddock, can I help you to some more cake?" "Well, thanks, just a mouthful, perhaps." The hostess nodded and called the maid. "Janet, fill Miss Craddock's plate."

3485   The alarm clock rang shrilly at 4.45 a.m. The young man got out of bed, shaved, made himself a quick breakfast, finished dressing by donning an elegant tweed suit, and rushed out of the house. He caught the early morning bus to town and from the bus station, took a taxi to the railway station. There he boarded a train. At five intermediate stations he changed trains and after a journey of some eighty miles across country he reached a remote and desolate little village. He waited thirty minutes for a bus and travelled for twenty minutes to the cross-roads where the bus turned off. Alighting there, the man set off to walk the remaining two miles across fields to a small cottage nestling at the foot of the hills. He tapped gently on the front door and a pretty young blonde woman came out and smiled a welcome at him. "Hello Sam," she said. "Oh, hullo kid," he grinned. "I just happened to be passing and I thought I'd look in on you."

3486   The Health Official was showing a party of overseas visitors around the town and after taking them to several interesting places, finished up at the Mental Home on the edge of the city. As they walked along the drive and entered through the gate they heard a loud noise coming from behind the high wall that surrounded the Institution. In the shadow of the bushes a perspiring young man was attacking the wall with a heavy mallet and a crowbar. The Health Official left his party and walked across to the man. "What the deuce are you doing?" he demanded. "Hush, hush," came the reply. "Can't you see I'm trying to break out." And he went on slamming away with the mallet, creating an ear-splitting din. "Look," said the Official, "there's a gate just over there." The inmate grinned knowingly. "I know that," he admitted confidentially. "But it squeaks."

3487   A party of explorers got lost in the heart of the Belgian Congo, many hundreds of miles from civilisation. The jungle was known to be the hunting ground of very ferocious tribesmen. In a swamp, on the way through the undergrowth they had lost all their weapons and ammunition, and their supplies of food were rapidly diminishing. One night they pitched camp and were alarmed by the whisper of voices in the creeping vegetation surrounding them. One of the members of the party noticed that another man kept walking up and down, up and down, with an expression of anxiety on his face. He went across to where the man was pacing and said: "Look, Mitchell, you might as well face facts and stop looking so worried."

Mitchell turned, and licking his dry lips, said soberly: "Oh, hullo Standish. I don't know why, but I keep thinking today is Tuesday."

3488   Looking as if he had lost all faith in mankind, a young timid man was sitting in a pub, slowly drinking a pint of beer. His friend found him there and asked him what was bothering him. "It's that fellow Pomfrett," he explained. "He's far too smart for me. Yesterday he sold me a plot of land to build a bungalow on, and when I went to see it, it was about five feet under water." "You should have gone for him—demanded your money back," his friend suggested. "I did," admitted the other man. "And instead of getting my money back, I was talked into buying a diving suit."

3489   They had finally got around to fixing the day for the wedding after a courtship of several years. She thought it would be only fair to confess to him. "Mike," she said, "to tell you the truth, I'm not much good at cooking." "Don't worry," Mike said. "On my salary we won't be eating often, anyway."

3490   It was just a quiet little wedding for a couple of hundred guests, and all the presents were on display as usual. Among these was a cheque for £3,000, a gift from the bride's father.

Suddenly one of the guests examining the presents was observed to pause in front of the cheque and start laughing. He laughed until tears rolled down his cheeks and he was doubled up.

In considerable annoyance the bridegroom whispered to his beloved: "Who on earth is that dreadful man laughing at your father's cheque?"

The bride answered: "No one important. He's Daddy's bank manager."

3491   A somewhat inoffensive-looking little man was spending his lunch-time with a former school-friend he had bumped into. Talking about the past, they forgot the time. Suddenly the little man looked at his watch and muttered: "Oh dear—it's nearly two and I have an appointment with my psychiatrist at two o'clock sharp—it'll take me five minutes to get to his consulting room . . ."

The friend said: "Take it easy, Horace—you'll only be a few minutes late —don't look so hot and bothered."

The man said earnestly: "You don't know the kind of man my psychiatrist is. If I'm not there on time he'll start without me."

3492   The Borsham Amateur Rugby League final was being played on a field just behind a chicken farm. Converting a try, the captain of the winning team sent the ball flying over a fence and it landed right beside a fat cockerel who was pecking corn outside the hen-house. The cockerel stared at the ball in amazement. Then he sauntered into the hen-house and snapped at all the hens: "Look, I don't want to sound critical, but have any of you seen what's being done in other poultry yards these days?"

3493   A small schoolboy was going home from school and the pretty young teacher of his class was walking beside him on her way to the village. As they reached the boy's home he said: "Why don't you come on in and see our new baby? We only had it yesterday."

The teacher smiled and said: "Perhaps I had better wait until your mother is a little better."

"Why?" the boy asked. "It ain't catching."

3494   The English film unit was on location in the wilds of Algeria many miles from the nearest centre of communications. An amazing local phenomenon was the uncanny accuracy of the weather predictions made by an old bearded Arab with no teeth. Because of the importance of knowing what weather was in store, the old boy was consulted daily by the director. But one day the old Arab was glum and unsociable, evidently annoyed about something, and he wouldn't co-operate.

"Look," said the film boss pacifically, "tell me what's the matter? Maybe it can easily be put right."

The Arab shrugged and said: "Radio. Bust."

3495   He was rather a good-looking fellow, with an athletic build, nicely spoken and gentlemanly. He was attending for a medical examination prior to going into the Navy. The doctor had given him a thorough going over and seemed delighted. The recruit said: "I must go and tell my wife; she's waiting in the next room."

The doctor frowned and said: "Not that big horsey woman with the straight hair, four chins and protruding teeth? The one who's sitting by the door?"

"That's her," said the recruit.

The doctor said: "I'm afraid you'll be rejected, old man. You'd never pass an eye test."

3496   Little Joan was just four, and she had been misbehaving herself with the result that Daddy had been forced to administer a sharp rebuke and a gentle spanking.

When he returned from the office that evening Joan watched him hanging up his hat and coat in the hall, and suddenly walked to the foot of the stairs and called up to her mother.

"Mummy, your husband's home."

3497   There were eight girls at the audition and the producer was having an awkward time trying to select the most suitable applicant for the important role of second female lead. Seven of the girls had everything: looks, shape, good voices and personality. The eighth girl was rather plain, tubby and ungainly, and her voice rather coarse; apart from which she was about forty.

When the final decision was made, the assistant producer called his chief aside and said: "Good grief, Bill! With seven beautiful and talented girls to choose from, you go and pick that stupid-looking misfit with the mouse hair. What are you trying to do—kill the production altogether!"

"No," snapped the producer. "I'm trying to give it a blood transfusion. That girl has something the others haven't got. Her old man's backing the show."

3498   St. Peter was interviewing new arrivals at the gates of Heaven. One little chap seemed to be worth special attention. St. Peter said: "While on earth, did you ever drink?"

"Gosh, no."

"Ever go with women?"

"Oh dear, no."

"Gamble?"

"No, no."

Said St. Peter: "Tell me, what kept you so long?"

3499   The Bishop was rather disturbed because his youngest daughter had taken up a theatrical career and was working in London, although he had no knowledge of her actual whereabouts. In fact he tried to forget the whole disgraceful thing. But one day he was having dinner with a very important business man who knew that the daughter was doing a strip-tease act in a West End cabaret. Over the liqueurs, the businessman said: "By the way, I saw your daughter's show last night. Wonderful! The way that girl gets unfrocked is no one's business."

3500   The preacher was giving a very warm sermon about the terrors of Hell. He was vigorous and animated, and the congregation looked very sheepish. At the end of the tirade the preacher ordered everyone who wished to go to Heaven to stand up.

Everyone rose except a young chap sitting near the front beside a very pretty young blonde.

"Young man," said the preacher sternly, "haven't you listened to my words? Do you want to go to Heaven or not?"

To which the man replied: "Look, I don't want to go anywhere. I'm perfectly satisfied where I am."

3501   The young man hadn't a great deal of money but wanted to buy a car to impress his girl-friend. He went to a second-hand dealer who promised to fix him up with a car for £40. When the man telephoned the following day to ask if the car was ready, the salesman replied: "Just come and pick it up."

The young man hurried along to the garage and when he arrived there found the salesman standing in the doorway of one of the workshops, the floor of which was littered with bits of metal, engine parts, wheels and tyres.

"Okay," said the salesman, jerking his head inside the workshop. "Start picking."

3502   The lavish bequest by a former rich inmate of a Mental Home was completely spent on the construction of a swimming pool for the occupants. When the pool was finished, the man's widow felt disposed to call at the Asylum and unveil the plaque. It was a beautifully sunny morning and she stood for a while watching some of the inmates having fun by climbing the thirty-eight steps to the high diving board and taking headers into the pool. She remarked to one of the warders: "By Jove, they're certainly pleased with the pool. Just look at them diving."

"Yes, Ma'am," nodded the warder sadly. "And they'll probably get even more excited when we put the water in."

3503   The door-to-door salesman looked very worried as he opened the gate leading to the big house. There was an enormous chow-like dog lying asleep just to the right of the drive.

He ventured forward when he saw the old lady who was sitting at the open bay window above the dog.

"Say, lady, that's a wonderful big dog you've got there. What breed is it?"

"Search me," replied the old lady. "Sister of mine sent it to me. She got married to a feller on the Gold Coast."

"It's the biggest, ruggedest dog I ever saw," admitted the salesman. "I never saw a dog with a head like that before."

"You should have seen him," the old girl said, "before I cut all the long hair off the back of his neck."

3504   She sent her boy-friend a telegram for his birthday: "Many Happy Returns and May All Your Dreams Come True."

She was surprised when an answer came back two hours later: "You'll be sorry."

3505   In the quiet reading-room of a reference library a rather unkempt character was busily poring over an erudite tome concerning birth and death statistics for the whole world.

Suddenly he turned to the dapper little man beside him and muttered in astonishment: "Do you know that every time I breathe someone dies!"

The stranger observed quietly: "Really? Have you tried sucking tablets?"

3506 She was very beautiful and a brunette, but still dumb. He bought her a book for her birthday.

"Oh, Cyril," she said, "it was very thoughtful of you, but I've already got one."

3507 The Eskimo boy was crazy in love with the Eskimo girl. One night he told her: "I've ridden over two hundred miles across the thick snow with my dog-team just to spend a few minutes with you."

Said she: "That sounds like a lot of mush."

3508 The hard-pressed husband finally got around to buying his wife the beautiful skunk coat she had been hankering after for years. Trying it on, his wife exclaimed in appreciation: "I can't understand how such a beautiful coat comes from such an insignificant repulsive little beast."

Said the husband: "Look, I don't expect any gratitude, but you needn't get personal, either."

3509 The doctor's infant son already had the makings of a wag. One afternoon he brought a small friend back from school for tea, and the doctor was out on his rounds. He took the other youngster into the surgery to impress him and the first thing the visitor saw was the skeleton in a glass case behind the door.

"Gee," he whispered to his small pal. "What on earth is that?"

"Oh, that! That's Dad's first patient," he was told.

3510 A Revivalist preacher was visiting a small village to address a meeting at the village hall. He had just arrived by train and was walking along to his hotel when he remembered he had to send a telegram to his agent. Seeing a small boy leaning on a fence reading an American comic he asked him to direct him to the Post Office. The boy showed the stranger the way and when they reached the Post Office he said: "Thank you, that was very kind of you."

The following afternoon the Revivalist was out and about superintending the posting of bills advertising the big meeting. He bumped into the same young lad, playing football with two other youngsters.

"Hello there, son," said the preacher. "Don't forget to come to the meeting tonight, and bring your friends with you. I will show you the way to Heaven."

When he'd gone on his way, the young lad turned to his friends and sneered: "Get that! He's going to show us the way to Heaven! He don't even know the way to the Post Office!"

3511 "What are you thinking about?" the sweet young thing asked him.

"Eh? Oh, nothing important," he said absently.

"Trouble with you," she complained, "is you're too durned introspective."

3512 The lazy young man had been sent to a farm to help out with the harvesting. At 3 a.m. on the morning following his arrival, he found himself being roughly shaken awake by the farmer.

"What's up?" he asked, sleepily.

"Three o'clock," explained the farmer. "Time to get up. There's work to do."

"What kind of work?" asked the new man.

"Reaping."

"Reaping what?"

"Oats."

"Are they wild?" asked the young man.

"Of course not," the farmer snapped.

"Then why the heck do we have to sneak up on 'em in the dark?"

3513 The night before, the man had had an interview with his prospective in-laws and the young couple were now discussing what chances they had of getting married.

"Dad's raising no objections," the girl reported, "but Mum is being difficult. I suppose you noticed how she bosses everyone? And she says she thinks you're a bit too effeminate."

"By comparison with your mother," he said grimly, "my war-time *sergeant* was effeminate."

3514 She had only had her fortune a few months and wasn't yet adapted to it. Trying to impress some friends at a hen party she said idly: "I clean my jewellery with champagne—it brings the sparkle up in the diamonds."

Another woman said quickly: "Oh, is that so? I always clean my diamonds with crème de menthe, but I use champagne for my rubies and emeralds."

A third woman said with studied indifference. "I always think cleaning the wretched things is tiresome. Once I dirty up a tiara or anything I usually hand it in for salvage."

3515 The American visitor was being driven around London by a sad little cab-driver. As they passed Buckingham Palace the American said: "Say, that's not a bad little joint. How long did it take to put that up?"

"Couple of years," said the cabbie.

"Gosh. We'd throw that up in six weeks back home."

Shortly afterwards they passed St. Paul's. The American said: "Gee, that's elegant. How long did that take to build?"

The cabbie, becoming irritable, said: "About three months."

"In America we'd have that up in a month," the visitor boasted.

Then they drove past the new Battersea power station.

"Jeepers, get a load of that!" said the American. "How long were they working on that?"

The cabbie sniffed, stared out of the window and grunted: "Well it wasn't there when I passed last night."

3516 She had just returned from a shopping trip in the car. She said: "Harry, don't you think it's time we had another car?"

"Look, Beryl, we already have one. It's good enough."

"Not now it isn't," she said. "A lamp-post backed into me."

3517 This is another little tale about a mental home, and the visitor to this one was surprised to see a group of men seated in a semi-circle, passing half a dozen sheets of paper back and forth.

"What kind of a game are they playing?" the visitor asked his guide. "Is it something to do with occupational therapy, or rehabilitation?"

"Not exactly," explained the official. "They're all ex-Civil Servants and they're imagining themselves back at work."

3518 Two medical students were talking about a certain doctor, lecturer in pathology. One of them remarked: "I've been told he's a lady-killer, but I don't think he really cares what sex they are."

3519 Salvador Dali, the artist, was staying in an hotel in New York when he was visited by a burglar who escaped before Dali could catch him. However, he had taken a good look at him and so was able to provide the police with a rough sketch of the miscreant. For eight days afterwards four thousand New York cops were scouring the underworld looking for a bent sword, two goldfish and a corkscrew with a human eye in the handle.

3520 A fellow-traveller was visiting the office of the mayor in a small Bulgarian town. While he was there the telephone rang and the mayor excused himself for interrupting their discussion. The visitor waited until the mayor replaced the instrument. Then he said: "That's a strange kind of telephone; I see it has a receiver but no mouthpiece."

The mayor nodded and said briefly: "It's a direct line from Moscow."

3521 The little Yiddisher man opened an office in town and advertised himself as a confidential inquiry agent. The telephone rang on the first morning he was in business: "Good morning, this is Epstein, the Private Isaac."

3522 Henry Koogan says of a friend: "He's only forty but he can't sleep, he can't eat and he daren't drink. I tell you he hardly notices the cost of living."

3523 A newly-degreed lawyer was present at the funeral of a millionaire who had not been particulary respected for his social conscience. A friend arrived a little late and the service was well advanced as he sidled into a seat beside the lawyer.

"How far has he got?" whispered the newcomer, nodding at the clergyman in the pulpit.

The lawyer whispered in reply: "Just opened for the defence."

3524 The hostess at the party remarked to a guest: "I see young Fothergill is showing some interest in that pretty daughter of Jervis's. About time, too; he's been a bachelor far too long." Sensing a gentle reproof for his own unmarried state the handsome guest returned: "I don't know. No man can really be a bachelor too long."

3525 Four sailors were marooned on a lonely island with three pretty girls. The sailors found a bottle and it was decided that they should send a message off in the hope that the bottle would be washed ashore somewhere. They were unanimous that the small, studious little matelot, George, should write the message. So George scribbled: "We are marooned on an island a hundred miles south-east of Picahito. Please send help. If you can't send help, send another woman."

3526 Down Haymarket they tell of the theatrical producer who insisted on two rehearsals for his wedding and at the second one decided that he'd have to get someone else to play the leading female role.

3527 A city financier, notoriously cynical, was talking about blondes, and one blonde in particular. "They're not as dumb as folks believe. Maybe their mathematics aren't so hot, but just ask 'em how many chinchillas make a wrap."

3528 Old Freddie Slocum's wife died on him and he was utterly distraught. At the funeral he practically collapsed with grief and all the way back to town in the carriage he was sobbing his heart out. "Look, Freddie," said his oldest friend, "don't take on so. It's tough, I know, but in six or seven months you'll have got over it, and who knows, you might meet another little woman and get married all over again." "Six, seven months," groaned Freddie, enraged. "What am I gonna do *tonight*."

3529 A commercial traveller made a snap decision to spend a week-end at home, a thing he hadn't done in months. He sent off a telegram to his wife Betty saying he'd be with her in a few hours, and then he took the first available train.

When he arrived home, to his consternation he found his wife in the arms of another man. After creating a violent scene he stomped out of the house with his clothes and threatened to divorce. He took a room in an hotel around the corner. The following morning his father-in-law went to see him in an effort to patch things up. He told the outraged husband: "I'm sure there's an explanation and I'm going to get to the bottom of this.

Hold everything until I get back." The old man then went to see his daughter. An hour later he returned, smiling all over his chubby face.

"You see," he told his son-in-law. "Didn't I say there was a perfectly good explanation. She didn't even *get* your telegram."

3530 "Gosh," declared Rube, "I sure do miss my wife's cooking."
"She gone away?" he was asked.
"Nope. I just don't go home. That's how I miss it."

3531 A jet-pilot in the R.A.F. was given a new prototype plane to test. It was estimated that the plane could touch 1,845 miles per hour. He got the crate into the sky and began to climb, speed increasing swiftly from 400 to 500 and up to the sound barrier. There was an enormous explosion as the plane smashed through, and on she went, hurtling through the heavens at 850 m.p.h. and on to 925 m.p.h. The pilot was petrified as he glanced at the clock and saw the needle hovering around the 1,000 m.p.h. mark, and the altimeter showing 98,000 feet.
"Good Lord!" he ejaculated.
A calm voice at his elbow said: "Yes, my son?"

3532 The general's pretty wife was ill in bed. The padre thought it only right that he should try to comfort the young woman in her trouble, so he invited himself along to the house after breakfast and told her: "I was praying for you last night." "Silly man," she smiled artfully. "You know perfectly well I'm on the phone."

3533 A few days after the floods in Norfolk a motorist was squelching along a muddy lane when he saw a man's head just sticking above the ground. Being a friendly sort of guy he stopped the car and called out: "Could I give you a lift?" "No thanks," came the reply. "I'm on my bike."

3534 The Rev. Duckley was a young and nervous clergyman and when the time came for him to preach his first sermon he was somewhat rattled. He stood in the vestry anxiously fingering his collar and wondering if his hair was tidy. Unfortunately there was no mirror in the place. Plucking up courage he asked the verger: "I say, do you think you could get me a glass?"
The verger went out and Duckley waited patiently for his return. He came back hiding something under his coat. Then he drew it out and passed it to the preacher saying gleefully: "I managed to get a whole bottle by mentioning your name."

3535 He had been courting her diligently for three weeks and one evening she was saying: "I like Keats and Shelley and Tennyson and Burns . . ."
He interrupted sheepishly and said: "Look, Gloria, I'm quite convinced that you're popular, but do I stand any chance at all?"

3536 Old Hogson said: "I sure miss those wonderful days of the silent pictures."

"Come, come, now," objected a friend, "what was so good about silent films?"

"Waal," mused Hogson, "I remember how restful it was to sit and watch a woman's mouth going for ninety minutes and never a single word coming out."

3537 Two Communists met on Broad Street in the early summer. It was a perfectly wonderful day, and all around them people were happily going about their business.

The first Communist, only slightly pink, was endeavouring to enter into the spirit of the sunshine and remarked: "Nice day we're having."

The second Communists scowled and retorted: "Yes, but the rich are having it, too."

3538 An industrial magazine insists that the latest edition of *Who's Who* quotes the recreations of the Chairman of British Rail as being "shunting and hooting."

3539 A wife seeking a divorce alleged that every time she and her husband drove past one of his girl-friends she was ordered to duck her head.

3540 Three citizens were having lunch together in a restaurant in a small town in Bulgaria. One of them was reading a newspaper. Suddenly he pointed to an article written by a leading Communist, and shaking his head slightly whispered: "Tut. Tut, tut."

One of the other men leaned over his shoulder and read bits of the article. He shook his head gently and said: "Tut tut."

The third man looked anxiously around the restaurant and, reaching for his hat, muttered: "Look, if you two are going to talk politics I'm getting out of here."

3541 Skeffingby was one of those low-brow comics who did nothing whatever for balletomanes except embarrass them. Nevertheless he was anxious to join the exclusive club to which a number of patrons of the Arts belonged. One of his theatrical friends finally agreed to sponsor Skeffingby's application for membership, and after considerable trouble on the friend's part, Skeffingby was reluctantly passed by the committee. His friend then called upon him at the theatre where he was playing and said: "All right, Skeff. I've fixed it for you. All you have to do now is pay your twenty guineas and you can make the club your second home."

Skeffingby pulled a wry face and exploded: "What? Do you think I want to belong to any club that has a character like me for a member?"

3542 A certain gentleman, noted for his die-hard principles, his vast estates and banking directorships, ancient lineage, and open dislike of the proletariat, was recently compelled to visit his dentist and part with his teeth.

The following day he was at his club, feeling somewhat sorry for himself. And inevitably he was dining off a couple of buttered rolls which he surreptitiously submerged in warm coffee before transferring them to his mouth.

Observing this phenomenon a passing friend observed drily: "Hello, Clifford. Why don't you adopt the democratic doughnut?"

3543 At the Head Office of the G.P.O. a well-dressed woman used to call three times a week, and on each occasion she would ask for a chair and a copy of the London 'phone directory, A–K. Armed with this bulky tome she would sit in a 'phone booth, avidly reading every page. This went on for a couple of months until the manager became both inquisitive and annoyed. He intended to speak to her but she beat him to it by smiling sweetly and saying: "Could I have the other book this time—the L—Z one."

The manager said gruffly: "What's the matter madam? Don't you like A–K?"

"Oh, yes, it was wonderful. I read every word," she said. "That's why I'm so anxious to read the sequel."

3544 All the money I earn goes to take care of the poor, sick horses. They are such poor, sick horses, they've never yet won a race.

3545 Have you heard of the latest miracle cure for bunions? Have your leg amputated.

3546 We're not rich, but at least we have lace on our beds. It's lace now, but before they went to the laundry they were sheets.

3547 A friend of mine has just got divorced because of something that came to his wife's ears. It was another man's mouth.

3548 I went out with a nurse last night. Soon my mother says I can take a girl out.

3549 Some girls can't be trusted too far. And some men can't be trusted too near.

3550 My wife keeps our home spotless. You never see a dirty dish. We eat straight out of the cans.

3551 We went to a restaurant where we had to sign the Poisons Register before they would serve us.

3552 He got a new job at the Eagle Laundry, but after a fortnight he left. He found it monotonous washing eagles all day.

3553 A man on the train was asked by the ticket collector for his ticket. He searched in all his pockets without finding it, then one of the other passengers said: "You're very absent-minded, you've got the ticket in your mouth." The traveller handed the ticket to the collector who punched it and moved on into the next compartment. When he had gone, another passenger said: "Fancy putting the ticket in your mouth and forgetting it"; and the traveller replied: "Don't be silly. I was chewing off the date."

3554 Lady (complaining to porter about his negligence): "I shall report you for insulting behaviour. I happen to be one of the railroad director's wives."
Porter: "I don't care if you're his only wife, lady."

3555 A drunk was staggering around the streets and eventually bumped into a stranger and asked: "Where am I?" The stranger said: "You're on the corner of Mason Street and First Avenue, you old fool," and the drunk said: "Cut out the details. Just tell me what town it is."

3556 A Scotsman walked into a bar and asked for a miniature bottle of whisky. The barman said: "Do you want to drink it here?" The Scot replied: "Nae, I'm takin' it hame and I'm throwing a party."

3557 Patient to doctor: "What can you do for me? I suffer terribly from insomnia."
Doctor to patient: "If I were you I'd go home and try to sleep it off."

3558 Pop singer: "All my new L.P.'s are unbreakable."
Girl-friend: "What a shame!"

3559 At the concert she turned to her boy-friend and said: "Isn't it a haunting piece of music?"
He: "It should be, the way the orchestra is murdering it."

3560 The vicar was marrying the young Scotsman to his lovely bride: "Throughout my career I have always maintained that it is an evil thing to marry for money."
Angus: "Then ye'll nae be wantin' your fee."

3561 Her husband was a member of the Musicians Union and when he died she benefited under the Pension Scheme. Every month she got a hundred sheets of music and a baton.

3562 The mistress of the house was downstairs organising a party and her maid was upstairs rearranging the dust.

3563   Whenever he goes away from Manchester he sits with his back to the engine because he enjoys looking at what he is getting away from.

3564   The sales manager of a washing-machine company called one of his salesmen into the office and complained: "Do you realise not one machine has been sold on your territory in the last two months?"

Salesman: "Can I help it if I'm working a territory in which there are three nudist camps?"

3565   Two drunks were walking home along a railway line in the heart of the country. One turned to the other and said: "I don't know about you—hic—Arnold, but I think this is the longest staircase I've ever walked up."

Arnold said: "I don't mind the stairs, Alf. It's these low banisters that's getting me."

3566   His wife has one habit that could be the death of her. Whenever she turns on the gas he hides the matches.

3567   A drunk was splashing about in the fountain at Trafalgar Square just as dawn broke. Suddenly he looked up the column and noticed Nelson standing there. He clung tightly to one of the lions and yelled up:

"Don't jump, don't jump! This is the shallow end."

3568   The ship was making its way up the Nile. Suddenly there was a harsh, scrunching noise and the vessel lurched to a grinding halt.

Captain (to Navigator): "I thought you said you knew every sandbank in the river."

Navigator: "Aye, sir, that's one of them."

3569   He said he was a soldier of fortune. He ran the Crown and Anchor Board in the barracks.

3570   The 'celloist played his solo walking up and down the rostrum. This was because the original music had been written for the bagpipes.

3571   The coastguard station thought they sighted a wreck off the coast near Eastbourne. It turned out to be a woman from Wigan, having a swim. I keep telling my wife not to bathe.

3572   The height of frustration. That was the time when Eve had a terrible argument with Adam, and there was no one to tell.

3573   Husband to wife: "I thought I asked you to put a bottle in the bed?"

Wife: "But I did!"

Husband: "I know that, but what's the good of the bottle without a corkscrew?"

3574 Harry: "My wife isn't a flighty sort of woman. She'd never do anything wrong. She's too decent, too fine, too loyal, too honest . . . and let's face it, Sid, she's too old."

3575 A group of young thespians put on an open-air show at Highfield Park, and it was such a bad effort, even the trees walked out.

3576 Then there's the knight of olden days who worked himself up into a terrible state trying to find a suit of non-iron armour.

3577 Tax Office: The only place on earth where people fight to be last in the queue.

3578 Two burglars broke into a government department in Whitehall and opened the safe. All they found there was a 4 lb. carton of tea and four chipped cups.

3579 Extraordinarily fat woman to husband: "I think I'll slip down to the Launderette and do my smalls."

3580 McTavish started an off-shore pirate radio station for broadcasting records. He advertised in the *Glasgow Herald* for a boy to sharpen the needles.

3581 Two men stopped at a remote country pub that was in an awful state of dilapidation. After a couple of drinks they asked the landlord if they could have a game of billiards. The billiards room was dusty and festooned with cobwebs. One of the travellers started to put the balls on the table and discovered that they were chipped and broken and all discoloured a shade of slate grey. He said to the landlord: "How are we supposed to know which balls are which?"
The landlord answered: "You'll soon get to know them by their shapes."

3582 A timid young man walked into an exclusive cocktail bar and asked nervously: "Do you serve women?"
Barman: "No, you're supposed to bring your own."

3583 An elderly spinster in a Scottish village was asked by the local reporter why, since she was such a good-looking woman, she had never been married.
Spinster: "Weel, my faither couldna bring himsel' to gie me awa'."

3584 When George met Alf, Alf had a beautiful black eye.
George: "Where did you get that shiner?"
Alf: "Well, all I did was kiss the bride after the ceremony."
George: "But that's normal procedure."
Alf: "Not eight years after the ceremony."

3585 Sign in a bar-room: "The customer is always tight."

3586 He's been studying medicine for six years—in chemists' windows.

3587 Some people like German pianos, and some like British. But Bert prefers an Italian model—named Gina.

3588 On one side of the record is his latest song—on the other a long apology.

3589 An old country inn, reputed to be haunted by a ghost, has a sign over the bar: "Licensed to Serve Spirits."

3590 Bride-to-be to mother: "Mum, do you believe in big weddings or little ones?"
Mother: "Well, I should have the big wedding first, dear."

3591 Wife (to husband): "Now look you, I don't want you to use any of your bad language before my mother."
Husband: "All right. I'll let her get hers in first."

3592 Bill: "She's as fresh as something out of a meadow!"
Ben: "A cow?"

3593 Diner: "Waiter, there's a button in my stew."
Waiter: "I'm so sorry, sir, that must have dropped off the jockey's blouse."

3594 Tom: "How about going to see the Folies Bergère this morning?"
Bill: "No, no. The show doesn't start till eight o'clock."
Tom: "I know, but we could watch the undress rehearsal."

3595 They were so rich, the Kaplans, they even had the family monogram embroidered on their paper tissues.

3596 The doctor examined Mrs. Hardcastle's husband and said to her: "It's his digestion that's at fault. You'd better put him on a stable diet." Forthwith she went down to the shopping arcade and laid in a stock of hay, oats and lump-sugar.

3597 There's a lot to be said for marriage, but try not to say it in front of the children.

3598 A husband is a man who has finally decided that he just can't go through life enjoying himself.

3599 "Is your wife a good dresser?"
"Well, I'd say she dressed rather casually."
"You would?"
"Yes. With the curtains wide open and a cigarette in her mouth."

3600 Wife: "It's Mother's birthday on Friday. I'd like you to send her some flowers."
Husband: "Okay. On my way to work I'll order some rock plants."

3601 He has two pairs of binoculars for studying heavenly bodies at night. A large pair for the stars above and a pair of opera glasses for the chorus girls at the Vaudeville theatre.

3602 "I'm taking that new body-building course, by post."
"I know. You've been at it for four months, and I can't see any difference."
"Can't you? Let me tell you I've got muscles I haven't even unwrapped yet."

3603 Road Signs Explained: Dangerous Curves Ahead—you are approaching a strip-tease club.

3604 A motorist going along the M1 tried to squeeze his shooting-brake between two enormous pantechnicons . . . anyone want to buy a long, thin station-wagon?

3605 The hotel advertised "running water in all rooms". What they meant was that the roof leaked.

3606 "That's a nice camera you have there."
"Yes. I'm a professional."
"Tell me, why does that camera have a keyhole-shaped lens?"
"I use it for taking blackmail pictures."

3607 "I hear that Jack has just passed his bar examinations."
"That's true. At the Star and Garter last night he drank ten pints in twenty minutes."

3608 He was a very accomplished organist but he had to give it up. His monkey died of exposure.

3609 We know a photographer whose speciality was taking portraits. He's in prison now. He took one from the Tate Gallery.

3610 "When I'm with Gladys," said Phil, "time stands still."
"I'm not surprised," said George. "She's got a face that would stop a clock."

3611   A somnambulist in Norfolk was so rich he didn't have to walk in his sleep. He took a cab.

3612   Georgina: "I'm never going out with Frank again."
  May: "Why not?"
  Georgina: "I can't stand a man who takes you to dinner and reads the menu from right to left."

3613   A Scotsman who had three beautiful daughters was glad when they were married off, one after the other. He had been unable to attend the first two receptions, but he went to the third. There was no further need to pick up the confetti outside the church.

3614   A businessman, harassed by overwork, advertised for a secretary: "Wanted, young lady assistant, who can type. One who has no bad habits and is willing to learn."

3615   The girl invited Ted into her flat and the first thing he noticed was a strange object over the mantelpiece. "What's that barber's pole doing up there?" he asked her. "Oh, that?" she said casually. "It's just to remind me of all the close shaves I've had."

3616   Letter from a cannibal chief to the Bishop of Barchester: "Your Grace, It was so kind of you to send our tribe a missionary. We found him very kind, most clever, terribly considerate and absolutely delicious."

3617   Wife: "Harry, who do you think I ran into today?"
  He doesn't answer—he goes out and looks at the car.

3618   On a little service station away out on the edge of a western desert there hangs a shingle, bearing this strange legend: "Don't ask us for information. If we knew anything we wouldn't be here."

3619   Wife to husband: "What shall we buy my mother for her birthday? She would like something electric."
  Husband: "How about a chair?"

3620   Recovering from an operation, a patient asked the doctor, "Why are the blinds drawn?"
  The doctor replied: "Well, there's a fire across the street, and I didn't want you to wake up and think the operation was a failure."

3621   His wife made him a chunky-knit sweater and it suited him perfectly. He was a chunky nit.

3622   A woman motorist, having trouble with her headlights, stops at a service-station and asks the mechanic to look the car over. After examining the electrical wiring the mechanic says: "It looks to me, Miss, as if you've got a short circuit between the fuse-box and the battery."

"Well don't just stand there," the girl snaps. "Lengthen it."

3623   Jonesey had a watch which had been given to him by his firm for good service. It went very well for thirty years and then suddenly stopped. The hair spring went bald.

3624   There's one very good reason why McKnee became an orchestra leader. When he was four his father bought him a lollipop and he didn't want to throw away the stick.

3625   "I hear that you went to the Subway Room for dinner last night. Did you leave a tip?"

"No. The place was a tip when we got there."

3626   Angeline: "Is it true that you are one of twins?" Beryl (opening photograph album) "Yes. Here's a picture of me when I was two."

3627   Leonard's wife ran away with the milkman. Now, every time he hears a van stopping outside the house he gets scared the milkman is bringing her back.

3628   There was once a famous musician who was invited by the Brighton Corporation to be a guest conductor for a month. But he didn't know how to punch the tickets.

3629   A man went to the doctor because he had spots before his eyes. The doctor examined him and sent him to a specialist optician. The optician examined him and put some drops in his eyes. "Is that any better?" he asked the patient. "Yes, much," came the reply, "I can see the spots much clearer now."

3630   The candidate made a sweeping statement, and cleared the Albert Hall.

3631   A debtor explained to his tailor: "I can't pay you this month. I have four lots of maintenance to keep up." The tailor said in surprise: "Four? You mean women?" "No," said the man; "bookmakers."

3632   Donald went fishing for the first time, armed with all the new equipment and Walton's book on angling. He baited the hook with a large worm, and cast it into the water. Suddenly there was a fierce tugging on the line. Donald fought and struggled to pull in the line as it threshed about and after half an hour's terrific battling, he managed to pull the worm back out of the water.

3633 She asked him in for a bite to eat. It was the nicest meal he'd ever had—simply melted in his mouth. All she gave him was an ice-cream wafer.

3634 Mrs. McPhee told her husband to call in at the store and buy her half a dozen coat hangers. He returned with six large nails.

3635 McTavish went into the lost property store to buy a trunk for his holidays. He finally found one reduced from six guineas to thirty shillings. The manager said: "Shall I wrap it up for you, Mr. McTavish?" McTavish said: "Nae mon, it doesna matter. Just put the brown paper and string inside."

3636 She was a good cook, so for an anniversary present he bought his wife a carving set—three chisels and a mallet.

3637 A parent is someone who spends hours and hours teaching his child to walk and to talk. But when the child starts school he tells him to sit down and shut up.

3638 Army life separates the men from the boys. It also separates the boys from the girls.

3639 The bookie slowly counted out the pound notes into the old lady's wrinkled hands. "Lady," he said, "I just don't understand. How ever do you manage to pick the winner?"
    The old lady patted her white locks in place. She looked a little bewildered.
    "Really," she said. "I don't know myself. I just stick a pin in the paper and . . . well, there it is."
    The bookie took a deep breath. "That's all very well, lady," he cried. "But how on earth did you manage to pick four winners in one afternoon?"
    "Oh," replied the old lady, "that was easy. You see I used a fork."

3640 He has a problem about the future. He's getting married in a month and he hasn't found her a job yet.

3641 Teacher: "Now, Freddie, tell me when Sir Walter Raleigh died." Freddie: "Heck, I didn't even know the poor fellow had been ill."

3642 We've just found out the truth about the Mary who used to take her little lamb to school. It was between two thick chunks of bread.

3643 "Has Cyril passed his 11-plus tests?"
    "Yes."

"That's good."

"What's good about it? He was 11-plus eight when he made it."

3644   "Where did you get that gorgeous silver rose-bowl from, Ken?"

"Oh, that? It was handed down to me by my father."

"Is he dead?"

"No. He's on Dartmoor. They caught him up the ladder while he was handing it down to me."

3645   Lord Hatchbuck to the new butler just arrived from the bureau: "And remember, Stevens, as soon as cook has everything ready, let us know. I shall be in the morning-room with our guests."

At eight sharp Stevens threw open the door of the morning-room, bowed low and bellowed: "Come an' get it!"

3646   They were about to embark for Carlisle, and his lordship was having a final word with his valet who was to accompany him. "Tell me, Jaggers, do we have to change at Crew?"

"I believe so, your lordship," said Jaggers. Said his lordship: "Well, it can't be helped. What do you suggest?—the striped worsted or the tartan smoking jacket?"

3647   Fond mother: "Look at my little Herbie. Isn't he cute? He's got his father's eyes, his father's nose, his father's mouth . . ."

Her sister: "Yes, it's no wonder your old man has such a vacant expression."

3648   Poor Matilda. Ten years ago she bought a love-seat from the department store—and half of it is still brand new.

3649   Sybil: "I feel rather sorry I turned Bill down. They tell me he's been drinking like a fish ever since."

Gracie: "Well, that's one way of celebrating."

3650   Last night Joe Perkins kissed a woman by mistake. It was his wife.

3651   Circus Owner to employee: "Davis, you fool, do you know you left the lion cage wide open all night?"

Davis: "So what? Who the heck would want to steal a lion?"

3652   Frank: "One thing about Stella, she knows all the answers."

Reggie: "What's the good? Nobody ever asks her the questions."

3653   Hollywood must be the only place on earth where brides keep the bouquets and throw away their grooms.

3654   A Civil Servant was transferred to a different town and another department. On his first day in the new office a file of correspondence came his way, bearing numerous inscriptions and memoranda, and pitted with the expression "Passed To You". The man checked the papers and signed them. Shortly afterwards an irate fellow-employee stormed into his office with the papers and threw them on to the desk. "You *signed* these, you fool," he exclaimed. "Do you know what you've done? You've gone and broken the chain."

3655   Miss Fatchwirth applied for a different job as she was tired of running a riding-school. The new job was that of a disc-jockey for a radio station in Cape Town. She used to put the records on, sitting side-saddle.

3656   A man in Edinburgh has invented something really new—coloured wireless. It's the same as ordinary radio, but you have to wear a pair of polaroid headphones.

3657   Harvey Johnson was given the lead role in a re-make of the film *Love Letters*. He was the postman.

3658   Arthur was saying to his pal: "Me and the wife don't quite know what to do with our youngster, he's one of those in-betweens, and we can't go out at night because he's too young to be left alone and too old to have a baby-sitter."

3659   When little Oliver was fourteen, his parents finally gave up trying and ran away from home.

3660   The beautiful Spanish senorita had a red, red rose between her teeth. She needed it to fill up the gap.

3661   Ghost to ghost: "I say, would you like to see where I had my apparition?"

3662   "My husband is as tough as a horse."
       "Is he? Race or clothes?"

3663   "Do you know that Albert was once the featherweight champion of Wales?"
       "How many fights did he win?"
       "All of 'em. He used to tickle his opponents to death."

3664   Young visitor from America: "Do you know where the British Museum is?"
       Old Man: "I should. I was an exhibit there for four years."

3665 Joy: "Your husband drinks an awful lot."
Agnes: "I'll say he does. He can hold his liquor better than the original cask."

3666 Newspaper Report: "On Wednesday, Lady Inchbottom will launch a new 100,000 ton oil-tanker on the Clyde."
There isn't much else they can do with it.

3667 Ivy: "I should imagine your boy-friend doesn't take his work home with him from the office. He always seems to spend the evenings at the pub drinking beer."
Joan: "Yes, but he says it helps. Two heads are better than one."

3668 Every night when he met her she used to give him the cold shoulder. Then he thought of a good idea. He took her to the local pub and filled her up with gin and anti-freeze.

3669 "Waiter, this cheese doesn't taste very good."
"It should be all right. We had it specially imported from Switzerland."
"Did you say imported or deported?"

3670 Notice on the garden gate of couple with delinquent child: "Please beware of our lad."

3671 "You know, Harriet, I've got no sympathy for a man who spends all his evenings drinking."
"A man who can spend all his evenings drinking doesn't need your sympathy, dear."

3672 Dinner at the Carlton-Ferris Hotel Restaurant is usually à la carte. Just round the corner at the Criterion Café it's à la pushcart.

3673 The commercial television station screened a notice which read: "This programme is unsuitable for children."
I've got news for them—the rest of the programmes are unsuitable for adults.

3674 Politician: a man who has been educated beyond his intelligence. A man who was born weak-minded and had a serious relapse at Westminster.

3675 Jack Harvester was a man with an inventive turn of mind. He crossed pigeons with woodpeckers. A friend asked him the motive behind this scientific miracle and Jack explained: "Well it's like this, when they come home, they can knock on the door to let me know."

3676   They must think an awful lot of Bert at the dog track. They keep a light burning for him in the   Tote window.

3677   Everyone knows that old saw about women dressing to kill, but lately the way they've been dressing is enough to ruin the textile industry.

3678   A man has been advertising in the Press for eighty years to the effect that: "You, Too, Can Have a Body Like Mine." Who the heck wants the body of an eighty-year-old body-builder?

3679   People who enjoy the majority of television programmes have special qualifications. They are deaf and daft.

3680   They offered Bill Williams a part in a new Tarzan picture. He was practising the dialogue, which runs: "You Jane, Me Tarzan", when the producer came up and told him he was to play the chimpanzee.

3681   Every time Percy drank too much it affected his eyes so much that print became blurred. Feeling that he ought to do something about it, he decided on a course of action. He stopped the papers.

3682   Eric is so concerned about inner-cleanliness that he takes some powder every morning. Soap powder.

3683   They were sitting in church listening to the vicar's lengthy and boring sermon. Little Alfie nudged his father and whispered: "Dad, can't we give him the money now, and go home?"

3684   Henry: "Is your wife hard to please?"
    Ron: "I don't know—I've never tried."

3685   Simpkins has found the way to double his money at the racetrack. He takes it out of his wallet, folds it, and puts it away in his hip pocket.

3686   When the Queen visited Aberdeen Mrs. McManus didn't have enough money to buy a flag, so she stood on the terrace and waved her hair.

3687   Passport Officer (looking at Kelly's passport): "Are you a pirate?"
    "Shure an' I'm as honest as the day is long," replied Kelly, his pinched face grimacing.
    "Then what's this skull and crossbones?" asked the officer.

3688   When two beatniks play the game of "boy meets girl", you can't tell the difference.

3689 Lester Morgan answered an advertisement in the newspaper for pen friends, and got replies from two pigs.

3690 A Women's Institute gathering is an assembly where the gossip goes twice as far as the sandwiches.

3691 Beatnik in coffee bar: "I'd like a coffee without cream."
  Snooty young waitress: "We ain't got no cream. You'll have to have it without milk."

3692 His new car is a five-seater. Two inside the car and three on the roof.

3693 A travelling salesman was recently committed to a mental home. He was suffering from chronic frustration after visiting a nudist camp every day for a month trying to buttonhole the manager.

3694 Albert's got one of those very small cars. The passenger seat is in his lap.

3695 A motor mechanic made an appointment to see a psychiatrist because he was suffering from sleeplessness. After asking the patient what his job was the psychiatrist said: "Okay, let's start. Get under the couch."

3696 Vera had the latest Italian-style hair-do. She looked like something that had been dragged by the scruff of the neck from a Venetian canal by a gondolier with greasy fingers.

3697 The theatre closed twenty-four hours after the opening of the production. A foul play was suspected.

3698 Here is some advice for you if you are likely to go into the jungle and be captured by cannibals. Do try to keep cool, calm and collected. There is no sense in getting in a stew.

3699 Garages are so grasping these days, when so many cars are on the road and motorists are ripe for the plucking. Geoffrey has just received his garage account which includes £1.50 for the grease which the mechanic smeared over the upholstery.

3700 He says that he doesn't mind in the least doing the washing-up for his wife. After all, she helps him with all the rest of the housework.

3701 "Stanley," said Mavis, studying hard for her degree in English, "do you understand syntax?"
  "Understand it?" said Stan. "I didn't even know it *was* taxed."

3702   Motorists should have their brakes checked regularly. But if, due to some negligence by the garage, you should ever find yourself behind the wheel of a car whose brakes have failed, here is the best tip the A.A. can offer you. "Aim the vehicle at something cheap."

3703   Whilst fishing off the beach at Briarmouth, an enthusiast caught five jelly fish. All different flavours.

3704   Psychiatrist: "You teenage beatniks are a national menace. The trouble with you is that you have no sense of social responsibility. Forget about material things and think of extraneous matters—science, mathematics, stuff like that. How are you on maths?"
    Patient: "What's maths?"
    Psychiatrist: "Oh, never mind. Look, I'm going to ask you some questions about arithmetic, to test your reactions to factual information. Give me a number."
    Patient: "Central 4556—that's the coffee-bar where my girl Edna works."
    Psychiatrist: "Forget about women. I don't want a 'phone number. Just an ordinary number."
    Patient: "Okay. Don't flip your lid. Er—thirty-eight?"
    Psychiatrist: "That's better. Now another one."
    Patient: "Twenty-two?"
    Psychiatrist: "And another one?"
    Patient: "Thirty-six?"
    Psychiatrist: "Excellent. See! You *can* get your mind working in other directions if you want to."
    Patient (dreamily): "Cor! 38–22–36—boy, what a figure. . . ."

3705   Man: "Excuse me, but have you got *Lady Chatterley's Lover*?"
    Girl: "Look, mister, if I had, do you think I'd be wasting time here selling books?"

3706   Customer (to manicurist): "You're far too pretty to be working in a dump like this. What you need is a good-looking young man to take care of you. How about you and me going places tonight? We'll have dinner, see a show, and then I'll take you back to my place for drinks, and things. . . ."
    Manicurist: "But I'm a married woman!"
    Customer: "So what! Stop quibbling. What your husband doesn't know won't hurt him."
    Manicurist: "But he's shaving you."

MISCELLANEOUS COMEDY
HUMOROUS PHRASES AND IDIOMS

MISCELLANEOUS COMEDY
HUMOROUS PHRASES AND IDIOMS

3707 ABACK: "Taken aback." Having bribed a rear player from a rival soccer team.

3708 ABOVE BOARD: "All above board." Everybody on deck.

3709 AIRS: "To give yourself airs." To play tunes like the *Londonderry Air* and *Air on a Shoestring* on a long-playing record.

3710 AULD REEKIE: An elderly gentleman who hasn't yet learned about deodorants.

3711 BAD FORM: "In bad form." In need of the support and encouragement of a good corset.

3712 A BAD LOT: Lot number 65, purchased at Hickinfield during an egg auction.

3713 BAT: "To carry one's bat." To give your wife a piggy-back.

3714 BALL: "To have the ball at one's feet." Being a member of a chain gang.

3715 BEAM: "On one's beam ends." Sitting down, anywhere.

3716 BEANS: "Full of beans." Aftermath of a very gluttonous beanfeast.

3717 BEARDED: "Bearded in his den." Portrait of a beatnik in his pad, or apartment.

3718 BED: "To get up on the wrong side of the bed." Stepping out of bed, accidentally, on the side where the linoleum is frozen stiff in mid-winter.

3719 BENEFIT: "Benefit of clergy." An amateur concert produced by the congregation to increase the vicar's income,

3720 BILLINGSGATE: "To talk Billingsgate." Telling fishy stories.

3721 BIRDS: "To kill two birds with one stone." Getting engaged to two blondes with the same engagement ring.

3722 BLACK: "In black and white." Wearing a white-striped dinner jacket.

3723 BLUE: "Feeling blue." When you are out in a stiff breeze.

3724 BOLT: "A bolt from the blue." Running swiftly from a policeman.

3725 BOOK: "It doesn't suit my book." The attitude of a turf accountant towards a punter who has backed a five-horse accumulator.

3726 BOW: "Two strings to one's bow." A girl who has roped in her boy-friend securely.

3727 BREAD: "To know which side one's bread is buttered." A test to find out if you can tell it from margarine.

3728 BREAST: "To make a clean breast." Having a bath.

3729 BRICK: "He's a regular brick." He's a very hard man to do business with.

3730 BRING: "To bring down the house." A vote taken at the end of a Parliamentary debate, which sometimes throws a government out of office.

3731 BROWN: "Brown study." A room in the house decorated, carpeted and furnished in brown throughout.

3732 BURN: "To burn the candle at both ends." A quick way to make ends meet, sometimes in less than a wick.

3733 CAP: "Cap in hand." Begging for an income at the edge of the pavement.

3734 CHANGES: "Ringing the changes." Laundering and squeezing out diapers.

3735 CHESHIRE CAT: "To grin like a Cheshire cat." A Persian cat doing feline impressions.

3736 CHAPTER: "A chapter of accidents." The first twenty paragraphs of the "Births" column in a local newspaper.

3737 CHICKEN: "She's no chicken." She is an old hen.

3738 CHIP: "A chip off the old block." One of the slices snipped from a potato on the antique chopping table.

3739 CLEAN: "Showing a clean pair of heels." A fastidious gentlemen with holes in the back of his socks.

3740 COAST: "The coast is clear." A message informing a coastguard that her husband is away for the week-end.

3741 COCK: "A cock and bull story." The shaggy dog tale about the Spanish Rhode-Island fowl who became a toreador.

3742 COLD: "Give the cold shoulder." Serving up some frozen mutton to her husband.

3743 COTTON: "To cotton on." Realising that the pure wool trouser-suiting is really blended, as soon as the seat wears through and you are on your own.

3744 COVENTRY: "To send to Coventry." What the post office usually does with the parcel boldly addressed to Chichester.

3745 DAN TO BEERSHEBA: A cheap inscribed locket given by Daniel to a drunken Sheba.

3746 DARBY AND JOAN: "A Darby and Joan man." One who thinks of nothing but horse-racing and women.

3747 HORSE: "To flog a dead horse." Serving a meaty stew to unsuspecting patrons of a wayside café, under the heading "Stewed Steak."

3748 DEVIL: "The devil's advocate." Your mother-in-law's solicitor.

3749 DOGS: "Gone to the dogs." Departed for the greyhound track.

3750 DOUBLE: "Double Dutch." When your old Dutch puts on weight.

3751 DOWN: "Down in the mouth." When you wake up in the morning after dreaming you were eating marshmallows in bed, and find you have been munching the bolster.

3752 DRAW: "Draw it mild." Telling an artist not to over-emphasise the attractions of his model.

3753 DUTCH UNCLE: "To speak like a Dutch Uncle." Giving your wife adequate reason to "not understand you" by discussing your absence the night before, in a foreign language.

3754 EAT: "To eat one's words." Dining off soup containing alphabetic noodles.

3755 ENDS: "Making both ends meet." Combing your hair with your toes.

3756 EYES: "Having eyes bigger than one's stomach." Wearing a monocle on your navel.

3757 FACE: "To lose face." Going to a cheap barber shop for a shave.

3758 FALL: "To fall flat on one's face." Something which the average show-girl finds very difficult to do.

3759 FAST: "Play fast and loose." A French farce.

3760 FAT: "The fat is in the fire." Meaning that you can grow rich on insurance money if you have a flair for arson.

3761 FAULT: "Generous to a fault." Being unselfish and always buying presents for an undeserving wife.

3762 FIGHT: "Fight shy." Blushing every time you enter the ring.

3763 FINGER: "Having a finger in the pie." The waiter who serves you with dessert.

3764 FRY: "Small fry." Of no use for large Tues.

3765 GO-BY: "To give the go-by." A motoring association's route map.

3766 GO: "It's no go." A red light.

3767 GRASS: "Let the grass grow under your feet." Never shaving your heels.

3768 GRAIN: "To go against the grain." Going teetotal after a lifetime of imbibing malt whisky.

3769 GREEN: "Green-eyed monster." See mother-in-law.

3770 HAND: "A poor hand." The supplicant palm of a beggar, usually fairly dirty.

3771 HAND: "To live from hand to mouth." Having nothing to eat and chewing your nails.

3772 HAVE: "To have it out with." A general anaesthetic, preferably.

3773 HEART: "Heart in one's boots." In love with your kinky footwear.

3774 HIP: "To smite hip and thigh." An enthusiastic masseur.

3775 HONOUR: "An affair of honour." A platonic friendship with a blonde.

3776 IVORY: "Living in an ivory tower." Occupying a whitewashed attic.

3777 JONESES: "Keeping up with the Joneses." Staying late at Jones's party although you are ready for bed.

3778 LETTERS: "A man of letters." A postman.

3779 LINES: "Read between the lines." Studying the messages scribbled on the brickwork.

3780 LIP: "Pay lip service to." To kiss your tennis partner.

3781 LOSE HEART: When someone trumps your ace.

3782 LIMB: "Out on a limb." A ladder in the stocking.

3783 MAIN: "Splice the main brace." Accidentally cut the thing that is holding up your trousers.

3784 MARE'S NEST: A stable.

3785 MISSING: "The missing link." Part of the golf-course which has been mislaid.

3786 MOLEHILLS: "Making mountains out of molehills." Wearing a padded foundation garment.

3787 NAP: "To go Nap." To fall asleep.

3788 NECK: "Neck and neck." To continue petting interminably.

3789 NINE: "Nine days wonder." British summer; when you wonder whether the weather will wander.

3790 NOD: "The land of Nod." An auction salesroom.

3791 NOSE: "Pay through the nose." People who buy expensive perfume.

3792 NOSE: "Nose to the grindstone." When you visit an inexperienced plastic surgeon to have your features improved.

3793 PALM: "Palmy days." Making a fortune as a quack fortune-teller.

3794 PEEPING: "Peeping Tom." A cat with poor eyesight.

3795 PIN MONEY: The entrance fee payable to see a leg-show.

3796 RAISE: "To raise the wind." To take bismuth, as usual.

3797 RAP: "Not worth a rap." When she is not worth buying a fur coat for.

3798 REEL: "To reel off." To stagger away from the local at closing time.

3799 RHYME: "Without rhyme or reason." A modern pop-song lyric.

3800 RIOT: "To run riot." To be in sole charge of the family.

3801 RIDE: "To ride rough-shod." To go hunting in old boots.

3802 ROUND ROBIN: An over-fed bird.

3803 SCOTCH MIST: Being a little hazy after drinking a bottle of whisky.

3804 SHOULDER: "Straight from the shoulder." A girl with a boyish figure.

3805 SLOW COACH: The average single-deck bus, which nevertheless puts on speed as it passes a bus-stop.

3806 STANDING DISH: A girl on the corner watching all the boys go by.

3807 STEALING A MARCH: The composer who can't write one himself.

3808 STIR: "To stir your stumps." Gnashing your teeth.

3809 TOP: "Sleep like a top." Twisting and turning in bed.

3810 TOUCH: "Touch and go." Borrow a fiver, and depart.

3811 UPPER CRUST: The top of a baldheaded man.

3812 WASH: "Washing your dirty linen in public." Taking your smalls to the launderette.

3813 WOOL: "To pull the wool over his eyes." Take off his socks by pulling them over his head.

3814 WRITING: "The writing on the wall." Inscriptions such as "Yanks go home" or "Bomb the Band".

HOWLERS AND BONERS

3815 Ancient Tyre was a wheel of a Greek chariot.

3816 Late invoices are things you hear in a haunted house.

3817 King Solomon had a thousand wives and also a lot of conquered turbines.

3818 An apiary is where the zoo keeps its monkeys.

3819 Lady Godiva rode bareback on a white charger through Coventry and all the people of the town tried to push to the front.

3820 A polar bear is a nude Eskimo.

3821 Florence Nightingale was a woman who used to sing in Berkeley Square.

3822 The mayonnaise is the name of a famous French marching song.

3823 Poetic licence is a certificate entitling you to make up rhymes and odours.

3824 Scotland Yard is a Scottish measurement which is a few inches shorter than an England yard.

3825 Nelson was an Admiral who commanded the *Victory* and died on a plaque which marks the place in the sea where he fell.

3826 Orpheus was the leader of the Underworld in Greece and was chased by the police.

3827 Mousse is a frozen sweet made from sugar mice.

3828   Aspiring is a drug on the market for headaches.

3829   Atlas carried the world on his head and later someone made maps with it.

3830   Bigotry is when you get married to two wives at the same time but at different addresses.

3831   In Venice they do not have any streets but a series of waterways on which they push boats to and fro with long Poles.

3832   People living on the Equator are called equations but they are imaginary.

3833   Yogis are thin people from India who do exercises to strengthen their characters. They sleep on nails and walk barefoot on hot coal which is good for their soles.

3834   Apostles are letters written in a dead language by four fathers from the Bible.

3835   Monotony is a word for when a man can only have one wife.

3836   The Philistines were people who collected foreign stamps in Egypt and Babylon long before anybody could read or write.

3837   Rabies are Jewish priests who have to be quarantined for six months.

3838   Geranium is a nuclear plant which is used to make atom bombs.

3839   A mongoose is a male French duck.

3840   Pidgin English is the language used to write messages sent by pigeons. The man writes on a slip of paper and ties it to his left leg.

3841   Avoir Dupois was a Frenchman who invented a way to count up to a ton in grains.

3842   Bamboo was a little fawn cartoon invented by Sir Walter Disney.

3843   Destitution is a woman who leads an immortal life and is on the telephone.

3844   Christianity first came to Britain around 42 B.C. by arrangement with the Roman evaders.

3845   The seven ages of man are baby, infant, child, schoolboy, youth, adultery and pensioner.

3846   A baboon is a musical instrument used in concerts for making low notes. You put one end in your mouth and stick your fingers in different holes.

3847   Africa is separated from Europe by the Sewers Canal which Disraeli dug for Queen Victoria.

3848   Expectation is when you spit on a bus and it is not allowed.

3849   A conservatory is a person in Parliament who is not in Labour and is not Liberal, but more to the right. They only use the end bit as this is a four-letter word for them.

3850   Doggerel is a puppy with a short tale and little pauses.

3851   Tranquilisers are little pills for cooling you off. They are only seen on a doctor's postscript.

3852   John Gay was an Irishman who wrote "The Begorrah's Opera."

3853   An antibody is someone who doesn't like nudist camps.

3854   Marie Juana was a Spanish woman who made hemp from rope.

3855   Continental drift is when everybody in England goes to France and Germany for their holidays.

3856   The Diet of Worms was an old-fashioned remedy for being fat.

3857   *Hors de Combat* was one of the horses used by knights of old, fighting in joists and tourniquets.

3858   The Lady of the Lake was a ballerina who was dancing "Swan Lake" and fell in.

3859   A mistrel is a man who puts burnt cork on his face and sings songs about Alabama on Radio Caroline.

3860   Bastille is a soft, French wine gum.

3861   Irrigation is when you have to scratch it.

3862   Newton invented the force of gravity after an apple fell out of a tree and struck him as being curious. Apples have played an important part in history. William Tell used one to teach his son how to use a bone arrow, and long before that Adam and Eve found one in the Garden of Eden. But Eve preferred figs because the leaves were more useful.

3863   The Colossus of Rhodes is the M.1.

3864   The Parthenon is a building in Athens, on the Apocalypse, and its roof is supported by several tall pillows. It was built by the master masons of Greece. There is a boy named Mason in my class but I don't think he is one of their ancestors.

3865   The Vikings were marauding Scandinavians who invaded England in large galleries driven by oars. They had horns growing out of the sides of their heads so they were called Great Danes.

3866   El Giza is the name for a Spanish water-heater.

3867   Alliteration is when a female dog has pups.

3868   Ariel is the name given to the spirit of television. It is a cabalistic spirit which comes down the co-axial cable.

3869   Beau Brummel was a well-dressed dandy from Birmingham.

3870   The earth comes round once every twenty-four hours and is the centre of the Solar Cistern. One of its main stalactites is the full moon which shines by reflecting the earth's light. Thus we can only see it at night when the earth's lights are switched on.

3871   The Boar War was when we fought the pygmies in Africa at the end of the nineteenth century.

3872   Shylock was a Shakespearean actor in Venice who fought a court case with a lady solicitor named Portion over a pound of flesh. The judge wouldn't let him cut the defendant up because Shylock was a Jew and Antonio wasn't Kosher.

3873   The main uses of cow-hide are for luggage and shoe-making but mainly for covering the cow.

3874   Caviare is a Russian dish made from rows of surgeons. It is very expensive but imported by wealthy people who like their food rich.

3875   Francis Bacon is one of the men suspected of writing Shakespeare's plays. A lot of the plays take place in Italy but Shakespeare hardly ever went farther than Anne Hathaway's cottage. He was known as the Bard, which is one of the other words for a poet.

3876   Bombay is the name given to that part of an aircraft where the missiles are kept. There is another one in India.

3877   Tobacco was bought by Sir Walter Rally from an American Irishman named Nick O'Teen who rolled it up and set fire to the end.

3878   A codicil is a small fish which grows up and has its roe removed for smoking.

3879   A mammal is a beast that suckers its young until they are old enough to do it themselves.

3880   Elizabeth I was so-called because she was the first Virgin King ever to sit alone on an English throne although she was in the Middle Ages.

3881   Louis XV was a French king who had a lot of antique chairs named after him and some of them are now collected by junk dealers covered in chintz.

3882   Crusaders were knights of old who went to the Holy Land to fight the Sassenachs but they were worried about leaving their wives unattended and so they came home fairly often. They sometimes got badly wounded.

3883   A termite is a boy who only stops at school for one term.

3884   Mercury was a god in Ancient Rome but he was known as Hermione by the Greeks. He was a weather expert and can now be found in thermometers.

HUMOROUS PROVERBS

3885   A drowning man will clutch at a strawberry blonde.

3886   A good wife makes a good husband suspicious.

3887   A man is known by the Company he floats.

3888   A penny saved is often false economy.

3889   A poet is born not made poor.

3890   A rolling seventeen stones gathers no sympathy.

3891   A short wife is a gay one.

3892   A woman's work is never done right.

3893   Accidents will happen—even to the best-regulated family planners.

3894 All is fair in love and the war that follows it.

3895 All roads lead to a traffic jam.

3896 All things come to those who are waited on.

3897 All work and no play is the occupational hazard of a dramatist.

3898 All's well that ends at the bottom of a shaft.

3899 An apple a day keeps the doctor going.

3900 An Englishman's home is his millstone.

3901 Any port in a storm is better than no rum.

3902 Anything for a quiet wife.

3903 Beauty is but skin-food deep.

3904 Beer is almost thicker than water.

3905 Beggars cannot be boozers.

3906 Better to have loved and lost than never to have lost at all.

3907 Birds in a feather prefer the warm weather.

3908 Boys will be buoys if girls want something to cling to.

3909 Caesar's wife must be above, by now.

3910 Clout not a cast till the first act has passed.

3911 Charity begins a Home.

3912 Children should not be on the scene and allowed to hear.

3913 Circumcisions alter cases.

3914 Civility cost nothing, but the Civil Service costs plenty.

3915 Do as you would be done by and no one will get done.

3916 Don't count your chickens until they have been defrosted.

3917 Don't meet trouble half-way: let your wife take a cab from the station.

3918 Don't put all your bags in one exit.

3919 Early to bed and early to rise, gives a bachelor time to dry his drip-dries.

3920 Even a woman will turn.

3921 Every crowd has silver in its pocket linings.

3922 It's every man for herself.

3923 Every Jock has his gill.

3924 Every dog has his day off.

3925 Every man has his salts.

3926 Faint heart never won funfair lady.

3927 Finding's housekeeping.

3928 Give him enough rope and he'll find a lasso will.

3929 God help those who help themselves.

3930 Half a loaf is better than no tea-break at all.

3931 Happy is the bride the son of a tycoon takes a shine to.

3932 He cannot say B.O. to a goose.

3933 He laughs best whose laughs last.

3934 He who fights and runs away, may live to take flight another day.

3935 Here today, and gone home to momma.

3936 His bed is buttressed on both sides.

3937 Honesty is not the bust policy.

3938 If at first you don't succeed, give up.

3939 In at one ear and out on the ether.

3940 It's easy to be wise after the blessed event.

3941 It's love that makes the world.

3942 It's never too late to men.

3943 Knees mushed when the old devil drives.

3944 Never put off till tomorrow what can be left today.

3945 No noose is good news to the condemned man.

3946 No smoking without fear.

3947 No present like the time if it's a diamond-studded cocktail-watch.

3948 None so blind as they who don't draw it.

3949 Like father, like son-of a-gun.

3950 Lover comes in at the window, but goes out at the fire escape.

3951 Love laughs at hotel-Smiths.

3952 Many a poodle makes a puddle.

3953 Many electricians make light work.

3954 Marriages are made uneven.

3955 Might is a good, straight right.

3956 Nature abhors a vacuum-cleaner salesman.

3957 Necessity is the mother of invective.

3958 One good turn gets most of the bedclothes.

3959 One half of the world doesn't know that a London property company owns the other half.

3960 One man's mate is another man's girl-friend.

3961 One swallow does not make a drunken orgy.

3962 People who live in glasshouses should watch out for jet aircraft.

3963 Pigs might fly but only as ham sandwiches on the stewardess's tray.

3964 Poverty is no sin. That's why people don't commit it.

3965 Practice makes perfect, but that's no consolation if you are the dentist's first patient.

3966 Prevention is better than being cured, as the fat pig said as he ran away.

3967 Procrastination is the thief of time especially if you can't spell it.

3968 A red spy at night is a secret agent's delight.

3969 Set a beggar on a horse, and having no shirt he will ride bare-back.

3970 Straws show which way the wind blows, especially in Hawaii.

3971 The darkest hour is just before you're overdrawn.

3972 The early bird makes the morning tea.

3973 The greater the truth, the smaller the label.

3974 The law does not concern itself with trifles, only with just desserts.

3975 The proof of the padding is in the seating.

3976 The road to Hell is paved with bad inventions.

3977 There are as good fish in the sea as ever came out of it—and fresher.

3978 Ruth is stranger than fiction.

3979 Two heads are better than one, if you are a Harley Street psychiatrist.

3980 Walls have ears, so you may just as well talk to the wall as to your wife.

3981 Waist not, wanted not.

3982 Where there's a Will, there's a lawyer to unsettle the estate.

FOREIGN PHRASES REDEFINED

3983 AD HOC. (L.)   To take something else to the pawnbrokers.

3984 AIDE DE CAMP (Fr.)   A spirit stove.

3985 ALLEGRO (It.)   Line of chorus girls.

3986 ALTER EGO (L.)   To change the look of his face.

3987 A POSTERIORI (L.)   A little behind.

3988 CASUS BELLI (L.)   A cummerbund.

3989 CHARGÉ D'AFFAIRES (Fr.)   The price of romance.

3990 CORDON SANITAIRE (Fr.)   Not while the train is standing in the station.

3991 EN BLOC (Fr.)   Waiting to be beheaded.

3992 ENTENTE CORDIALE (Fr.)   Campers' refreshment.

3993 ENTRECHAT (Fr.)   Let the cat in.

3994 ET EGO IN ARCADIA (L.)   Had an omelette in the Arcadian Restaurant.

3995 FAUX PAS (Fr.)   Not his real father

3996 FLOREAT (L.)   An Easter bonnet.

3997 HIC JACET (L.)   Drinking jacket.

3998 HOC AGE (L.)   Vintage wine.

3999 IN FORMA PAUPERIS (L.)   Tell her father.

4000 IN POSSE (L.)   The cat's eaten the goldfish.

4001 PARI PASSU (L.)   Going through Paris.

4002 PIÉCE DE RÈSISTANCE   "Pas ce soir, Napoleon."

4003 POT-POURRI (Fr.)   Teapot.

4004 QUIDNUNC (L.)   Give uncle a pound note.

4005 SIC TRANSIT GLORIA MUNDI (L.)   Gloria was sick on the bus last Monday.

4006 TOUR DE FORCE (Fr.)   Walk around the police station.

4007 VICE VERSA (L.)   A coarse poem.

ARTICLES

4008   OPERA IN ONE EASY LESSON.

A large number of people don't understand Italian Opera. There is only one basic story, and different Operas serve it up in various guises. To be a fully conversant operagoer, all you need to do is memorize this outline, then whenever you go to an Italian Opera, you can listen to the music in comfort and not bother any more about the plot.

Arabella, the poor but proud daughter of the illiterate inn-keeper is secretly in love with the influential Duke of Bosnia, who having become crazed with love for the delectable Countess D'Orsay of Orlando, spends most of his time writing passionate love letters to her, which the Countess flings aside with a high-pitched scream. The Countess is secretly in love with Captain Trevellis, a handsome Irish Guardsman, who pays no attention to the Countess because he is secretly pining for Arabella, whom he serenades with an electric guitar, singing in a sweet tenor voice the theme music, "Love Will Conquer Fear," one of the highlights of the Opera.

In the meantime, the Countess learns that Trevellis is actually Pretender to the throne of Uravia, in disguise, so she begins to plot the assassination of Trevellis's twin brother, Alberto, who is secretly in love with Arabella's half-sister Martha, a victim of a conjuror's trick that went wrong. Martha, who knows what it is all about, then sings the famous aria, "Bliss is Joy, I Love All Men," which is another of the highlights of the Opera. Countess D'Orsay now comes to the inn where she is aghast to find Trevellis gazing with wrapt attention at Arabella who is gazing affectionately at the Duke of Bosnia, who is giving sly oblique glances at the Countess; this provides a great opportunity for the famous quartette, "Nobody knows but us," . . . which is another highlight of the Opera.

In the meantime Arabella's father has become suspicious that something is wrong and his suspicions are borne out when he discovers that thirty-two of his best paying customers have been secretly poisoned and that the local constabulary, played by Kirk Schusselmeister, is demanding overtime. The harassed inn-keeper, now comes down stage to sing in a deep Bass voice, the famous aria: "We Must Hasten, Trouble's Nigh." Arabella is now so desperate that she pulls a knife from the cleavage of her bosom and stabs Trevellis. Then she comes to her senses and realises that it was Trevellis she loved all along. Trevellis sinks to the stage floor mortally wounded, and sings the twelve choruses of the secondary theme of the Opera: "My Love Lives On No Matter How Much I Die." Wringing her hands in misery Arabella counters with her own famous aria: "Hope Is Gone When Love Recedes." After which she grabs a tankard of poisoned ale and drinks it, to fall lifeless across the body of Trevellis. Seeing this travesty of justice, the inn-keeper pulls out a flintlock pistol and shoots at the Countess, but the Duke dashes across the stage and intercepts the bullet with his stomach. The Duke falls dead across the bodies of Trevellis and Arabella. With dignified nonchalance, the Countess picks one of the crossed swords from the wall of the inn and rushes the inn-keeper, who draws his own rapier and proceeds to fence with the Countess. Suddenly they stop fighting and the Countess tosses aside her sword and leans over the refectory table weeping copiously. The inn-keeper goes to her, gathers her into his arms and consoles her with the famous air: "Weep Not, Fair Lady, Our Love Will See Us Through." And so into the final ensemble with the villagers crowding around the coach as the inn-keeper and the Countess depart for a honeymoon in Geneva, singing: "Folderolderoldeo, Hey Nonny No We Go." And the curtain falls.

4009   THE BED.

There are two very important rooms in any home, and the second one is the bedroom. Inside the bedroom there are several pieces of furniture, and the most important item of furniture is the bed. Why is a bed so important in the life of a human being? Well, you get born in a bed; you spend more than half your life resting or sleeping in bed, and in the final analysis, you get laid out on it. In between times it acts as a very useful accessory for married couples—unless of course they use twin beds, which they will do if they happen to have twins.

There are all kinds of beds—iron beds, wooden beds, divan beds, single beds, double beds, four poster beds, oyster beds, day beds, hospital beds, camp beds, flower beds and ocean beds for mermaids. Scientists have worked out that single people spend an average of eight hours a night sleeping in beds. They are not so sure how much time married people spend sleeping because no statistics are available.

The most modern type of bed is the one which folds up. When not in use it can be pushed back flush with the wall; sometimes it is very handy to do this while the wife is still in it. Long ago in England the iron bedstead was very popular. Awakening dreamily in the morning, people could stare at the bars and imagine for a moment that they were still in prison. Iron bedsteads of this age were fitted with monstrous brass knobs at each corner. You could use these for stretching your socks, hanging your hat on, or in cases of emergency you could screw one off and chastise your wife with it by bouncing it against her head. The main trouble with iron bedsteads was the awful way they squeaked. Inventors remedied this fault easily enough—they invented sound-proof floors.

The worst bed of all is the camp bed. It is such a complicated piece of mechanism that by the time you've finished struggling to put it together, daylight is streaming through the window and it's morning. You can dispense with a camp bed by using a sleeping bag.

Spinsters prefer the high bed to the low bed; this is because when they go to bed they like to look underneath to see if there is anything there—such as a man.

Beds need mattresses. Some mattresses are stuffed with kapok, some with down and some with horse-hair. One or two bed mattresses have also been known to be stuffed with money. Feather beds can be bought on hire purchase; so much "down" and the rest spread over twenty-four hours. Every time you pay an instalment they give you another feather. On H.P. the finance company sometimes does not get the rest it deserves—the rest of the money. Coil-wire mattresses are all right in their way but when they break they are uncomfortable—who wants to dive into the bright spring on a cold winter's night?

There are people who dislike beds and who prefer to sleep out of doors under the twinkling stars. What could be more romantic, more idyllic, more rapturous than sweet, refreshing slumber in the balmy open air?—with rain splashing into your face, the wind howling up your pyjama leg, leaves blowing into your mouth, and ants and tarantulas crawling all over you.

Invalid beds are specially constructed so that they can be raised as much as two feet from the floor. The idea of this is that if you are ill and need all-night attention, when you fall two feet out of bed, the nurse can hear you.

It is usual when married couples are sleeping in a double bed for the wife to keep to her own three-quarters of the bed.

In some countries there are interesting customs connected with beds. In Finland for instance, all betrothed couples are permitted to sleep together in a double bed before marriage, provided that a long bolster is laid down the middle. This was all right in practice, but a number of young men, came down to breakfast with mouths full of feathers.

Some people cannot sleep in a cold bed, hence the invention of various kinds of bed warmers. Some bed-warmers are dark and brassy affairs. In later years came the hot-water bottle, but long before this it was just as easy to get into hot water. Some beds get woodworm in them; others get husbands. Some people sleep in their pyjamas, some in nightshirts and others in birthday suits.

In America they have a wonderful invention called the Murphy bed, which is invaluable in small homes. The Murphy bed folds back into a hole in the wall, completely out of sight. But in some American apartments the walls are so thin that it is a frequent sight to see someone pull the Murphy bed out of the wall at night and find the next-door neighbours fast asleep in it.

Going to bed is a common occurrence among mankind; nearly everyone does it sooner or later—either at 8 p.m. or 4 a.m. Men going to bed sling their clothes any old where around the room, swill their teeth and jump straight between the covers. Women are different. They put their clothes away tidily, cream their faces, wash their smalls, remove nail varnish, brush their hair and do their exercises. It takes them about forty minutes and often gives rise to grounds for divorce.

4010 THE COMIC ART OF HOW TO GIVE A SPEECH.

The first essential about giving a speech, is having something to talk about. Make sure your audience will react to your subject. If the audience is all men, you are safe on subjects of such cultural topics as "women", "beer", "the dogs", "football pools" and "girls". If the audience is all women, your safe subjects are "men", "fashions", "slimming", "other women" and "film stars". Teenage audiences are always interested in "men" (if they are girls) and "girls" (if they are boys). You could also interest them in such things as "hot-rod cars", "skiffle discs" and the history of drain-pipe trousers through the ages".

The clever speaker goes into action well armed. He needs a good strong suit of armour plate, a steel grill to ward off ballistic missiles flung from the auditorium, and a good supply of water to quench his thirst. The water can be mixed with gin or vodka, or anything else that looks like water but isn't.

The biggest enemy of the speaker is the heckler. The heckler usually arrives at the meeting with pockets full of bad eggs, over-ripe tomatoes, squashy grapefruit and split peas which he shoots through a lethal weapon called a pea-shooter. He sometimes sits close to the rostrum and has a nasty habit of sliding stink-bombs under the platform. If you are big and strong you can always deal with a heckler by shouting back at him such insults as "Why don't you take one of your heads home?" or "If you open your mouth again I'll come down there and push your flat feet in it" or "When did you last see your father, or are you still trying to find out who he is?" But if you are a short, thin, weak sort of speaker, hecklers can only be dealt with by subtle remarks such as "I'll tell my mother about you when I get home" or "You ought to be ashamed of yourself". Or if you want to get the sympathy of the audience, just burst out crying.

Some speakers are so good that they keep their audiences glued to their seats. For this purpose you can use either resinous glue or flour paste.

When things get rough during a speech, the chairman will sometimes yell out "Order! Order!" That's when you turn to him and say with a smile "I'll have a large brandy".

Never accept an invitation to give a speech at a large Civic meeting. Such affairs are attended by many dignitaries and you have to start your speech like this: "My Lord Mayor, Lady Mayoress, Alderman, my Lords, Ladies, Mr. Chairman, Mrs. Chairman, Deputy Sewerage Convenor,

Mr. Toastmaster, Uncle George, et cetera—usually the list is so long that before you can start your speech you are breathless from voicing two or three hundred titles and names, as if you were reading extracts from Burke's Peerage. Not that all peers are Burkes.

Safety precautions are always taken at a large meeting. The most important of these so far as the speaker is concerned is to ensure that you are as close to a convenient exit as possible. Make a note of where the "Fire" exit is as many people in the audience may be armed and firing at you.

At some meetings you will be called upon to answer questions from various parts of the hall or stadium. Usually it is impossible to hear these questions that are shouted, and even if you do hear these questions it is quite possible that you won't know the answers. The way to deal with this problem is easy: First of all pretend that your hearing-aid is broken, and shrug apologetically as you fiddle with the volume control. Secondly smile broadly in the direction of the questioner and say, "That's a very good question. Why not bring it up at a more important session?" Or "I must have notice of that question—come back in nine or ten years time . . ." If the questioner becomes insistent and aggressive say: "Why, anybody knows the answer to a stupid question like that—you shouldn't parade your ignorance by asking such trivial, foolish questions." This usually squashes the questioner who sulks out with his shoulders drooping.

Sometimes you will be asked to speak at a meeting and on arrival you will find that only two people are in the audience. The first thing you do is to offer them their money back, but if it's a free meeting, ask them to sit together so that you can keep your eyes on them. The best thing about a two-person audience is that if things get rough, the people on the rostrum invariably outnumber the audience, and this can give remarkable confidence to the speaker. Taking the other extreme, where the audience is so packed that people are standing on people who are sitting on people who are kneeling at the back—demand danger-money from the committee.

Always time your speech, so as to keep it taut, precise and to the point. Use either a wrist-watch or an alarm clock. Never use an egg-timer—this gives the audience ideas of thought-association and you might get a raw pancake in your eye or even a hard-boiled ostrich egg.

When talking, don't gape at the audience, but keep your eyes fixed on a spot at the back of the hall. . . . If there is a good-looking blonde there, it's very easy. Good-looking blondes are available for this purpose from any modelling school, and you can always take her home after the meeting.

After a speech some of the audience might rush forward clapping and stamping their feet—clapping your head and stamping their feet all over your face. 'Phone the riot squad.

INDEX

INDEX

A

Absent-minded, 158, 2835, 3316
Accident, 1159, 1293, 1458, 3409, 3438
Actor, 318, 615, 701, 1089, 1140, 1207, 2555, 2638, 2648, 2883
Actress, 579, 719, 725, 843, 1068, 1146, 1364, 1448, 2574, 2679, 2703
Adam, 1566, 2926, 3334
Adolescence, 630, 1741
Adverbs, 2378–2431
Advertising, 121, 255, 430, 500, 568, 1111, 1118, 1758, 2654, 2734, 2781, 2922, 3003, 3040, 3131, 3177, 3403, 3445
Advice, 3073, 3181, 3698
Africa, 1828
Age, 615, 1477
Air Force, 656, 784, 2522, 2532, 2590, 3192, 3353, 3531
Air mail, 47, 1229, 3296
Airways, 803, 1798, 2542, 2723, 2737, 2962, 3081, 3176, 3190, 3192, 3193, 3194
Aisle, 681
Alibi, 2606
Alps, 292
Ambition, 378
Ancestors, 424, 1142, 1203, 3413
Ancient Language, 2910
Anger, 544
Angling, 196, 363, 2518, 3632
Anniversary, 1215, 2834
Anti-freeze, 596
Antiques, 268, 429, 718, 1326, 1732, 2677
Aphrodite, 2460
Appearance, 911
Appetite, 1698
Apple, 1106
Appreciation, 462
Aquarius, 2432
Arabia, 256
Architect, 1712
Aries, 2434
Aristocracy, 1580, 2490, 2695, 2731, 2755, 2783, 2938, 3209, 3444, 3646
Armada, 30
Army, 52, 94, 114, 116, 148, 178, 235, 241, 247, 343, 445, 500, 654, 656, 675, 1003, 1145, 1314, 1389, 1598, 1649, 1714, 2523, 2543, 2580, 2738, 2757, 2802, 3021, 3025, 3105, 3144, 3159, 3210, 3232, 3638
Art, 528, 589, 1017, 1516, 2517, 2558, 2907, 3085, 3091, 3134, 3154, 3175, 3216, 3218, 3461, 3609
Artist, 213, 216, 774, 793, 1219, 1228, 1449, 1683, 2783
Artist's Model, 221, 899, 2496, 2705, 2785
Aspirin, 1157, 1225
Astronomy, 532
Auctioneer, 329, 3291

Audience, 82, 695, 871, 971, 1068, 1780, 2548, 2638
Audition, 1749, 2892
Authorship, 166, 167, 244, 253, 322, 373, 478, 1005, 1121, 2513, 2607, 2693, 2712, 2727, 2914, 3343, 3446
Automation, 2791

B

Baby, 561, 745, 972, 1039, 1146, 1206, 1232, 1424, 1677, 1765, 1797, 2549, 2557, 2611, 2658, 2689, 3058, 3493
Baby-sitting, 585, 948, 3658
Bachelors, 435, 470, 731, 857, 1115, 2468, 2862, 3028, 3418, 3524
Bacon, 728
Badges, 2541
Bagpipes, 1537
Bakery, 215
Baldness, 79, 280, 304, 638, 859, 1211, 2539, 2632, 2674, 2690, 2714, 3195
Ballet, 1112
Ballpen, 1256
Banana, 1179
Banking, 463, 842, 1099, 1678, 1702, 1790, 3063
Bank notes, 1705, 1811, 2598
Bank robbery, 2780
Barber shop, 483, 754, 936, 965, 1016, 1161, 1344, 1381, 1776, 2547, 2732, 2762, 2784, 2909
Bargain, 472, 689
Barmaid, 951
Bashfulness, 2800
Bathing-belle, 419, 1441
Bathroom, 78, 98, 776, 1107, 1167, 1384, 2786, 2843, 2984, 3448
BBC, 1574, 1780, 2624, 2669
Beach, 261, 367, 692, 741, 813, 991, 1029, 1096, 1190, 1195, 1276, 1301, 1433, 1498, 1578, 2664, 2773, 2795, 3309
Beads, 1051
Beard, 2951
Beatniks, 3, 117, 713, 848, 1161, 1427, 1436, 2588, 2744, 2775, 3019, 3091, 3227, 3688, 3691
Beauty, 136, 192, 249, 340, 389, 426, 461, 488, 707, 750, 964, 1063, 1066, 1679, 2470, 2586, 2807, 3120
Beauty Contest, 165, 807, 1416, 1587
Bed, 917, 1111, 1244, 1282, 1338, 1418, 1493, 2456, 2584, 2595, 2686, 2844, 3573, 4009
Bedroom, 1815, 2460, 3031
Bedtime-story, 2758
Beehive, 425
Beggar, 2528, 2529
Bible, 3158
Bigamy, 1124
Bikini, 1585, 2449, 2509
Billiards, 1557, 1779, 2630, 3581